HOUSING

HOUSING

ROBINSON O. EVERETT
JOHN D. JOHNSTON, JR.
Editors

OCEANA PUBLICATIONS, INC.
Dobbs Ferry, New York
1968

Originally published in Spring and Summer 1967

by

LAW AND CONTEMPORARY PROBLEMS

DUKE UNIVERSITY SCHOOL OF LAW

PRINTED IN THE UNITED STATES OF AMERICA

Titles Published in

The Library of Law and Contemporary Problems

POPULATION CONTROL, The Imminent World Crisis
MELVIN G. SHIMM, *Editor*

EUROPEAN REGIONAL COMMUNITIES,
A New Era on the Old Continent
MELVIN G. SHIMM, *Editor*

AFRICAN LAW, New Law for New Nations
HANS W. BAADE, *Editor*

ACADEMIC FREEDOM, The Scholar's Place
in Modern Society
HANS W. BAADE, *Editor*

THE SOVIET IMPACT ON INTERNATIONAL LAW
HANS W. BAADE, *Editor*

URBAN PROBLEMS AND PROSPECTS
ROBINSON O. EVERETT and RICHARD H. LEACH, *Editors*

ANTIPOVERTY PROGRAMS
ROBINSON O. EVERETT, *Editor*

INTERNATIONAL CONTROL OF PROPAGANDA
CLARK C. HAVIGHURST, *Editor*

HOUSING
ROBINSON O. EVERETT and JOHN D. JOHNSTON, JR., *Editors*

CONTENTS

Part I: Perspectives and Problems

Part II: The Federal Role

Part I

Perspectives and Problems

FOREWORD

The continuing population explosion threatens to overwhelm the national inventory of housing. Housing codes, urban renewal programs, and public housing projects have not yet sufficed to put every American family in a home that meets minimal standards. Instead, despite our efforts, we seem in some respects to be falling farther behind in attaining the goal of adequate housing for everyone.

Moreover, housing problems have taken on added dimensions. Adequate housing now signifies much more than a well-built structure. It includes accessibility of schools, parks, playgrounds, highways, public tranportation, and shopping facilities. Since the desirability of a site for housing purposes will depend to a significant degree upon the availability of public improvements and facilities, governmental decisions as to their location will materially influence the choices of site made by developers of housing. Similarly, governmental action in the form of zoning ordinances, subdivision controls, and building and housing codes will have great impact on decisions which private entrepreneurs make with respect to housing.[1]

In some quarters the complaint is voiced that government officials have made excessive use of the broad authority vested in them and that, by imposing unnecessary controls on residential development, they have added to the expense of, and have thereby deterred, construction or rehabilitation of housing. According to this view, the untrammeled operation of the laws of supply and demand would often have resulted in more, and even better, housing than was feasible in light of the strict governmental restrictions. And certainly in the face of a vast need for new housing, city planners are sometimes open to the charge that the requirements they have promulgated involve "gold-plating"—demanding that any housing be constructed or rebuilt in such a way that it will meet adequately the needs of all foreseeable future generations, thereby adding costs and delays that may prevent the fulfillment of present housing needs.

Frequently it is asserted that government's sin has been inertia, rather than hyperactivity and excessive use of authority. For example, the criticism is stated that municipal authorities have tolerated or condoned slums by reason of failures to enforce housing codes which preclude the occupancy of seriously substandard buildings. Sometimes the issue is complicated by the likelihood that unbending

---

[1] Over the years the courts have been willing to broaden the spectrum of factors which government officials may weigh in the planning and control of land use. Even aesthetics may now be considered in this regard—an evolution which contains an element of irony since, in today's society, a consensus of views as to aesthetic values is especially difficult, if not impossible, to achieve.

enforcement of the codes may remove dwellings from the housing market and thereby exacerbate existing housing shortages.

There have been attacks on the process by which such difficult issues are decided. Some groups maintain that they are underrepresented on the local commissions or groups which make the decisions. And the suggestion has been made that local and state governmental processes should be somewhat restructured to assure greater citizen involvement in the decision-making which affects housing. It is argued that, even if such involvement does not lead to wiser decisions, it may give rise to more acceptable ones.

In some respects the mortgage lender is the most important decision-maker in the process of adding to the national housing inventory. In practice, availability of a "permanent" mortgage loan is usually a requisite for constructing a project; indeed, a developer will frequently defer his architect's preparation of detailed working drawings until, on the basis of preliminary plans and specifications, he has received a satisfactory loan commitment.

The mortgage lender is himself profoundly influenced by governmental action, especially action at the national level which affects interest rates or tends to direct personal savings to one type of financial institution instead of another—for example, to commercial banks instead of building and loan associations. However, the lender has a considerable sphere of autonomy, as most builders are well aware. Unfortunately, many mortgage lenders have occasionally imposed severe limitations upon their own autonomy and have contented themselves with applying rules of thumb and rigid formulae, with almost no consideration of design criteria. Obviously good design should have in the long run a positive effect on value; but many lenders have given only lip service to design.

The mortgage lender, the government official, the developer, and others involved in the effort to supply the existing vast housing demands will be materially aided by advances in technology. For instance, systems analysis utilizing computer techniques can be applied to identify the types of housing that are, and will be, needed, and to compare the costs of the alternatives available for meeting those needs; it can assist the architect in achieving improved design at reduced cost; it can help reveal the added expense of construction that results from obsolete municipal land-use controls; and it can predict the effects on housing construction of new fiscal and monetary policies.

The available technological advances include more extensive use of prefabrication —a construction technique which is carried to its logical conclusion by the mobile home.[2] Progress in "legal technology" also affords help in the solution of housing

---

[2] Unfortunately, the introduction of new technology for construction of housing must often take place over considerable opposition. For example, carpenters have resisted from time to time the installation of pre-hung doors; and the substitution of performance criteria in many building codes may be opposed by suppliers of materials which have an entrenched position under the wording of the existing codes.

problems. The development of residential condominia provides a good example in this respect. Also, skilled lawyers have played a role in meeting housing needs by encouraging and supervising the organization of nonprofit sponsors to participate in certain federal housing loan programs and by familiarizing their builder clients with tax advantages available through accelerated depreciation, capital gains, land leases for the construction of multifamily housing projects, and so on.

Certainly there exists a need for every new tool that can be forged for use in attaining the national goal of adequate housing for all citizens. And the events of recent summers suggest that the time left for us to meet housing demands within our traditional social framework may be extremely short. Yet it is inconceivable that a society which can mobilize its resources on short notice to fight wars abroad or to place a man on the moon cannot solve its housing problems. Perhaps part of the difficulty stems from the failure in many quarters to appreciate the urgency of the situation, the absence of a general outcry from the populace demanding effective action, and the lack of more forceful exhortations by influential leaders of government, business, or labor. It is unknown how much substandard housing our society can tolerate before irreversible deterioration in the quality of national life sets in. We may be perilously close to that point now; unless heroic measures are taken soon, we shall surely reach it in the near future.

ROBINSON O. EVERETT.
JOHN D. JOHNSTON, JR.

POPULATION PRESSURE, HOUSING, AND HABITAT

[F]or life to run smoothly, for the living organism to remain healthy in the highest degree, the environmental complex must be made as perfect as possible.

—J. W. Bews, *Human Ecology* 79 (1939).

Woe unto them that join house to house, that lay field to field, till there be no room.

—*Isaiah* 5:8.

Very few people, indeed, want to be better than they are; or . . . hunger and thirst after righteousness.

—T. S. Eliot, *Essays, Ancient and Modern* 115-16 (1936).

INTRODUCTION

A house is not a home. This aphorism is usually held to possess validity only in the demimonde. Brief consideration suggests, however, that the validity of this aphorism is not so confined. It fits other worlds as well; in particular, the world of housing upon which the current issue of this journal is focused.

It may still be true in this age of insecurity, anti-privacy, and emerging police states, that "the house of everyone is to him," as Sir Edward Coke declared four centuries ago, "as his castle and fortress, as well for his defense against injury and violence as for his repose." It is also true that a man's house means a great deal more, even to those who agree with Samuel Butler that occasional absence from one's house enhances its attractiveness.

In this article I argue (a) that the subject of housing must be examined in terms of the larger set of *gesellschaftliche* and *gemeinschaftliche* relations within which the house, together with its occupying household, is situated; (b) that this set of relations and hence the role of housing is significantly affected by the growth and concentration of population, control of which is essential to the easing of the so-called housing problem.

The underlying issue is clearly recognized by architects such as Doxiadis who see in the expansion of the impersonal city and the associated elimination of nature a process that is destroying neighborhood and community units and making of man a building-occupying troglodyte subject to "instructions issued from the peak of the pyramid." He suggests that we once again create human communities in our cities, "operating neighborhoods, downtown shopping centers where people can walk freely, can come into natural contact, can enjoy quiet surroundings and create and admire art. These human communities should become the cells which will be interconnected

---

*A.B. 1926, M.A. 1929, Ph.D. 1930, Ohio State University. James B. Duke Professor of Economics, Duke University.

by mechanical means of transportation and communications to form major systems and major cities."[1] While Doxiadis is here referring mainly to communities within large cities he recognizes the interrelation of housing and community and the importance of how man can spend his time, especially in a modern world in need of a moral equivalent to work.

I

HOME VERSUS HOUSE

How the Greeks, Aristotle in particular, viewed housing may be suggestive since concern for the eudaemonic aspect of life played a very important role in their view of housing—a concern honored more in the breach than in the observance in the United States.[2] Aristotle approaches housing in terms of the overall community and the pursuit of the "highest good." The polis, or city state, as he conceived of it, was a community which, embracing all other communities, aimed at the "highest good." The elemental community of which the state was composed was the household, to whose management Aristotle and those influenced by him devoted attention.[3] Aristotle, defender of simplicity in a simple age, pointed to the smallness of the number of instruments needed within a household to make the "good life" possible.[4] Presumably he agreed with Hesiod that a house was the "first and foremost" requisite of a household[5] and with the statement that "a house must be arranged both with a view to one's possessions and for the health and well-being of its inhabitants." A house must, therefore, "be airy in summer and sunny in winter"; whence it needs to face "north" and be longer than wide.[6] These and other aspects of a house were stressed several centuries later by the architect Vitruvius, a contemporary of Nero, who designed and situated several types of houses to meet specific occupational and climatic requirements.[7]

Aristotle looked upon a house as one of a triad of interrelated elements: house, household, and organic urban community. The house sheltered the members of the household and afforded them access to a good and healthy life. The household itself was relatively self-sufficient, as a rule. The head of a household was united with other household heads in that network of reciprocity which undergirded the state or urban community.

The problems confronting a household in Aristotle's day were fewer and simpler than those confronting a household in the affluent present. Cities usually were small

---

[1] Doxiadis, *Topics: Of Inhuman and Human Cities*, N.Y. Times, March 11, 1967, at 28, col. 5. *See generally* on *gemeinschaft and gesellschaft*, T. PARSONS, STRUCTURE OF SOCIAL ACTION 686-94 (1937).

[2] *See, e.g.,* R. E. WYCHERLY, HOW THE GREEKS BUILT CITIES (2d ed. 1962).

[3] POLITICA I:2. *See generally* OECONOMICA I:I, a work partly Aristotelian and partly reflective of the influence of Xenophon and others.

[4] POLITICA I:8-9.

[5] OECONOMICA I:2.

[6] *Id.* at I:6.

[7] VITRUVIUS, THE TEN BOOKS ON ARCHITECTURE 24-26, 38-41, 170-92 (M. H. Morgan transl. 1960).

and relatively free of congestion, even of that congestion of which Juvenal was later
to complain in Imperial Rome. Getting to work, to recreational and religious
centers, or to political responsibilities, presented no serious difficulties. Aristotle
wanted to keep the Greek city that way. Not only did he insist that a city not be
large, since "a very populous city can rarely, if ever, be well governed." He even
suggested that its population not exceed "the largest number which suffices for the
purposes of life, and can be taken in a single view."[8] Had he anticipated today's
opulent society, he would have found it wanting, along with its conception of housing.

The observations made by Aristotle or imputable to him call attention to the fact
that a house is not a solitary, autonomous, self-subsisting unit, even when occupied
by a household, but rather a locus in many partially overlapping environments or
complexes. It is a locus in the spatial economy of the household; it is a locus in a
social environment; it is a locus in a physical environment that varies in salubrity
and conduciveness to health. In the parlance of today, we may conceive of a house
as a micro-habitat within a larger but highly relevant macro-habitat. The house-
holder may be said to dwell in the former and carry on his extra-dwelling roles and
functions in the latter. It is quite evident, therefore, that his well-being and the
extent to which he can attain the good life depend in large measure upon the quality
of each of these two habitats. This inference is borne out by data assembled on the
amounts of time spent by various types of families, upon in-home and extra-house
activities, respectively.[9]

Since a house is a micro-habitat within a macro-habitat, it is improper to conceive
of housing independently of and in isolation from the macro-habitat within which
houses are situated. To do so is on a par with conceiving of Gettysburg in terms of
Edward Everett's prolix but forgotten oration. That housing often is so conceived of
is a result of the absence of order, or even of ordering values, from the determinants
of the growth, organization, and construction of cities. The outcomes resulting are
accepted as parts of the scheme of things, with the result that the fundamental significance of the macro-habitat for the quality of housing is underestimated. In consequence, the impact of the growth and concentration of population upon man's
macro- and micro-habitats receives little attention.

II

The Macro-Habitat

The macro-habit, within which household, house, and micro-habitat are situated,
embraces a number of environments. For purposes of illustration we need discuss
only a few. Perhaps the most important is the set of spatial economies within which
the individuals composing a household seek the good life, directly and/or indirectly

---

[8] Politica 7:4.

[9] *E.g.*, the excellent account given in J. N. Morgan, I. A. Serageldin & N. Baerwaldt, Productive
Americans (1966).

through pursuit of material means. Almost equally important are the social, physical, and health environments of the micro-habitat. It is sometimes said, of course, that modern man has become largely free of his external environment.[10] This exaggerated view suggests a modern Daedalus who pretends to have risen above his physical environment. One must, therefore, agree with Dubos's comment: "As happened to Antaeus of the Greek legend, his [man's] strength will probably wane if he loses contact with the biological ground from which he emerged and which still feeds him, physically and emotionally."[11]

A house is always a locus of household activities and a base from which members of a household operate. The household is situated in a net of activity-loci interrelated from the vantage point of members of a household even if not always connected by exchange as are interrelated markets. Each member of a household moves from his house to a locus of activity and back to his house either directly or via a path connecting diverse activities participated in sequentially. The problem confronting each member of a household is that of minimizing time utilized in moving from house to activity, from activity to activity, and from activity to house. His capacity to minimize time thus expended is quite limited, however, since the loci of these activities, together with the house, are not easily modified.[12]

Economy of time must be mainly sought, therefore, via economy of space, though some economy of time is achievable through reducing the actual time cost if not also the pecuniary cost of traversing space. Economy of space in turn must be sought through optimizing the spatial arrangement of relevant activities in the urban environs of the house and household.[13] When this is done a house begins to be viewed as a home, as the focus of man's search for the good life. This outcome is not likely to be emphasized, however, until both social scientists and those who manage the allocation of resources become space-minded—concerned about terrestrial and urban space rather than about mere lunar and martian space. For, as Isard observes, excessive emphasis upon time in economic analysis long made for neglect of the role of space in the theoretical and empirical structures of Anglo-Saxon economists.[14]

What constitutes a satisfactory social environment is not easy to define or to realize empirically. It is evident, however, that occupants of micro-habitats or

---

[10] For example, R. W. Gerard writes: "Man has, in fact, largely cut himself off from the external environment and created a hothouse internal environment of culture in which he lives in remarkable physical comfort. . . . Our lives are spent overwhelmingly at the symbolic level, and we live in a man-made sea of meanings. And the sea is still rising more or less exponentially." Gerard, *Intelligence, Information, and Education*, 148 SCI. 762, 763 (1965).

[11] R. DUBOS, MAN ADAPTING 279 (1965).

[12] An extended inquiry into the relationships between time, space, and activity is being conducted by G. C. Hemmens. A recent progress report is available: The Structure of Urban Activity Linkages, 1966 (mimeo., Center for Urban and Regional Studies, University of North Carolina, Chapel Hill).

[13] W. ISARD, LOCATION AND SPACE-ECONOMY (1956).

[14] *Id.* at 24-27.

neighborhoods are not likely to agree upon what makes a social environment satisfactory unless they agree on many things. This condition is overlooked, of course,
in much of the discussion of housing that involves the intermingling of households
which are quite dissimilar in tastes and conduct-determining norms. Even within
a household common standards of value must be present to permit passage from
the preference patterns of its individual members to a preference pattern representative of the household as such.[15] At the neighborhood level where the tastes of
individuals must be sufficiently similar to permit the construction of "suitable social
welfare functions,"[16] a minimal though not excessive degree of similarity of tastes is
essential to insure agreement on what constitutes a satisfactory social environment.
The degree required is less when there is agreement both on the need for day-to-day
decisions and on the mechanism or process whereby these decisions are reached.[17]
The market mechanism alone is unlikely to bring about this minimal degree under
all conditions, though it can be enabled to do so if certain conditions are met.[18]
It is true, as a rule, therefore, that a considerable though variable degree of homogeneity in the tastes of those inhabiting a neighborhood or macro-habitat is essential
to their settling upon what makes a social environment good. When this degree
is not fully attained, whether because of class or other differences, the macro-habitat
becomes instable.[19] It can become instable also if the inhabitants and their children
become too standardized.

While it appears to be true that whatever unduly reduces the degree of homogeneity of any particular neighborhood or macro-habit affects it unfavorably, this
inference does not support the view that cultural differences *between* macro-habitats
should be reduced. There must be room in the all-inclusive community for a
sufficiency of diversity which, while a characteristic of individuals, is in part a
concomitant of differences between macro-habitats.[20] It may be well, therefore,
that the overall community resemble a sea dotted with islands which differ culturally
from one another.[21] Unfortunately, the "formal elegance of welfare economics"

---

[15] K. J. ARROW, SOCIAL CHOICE AND INDIVIDUAL VALUES 9 n.1 (Cowles Comm'n for Research in
Economics Monograph No. 12, 1951).

[16] *Id.* at 81. "[I]t must be demanded that there be some sort of consensus on the ends of society,
or no social welfare functions can be performed." *Id.* at 83.

[17] Arrow concludes that "we may expect that social welfare judgments can usually be made when
there is both a widespread agreement on the decision process and a widespread agreement on the
desirability of everyday decisions." *Id.* at 91.

[18] The market mechanism does not always take into account all relevant matters, although it can be
manipulated to this end. *See* Arrow's discussion, *id.* at 81-86.

[19] For example, a retirement city built outside Sacramento for retired military personnel proved a flop.
"[I]t turned out that retired colonels did not like to live beside retired sergeants, and neither liked the
idea of living on streets named Billy Mitchell Boulevard and Hap Arnold Court." FORTUNE, Feb. 1966,
at 158.

[20] *See generally* Platt, *Diversity*, 154 SCI. 1132 (1966), for a discussion stressing the importance of
cultural and other diversity.

[21] In the United States, for example, though unifying common values are present, there are also many
local communities which, though they include diverse elements, have evolved each into a somewhat unique
constellation of values and institutions. *See, e.g.*, R. E. ENGLER, JR., THE CHALLENGE OF DIVERSITY
(1964).

does not tell us how much homogeneity is essential to a people's happiness.[22]

It may be noted parenthetically that economic as well as social factors have to be taken into account if the current housing shortage confronting nonwhites is to be greatly reduced. For, while housing values in nonwhite areas tend to lie below those for comparable housing in nearby white areas,[23] and while block-busting can enlarge nonwhite housing areas, urban renewal programs tend to raise the price of affected urban land above the level at which it is economically attractive to most nonwhites.[24] Emphasis upon residential desegregation, it is said, is retarding the construction of low-income housing.[25]

The degree of attractiveness of the physical environment of a macro-habitat enveloping a dwelling unit depends upon many circumstances, some of which seem to have been taken into account even in ancient ghetto-ridden Egypt.[26] Among these circumstances are absence of disorder and traffic congestion, the availability of private and public space, and general attractiveness, now usually lacking within as well as outside American urban centers.[27] Closely related is the healthfulness of this environment and its freedom from noise and pollution both of which are inimical to good health.[28]

An environment's healthfulness usually depends, at least in advanced countries, upon its freedom from pollution, especially chemical pollution of the water and the atmosphere. "[T]he few facts available demonstrate," René Dubos states, "that

---

[22] Mishan, *A Survey of Welfare Economics, 1939-59*, in 1 SURVEYS OF ECONOMIC THEORY 154, 211-13 (American Economic Ass'n & Royal Economic Soc'y 1965).

[23] Bailey, *Effects of Race and of Other Demographic Factors on the Values of Single-Family Homes*, 42 LAND ECON. 215 (1966).

[24] *See* J. ROTHENBERG, ECONOMIC EVALUATION OF URBAN RENEWAL (1967); Bailey, *Note on the Economics of Residential Zoning and Urban Renewal*, 35 LAND ECON. 288 (1959); Nourse, *The Economics of Urban Renewal*, 42 LAND ECON. 65 (1966).

[25] "The Achilles heel of housing programs has been precisely our insistence that better housing for the black poor be achieved by residential desegregation. This ideal glosses over the importance of the ethnic community as a staging area for groups to build the communal solidarity and power necessary to compel eventual access to the mainstream of urban life. . . .

"If group conflict is at the root of past failures, strategies must be found to improve ghetto housing without arousing the ire of powerful segments of the white community." Piven & Cloward, *Desegregated Housing, Who Pays for the Reformers' Ideal?*, NEW REPUBLIC, Dec. 17, 1966, at 17, 21. That this proposal for the improvement of ghettos is not impractical is suggested by the actions of a number of large building supply companies that are rebuilding parts of slums, to be turned over to nonprofit sponsors, and by plans to establish corporations that can produce housing competitive with public housing. *See* Ridgeway, *Rebuilding the Slums*, NEW REPUBLIC, Jan. 7, 1967, at 22.

[26] Perhaps the world's first model village for workmen was that built in Amarna in Egypt in the 14th century, B.C. *See* E. WELLS, NEFERTITI 162-63 (1964).

[27] *See* L. HALPRIN, FREEWAYS (1966); Faltermayer, *How to Wage War on Ugliness*, FORTUNE, May 1966, at 130; Larremore, *Public Aesthetics*, 20 HARV. L. REV. 35 (1906). *See generally* R. STARR, THE LIVING END: THE CITY AND ITS CRITICS (1966); Spengler, *The Aesthetics of Population*, 13 POPULATION BULL. 61 (1957).

[28] *See generally* on the adverse effects of noise, Beranek, *Noise*, SCIENTIFIC AM., Dec. 1966, at 66; Kryter, *Psychological Reactions to Aircraft Noise*, 151 SCI. 1346 (1966); *Silence at Less than $35 an Ounce*, FORTUNE, Dec. 1966, at 191; *When Noise Annoys*, TIME, Aug. 19, 1966, at 24, and on the destructiveness of the "sonic boom," offset only by an increase in the egg-hatching rate among chickens, THE NEW YORKER, Dec. 18, 1965, at 41.

pathological states can be caused by exposure to concentrations of pollutants of the order of those which exist in the urban atmosphere. On the basis of these results, it can be surmised that pollution can also have deleterious and lasting effects on human beings."[29] "The possibility of delayed and cumulative effects is not limited to any particular class of agent."[30] Dubos, therefore, stresses the "need for *striking* information" because "environmental pollution will not be controlled until physicians and scientists take an active part in its study."[31] Response to this same need on the part of students of urban and housing environments will help place efforts to solve housing problems in a more general context than is common at present; it will help men recognize that since, as Commoner shows, the elements of nature constitute an integrated totality,[32] it must be dealt with as a whole and not in a piecemeal fashion.[33]

III

POPULATION TRENDS

The rate of population growth has fallen below 1.5 per cent per year, at which rate it increased in 1960-64 when natural increase accounted for eighty-seven per cent of the total growth. Natality has since descended enough to reduce the current rate of natural increase nearly to one per cent per year. In the years just ahead, however, the large increase in the number of females aged 20-29, an echo of the upsurge of natality after the war, should push natality up somewhat. It is likely that the nation's population, nearly 198 million at the beginning of 1967, will number over 250 million by 1985 and 300 million or more by the close of the century. Should this population continue thereafter to grow 1¼ per cent per year it would number a billion or more by the year 2100, by which time population density might exceed 350 per square mile in the conterminous United States. Acres of all sorts per person would then average less than two.

The nonwhite population will increase somewhat faster than the white population, rising from twelve per cent of the total at present to about 13.5 per cent by 1985. At that time the rate of natural increase of the nonwhite population may be somewhat in excess of two per cent whereas the white rate will be about 1⅓ per cent. Should that rate differential persist, around one-fourth of the nation's population would be nonwhite by 2085.

[29] DUBOS, *supra* note 11, at 209-10. *See generally* ENVIRONMENTAL POLLUTION PANEL, PRESIDENT'S SCIENCE ADVISORY COMMITTEE, RESTORING THE QUALITY OF OUR ENVIRONMENT 1-9, 91-101 (Report of the Environmental Pollution Panel, 1965).

[30] DUBOS, *supra* note 11, at 221. *See generally* B. COMMONER, SCIENCE AND SURVIVAL (1966); *Ecology*, TIME, Jan. 27, 1967, at 48.

[31] DUBOS, *supra* note 11, at 225. (Emphasis added.)

[32] COMMONER, *supra* note 30.

[33] *See, e.g.*, COMMITTEE ON POLLUTION, NATIONAL RESEARCH COUNCIL, NATIONAL ACADEMY OF SCIENCES, PUB. NO. 1400, WASTE MANAGEMENT AND CONTROL (1966); SUBCOMM. ON SCIENCE, RESEARCH, AND DEVELOPMENT, HOUSE COMM. ON SCIENCE AND ASTRONAUTICS, 89TH CONG., 2D SESS., ENVIRONMENTAL POLLUTION—A CHALLENGE TO SCIENCE AND TECHNOLOGY (Comm. Print 1966).

While the farm population has continued to decline, from 32 million in 1920 to less than 12 million, increase in population concentration has been extensive rather than intensive. The population formerly defined as rural has continued to increase, though only about half as fast as the nation's population—in 1940-60 about sixteen per cent instead of thirty-five per cent as in the aggregate. The urban population increased more rapidly, of course, about fifty-two per cent; that in places under 100,000 increased about seventy-one per cent while that in places of 100,000 and over grew about thirty-four per cent. Even so, the proportion which the population in places of over 100,000 constituted of the total population changed only slightly.[34] The data just presented do not, however, fully reflect the implosion and megalo-politanization of population in process. But they do reveal how a shifting urban frontier has replaced that westerly moving rural frontier in terms of which some seventy years ago Frederick Jackson Turner interpreted the course of American history up to the 1890s. For a real sense of the change we must turn to metropolitan data.

Continuing population growth may intensify population concentration and urban crowding in two ways. First, it may simply add to the population situated in places of all sizes. Second, should the population-attracting power of cities increase more than in proportion to their numerical size, the rate of growth will be greatest in larger centers and the fraction of the nation's population concentrated therein will increase. This did happen between 1900 and 1930 when the rural fraction of the population fell from 60.3 per cent to 43.8 per cent and when the population in places of 100,000 and over rose from 18.7 to 29.6 per cent of the total population and from 47.1 to 52.7 per cent of the urban population. Then the process slowed down. Between 1930 and 1950 none of these percentages changed markedly. More recently some dispersion has set in. Between 1950 and 1960 the fraction of the nation's population situated in places of both above 500,000 and above 100,000 declined. This increase in dispersion may reflect in part a forty-two per cent increase in 1940-60 in the number of places under 100,000—of which nearly three-fifths were added in 1950-60.[35]

Whether an increasing fraction of the nation's population does become concentrated in the larger centers turns on the strength of the stochastic process apparently underlying what Kendall, describing the work of Zipf and others, calls "a kind of the-higher-the-fewer rule." This rule "says, in effect, that for certain kinds of activity with a measurable size x, the number y of individuals greater than or equal to x is given by

$$y = A/x^p$$

---

[34] In 1940, 28.8 per cent of the total population and 51 per cent of the urban population lived in places of 100,000 and over. The corresponding percentages in 1960 were 28.4 and 45. I have used the former census definition of "urban" in order to make the data of 1940 comparable with those of 1950 and 1960.

[35] U.S. BUREAU OF THE CENSUS, DEP'T OF COMMERCE, STATISTICAL ABSTRACT OF THE UNITED STATES 1965, at 15 (1965); C. TAEUBER & I. B. TAEUBER, THE CHANGING POPULATION OF THE UNITED STATES 114-15, 118 (1958).

where p is a constant which is often quite close to unity."[36] Here y stands for the rank of a particular city in size of population, x for its size, and p and A are constants, with A denoting the population of the largest center and p approximating unity. Now if A grows faster than a nation's population it will, after the manner of a Saturn eating his own children, increase at the expense of other communities, especially the smaller ones;[37] but if the number of communities grows rapidly enough, the population will tend to become more dispersed.[38]

It is within the metropolitan population that we find changes taking place of great significance for housing and its macro-habitats. First, the population of metropolitan areas is growing much faster than that lying outside these areas—2.3 per cent per year in the 1950s and 1.9 per cent per year in 1960-65 when the corresponding rates for the nonmetropolitan population were 0.8 and 0.7 per cent per year. The fraction of the nation's population living in metropolitan areas rose from about 60.5 per cent in 1950 to about sixty-three per cent in 1960 and sixty-four per cent in 1965. The metropolitan population in 1960 already approximated nine-tenths of the urban population and it could easily rise to seventy-five per cent of the nation's total population within 40-50 years. Second, while the proportion of the nation's population growth taking place in metropolitan areas is greater than before the Second World War, the proportion taking place in central cities situated within metropolitan areas is declining, especially in those with over a million inhabitants.[39] In sum, while the nation's population is becoming more concentrated, within the larger areas of concentration a redistribution of population is taking place and thus changing or threatening to change many of the macro-habitats within which housing is located. The rate of change underway can be especially significant because it is made up of net in-migration as well as of natural increase. For example, between 1950 and 1960 about thirty-five per cent of the increase in metropolitan population was due to in-migration.[40]

The long continued migration of the Negro to the city in search of better economic opportunity and housing, coupled with the decline in foreign immigration, is bringing about a redistribution of population within metropolitan centers.[41] This redistribution is of very great significance for housing problems since in 1965 about sixty-four per cent of the white population of the United States and about sixty-eight per cent of the nonwhite population lived in metropolitan areas. This

---

[36] Kendall, *Natural Law in the Social Sciences*, 124 J. THE ROYAL STATISTICAL SOC'Y (ser. A) 1, 4 (1961). *See generally* ISARD, *supra* note 13, at 55.

[37] G. K. ZIPF, NATIONAL UNITY AND DISUNITY 55 (1941). In the United States the ratio of New York's population to that of the nation rose between 1880 and 1930 and thereafter fell. *Id.* at 56. I have computed the ratios for 1950 and 1960.

[38] The ratio of places to population rose from 100 in 1900 to 115 in 1930, 118 in 1940, and 126 in 1960.

[39] W. S. THOMPSON & D. T. LEWIS, POPULATION PROBLEMS 141-48, 156 (5th ed. 1965).

[40] *Id.* at 151-52.

[41] *See* Newman, *The Negro's Journey to the City* (pts. 1 & 2), 88 MONTHLY LABOR REV. 502, 644 (1965).

redistributive process reflects forces affecting both concentration and congestion as well as the passage of a city's racial composition beyond a so-called tipping point.[42] First, the population outside the central cities has been growing much faster than that in these cities, four per cent per year in 1950-60 and 3.3 per cent per year in 1960-65 compared with annual increases in central cities of one per cent in the 1950s and 0.6 per cent in 1960-65. Second, the nonwhites are displacing the whites in central cities with the result that if this process continues, by 1980 seven or more large cities will be predominantly nonwhite (mainly Negro) and perhaps thirty more about one-third nonwhite. Of the top ten cities in the United States only Houston and Los Angeles will be predominantly white thirty-five years from now.[43]

Illustrative of current redistributive tendencies are those of 1960-65 when the nonwhite population of metropolitan areas increased 2,508 thousand, of whom 2,096 thousand settled in central cities. Meanwhile, the metropolitan white population increased 8,982 thousand, *all* of whom settled outside central cities, together with about 470 thousand who migrated there on balance from central cities. The non-white fraction of the total central-city population thus rose from about eighteen per cent in 1960 to nearly twenty-one per cent in 1965; in 1950 it was only about thirteen per cent.[44] Meanwhile the nonwhite fraction of the metropolitan population in the ring of areas outside central cities, about 5.5 per cent in 1950, had declined to five per cent by 1960. An unpublished study of eleven central cities, by my colleague Reynolds Farley, indicates that residential segregation is again increasing.

So alarmed has the present administration apparently become at the current drift and its implications for desegregation of the school system that what amount to legislative and administrative efforts to countervail or reverse the drift are being initiated.[45] This approach not only is unmindful of potential boomerang effects; it overlooks the advantages to be had from the proposal made below to multiply the number of urban centers to which Negro and white can migrate and through which the problem of concentration can be greatly alleviated, though not solved altogether.

IV

POPULATION EFFECTS

The effects of the population trends described in the preceding section are of two sorts, sequelae to population growth and sequelae to population concentration. Four

---

[42] *See, e.g.,* Grodzins, *Metropolitan Segregation,* SCIENTIFIC AM., Oct. 1957, at 33; Tauber & Tauber, *White Migration and Socio-Economic Differences Between Cities and Suburbs,* 29 AM. SOCIOLOGICAL REV. 718 (1964); Winsborough, *An Ecological Approach to the Theory of Suburbanization,* 68 AM. J. SOCIOLOGY 565 (1963); Winsborough, *City Growth and City Structure,* J. REGIONAL SCI., Winter 1962, at 35.

[43] U.S. NEWS & WORLD REPORT, Feb. 21, 1966, at 72-73; U.S. NEWS & WORLD REPORT, March 6, 1967, at 58-62.

[44] The fraction that was Negro was slightly smaller than the nonwhite. *See generally* on the suburbanization process, Winsborough, *An Ecological Approach to the Theory of Suburbanization, supra* note 42.

[45] *See* U.S. NEWS & WORLD REPORT, Feb. 27, 1967, at 68-69.

sequelae to population growth may be noted. The first of these, the accentuation of population concentration or density, has already been touched upon. The second, increase in overall population, is treated largely under the head of population concentration, of which it is a source. Of course, enlargement of areas of population density outside areas of heavy concentration do produce effects of the sort discussed below, though less intense than those found in areas of heavy concentration.

The third effect of population growth is the absorption of inputs which might otherwise have been used to improve the material condition of the existing population and its replacement. Here we may indicate only the order of magnitude of this cost which may then be compared with fixed investment in residential construction that has been running about $22 billion a year. If we conceive of capital only in terms of hard goods and suppose it costs about four per cent of the national income to support a rate of population growth of one per cent per year, then the cost of America's population growth has been in the neighborhood of $30 billion a year since 1964. If we include under the head of "capital" all expenditure which serves to increase the stream of income in the future and allow as well for the adverse effect of population growth upon the age composition of the population, we may raise this figure to around $45 billion. Another way of arriving at an estimate is to suppose that the cost of adding a cross-sectional thousand people to the nation's population costs between $10 and $20 million. On this supposition, adding about 2.5 million persons a year to the population costs between $25 and $50 billion a year. Whatever be the correct estimate, it represents an annual expenditure far in excess of the current rate of expenditure upon residential construction. Of course, even should fertility fall to the replacement level, it would take a few years for the benefits to materialize fully and then they might be utilized in part in the form of leisure.[46]

The fourth effect is associated with the continual change in city size produced by population growth and discussed earlier. Let us suppose that a country's population is stationary. Its population distribution will then be fairly stable, affected by changes in technology, incomes, and the composition of tastes and amenities, but *not* by the main source of distributive change operative in the past—namely, increase in the nation's population. The urban problem would then become mainly one of keeping particular cities and their macro-habitats intact; it would thus resemble maintaining a stationary economy's capital intact.[47] Financial provision for the maintenance of all components of a city including its housing and macro-habitats could then easily be put on an orderly basis. Planning for changes could be carried out readily since almost any particular change would be but a wave in a sea of stability. Short and long time-horizons would differ less than now. The remaining changes would be

---

[46] When families earn less than $6,000 per year they tend to put forth extra effort. *See* MORGAN, SERAGELDIN, & BAERWALDT, *supra* note 9, at 191. *See generally* on choosing between more work and more leisure, *id.* at 198-202.

[47] *See generally* on "maintaining capital intact," A. C. PIGOU, ECONOMICS OF WELFARE 43-49 (4th ed. 1932).

small enough so that, were they met sub-optimally, corrective action would be easy and not very costly. Under these conditions demographic metabolism, the replacement of old families nearing or beyond retirement by younger families, would entail little unfavorable change in the quality of the environment.

Population concentration and density produce a number of somewhat distinct effects, all of which, when intensified beyond a critical point, outweigh the advantages associated with a lesser amount of population agglomeration. These effects are incident on some or all the macro-habitats constituting a community, though in varying degree, and they reduce the contribution that housing can make to welfare. "Welfare," in other words, may be viewed as a joint "product" of (*inter alia*) that which a household's housing and macro-habitat make possible and that which the larger, all-inclusive community makes possible. Agglomeration of population continues to increase the latter contribution after it has begun to diminish that of housing and habitat, until a point is reached where the positive effect is offset at the margin by the negative effect. This is the optimum point; it varies with household, of course, and this variation affects how population distributes itself within urban or metropolitan space.

It is not possible here to catalog and describe all the effects associated with excessive population growth and concentration, but the main ones may be touched upon in order to illustrate the theme of this paper. These effects are contraction of space, pollution, congestion, unproductive use of time, and sub-optimal distributions of population.

Population concentration reduces the ratio of space available per person for household and/or other activities and thus diminishes the contribution of space to the city-dweller's standard of life. In 1960 about twenty-eight per cent of the nation's population occupied only 0.23 per cent of its land area, and about forty-five per cent occupied just under one half of one per cent of this area. Population density ranged from 13,870 persons per square mile in places of a million or more to just over 3,900 per square mile in places of 50-100 thousand and about 2,290 per square mile in places of 10 to 25 thousand. Expressed in terms of acres per person, ground space per person ranged from about one twenty-fifth of an acre in places of over a million to one-sixth of an acre in places of 50-100 thousand and nearly three-tenths of an acre in places of 10-25 thousand. Even if we allow four persons per household, the pinch of space is pronounced, for part of this average land quota is required for streets, structures other than housing, and very rarely for parks. Moreover, since the daytime population of cities is much greater than their nighttime population, density within the city in daytime is more pronounced than our data suggest.

Second, population concentration increases the exposure of housing and macro-habitats to pollution of all sorts. Most of it is ultimately of human origin and therefore is in greatest amount where men are concentrated and live, work, and consume, and hence manufacture debris, pollutants, and contaminants of all sorts.

Moreover, the impact of this unwelcome product is hard to cushion. For example, since about nine-tenths of United States air pollution "consists of largely invisible but potentially deadly gases," air conditioners cannot defoul the atmosphere; at best they can remove particles.[48] It is doubtful, therefore, if man's natural right to breathe clean air can be made realizable in megalopolitan or other large centers. Indeed, he may find himself hard pressed even to dispose of his refuse and get a sufficient supply of usable water.[49]

We may state the problem generally and in terms of a set of hypothetical flows. Modern life is subjective and objective; it consists largely in symbolic communication and in the flow of men and matter. The volume of each stream tends to increase faster than population, especially in urban settings. Indeed, an urban center, above all, a megalopolis, may be thought of as a network of channels for the conduct of men and matter, together with information, within that center and between it and the world outside its environs. Channel capacities are limited and so are the number of channels actually or potentially available. Let R_e represent the rate of flow of effluent e and C_e the capacity of channels existing for the conveyance and disposal of e into the atmosphere, into waters, and elsewhere, but always in keeping with the health and good life of all concerned. If $R_e > C_e$, portions of e must be destroyed at points of origin, or stored until R_e falls below C_e. Otherwise e will accumulate within the population center and perhaps in areas immediately nearby. Presumably R_e grows at least as fast as $(p' + g')$ where p' denotes the rate of population growth of an urban center and g' denotes the rate of growth of per capita consumption and/or production of output which gives rise to various forms of effluent within the urban center. Since C_e has upper limits, it is inevitable that as a center's population grows, the probability of pollution of the macro-habitats of housing increases.

Third, congestion of channels for the conveyance of people and perhaps also of those for the conveyance of information tends to increase with population growth and concentration. Consider for example the movement of traffic through the center of a metropolitan area; it can grow nearly as the square of the population. "To keep the degree of traffic congestion constant, road traffic capacity must rise far more than in proportion with the rate of increase of population, and sheer problems of geography and land availability practically preclude such a possibility. Of course, the fact that population tends to cluster and is not spread evenly throughout the city only adds to these congestion problems."[50] This congestion, together with the accompanying noise and disorder, tends to accentuate two interrelated forces which generate

---

[48] *Ecology*, TIME, Jan. 27, 1967, at 48, 49-50; *See generally* RESTORING THE QUALITY OF OUR ENVIRONMENT, *supra* note 29, at 1-9, 62-69.

[49] New York's garbage dumps will be filled in eight years. N.Y. Times, Feb. 20, 1967, at 27, col. 1. *See generally* on the water problem, Wolman, *The Metabolism of Cities*, SCIENTIFIC AM., Sept. 1965, at 179, 181-85.

[50] Baumol, *Urban Services: Interactions of Public and Private Decisions*, in PUBLIC EXPENDITURE DECISIONS IN THE URBAN COMMUNITY 1, 7-8 (H. G. Schaller ed. 1963).

the cumulative deterioration of local environment and macro-habitats—namely, urban blight and flight to the suburbs.[51] Dense traffic is not the only form of congestion that inflicts uncompensated costs upon a large fraction of the population. There is also, as Colin Clark points out, a second type, "zonal congestion," the dearth of open space for recreational and other purposes.[52] Oddly enough, another British author argues for the "concentration of future population growth in a limited number of major cities as opposed to a balanced and uniform expansion of all existing urban centres."[53] Such concentration will economize on land and thus preserve more land for agriculture and the amenities.[54] He has in mind England where overall population density is very high, greater even than in Japan.

Fourth, two further concomitants of population concentration may be noted, each of which may affect man's macro-habitat adversely. First, a population and its activities may become sub-optimally dispersed within a metropolitan region and then perpetuated because the totality of public and private fixed capital outlays undergirding this distribution is so great as to render modifications very expensive. Herein, it is to be noted, we find support for careful anticipational urban planning, together with emphasis upon the preservation of flexibility and the retention of options realizable in the future. Since urban decisions tend to become frozen in steel and concrete as well as in transport systems, they should not be taken and acted upon until and unless the future is relatively clear. Second, a sub-optimal distribution of population and activities makes for high consumption per capita of modern man's most precious possession, time that might otherwise be discretionary and hence contributive to his well-being. Perhaps increasing education will result in countervailing measures. Did not Dante write: "Who knows most, him loss of time most grieves."[55]

V

POLICY IMPLICATIONS

Certain policy implications may be derived from what has been said. First, it is unlikely that the housing problem can ever be solved satisfactorily so long as population continues to grow and with it the excessive size of cities. For the impact of growth, unless carefully planned for and counterbalanced, will make for continual decay of parts of cities and hence of macro-habitats. Not only central cities but suburbs as well will continue to be subject to this process of decay which steals in unobtrusively, not as a fast-working pestilence that comes in the night but as a slowly working mutagen which produces a bodily change that in time metastasizes.

---

[51] *Id.* at 11-14; G. NEUTZE, ECONOMIC POLICY AND THE SIZE OF CITIES (1965).

[52] Clark, *Industrial Location and Economic Potential*, LLOYDS BANK REV., Oct. 1966, at 1, 3-4.

[53] Bellan, *The Future Growth of Britain's Cities*, 37 THE TOWN PLANNING REV. 173, 183 (1966).

[54] *Id.* at 183-84. *See generally* G. P. WIBBERLEY, AGRICULTURE AND URBAN GROWTH 201-29 (1959).

[55] PURGATORY, Canto I.

It will probably be many years, however, before population growth ceases, or, in the absence of nuclear war, becomes negative.

Second, contemporary tax and subsidy systems conduce to the deterioration of many macro-habitats, together with housing, by putting a premium on deterioration or by shunting its costs from those responsible to non-responsible third parties. (a) Buildings and land need to be differentially taxed in order that taxation of real property, usually a deterrent to its maintenance and improvement, will cease to be so.[56] (b) Every business firm or organization must be made to bear *all* congestion and related costs to which it gives rise, costs currently borne in part by others. (c) Impose the entire cost of urban expansion upon those responsible for this cost, instead of partly upon non-responsible parties as at present.

Third, current financial arrangements for maintaining housing and other forms of urban capital are inadequate to keep this capital intact through repair and/or replacement. Two approaches seem indicated. (1) Requiring the accumulation of adequate, earmarked liquidable assets to permit repair or replacement as it becomes necessary. (2) Require architects to plan construction in much greater measure than now in terms of easily replaceable parts, a point insisted upon by A. Spilhaus in his plan for an experimental city of about 250,000.[57]

Fourth, many problems associated with urban growth and housing flow from in-attention to the need to balance *total* costs and benefits at the margin; and this form of inattention tends to grow faster than the size of urban centers. Pollution, congestion, and related costs are among those that need to be offset. A variety of measures is available for this purpose, some of which are better suited than others to particular cases.[58]

Fifth, several implications follow from the irreversible character of decisions or processes determining urban growth after it has taken place. It sometimes happens, as Lösch has pointed out, that production, having been initiated in the wrong place, will be continued there.[59] For such mislocation imperfectly planned investment is responsible. Urban growth and extension entail heavy fixed-capital investment the sacrifice of which, along with that of economy-yielding business connections, makes decision-makers loath to shift location. Given this heavy *ex-post* anchor, should not *ex-ante* decision-making be forced to take into account all expected costs as well as all suppositious advantages? Should not the set of forces

---

[56] M. M. Gaffney writes of building taxes as distinguished from land taxes that "it would be hard to contrive a tax calculated to throw more risk onto the builder in proportion to the revenues raised." Gaffney, *Property Taxes and the Frequency of Urban Renewal*, in PROCEEDINGS OF THE FIFTY-SEVENTH ANNUAL CONFERENCE ON TAXATION 272, 284 (National Tax Ass'n 1964). The builder responds by not making improvements since the assessment of his land moves with the assessment of the structure on it. If, however, land is assessed and taxed at its true opportunity cost, it can no longer be economically allocated to sub-optimal uses. *See id.* at 272-85. *See generally* Woodruff & Ecker-Racz, *Property Taxes and Land Use Patterns in Australia and New Zealand*, THE TAX EXECUTIVE, Oct. 1965, at 16.

[57] Spilhaus, *The Experimental City*, The News and Observer (Raleigh, N.C.), Jan. 22, 1967, § 3, at 1.

[58] *See, e.g.,* Ogden, *Economic Analysis of Air Pollution*, 42 LAND ECON. 137 (1966).

[59] A. Lösch, THE ECONOMICS OF LOCATION 258, 330-31 (1954).

currently shaping city growth be brought under more effective control, at least so long as these forces resemble those governing the growth of polyp colonies? Of course, city size could be explicitly limited, and the ownership of all urban land could be vested in cities. Such controls might, however, run counter to economic flexibility and American ideology. The same objectives could probably be achieved through use of a system of taxes and subsidies, calculated to influence population distribution and provide compensation to those on whom discretionary decision-makers imposed unrequited direct and indirect costs. These tax and subsidy arrangements would be reinforced if a rent-absorbing tax in keeping with, say, the *zonal* opportunity cost of land were imposed on all *land* in and around cities.

Sixth, perhaps the greatest promise lies in the development of an adequate number of additional cities of such size—say, 100-200 thousand—as provides adequate communal opportunity, together with near-optium conditions for housing and macro-habitats as well as abundant access to amenities and recreational space. Suppose that 600 such cities were established during the next thirty-five years. They could absorb 60-90 million or more inhabitants, or something like 60-80 or more per cent of the prospective population increase, most of which will settle in urban centers. If, say, as much as one-fourth of the population absorbed into these cities were nonwhite, it is possible that more than the anticipated increase in the nonwhite population would be settled there; then the current drift into central cities and ghettoes would be checked and perhaps reversed. Should such cities not be established, the population of most cities now over 100,000 would be greatly increased, for the next thirty-five years will witness the addition of 100 or more million to this nation's population and perhaps that of an equal number to the urban population, which in 1960 already numbered 113 million on the old census definition and 125 million on the new definition.

That this promise is realizable is suggested by two facts: (a) the relevant Key Decisions regarding location and many other matters are made by a very small number of business men; (b) big business men and corporations are becoming increasingly interested in the development of attractive, rationally-organized cities. We may divide a working population into Primary Job Makers and Job Takers, in which category may be placed Secondary Job Makers. The Primary Job Makers establish and locate the basic enterprises and employments. Around these gather Secondary Job Makers whose enterprises service and meet the needs of the Primary Job Makers and their employees as well as those of all persons who fall in the Job-Taker category. The heads of some but not all governmental agencies and foundations belong in the Primary Job-Maker category as they make Key Decisions affecting location of activities.

(a) That the making of Key Decisions respecting location is highly concentrated is suggested by the following data. In 1965 twenty-one out of each 100 persons employed in the United States were employed by 750 companies, many of which are describable as Primary Job Makers. About 55.1 per cent of all industrial workers were employed by 500 industrial companies.[60] Brian Berry reports that in the area around Chicago the location decisions of about twenty retailers control those of about 20,000 lesser retailers respecting where they will carry on for the next twenty-five years.[61] It is evident, therefore, that the Key Decisions essential to locating basic employment in new cities may be made by a small number of business firms. The implementation of such locational decisions would entail a redistribution of "brains," now most unevenly distributed because of unequal distribution of economic activities and educational institutions.[62] For "brains" have not merely replaced muscle; they now constitute the most strategic form of mobile and creative capital. "Brains," however, insist on access to cultural and other amenities as well as to good housing and attractive macro-habitats. Of this Key Decision Makers are becoming increasingly aware even if the current urban power structure is not.

A Key Decision Maker or two can launch a new city destined to number 100-200 thousand inhabitants by establishing an economic base capable of multiplying and expanding into around 40-80 thousand jobs.[63] If such base is established, say by introduction of manufacturing plants that employ 10-20 thousand persons, the labor force will expand sympathetically to something like 40-80 thousand gainfully employed. Manufacturing is not, of course, the only possible source of an initiating economic base, particularly in the United States where the ratio of employment in manufacture to all employment is falling. Other activities, among them collections of services, may provide a base; they need only to supply the exports that enable the community to purchase goods and services not supplied locally.

(b) A Key Decision Maker may be interested in doing more than locating activities at a point in space where, he believes, a city with attractive environs will come into being. He may want to establish a more complete city, one providing not only basic employment but also ordered and abundant space for all ancillary activities and amenities (including even such activities as amateur theatricals and similar activities which seldom yield returns even equal to private monetary costs). In such a city far more than in those described under (a) high priority must be given to housing and its macro-habitats and to averting the diverse costs and dissatisfactions associated with both life in central cities and life in isolated suburbs. Otherwise the collection of houses and macro-habitats constituting this city will not prove convertible into

---

[60] *Big Business in American Society, Is It Really Taking Over?*, BUSINESS IN BRIEF (Chase Manhattan Bank), Oct. 1966.

[61] NORTH EASTERN ILLINOIS PLANNING COMMISSION, METROPOLITAN PLANNING GUIDE LINES, COMMERCIAL STRUCTURE 94, *cited in* Clark, *supra* note 52, at 3.

[62] *See* Lapp, *Where the Brains Are*, FORTUNE, March 1966, at 154.

[63] In 1960, 40% of the population was in the labor force. Given lower fertility this fraction might rise slightly.

a community that generates a degree of loyalty and collective responsibility. It is probable that planned cities of this sort, together with those referred to under (a), can absorb most of the prospective increase in urban population. Illustrative of the planned type of community is that near Clear Lake, Texas, sponsored by the Humble Oil Company and the National Aeronautics and Space Administration, and intended to evolve over a fifteen-year period into a city of some 140,000 residents living in some 40,000 houses situated in an area of twenty-four miles square that includes a 365 acre town center and a 1,000 acre research park.[64] Somewhat similar cities are planned by General Electric Company, Goodyear Tire and Rubber Company, Westinghouse, and other large corporations. Several are well along—Robert Simon's Reston, Virginia, intended to house about 75,000 people, and James Rouse's Columbia, Maryland, intended to house about 110,000 people. All follow Secretary Udall's advice that "city planning should put people first."[65]

The types of towns referred to have a localized primary base, supplemented in several instances by the activities of inhabitants destined to work in nearby metropolitan centers. The housing problem is solved, though sometimes at the expense of considerable cost in potentially discretionary time. This time-cost must be borne also by some of those who live in small planned communities (other than retirement communities) situated near metropolitan centers to which many must journey daily for employment. Again, however, the housing problem is solved.

CONCLUSION

The argument permeating this essay is that the housing question must be examined and carried toward resolution through a systematic approach rather than through the piecemeal approaches of speculators and others who neglect the fundamental importance of macro-habitats and their relations to each other and the larger urban unit. This approach is of increasing significance in an age when discretionary time is increasing and the challenge of the inept may be undergoing intensification, perhaps with Toynbeean implications.[66] It is not inferred that improvement in housing or even in macro-habitats will solve the ills of the day though it may contribute to solutions under appropriate conditions. It is suggested, however, that we are in need of innovation of systematic though diverse arrangements suited to the housing, habitat, and related needs of communities of varying size and situation. It is emphasized finally that our capacity to meet these needs is likely to be inversely related to our rate of population growth.

---

[64] The Birth of a City, THE HUMBLE WAY, No. 4, 1963, at 1-3.

[65] S. L. UDALL, THE QUIET CRISIS 170 (1963).

[66] See Goode, The Protection of the Inept, 32 AM. SOCIOLOGICAL REV. 5 (1967). See generally on the internal proletariat, 5 A. TOYNBEE, A STUDY OF HISTORY 58-194 (1939).

AN ASSESSMENT OF NATIONAL HOUSING NEEDS

Nathaniel S. Keith*

Introduction

It is clear that total housing needs in the United States, in terms of existing and projected future requirements, are a product of four principal factors:

First, the needs of the current population and the future needs for housing based on the official projections of population growth and net household formation.

Second, the condition of the existing housing supply.

Third, the financial ability of the various segments of the U.S. population to pay for shelter.

Fourth, the accepted goals and standards of the nation for the housing of the population as a whole.

To reverse the sequence of these four factors, since 1949 it has been the official policy of the United States to achieve eventually a "decent home and a suitable living environment for every American family." This policy was established by the preamble of the Housing Act of 1949[1] and has remained the official national goal through succeeding Congresses and presidential administrations. The main purpose of this article is to appraise the progress—or limitations—in meeting this goal during the eighteen years since its establishment, to assess the related implications springing from the rapid population growth, to examine the performance of the housing industry and of special federal programs in advancing toward the goal, and to consider particular problems affecting that progress and various proposals to meet them.

I

National Housing Needs

The general dimensions of the prospects for massive population growth in the United States are presumably well recognized. However, it seems doubtful that the full import of this growth in terms of future housing needs has as yet penetrated the national consciousness.

With total population soon to reach the 200 million mark, the median official projection is that there will be further growth to about 260 million by 1985. This

---

* A.B. 1929, Brown University. Urban Renewal and Housing Consultant. President, National Housing Conference, Inc.; Trustee, Foundation for Cooperative Housing; Member, Advisory Committee on Housing and Urban Development, Agency for International Development, U.S. Department of State. Author, University Hill, Syracuse, N.Y. (1967); The Future of Downtown Rochester, N.Y. (1965); co-author [with Carl Feiss], The Community Renewal Program for the U.S. Virgin Islands (1966); The Community Renewal Program for Rochester, N.Y. (1963); The Future of Buffalo, N.Y. (1958); The Renewal Possibilities of the Historic Triangle of San Juan, Puerto Rico (1955); [with James Rouse], No Slums in Ten Years, Washington, D.C. (1955).

[1] 42 U.S.C. § 1441 (1964).

TABLE 1

CONDITION OF OCCUPIED HOUSING UNITS, INSIDE AND OUTSIDE STANDARD METROPOLITAN
STATISTICAL AREAS, 1960

Subject	Thousands of Housing Units			Percent Distribution		
	United States	Inside SMSAs	Outside SMSAs	Total	Inside SMSAs	Outside SMSAs
All occupied units........	53,024	34,000	19,024	100.0	100.0	100.0
Sound.................	43,812	29,564	14,248	82.6	87.0	74.9
With all plumbing facilities..............	40,432	28,268	12,165	76.3	83.1	63.9
Lacking some or all facilities..............	3,380	1,296	2,084	6.4	3.8	11.0
Deteriorating...........	6,944	3,456	3,487	13.1	10.2	18.3
With all plumbing facilities..............	4,118	2,521	1,597	7.8	7.4	8.4
Lacking some or all facilities...........	2,826	936	1,890	5.3	2.8	9.9
Dilapidated........	2,268	979	1,288	4.3	2.9	6.8

Source: U.S. Bureau of the Census, Department of Commerce.

will represent an increase of about one-third in two decades, representing 65 million people and about 20 million households.

In relation to the national goal of achieving a satisfactory standard of housing for the entire population, the implications of this sharp population growth on future housing needs are compounded by the unsatisfactory condition of much of the existing housing supply. As shown in table 1, the 1960 Census of Housing reported that close to 12.6 million occupied housing units, or twenty-four per cent of all occupied units, were deteriorating, dilapidated, or lacking some or all plumbing facilities. Within the standard metropolitan areas, the percentage of deficient units was seventeen, or a ratio of about one in six; outside metropolitan areas, the percentage was thirty-six per cent, or a ratio of more than one in three, reflecting in part the high incidence of deficiencies in farm and rural non-farm housing.

In addition, from observation it is clear that many of the so-called standard dwellings are obsolete or obsolescent, poorly located, or deficient in modern facilities, and will require replacement before the end of this century.

There may have been some improvement in this situation during the past seven years, although comprehensive national statistics will not be available until the 1970 Census is tabulated. However, as will be discussed later in this paper, on the basis of the slow rate of progress in corrective programs, it is doubtful that there has been any marked decrease since 1960 in the percentage of deficient housing in the nation as a whole.

The correlation between occupancy of substandard housing and substandard incomes is obvious. However, the implications of this correlation from the standpoint of housing needs are emphasized by the significant statistics on poor households

TABLE 2

NUMBER OF POOR HOUSEHOLDS AND INCIDENCE OF POVERTY, 1959, 1962, AND 1965

	Number of Poor Households (Millions)			Incidence of Poverty (percent of total households in the category)		
	1959	1962	1965	1959	1962	1965
Total...................	13.4	12.6	11.5	24	22	19
Aged (65 and over)[1].......	3.9	3.8	3.8	49	41	39
White................	3.5	3.3	3.4	47	39	37
Non-white............	.4	.4	.5	73	64	65
All other[2]................	9.4	8.9	7.6	20	18	15
Farm................	1.5	.9	.7	40	31	24
White...............	1.1	.7	.5	34	25	18
Non-white...........	.4	.2	.2	86	81	76
Non-farm..............	8.0	7.9	7.0	18	17	15
White..............	5.7	5.5	4.9	15	14	12
Non-white..........	2.2	2.4	2.0	47	47	37
	Billions of Dollars			Percent of GNP		
Poverty Income Gap[3]........	13.7	12.8	11.0	2.8	2.3	1.6

[1] One- and two-person households with head aged 65 and over.
[2] All households headed by a person under 65 and families of three or more headed by an aged person.
[3] The poverty income gap is the amount which would raise money income of all poor households over the poverty threshold.
Source: U.S. Department of Commerce; U.S. Department of Health, Education & Welfare.

and incidence of poverty set forth in table 2. In this table, a household is statistically classified as poor if its total money income falls below levels specified by the Social Security Administration, currently $1,570 for an unrelated individual, $2,030 for a couple, and $3,200 for a family of four. (Median family income is estimated at $6,569 as of March 1965.)

While considerable improvement has been shown since 1959, the fact that 11.5 million households, or almost one out of five, were in the poverty area in 1965 gives further weight to the crucial nature of housing needs among the poor. Aside from the six per cent of poor families living in low rent public housing, the realistic assumption is that the great predominance of poor households is occupying substandard housing.

To meet the combined objectives of accommodating the housing needs generated by population growth and eventually replacing present substandard dwellings, there is a growing consensus that gross annual housing production in the general range of 2.5 million units per year will be essential. The Board of Directors of the National Housing Conference, Inc., representing a clearing house of public interest organizations, professional groups, and organized labor on housing and community development matters, recently expressed this consensus as follows:[2]

Here is a suggested schedule of programs needed to accomplish our objectives now and for the coming decades:

[2] National Housing Conference Legislative Proposals, approved April 9, 1967. (These proposals have been reprinted in 113 CONG. REC. H4799 (daily ed. April 27, 1967).)

1. Massive programs to increase and improve the national housing supply through measures which will raise production to the absolute minimum of 2.5 million dwelling units per year, eliminate slums, blight and deterioration within 20 years, and provide for other needed replacements and for housing mobility.
. . . .

To achieve the housing priority proposed above, it will be necessary to build a total of 45 to 57 million new dwelling units in the next 20 years; the high range in this projection would represent in effect the equivalent of the entire national housing stock in existence in 1960. This would represent an average 20-year annual production rate of between 2.2 million and 2.8 million units a year, with a rate in excess of these averages during the closing years of these decades in order to offset the lead-time which would be involved in expanding production up to the required levels. These projections contemplate accommodating the anticipated net household formation over the next 20 years, the replacement of existing substandard housing as well as of the units which will be eliminated by other demolition or losses, and the replacement of other presently existing housing at an annual rate of one percent to two percent of the present national inventory.

As shown in table 3, actual total housing production has consistently fallen far below this target. In fact, in 1966 total housing starts declined to the lowest annual level since 1946, reflecting in large part the shortage of private mortgage funds and the rise in conventional mortgage interest rates to 6.44 per cent in December 1966, from 5.78 per cent in December 1965, an increase of about one-ninth.[3]

TABLE 3

NEW HOUSING UNITS STARTED (PRIVATE AND PUBLIC)

	Total Farm and Non-Farm	Non-Farm Private Single-Family	Non-Farm Private 2-Units or More
1960	1,296,000	973,000	257,000
1961	1,365,000	946,000	339,000
1962	1,492,000	968,000	471,000
1963	1,640,900	993,200	588,500
1964	1,590,700	944,500	585,900
1965	1,542,700	940,000	542,700
1966	1,252,300	771,000	426,000

Source: U.S. Bureau of Census, Department of Commerce.

This disparity between actual housing production and recognized total needs reflects primarily the fact that new housing construction costs plus related costs for improved land can be absorbed at market financing rates only by the upper half of the income ranges of the national population. Thus, the lower income range of the population, where housing needs are the most acute, is generally outside the market which can be served by the private housing industry in so far as new dwellings are concerned.

---

[3] This data was obtained from the Federal Home Loan Bank Board.

Currently, this disparity is further accentuated by the shortage of private mortgage funds and the inflation in mortgage interest rates. Over the long term, it also reflects the rise in construction costs which historically have risen at a faster rate than the consumer price index as a whole. Between 1959 and 1966, while the Bureau of Labor Statistics consumer price index was rising from 101.5 to 112.9, an increase of 11.4 points, the Boesch residential construction cost index was increasing from 102.5 to 120.1, an increase of 17.6 points.

As shown by table 4, the average estimated construction cost of privately-owned dwelling units increased by fourteen per cent between 1963 and 1966. While part of this rise may reflect an increase in the average size and equipment of private housing, examination of the construction cost index indicates that rising costs are the principal factor. The statistics in table 4 represent construction cost only. The estimated median sales price of a single-family home in December 1966 was $20,700, including land, according to the Bureau of the Census.

TABLE 4

AVERAGE CONSTRUCTION COST OF PRIVATE AND PUBLIC NON-FARM HOUSING STARTS, 1963-1966

	Privately-owned		Publicly-owned
	1-family	Total	
1963......................	$14,825	$12,625	$11,925
1964......................	15,600	13,125	12,450
1965......................	16,250	13,650	12,625
1966......................	17,000	14,375	12,625

Source: U.S. Bureau of Census, Department of Commerce.

II

MEETING THE UNSERVED HOUSING NEEDS

There has been growing recognition over the years of the necessity for supplemental financing programs to meet the needs of families and individuals with incomes below the level at which new standard private housing could be afforded.

The initial major step in this direction was, of course, the enactment of the Housing Act of 1937[4] which established the federally-aided, low rent public housing program. After a lapse during the Second World War period and the immediate postwar years, the program was reactivated and expanded by the Housing Act of 1949.[5] Again, additional annual federal subsidy was authorized by the Housing Act of 1961[6] and by the Housing and Urban Development Act of 1965.[7] The latter statute contemplated annual production of 35,000 new public housing units per year and

---

[4] United States Housing Act of 1937, ch. 896, 50 Stat. 888.
[5] Ch. 338, 63 Stat. 413 (codified in scattered sections of 12, 42 U.S.C.).
[6] Pub. L. No. 87-70, § 303, 75 Stat. 166.
[7] 42 U.S.C. § 1453(b) (Supp. II, 1965-66).

the provision of approximately 25,000 units per year through rehabilitation or through the leasing of existing private housing suitable for this purpose. Through administrative action, efforts are also currently being made to further broaden the base for the production of public housing through the so-called "turnkey" approach under which private developers may submit proposals to local housing authorities for construction of public housing units based on their own sites and their own plans for sale to the local authorities upon completion. The objective is to increase the flexibility of the program by introducing private initiative and to substantially shorten the long lead-time required for the development of new public housing through the conventional channels.

The Housing Act of 1961 also initiated a program for the private development of housing for low or middle income families at a subsidized interest rate.[8] Under this program, FHA insurance commitments are issued to nonprofit, cooperative, or limited distribution sponsors for the development of new or substantially rehabilitated housing for occupancy by families or individuals in moderate income brackets, which are administratively defined as below the median income in the particular locality. The mortgage interest rate is limited to three per cent, the FHA mortgage insurance premium is waived, and the permanent mortgage is purchased by the Federal National Mortgage Association.

Another major innovation in federal housing programs to meet the special housing needs of low income families and individuals was the rent supplement program enacted by the Housing and Urban Development Act of 1965.[9] Under this program, the FHA insures mortgages at market interest rates (currently six per cent) to private nonprofit, limited distribution, or cooperative mortgagors for new or substantially rehabilitated housing. In order to accommodate low income families and individuals in such housing, the Secretary of the Department of Housing and Urban Development is authorized to enter into contracts with such mortgagors to provide annual rent supplements covering the difference between the full rents required to support the project and twenty-five per cent of the total family income of low income occupants, who are required by statute to have incomes at admission within the eligibility ceilings for admission to federally-aided low rent public housing in the particular locality.

These three programs are also intended to give special relief to the housing needs of low and moderate income elderly couples and individuals. In addition, section 202 of the Housing Act of 1959[10] established a program of direct low interest federal loans (currently limited to three per cent) from the Department of Housing and Urban Development to finance housing by nonprofit sponsors for elderly couples and individuals. As was shown in table 2, the incidence of low incomes among the

---

[8] 12 U.S.C. § 1715*l*(d)(3) (Supp. II, 1965-66).

[9] 12 U.S.C. § 1701s (Supp. II, 1965-66).

[10] 12 U.S.C. § 1701q (1964, Supp. II, 1965-66).

elderly is especially pronounced. There also exists a special FHA market rate insurance program for housing for the elderly.[11]

While these programs represent important steps in meeting unserved housing needs, the volume of accomplishment has been marginal in relation to the overall dimensions of the needs. This has reflected in part the political controversy still generated by the use of direct federal subsidy for housing. In the case of the federally-aided low rent public housing program, the limitations have been compounded by local difficulties in securing agreement on acceptable sites, which have frequently involved racial overtones, and by the tax exempt status of public housing projects. In the case of the special FHA programs, the limitations appear to reflect the absence of any strong financial incentive to the overall private housing industry to undertake such projects on a broad scale and the difficulties encountered in developing effective nonprofit organizations as an alternative source for volume production.

In the thirty-year history of the federally-aided, low rent public housing program, total production has amounted to only 636,000 completed dwelling units, representing little more than one per cent of the total existing housing supply in the nation. While the broadened and more flexible approaches toward providing public housing as previously described may hopefully expand future accomplishment, the production record through 1966, as shown in table 5, does not reflect such a trend.

TABLE 5
PUBLICLY-OWNED HOUSING STARTS (UNITS)

	Federally-assisted	Other	Total
1960	26,500	17,400	43,900
1961	28,200	23,800	52,000
1962	19,800	9,900	29,700
1963	24,000	7,800	31,800
1964	22,700	9,400	32,100
1965	30,100	6,800	36,900
1966	28,700	2,500	31,200

Source: U.S. Bureau of Census, Department of Commerce.

In the case of the FHA below market interest rate program for moderate income families and individuals under section 221(d)(3), the total insurance written from the establishment of the program in 1961 through the end of 1966 involved only 52,000 dwelling units, of which 13,000 were insured during 1966. Likewise, as shown by table 6, the rate of production under the special program for housing for moderate and low income elderly families and individuals has been of very modest proportions (it is significant, however, that about two-thirds of the federally-aided low rent public housing units started in 1966 were for the elderly, indicating substantially greater local political acceptance for this phase of the public housing program).

[11] 12 U.S.C. § 1715v (1964, Supp. II, 1965-66).

TABLE 6

FEDERALLY-ASSISTED HOUSING CONSTRUCTION FOR SENIOR CITIZENS BY DWELLING UNITS,
1963-1966

	Direct Loans (Net Loans Executed)	Low-Rent Public Housing (Units Started)	FHA Insured (Units Started)
1963	4,350	8,810	8,267
1964	4,753	12,401	5,005
1965	4,641	17,420	5,237
1966	5,707	19,780	1,349

Source: HOUSING ASSISTANCE ADMINISTRATION AND FEDERAL HOUSING ADMINISTRATION.

Actual development of housing under the rent supplement program has been slow because of delays in funding the program in Congress. The initial appropriation of $12 million (representing contract authority for annual rent supplement payments) was not voted until May 1966 and the second appropriation of $20 million occurred in the fall of 1966. The combined appropriation was less than half the $65 million authorized by the 1965 act and is sufficient to cover about 53,000 dwelling units at an assumed average rent supplement of $600 per year per unit or $50 per month. Under the 1965 act, additional appropriations are authorized in the amount of $40 million in the fiscal year beginning July 1, 1967 and $45 million in the fiscal year beginning July 1, 1968. If fully funded (which appears doubtful on the basis of past congressional action), these would be sufficient to cover an additional 142,000 units.

As of August 11, 1967, funds had been earmarked in the amount of $32,000,000 by the Department of Housing and Urban Development for 431 rent supplement projects in 284 cities involving 33,961 rent-supplemented dwelling units.

Later in this article there will be a presentation of current recommendations for measures to substantially enlarge the production of housing in the areas of the most critical needs among moderate and low income families and individuals. However, the dimensions of these needs as previously cited together with the large volume of deficient housing now in use, predominantly by the low income segment of the population, emphasizes the potential importance of large scale rehabilitation of existing housing at least as an interim supply of decent shelter.

Such large scale rehabilitation has in principle been a major objective of the federally-aided urban renewal program since 1954 when the Housing Act of 1954 was enacted. Here again, however, the overall accomplishments in relation to the total volume of deficient housing have been small. On the basis of statistics from the Renewal Projects Administration of the Department of Housing and Urban Development, the status of rehabilitation in urban renewal projects as of June 30, 1966 is shown in table 7.

Evidence of increasing local interest and activity in rehabilitation as part of urban renewal is indicated by the fact that as of December 31, 1966, 231 (forty-eight per

TABLE 7
STATUS OF RESIDENTIAL REHABILITATION IN FEDERALLY-AIDED URBAN RENEWAL PROJECTS,
JUNE 30, 1966

Total number of projects in execution	1,119
Projects involving some rehabilitation	307
Number of residential structures scheduled for rehabilitation	72,387
Number of dwelling units scheduled for rehabilitation	185,267
Dwelling units with rehabilitation completed	60,319
Dwelling units with rehabilitation in process	26,396

Source: U.S. RENEWAL PROJECTS ADMINISTRATION, DEPARTMENT OF HOUSING AND URBAN DEVELOPMENT.

cent) of the 485 urban renewal projects in the planning stage will involve rehabilitation of existing housing in various proportions.

In efforts to stimulate greater activity in rehabilitation of existing housing, special provisions have been enacted by Congress to facilitate the financing of such rehabilitation. These have included special FHA insurance for residential rehabilitation in urban renewal areas under section 220(h) of the National Housing Act of 1934, as amended;[12] direct federal loans at three per cent interest rate up to $10,000 per dwelling unit for rehabilitation in code enforcement areas;[13] and direct grants of up to $1500 to enable low income homeowners in urban renewal areas and code enforcement areas to bring their homes up to required standards.[14] The latter two provisions were incorporated in the Housing and Urban Development Act of 1965. Here again, actual performance has been of small proportions.

The special FHA section 220(h) program has been virtually inoperative, presumably because of lack of interest on the part of private lenders in making such loans. Under the three per cent direct rehabilitation loan program, as of December 1966, 649 loans involving 916 dwelling units in the amount of $3,200,000 had been issued. On that same date, 1,919 rehabilitation grants to low income owner-occupants in the amount of $2,784,000 had been approved.

It is therefore apparent that most of the rehabilitation which has been actually carried out in urban renewal areas has been conventionally financed rather than undertaken under the special federal program.

Still another approach to broadening the use of the existing housing supply and improving its quality is a program for two-thirds federal grants to localities for carrying out concentrated code enforcement programs in areas where the existing housing can be brought up to local code standards at reasonable costs.[15] This program was established by the Housing and Urban Development Act of 1965 and is still in its early stages. However, as of June 1966, code enforcement grants, which can also cover

[12] 12 U.S.C. § 1715k(h) (1964, Supp. II, 1965-66).
[13] 42 U.S.C. § 1452b (1964, Supp. II, 1965-66).
[14] 42 U.S.C. § 1466 (Supp. II, 1965-66).
[15] 42 U.S.C. § 1468 (Supp. II, 1965-66).

up to two-thirds of the costs of improving public facilities in an area, had been approved for twelve projects containing 38,382 dwelling units of which 20,134 involved one or more local code violations.

CONCLUSION AND RECOMMENDATIONS

From the previous discussion in this paper of the nature and dimensions of the national housing needs not now being adequately served by the private housing or by existing federal-aid programs, it is clear that massive expansion in those programs and no doubt the establishment of additional and broader approaches will be necessary if the ultimate goal of satisfactory housing for the entire population is to be substantially achieved in the foreseeable future.

Over the near term, the fiscal demands of the Vietnam war constitute a barrier against expansion of existing programs or the enactment of new ones.

In the previously cited report of the Board of Directors of the National Housing Conference on March 17, 1967, these questions were examined. The conclusions and recommendations of this professional group with respect to matters discussed in this article may be summarized as follows:

1. The administration of existing programs for low and moderate income housing and rehabilitation should be made more forceful, more expeditious, and more sympathetic to the objectives of these programs.

2. Program funds for moderate income housing temporarily impounded by the Administration because of fiscal stringencies should be released. Some relief in this direction has already occurred with the lessening of inflationary pressures.

3. The Congress should fully fund the rent supplement and model cities programs which it authorized in 1965 and 1966.

4. A national goal should be established to expand production of housing for low and moderate income families and individuals to an annual average of 500,000 dwellings to produce a total of 10 million dwellings for this critical segment of national housing needs by 1987. This should include expanding the public housing program to a rate increasing the supply by 125,000 units a year, including full use of the new approaches previously described. It should include an expansion in the mortgage backing of the section 221(d)(3) below-market interest rate program for moderate income families and individuals by the Federal National Mortgage Association so as to permit the financing of 140,000 units per year. Ultimately, it should include the establishment of broader programs which would stimulate greater participation by the private housing industry in this market.

5. A national objective should be to establish vacant land development programs and land reserve programs to provide the new housing and related facilities needed to accommodate population growth in urban centers, to permit the renewal and redevelopment of slums and blighted areas, and to support the model cities program.

6. In order to expand the rehabilitation of existing housing to significant levels, there should be recognition that large-scale rehabilitation programs will require capital and other subsidies comparable to those involved in acquiring and clearing slum properties. Because most properties suitable for rehabilitation are occupied by families and individuals of low and moderate income, there should likewise be recognition that write-offs of part of the costs of rehabilitation will be generally required in order to produce monthly charges within the financial capacity of that market.

CITIZEN PARTICIPATION: A SUBURBAN SUGGESTION FOR THE CENTRAL CITY

Richard F. Babcock* and Fred P. Bosselman†

Municipal building, zoning, and housing codes have traditionally been characterized by (1) centralized municipal administration and (2) comprehensiveness of their application within the political jurisdiction to which they are applicable. These distinctive features may be consistent with the goals of the residents of small, homogeneous suburbs. Within our large cities, however, these same characteristics explain much of the failure of such codes to come to grips with the problems of lower income residents of blighted neighborhoods.

It is the purpose of this paper to propose a line of examination that will question the relevance of these orthodox rules to current urban conditions and to suggest the testing of a system of code administration and enforcement in our big cities that is not bottomed on those two ancient premises.

I

The Need for Decentralization

A mass of literature has accumulated in the past few years advocating "citizen participation" as the latest tactic for solving the problems of deprived neighborhoods, now that public housing and urban renewal have "failed." These "People people" as Roger Starr might characterize them,[1] urge us to emphasize the needs and desires of the people in each neighborhood and block rather than the needs of the city as a whole. They suggest that we adopt "the microscopic or detailed view."[2]

The methods that they have advanced for achieving participation in governmental affairs by residents of deprived neighborhoods unfortunately fall, for the most part, into two self-defeating categories.

The first might be called the "burn, baby, burn" theory. This holds that the urban establishment will never voluntarily pay any attention to poor people unless poor people make themselves obnoxious. To achieve this end various organizers, professional or otherwise, are employed to activate groups in support of particular issues,[3] and to bring pressure to bear upon the city administration, through adversary methods ranging from noisome irritation to guerilla warfare.

---

* A.B. 1940, Dartmouth College; J.D. 1946, M.B.A. 1951, University of Chicago. Member of the law firm of Ross, Hardies, O'Keefe, Babcock, McDugald & Parsons, Chicago, Ill. Author, The Zoning Game (1966).

† A.B. 1956, University of Colorado; LL.B. 1959, Harvard University. Member of the law firm of Ross, Hardies, O'Keefe, Babcock, McDugald & Parsons, Chicago, Ill.

[1] Starr, *The People Are Not the City*, in American Soc'y of Planning Officials, Planning 1966, at 125 (1966).

[2] J. Jacobs, The Death and Life of Great American Cities 439 (1961).

[3] The leading text is, of course, S. Alinsky, Reveille For Radicals (1945).

The second tactic—often a self-conscious riposte to the first—might be called the "figurehead" method. This calls for the placing of a number of "leading" residents from deprived areas on advisory boards and commissions where they can meet and nod their heads when their sponsors tell them what is good for them,[4] while the rest of the populace is overwhelmed by a swarm of social workers skillfully trained in head-patting.[5]

Neither of these strategies offers the citizen of the urban neighborhood *real* participation in the actual decision making process. At a recent conference in Chicago, Daniel Watts, editor of *Liberator*, a "new left" magazine, bluntly described the failure of the figurehead method:[6]

> The negro preacher has been the self-appointed leader of the community and the white power structure of the city would like to deal with him. But this doesn't get through to the "soul brothers" who could get the idea to burn the community down. You've got to get them to feel that this is their community and it would be their community that they would put to the torch.

The "burn, baby, burn" method may achieve a few additional neighborhood swimming pools, tot lots, and similar short-range goals, but at what cost?[7] The technique creates so much antipathetic reaction that it carries the seeds of its own destruction by a fierce response from the majority.

Neither of these responses to the growing restlessness in our cities offers a constructive solution to what Richard Goodwin has recently called "the most troubling political fact of our age: . . . [the] swift and continual diminution in the significance of the individual citizen, transforming him from a wielder into an object of authority."[8] Nor are traditional political processes satisfactory means of obtaining citizen participation. It may be true, as one politician suggested, that every good precinct captain is an ombudsman. The rub is that in an age when a real understanding of government requires familiarity with electronic machines as well as political machines it is hard to find good precinct captains. The distance between the increasing complexity and professionalism of City Hall and the malaise of the poor citizen has widened appreciably since the days of the Curleys and Crumps.[9] As David Hunter puts it: "Slum people are out!"[10]

[4] *See, e.g.*, CITY PLANNING ASSOCIATES, SUGGESTIONS FOR ENLISTING CITIZEN PARTICIPATION IN URBAN RENEWAL (1962), a guide for the creation of such groups; ARTHUR D. LITTLE, INC., STRATEGIES FOR SHAPING MODEL CITIES 22-27 (1967).

[5] *See, e.g.*, David & Lewis, *Citizen Participation*, 20 J. HOUSING 472, 474 (1963), discussing the creation of tenant organizations in public housing in New York City: "The most helpful relationship between authority staff and tenant organization would seem to lie in an educational and training role." (Original in italics.) *Compare* G. ORWELL, THE ROAD TO WIGAN PIER 70-73 (1st Am. ed. 1958).

[6] Chicago Daily News, June 7, 1967, at 9, col. 1.

[7] *See generally* Twomey, *Citizen Participation*, 20 J. HOUSING 463 (1963).

[8] Goodwin, *The Shape of American Politics*, COMMENTARY, June 1967, at 25. *Compare* W. LIPPMAN, THE PHANTOM PUBLIC 174-83 (1925).

[9] *See* R. WOOD, SUBURBIA 165, 197 (1959). This is not to deny that many municipal governments have a good record of employing residents of deprived neighborhoods in city jobs, but commuting to city hall creates little feeling of participation in the neighborhoods.

[10] D. HUNTER, THE SLUMS, CHALLENGE AND RESPONSE 221 (1964).

Real citizen participation is possible—in an era when HUD has replaced Hague—only if real governmental power is delegated to the neighborhood level. It is past time that we begin directing imaginative debate toward the formulation of a legal and administrative system that may achieve real decentralization of governmental power in our large cities and still leave to the central city government control over those features of the urban environment that require centralized administration.

It is significant that precisely such an exercise in the re-allocation of power is now going on in the metropolitan areas outside the central city. The suburbs, large and small, long accustomed to wielding all the powers of government, are faced with demands that they divest themselves of control in those areas of power where the facts of our untidy environment require a wider consensus of decision making. In the case of the metropolitan area the transference of power is upward to state and regional agencies, impelled by the inability of the suburbs to deal individually with the exploding problems of transportation, the pollution of our air and water, our shriveling open spaces, and overwhelming densities. In the case of the central city, however, a similar and consistent re-appraisal requires the transfer of some power downward to the individual neighborhood. In each case, the hard job is to make a reasonable allocation of power that will recognize the legitimate interests of the neighborhood (or suburb) on the one hand, and the city (or region) on the other.

The enforcement and administration of housing, zoning, and building codes and related ordinances may be a fair area in which to test out the feasibility of such a delegation of power, for in these spheres of government all would have to agree that those regional neighborhoods, the suburbs, should retain considerable administrative authority. No more is here proposed to be given to the city's neighborhoods than would be left to the suburbs by even the most intransigent regionalist.

Before delving further into the theoretical advantages of this type of decentralization, we propose to suggest a way in which such decentralization might operate in practice.

II

DECENTRALIZATION: A PROPOSAL

Under our hypothetical system the city would be subdivided into administrative districts following historic neighborhood boundaries, probably with no less rational bases than are apparent in many suburban municipal boundaries. (Certainly the variations in population and "motivation" among these "suburbs in the city" would not be significantly greater than now exist among such suburbs as Winnetka and Robbins, Illinois, each of which enjoys substantially all the powers vested in municipal corporations.)

Within each of the districts of the city in which the technique is adopted would be chosen a Board of Compliance and Appeal made up of residents of the

neighborhood.[11]   The neighborhood Board would have three types of powers: it
would set standards, it would enforce them, and it would grant variations from them.
The standards created by the Board and its administration of them would be subject
to overall policies and guidelines laid down by the central administration.

Each Board would have its own staff of engineers, planners, and attorneys who
would be available to provide information on codes to the residents of the neighborhood and to conduct inspections of housing units for code violations.   The staff could
also conduct schools on housing maintenance for under-urbanized tenants and
fledgling landlords, similar to the "traffic schools" so commonly used in modern
traffic courts,[12] and could engage in other advisory and educational activities.[13]

The neighborhood Board could play a major role in code enforcement.   When
violations are found, the offender would be brought before the neighborhood Board
as the first step in obtaining compliance.   The Board would set a timetable for
making repairs and would offer advice and supervision.   The neighborhood Board
would be better able than any housing court judge to tell whether a property owner
is making a bona fide effort at compliance with the codes, and can far more easily
ascertain the number of families living in a building than can any building department—a problem of increasing importance in view of the new restrictions on housing
inspection laid down by the United States Supreme Court.[14]   The Board, not just
the city, would have the power to seek judicial implementation of its decisions,[15]
and in chronic cases of noncompliance a court order might be obtained making the
Board the receiver of the property.[16]

There are many subjects of code regulation that could be varied from neighbor-

---

[11] The city might well choose to begin use of the technique on an experimental basis in a limited
number of neighborhoods, retaining for the rest of the city the existing city-wide code administration
which would be gradually phased out as new neighborhood boards are phased in.   It is recognized,
of course, that constitutional problems of equal protection, as well as numerous questions of state law,
will need to be considered in instituting this type of system.   Cf. the Texas statute authorizing the City of
Houston to sue to enjoin violations of private covenants.   TEX. REV. CIV. STAT. ANN. art. 947a-1 (Supp.
1966).   See also the prezoning era techniques by which the residents of particular neighborhoods were
given governmental authority to control new construction through the creation of restricted residence
districts.   E.g., State ex rel. Twin City Bldg. & Inv. Co. v. Houghton, 144 Minn. 1, 174 N.W. 885, 176
N.W. 159 (1920).   The State of Washington has recently enacted a statute permitting a form of consolidation of municipalities in which each former municipality retains separate powers in regard to zoning,
subdivision control, and "comprehensive planning."   Ch. 73, [1967] Wash. Laws.

[12] Pioneering in this type of educational treatment is the Baltimore Housing Clinic.   See generally
Bateman & Stern, Housing Clinic for Code Violators, 23 J. HOUSING 203 (1966); Note, Enforcement
of Municipal Housing Codes, 78 HARV. L. REV. 801, 825-26, 859 (1965).

[13] The use of neighborhood information centers in which municipal employees are station in the
neighborhoods to advise and assist the residents has received enthusiastic and rapid acceptance in the past
few years.   See A. KAHN, NEIGHBORHOOD INFORMATION CENTERS: A STUDY AND SOME PROPOSALS (1966).
The present suggestion would expand on this idea by giving the neighborhood centers greater power, and
giving the residents of the neighborhood the immediate supervision of them.

[14] Camara v. Municipal Court, 387 U.S. 523 (1967).   See also R. POUND, SOCIAL CONTROL THROUGH
LAW 53-55 (1942).

[15] In a number of states zoning boards now have the right to litigate independent of the city.   See,
e.g., Dion v. Board of Appeals of Waltham, 344 Mass. 547, 183 N.E.2d 479 (1962).

[16] See generally Gribetz, New York City's Receivership Law, 21 J. HOUSING 297 (1964); Note, supra
note 12, at 828-30.

hood to neighborhood, as the citizens of the neighborhood may choose. Consider the control of housing density: the number of housing units to be permitted per acre. The city's interest in the gross density of its component parts is indisputable, though no more than is the region's concern over the densities of the multitude of municipalities of which it is made up. Control over housing density is crucial in the planning of transportation, recreation, and other public facilities. Trying to plan highways or sanitary systems for regions containing communities which may have five-acre lots today and quarter-acre lots tomorrow makes transportation or sanitary planning more of an intellectual exercise than a meaningful occupation. Only if the governmental unit that plans the highways or sewers also has a voice in the control of the overall number of housing units per acre could economical planning of public facilities be achieved.

But the proposition that gross density of population is not a matter for neighborhood control should not necessarily result in a legal system that leaves a neighborhood with no voice in whether Mrs. Schultz should be able to convert her two-family dwelling into a four-family flat. For example, within general policies set by the city (e.g., that housing in a particular neighborhood should not exceed an average of x units per acre, or that in the next ten years the population of the neighborhood should not increase by more than 20,000), the neighborhood Board rather than City Hall could be given the power to pass upon specific proposals by would-be builders or landlords. Thus the actual decisions as to where and how many new housing units would be permitted, and whether remodeling and conversions of old housing would be allowed, could be delegated to the neighborhood Board, while the city retains control over the overall number of housing units that would be permitted in the neighborhood as a whole. Of course the scope of the neighborhood Board's discretion would need to be kept within limits of city-wide concern over the efficiency and availability of major public services such as sewer and water facilities and traffic.

Another area of potential decentralization is the administration of "open space" requirements. Why must every R-2 single-family district or every R-5 multiple-family district, wherever located in the city, have the same setbacks and side yards? "More Open Space for what?" as Jane Jacobs asks.[17] And why must departures from those uniform patterns—probably originally copied out of some other city's ordinance—require a petition to City Hall? Is there any reason why the residents outside an immediate neighborhood should care how much open space is provided on each private parcel, assuming that overall density is controlled? Despite Lewis Mumford's claim that the residents of Park Avenue, being deprived of open space, live in a slum and don't know it,[18] it seems perfectly appropriate to let the citizens of Park Avenue or Brooklyn Heights or East Harlem determine the extent to which open space

---

[17] J. JACOBS, *supra* note 2, at 90.

[18] L. MUMFORD, THE CITY IN HISTORY 428 (1961). *See also* H. KOBBE, HOUSING AND REGIONAL PLANNING 19 (1941).

must be maintained on individual lots as long as a larger jurisdiction controls the overall density of the neighborhood as a whole.

Then there is the familiar and often litigated problem of "home occupations." Should Mrs. Jones be allowed to run a beauty shop in her basement? Should a real estate broker be allowed to erect an advertising sign in front of his home? There is no reason why anyone at Boston City Hall knows more about these questions than the residents of the neighborhoods of Allston or Roxbury. And would not the municipal officials be happy to free themselves from the responsibility for resolving these emotionally charged but basically petty quarrels?

As a last example, consider the control of architectural design of individual housing structures, an issue which appears to be of great importance to many suburbs and which may become of more interest to deprived neighborhoods in central cities as the paint manufacturers and social psychologists assume a more significant role in urban renewal. There are, of course, selected locations where the control of architecture and design has major regional impact—the preservation of the aesthetic beauty of the Potomac, the maintenance of the charm of the Vieux Carre, or the creation of "gateway" districts to give arriving travelers an unobstructed view of the San Francisco skyline. But in most locations architectural style has no impact outside the immediate neighborhood, and its regulation (if any) could best be left to the neighborhood.[19]

A few aesthetes may insist that the residents of neighborhoods, deprived or otherwise, lack the keen artistic sense necessary to provide meaningful standards of architectural design or decoration. We suggest that in these days when pop art and "indigenous architecture" are so fashionable it would be difficult to deny anyone the right to become his own judge of artistic merit. "The human being is an unproclaimed architect," proclaims Charles Abrams; "the touch of a hundred hands can have the patina of humanity."[20] One only needs to look at a few typical examples of public housing design to conclude that the neighborhood would be hard put to do worse than City Hall.[21]

The above illustrations are only a few of the many suggestions for experiment that could be given. The only missing link is an administrative and legal system for partial decentralization of code administration.

We should not be misunderstood. The authors are as aware as the reader of the host of difficult legal, administrative, and political hazards that such a scheme must

[19] See Babcock, *Billboards, Glass Houses, and the Law*, HARPER'S MAGAZINE, April 1966, at 20.

[20] C. ABRAMS, THE CITY IS THE FRONTIER 320 (1965). Lest this be thought to be purely an American phenomenon it should be noted that the Louvre recently featured an exhibition entitled "Selection des Collections de la Compaignie de l'Art Brut" consisting of art works created by "schizophrenic or psychopathic patients from special institutions" who are described by their patron, artist Jean Dubuffet, as "persons who are strangers to cultural milieus, have been preserved from their influences, and, for the most part, have had only a rudimentary education." THE NEW YORKER, April 29, 1967, at 169-70. Ironically, many ghetto residents might feel that they also meet those criteria.

[21] See Mayer, *Public Housing Architecture*, 19 J. HOUSING 446 (1962).

overcome. All we suggest is that an analysis be made, unhindered by traditional assumptions about the structure of city government, of all phases of the codes which control housing and land development to determine the extent of the impact of each phase of governmental control. Those aspects which have broad impact should be under broad control. Conversely, those powers which have no significant impact outside a small locality should be under local control. For such latter functions, enforcement and administration could be decentralized right down to the neighborhood level.

III

THE LIMITS OF DECENTRALIZATION

There are, of course, many aspects of the traditional municipal codes that cannot and should not be delegated to the neighborhood level. These nondelegable features fall into two categories. First and most important are matters of indivisible city policy, and where such policies are involved the least to be expected from City Hall is that it articulate those policies that demand city-wide decisions. The planning profession is turning away from the mapped master plan showing specific locations of land use and toward the "policies plan" in which the city states the basic policies that should guide the particular location of land uses.[22] Too often, however, these policies plans are being formulated in such ambiguous terms that they can be employed to justify almost any decision which subsequently proves to be expedient. Because the policies have no legal significance there is no compulsion to assure that their meaning is precise. However, if the city's planning policies were to be legal limitations on the powers of neighborhood Boards to set neighborhood standards and dispense variations from them, the pressure would be on the planners to formulate real policies in definitive fashion. The city's policies plan would then at last perform a useful function.[23]

The second area in which delegation of power to neighborhood boards should not be permitted is in regard to those code provisions which are so essential to the health and safety of the entire population that no variance from them should be permitted regardless of the desires of the local residents. The basic policies underlying the codes, involving such things as fire protection and public health, cannot be delegated to the neighborhood level.

It is easy, of course, to state the general proposition that overall policy matters and basic health and safety matters should not be delegated. The difficulty lies in actually drawing lines. Where does policy end and implementation begin? Which aspects

---

[22] Aschman, *The "Policy Plan" in the Planning Program*, in AMERICAN SOC'Y OF PLANNING OFFICALS, PLANNING 1963, at 105 (1963); Fagin, *Planning for Future Urban Growth*, 30 LAW & CONTEMP. PROB. 9, 19 (1965); F. S. CHAPIN, JR., URBAN LAND USE PLANNING 349-54 (2d ed. 1965); AMERICAN SOC'Y OF PLANNING OFFICIALS, POLICY STATEMENTS: GUIDES TO DECISION-MAKING (ASPO Planning Advisory Service Information Rep. No. 152, 1961).

[23] *See* Williams, *Development Controls and Planning Controls: The View From 1964*, in PROCEEDINGS OF THE 1964 ANNUAL CONFERENCE OF THE AMERICAN INSTITUTE OF PLANNERS 70, 78 (1964).

of building codes are in fact designed to protect basic health and safety and which are attempts to protect union privileges or vestiges of long-forgotten purposes?[24]

For example, the desire to reduce costs of rehabilitation will need to be balanced against the concern of all residents of the city over adequate fire protection. Yet this relationship between neighborhood and city is a two-way street, and even some of those aspects of municipal codes that are often thought of as intimately related to health and safety may be susceptible to modification in individual neighborhoods. To alleviate the drastic problems of some deteriorating neighborhoods it may be necessary to sacrifice the ideal for the feasible, and the opportunity to try out new ideas in building construction should not be hamstrung by the reluctance to extend the experiment to all neighborhoods.[25] The willingness of the United States Gypsum Corporation to experiment in Harlem with new techniques should not be frustrated by codes that know no difference between Harlem and Staten Island.[26]

Those who instinctively oppose any "weakening" of code requirements must face an undeniable fact of life. Our present codes are not effectively helping to remedy housing deterioration. In his recent testimony before the Ribicoff Committee, George Sternlieb emphasized that rigid code enforcement does not have uniformly desirable effects:[27]

The cry goes out for code enforcement, and code enforcement obviously is essential, but not uncommonly, when you put the screws on for code enforcement, what you

---

[24] Florida planning consultant Fred Bair described the origin of the common requirement that each dwelling unit have a minimum of 600 square feet:
You go up and talk to the American Public Health Association and say:
"Look—we've been reading this housing code of yours with considerable interest. Where did you come up with the figure that you had to have 600 square feet of floor space in a house to be reasonably healthy, safe and moral—or whatever it is that you're trying to do with that regulation?" And they say, "Well—what was that again?" And you say, "Well, where did you get that 600 square foot figure?" "Well, gee, let's see—who was on that committee?" So you find out that Stu Chapin and so-and-so and so-and-so were on that committee in 1952 and they reached up and picked a figure out of thin air. This conclusion is inescapable. But because the figure was published by APHA, it became a religious symbol. And now you go into them and say, "Well, look—we've got air conditioning. We've got heating. We've got artificial light. Got any number of things that we didn't have generally in 1940 or 1950 or whatever. Does this change the picture?" And they say, "Well, no—it doesn't change the picture. It is printed right there—600 square feet." And you can pursue our symbols and shibboleths back to their origins. But because these things are universally worshipped now, the fact that the origins were a little weak doesn't make too much difference any longer.
R. BABCOCK, THE ZONING GAME 16 (1966).
[25] The feeling of being a guinea pig which might prevail if experimental techniques are imposed from city hall would be alleviated if a neighborhood board were to control the extent to which experimentation was to be permitted. Of course a number of constitutional and legal problems will have to be faced; for a summary of the legal problems of zoned housing codes, see NAT'L ASS'N OF HOUSING AND REDEVELOPMENT OFFICIALS, THE CONSTITUTIONALITY OF HOUSING CODES 43-45 (2d ed. 1964).
[26] See address by H. Ralph Taylor, Assistant Secretary of the Department of Housing and Urban Development, 1967 Spring Conference of the Building Research Institute, May 3, 1967 (mimeo. ed. at 7).
[27] Hearings on the Federal Role in Urban Affairs Before the Subcomm. on Executive Reorganization of the Senate Comm. on Government Operations, 89th Cong., 2d Sess., pt. 8, at 1686 (1966). See also Comment, Building Codes, Housing Codes and the Conservation of Chicago's Housing Supply, 31 U. CHI. L. REV. 180 (1963).

get are one of three patterns of conduct. One pattern is the one that you would really like. People fix up the parcel. That is fine. Another pattern is people basically avoiding the code one way or another. The third pattern is that of people basically abandoning the parcel, and, in a weak market, there is a tendency toward abandonment. There is a tendency toward burned-outs. . . .

If you do get code enforcement, not infrequently you get it at the cost of raising rents and driving the poor out. So we have a very complicated picture before us.

In his study of slum housing conditions in Newark, Mr. Sternlieb pointed out the failure of the codes to reach the real needs of the residents: "[A]dequate insect and rodent control, plumbing that works, paint, and general cleanliness may be much more significant to the inhabitants of a tenement, both physically and spiritually, than the existence of central heat and/or plaster walls."[28] The slum resident lacks a feeling of identification with the code enforcement process in part because the codes appear arbitrary and mechanical. They are not *his* codes.

But if the residents of each neighborhood were given the power to set their own housing and building code standards, within relatively broad perimeters of health and safety criteria, and were given the power to enforce these standards and grant variations where appropriate, the codes and their enforcement would begin to be tailored to the actual needs of neighborhood residents. In this way a step would be taken toward the goal of, as Senator Joseph Clark has put it, "design[ing] cities so that the pattern of the city complements the individual's pattern of living."[29]

IV

ADVANTAGES OF DECENTRALIZATION

It is a sardonic fact that the gripes of deprived neighborhoods are directed at both the severity of enforcement and the looseness of enforcement, and frequently simultaneously. The neighborhood Board would serve as a forum not only to enforce compliance but to dispense benefits. It would provide an arena for debate and decision making by low- and middle-income tenants and landowners that would be much more accessible to them than the distant and little understood machinery at City Hall.

One of the major difficulties of achieving any progress in slum neighborhoods

[28] G. STERNLIEB, THE TENEMENT LANDLORD 233 (1966).

[29] Clark, *Planning for People*, in AMERICAN SOC'Y OF PLANNING OFFICIALS, PLANNING 1966, at 119 (1966). Carl Friedrich has summarized the idea very well: "[P]*olicies deal with average acts of average persons.* It is with reference to these that the judgment of the uncommon man is untrustworthy, just because he is an uncommon man." C. FRIEDRICH, THE NEW IMAGE OF THE COMMON MAN 37 (1950).

The importance of local initiative was well summarized by Pastor Leopold Bernhard, founder of the highly successful East Central Citizen Organization of Columbus, Ohio, in his testimony before the Ribicoff Committee. "Our experience . . . [is] that when we come with something from the outside, however good it is, it will not be received and it will not work as well as something that has been arrived at with the decision of the people." *Hearings, supra* note 27, pt. 9, at 2084. As Henry Churchill said: "A city plan is the expression of the collective purpose of the people who live in it, or it is nothing." H. CHURCHILL, THE CITY IS THE PEOPLE 186 (1945).

is the sense of alienation the residents feel toward society. "They see life rather as unpatterned and unpredictable, a congeries of events in which they have no part and over which they have no control."[30] The residents of slums feel that they lack "access" to the government in the sense that they are not confident of their ability to transmit their views to the city administration and have them taken seriously.[31] "One of the greatest single problems of the people who live in the slums," Secretary Weaver has said, "is lack of knowledge, and that leads to fear."[32] Decentralization of big city government offers a means of providing this access.

A larger degree of participation by slum dwellers in their local government should give them a greater sense of identification with the city government, and reduce their antagonism toward City Hall. As sociologist Marshall Clinard puts it, "A certain degree of decentralization of civic authority in the slums might result in greater support for government and thus help to overcome some of the apathy and hostility displayed by many slum dwellers."[33]

Decentralized code enforcement and administration should also help in overcoming the often prevalent hostility toward the city administration by the middle-class resident. This attitude is well summarized by the New York woman whose response to the city's proposal to change the name of Third Avenue was quoted by Bernard Frieden: "They should leave this city alone! They should keep their cotton-pickin' fingers off!"[34]

Another of the major benefits of decentralization of code enforcement and administration in large cities is that it would reduce the advantages now obtained by the large scale slum landlord who is able to develop or hire the expertise necessary to cope with the complexities of the central building department and housing court, and who is able to spread the costs of legal fees, fines, and the other overheads of his trade over a large number of units. The resident owner of a small apartment building finds dealing with these centralized agencies mysterious and expensive.[35] But the opposite result would obtain if code enforcement and administration were handled at the neighborhood level. Then it would be the local landlord who would have more empathy with the administrators—now his neighbors and social equals— while the large scale slumlord would have difficulty dealing with a number of

[30] U.S. WELFARE ADMINISTRATION, DEP'T OF HEALTH, EDUCATION, AND WELFARE, LOW-INCOME LIFE STYLES 3 (L. Irelan ed. 1966).
[31] See J. C. DAVIES III, NEIGHBORHOOD GROUPS AND URBAN RENEWAL 191 (1966).
[32] Address by Robert Weaver, Secretary of the Department of Housing and Urban Development, Conference on the Rights of Tenants, Washington, D.C., Dec. 9, 1966 (mimeo. ed. at 4).
[33] M. CLINARD, SLUMS AND COMMUNITY DEVELOPMENT 129 (1966).
[34] B. FRIEDEN, THE FUTURE OF OLD NEIGHBORHOODS 124 (1964).
[35] In some cases he may also feel that the city's building department is actually hostile toward him. See HOUSING AND REDEVELOPMENT BOARD, NEIGHBORHOOD CONSERVATION IN NEW YORK CITY 88 (1966). David Hunter suggests that the resentment of the residents of underprivileged areas toward what they often feel to be discriminatory imposition of penalties might be alleviated by obtaining "the support and cooperation of the residents of a slum area in the inspection process and follow-up." D. HUNTER, supra note 10. See also Davison, On the Effects of Communication, 23 PUB. OPINION Q. 343, 360 (1959).

separate neighborhood agencies with whom he would have less "kinship" than with the central city leaders.[36]

The decentralization of any part of code enforcement and administration is not a simple matter. Comprehensive study of the detailed legal and administrative problems in each jurisdiction would be required, and state legislation would be needed to implement the needed changes. After some experimentation, however, there is no reason why a practical and workable method of delegation of authority could not be feasible.

V

PARALLELS IN THE SUBURBS

Is increased citizen participation feasible in view of the increasing complexity of government in our mushrooming metropolitan areas?

It is one of the ironies of land development policy in our era that the strident cry within the neighborhoods of our big cities for dispersion of power arises at the same time as the emergence of a justified criticism of the fractured and dispersed condition of land use controls in the suburban areas due to the multiplicity of political jurisdictions. In the outer parts of the metropolitan area the suburban duchies are manning the battlements to ward off the attacks of the regionalists who seek to transfer control over schools, air pollution, open space, and other traditional concerns of suburban governments to larger governmental units. The "big picture" planners urge us to "conceive Ecumenopolis, the universal city" and to institute "a unity of command for the broadest possible urban area so that we have unified programs, plans, and implementation efforts."[37] Both the states and the federal government are relentlessly chipping away at the suburb's exclusive powers over the control of land use.

Nevertheless, the pressure for increased citizen participation in the big cities parallels the equally strong drive toward state and regional control of land-use issues that have a metropolitan impact, and both of these apparently contradictory goals of centralized policy-making and local citizen participation can be rationalized into one logically consistent policy. To put it more bluntly, the same authors who have previously urged a reduction in local control of housing in the suburbs can now urge a greater localization of housing control in the central city.[38]

The reason lies in the nature of our existing legal system of local government. The central city is a conglomeration of many neighborhoods, each of which may well attain as much social and historic unity as the average suburb. The suburb, however,

---

[36] See G. STERNLIEB, supra note 28, at 137-41.

[37] C. A. DOXIADIS, URBAN RENEWAL AND THE FUTURE OF THE AMERICAN CITY 131 (1966). See also L. MUMFORD, supra note 18, at 576: "The final mission of the city is to further man's conscious participation in the cosmic and the historic process."

[38] See Babcock & Bosselman, Suburban Zoning and the Apartment Boom, 111 U. PA. L. REV. 1040 (1963).

enjoys virtually absolute control over the location, size, style, and characteristics of housing and other land uses, while an equivalent neighborhood in the city has no control whatsoever over its own affairs. Usually the sole requirement for the exercise of such control is that a group of people in a contiguous geographical area shall have formed a municipal corporation. It's all or nothing. As with so many aspects of land use control, only black and white solutions are available and there is no middle ground.[39]

If even those who most outspokenly advocate regional solutions for regional problems would agree that only a limited number of basic policies should be enacted at the regional level, and that most of the actual implementation and decision making relating to specific parcels of land should be retained by the suburbs, would it not be consistent to apply a similar logic in the communities within our central city and to conclude that some of the powers now centralized in the city administration should be delegated back to the neighborhood level?

In our opinion the type of decentralization advocated in this article is consistent with the view that the states should exercise greater policy-making authority over problems of regional impact.[40] It seems apparent to us that this proposition is fully consistent with the principle that policies should be formulated at the level of their impact. Policies which affect the entire nation should be formulated on the national level; policies which affect a whole state should be formulated at the state level; decisions which affect only the neighborhood should be made at the neighborhood level. And it matters not whether the neighborhood be an incorporated suburb or an undivided portion of a central city. Under this banner the Jacobses and Doxiadises could join hands and get on about improving the neighborhood as well as the region rather than criticizing each other.

No one would seriously claim that neighborhood participation in local code administration and enforcement would be successful in solving all of the problems of our urban areas. But, as Peter Blake recently pointed out, nobody guaranteed that space exploration would be successful before it was tried:[41]

> To achieve that ambitious goal, much planning at Cape Kennedy had to be based on educated guesswork—before all the facts were in. As a result, a great deal of time was saved—the kind of time that is often wasted in attacks on urban problems, because no one is willing to take a chance until every theory has been tested over and over again.

Our federal system offers an ideal laboratory for experimentation with methods of solving urban affairs. The time has come to initiate such experiments in the decentralization of local governmental power within the large cities. What is claimed to be good for the suburban goose should be tried with the urban gander.

---

[39] See Bosselman, *The Third Alternative in Zoning Litigation*, 17 ZONING DIGEST 73, 113 (1965).
[40] See R. BABCOCK, *supra* note 24, at 159-66.
[41] Blake, *Cape Kennedy*, ARCHITECTURAL FORUM, Jan.-Feb. 1967, at 50, 59.

LOCAL PUBLIC POLICY AND THE RESIDENTIAL DEVELOPMENT PROCESS*

Edward J. Kaiser† and Shirley F. Weiss‡

Although local public policies must be legally sound and administratively feasible, they must also adapt to the urban social, economic, and political processes with which they are merged if they are to be effective in influencing those processes. This article considers the nature of one such process, the residential development process by which land is changed from nonurban use to urban residential use and the implications for local public policies. By conceptualizing the development processes and the role of public policy within these processes, we attempt to gain insight into the problem of designing local public policies to guide residential development.

Our approach views the residential process as the cumulative result of a complex of decisions and actions by individuals and groups, each being guided by his own incentives—the household consumer by basic needs and preferences, the developer-entrepreneur by the profit motive, the predevelopment landowner by a mixture of pecuniary and personal motives. The approach is also based on the micro-behavioral aspects of the development processes—individual units of property, individual pre-

* The research reported in this paper was financed in part by the Environmental Engineering Policies and Urban Development Project, Public Health Service Research Grant EF 00407-05, of the Division of Environmental Engineering and Food Protection. The material reported in this paper draws from a larger study and a larger team effort in the area of "Environmental Engineering Policies and Urban Development." The authors acknowledge the major contributions of present and former colleagues who have been actively associated with various stages of the research and who have participated in the Development Decisions Seminar. In particular, the following were intimately involved in the ongoing research while in residence in Chapel Hill as graduate students in the Department of City and Regional Planning and as research assistants or research fellows at the Center for Urban and Regional Studies: Kenneth B. Kenney, Assistant Professor of Planning, University of Tennessee, Knoxville; John E. Smith, Planning Economist, Office of Planning Coordination, State of New York Executive Department, Albany; L. Earl Armiger, Community Planner, Brevard County Planning Department, Titusville, Fla.; Roger C. Steffens, Principal Planner, City Planning Commission, Huntsville, Ala.; and Donald A. Stollenwerk, Chief Community Planner, Lancaster County Planning Commission, Lancaster, Pa.

† B.Arch. 1958, Illinois Institute of Technology; Ph.D. 1966, University of North Carolina. Assistant Professor of Planning, Department of City and Regional Planning, and Research Associate, Institute for Research in Social Science, University of North Carolina at Chapel Hill. Co-author [with S. F. Weiss, J. E. Smith & K. B. Kenney], RESIDENTIAL DEVELOPER DECISIONS: A FOCUSED VIEW OF THE URBAN GROWTH PROCESS (Urban Studies Research Monograph, Institute for Research in Social Science, University of North Carolina, 1966); author, Toward a Model of Residential Developer Locational Behavior, 1966 (unpublished thesis in University of North Carolina Library).

‡ A.B. 1942, Rutgers University; M.R.P. 1958, University of North Carolina. Associate Research Director, Center for Urban and Regional Studies, Associate Professor of Planning, Department of City and Regional Planning, and Research Associate, Institute for Research in Social Science, University of North Carolina at Chapel Hill. Co-editor and co-author [with F. S. Chapin, Jr.], URBAN GROWTH DYNAMICS IN A REGIONAL CLUSTER OF CITIES (1962); co-author [with F. S. Chapin, Jr. & T. G. Donnelly], FACTORS INFLUENCING LAND DEVELOPMENT: EVALUATION OF INPUTS FOR A FORECAST MODEL (1962); A PROBABILISTIC MODEL FOR RESIDENTIAL GROWTH (1964), and SOME INPUT REFINEMENTS FOR A RESIDENTIAL MODEL (1965) (Urban Studies Research Monographs, Institute for Research in Social Science, University of North Carolina, in cooperation with the U.S. Bureau of Public Roads, Dep't of Commerce).

development landowners deciding to sell or to hold property, individual developers purchasing sites and producing individual residential products for sale, and individual households choosing among alternative residential units.

Although the approach in this article is primarily conceptual, it is firmly based on a series of in-depth interviews and other extensive field data concentrating on Greensboro, North Carolina, but including other North Carolina Piedmont cities as well. The empirical approach, relying heavily on tape-recorded interviews, is experimental. It is being tested in other cities of different sizes and different growth characteristics and is being extended to other decision agents in both the development and the redevelopment processes. In addition to our own empirical work at the Center for Urban and Regional Studies, the conceptualizations also draw upon related literature and research done in other areas of the country. Because of this, we feel the basic conceptualizations about public policy merged with the residential processes should have general nationwide applicability to urban areas, although many of the specific findings would require recalibration in applications to specific urban areas due to our primary dependence upon one study area.

I

CONCEPTUAL OVERVIEW OF THE RESIDENTIAL DEVELOPMENT PROCESS

Residential development may be seen as land in an urban area passing through a sequence of states over time. Beginning with a unit of land in nonurban use on the periphery of an urban area, one could trace the transition from an initial state of nonurban use through several stages of development to a state of active residential use by a household. A typical chain of states for a unit of land is shown in the top row of figure 1. Local public policies for urban residential growth might be conceived as an attempt to control the spatial and temporal probabilities of units of land changing from one state to another.

The evolution of the property through this observable chain of sequences is a result of another process not quite so easily observed. This is the complex set of critical decisions which are made over time by a group of key and supporting decision agents. The key decision agents include the landowner, the developer, and the household. Their decisions are necessary in order for land to evolve through the sequence of states. The relationship of these decisions and decision agents to the sequence of states is illustrated in figure 1. For example, at the beginning of the process at the left side of the figure, for land to move into the state of active consideration for residential development, both the developer and the landowner must decide to consider the land for purchase and sale in anticipation of residential development.

Going one step deeper into our conceptual framework, we introduce three sets of decision factors to explain the decisions which in turn explain the evolution of

FIGURE 1

THE RESIDENTIAL LAND DEVELOPMENT PROCESS: SEQUENCE OF STATES, KEY DECISIONS, DECISION FACTORS, AND LOCAL PUBLIC POLICIES

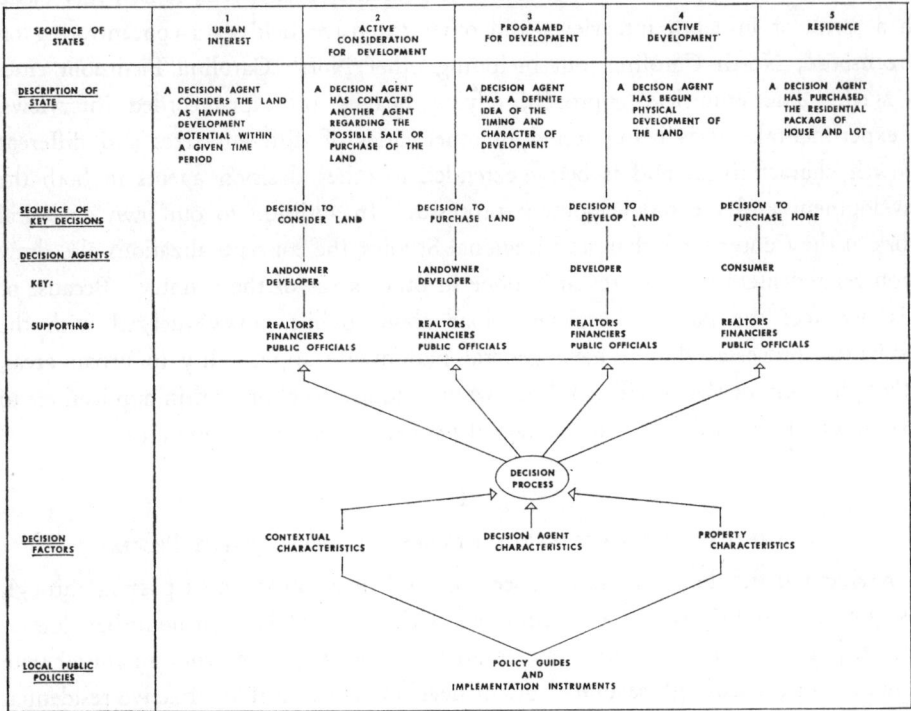

SEQUENCE OF STATES	1 URBAN INTEREST	2 ACTIVE CONSIDERATION FOR DEVELOPMENT	3 PROGRAMED FOR DEVELOPMENT	4 ACTIVE DEVELOPMENT	5 RESIDENCE
DESCRIPTION OF STATE	A DECISION AGENT CONSIDERS THE LAND AS HAVING DEVELOPMENT POTENTIAL WITHIN A GIVEN TIME PERIOD	A DECISION AGENT HAS CONTACTED ANOTHER AGENT REGARDING THE POSSIBLE SALE OR PURCHASE OF THE LAND	A DECISION AGENT HAS A DEFINITE IDEA OF THE TIMING AND CHARACTER OF DEVELOPMENT	A DECISON AGENT HAS BEGUN PHYSICAL DEVELOPMENT OF THE LAND	A DECISION AGENT HAS PURCHASED THE RESIDENTIAL PACKAGE OF HOUSE AND LOT
SEQUENCE OF KEY DECISIONS	DECISION TO CONSIDER LAND	DECISION TO PURCHASE LAND	DECISION TO DEVELOP LAND	DECISION TO PURCHASE HOME	
DECISION AGENTS KEY:	LANDOWNER DEVELOPER	LANDOWNER DEVELOPER	DEVELOPER	CONSUMER	
SUPPORTING:	REALTORS FINANCIERS PUBLIC OFFICIALS	REALTORS FINANCIERS PUBLIC OFFICIALS	REALTORS FINANCIERS PUBLIC OFFICIALS	REALTORS FINANCIERS PUBLIC OFFICIALS	
DECISION FACTORS	CONTEXTUAL CHARACTERISTICS	DECISION AGENT CHARACTERISTICS (DECISION PROCESS)	PROPERTY CHARACTERISTICS		
LOCAL PUBLIC POLICIES		POLICY GUIDES AND IMPLEMENTATION INSTRUMENTS			

property through the development process. The lower portion of figure 1 shows the three sets of decision factors: contextual, decision agent, and property characteristics. Each of the sets of factors influences the decision process in a unique way. The contextual factors provide the macro environment for development decisions—namely, the considerations which limit and determine the overall rate and type of change in the urban community and the general structure of the population of decision agent characteristics and property characteristics. Property characteristics describe the property about which decisions are made. Finally, decision agent characteristics are crucial in explaining important variation in decisional behavior among decision makers in the face of similar contextual and property characteristics.

At this point we can introduce the relationship of local public policy to the conceptualization of the residential process. We see local public policy as an attempt to influence the residential evolution of land by affecting the basic decision factors. As shown in the bottom of figure 1, the influence of local public policies on the evolution of land is indirect, being channeled through constraining contextual and property characteristics; policy does not affect landowner characteristics directly.

The important aspects of the public policy are its content, the differentiation of the application of this content to properties over space and time, and finally the expected variation in reactions of the different decision makers to the policy content.

Let us conceptualize an overview of local public policy merged with the residential development process by integrating the relationships discussed above. The evolution of urban property through a sequence of states is the result of a series of decisions. Inputs to each decision process in the sequence consist of three sets of decision factors. The output of the decision process is a determination of whether or not there is to be a change in the state of the property. The influence of local public policy on the outputs of these decision processes and hence on the evolution of property is channeled through the input decision factors. Figure 2 illustrates the relationships between the decisions, the decision factors, and the policy factors to be explored in this paper.

FIGURE 2

ELEMENTS IN THE RESIDENTIAL DEVELOPMENT PROCESS: AN ANALYTICAL FRAMEWORK

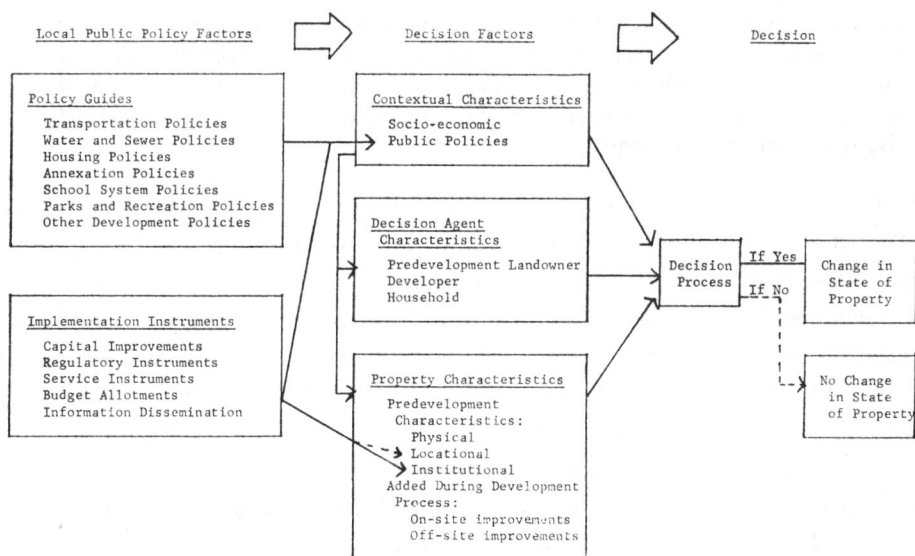

In the following three sections we utilize the above conceptualizations in discussing the decision of the predevelopment landowner to sell or not to sell, the locational decision of the developer-producer to develop a property or to look for another location, and the selection of a residential place by a household consumer.

II

THE DECISIONS OF THE PREDEVELOPMENT LANDOWNER

Land assumes the state of urban interest when a decision agent considers the land as having urban development potential. With the attainment of this state, the prevailing use, usually agricultural, begins to share the determination of the value of the land with the potential urban use of the land. The land use thus becomes transitional.[1] It generates an income stream which, when capitalized, supplements the speculative value of the land based on its potential urban use. Sometimes this transitional nature of the use is obvious—e.g., junk yards and used car lots. But sometimes it is disguised as the old use which is carried on to help tide the landowner over the transitional period when the land is in the state of urban interest, but is not yet under active consideration for development by a developer or the current landowner. Nevertheless, the old use is actually being made increasingly obsolete by the increasing proportion of the value of the property attributable to existing and anticipated land use changes and urban investment all about.

Let us examine the transitional landowner's decision to hold or to sell in order to try to explain why some land in the urban fringe becomes residentially developed and why other land does not. A useful conceptualization of the landowner views him as a

> rational individual who attempts to maximize his satisfaction from a given stock of pecuniary and nonpecuniary assets, including the land. Primarily, the landowner's decision to sell or hold the land depends upon his satisfaction from the pecuniary income from the land in the form of current and expected income, relative to income from alternative investments.[2]

The pecuniary aspect of the landowner's decision to sell or to hold the land relates to the net annual holding cost of the land, the costs that would be incurred in shifting to another investment, the opportunity costs of capital, and the time period of the investment.[3] "Secondarily, the landowner's decision depends upon his relative satisfaction from nonpecuniary income from the land in the form of 'farming as a way of life,' the land as a residence, 'love of the land,' or privacy and status."[4]

It appears that both pecuniary and nonpecuniary motives are too important to be ignored in the explanation of the predevelopment landowner's decision to sell or to hold. Some research stresses the pecuniary and other research suggests the importance of the nonpecuniary. Speculative pecuniary motives were found to be most important in separate studies by Maisel and by Lessinger in California. Maisel tentatively concluded that "the possibilities of capital gains have become the dominant factor influencing ownership of land upon which urban development would be expected in the next decade or two. . . . In the past 12 years [1959-1962], almost half of the land held by the earlier owners was sold to those primarily interested

---

[1] See J. Lessinger, The Determinants of Land Use in Rural-Urban Transition Areas: A Case Study of Santa Clara County, California, 1957 (unpublished thesis in University of California Library).

[2] See J. E. Smith, Toward a Theory of Landowner Behavior on the Urban Periphery, 1966, at 53 (unpublished thesis in University of North Carolina Library).

[3] Id. at 32-46.

[4] Id. at 53-54.

in capital gains."[5] Lessinger also found that although the fruitgrowers' willingness to hold the land in transitional agricultural use "could theoretically result either from expectation of speculative rates of return or from intangible returns . . . [i]n the actual case area under study, speculative interests predominate."[6] But in support of the importance of nonpecuniary motives, Kenney found that "while price and profit motivations loomed large as both primary and secondary factors affecting the decision to sell, personal circumstances and land oriented factors (property characteristics) play key roles in these decisions."[7] Kenney's conclusion is reinforced by Bahl, who commented on why intervening land in his study area was passed over: "Information which could be gained from the owner of one of the large intervening tracts of land and from many secondary sources suggests that the land in question was withheld, at least partially, for personal reasons."[8]

The following equation, formulated by Smith, is a concise statement of the factors entering into the conceptualized decision of the landowner to hold or to sell:[9]

$$PV = \sum_{t=1}^{n} \frac{(a_t^p + a_t^{np}) - (e_t^p + e_t^{np})}{(1+r)^t} + \frac{EV - C}{(1+r)^n}$$

PV—the present value of the land, where:

a_t^p—the annual pecuniary income from the property in year t

a_t^{np}—the annual nonpecuniary income from the property in year t

e_t^p—the annual pecuniary expense on the property in the year t

e_t^{np}—the annual nonpecuniary expense on the property in the year t

r—the opportunity cost of capital, *i.e.*, the rate of return foregone on a possible alternative investment

n—the number of years that the land would be held

EV—the expected value or market price in the year of sale, n

C—the transfer and transaction costs associated with a shift in investment

Upon estimation of the present value, PV, the landowner follows the traditional decision rule: sell the land if his (landowner's) estimated present value falls below the present market price of the land.

Factors which tend to encourage the sale of the land are those which lower the present value estimate or raise the current market price. Factors which lower the present value estimate are those that decrease the numerator and increase the denominator of the equation. Thus, factors that decrease the estimates of annual

[5] Maisel, *Land Costs for Single-Family Housing,* in CALIFORNIA HOUSING STUDIES 1, 56 (Center for Planning and Development Research, University of California at Berkeley, 1963).

[6] J. Lessinger, *supra* note 1, at 221.

[7] K. B. KENNEY, PRE-DEVELOPMENT LAND OWNERSHIP FACTORS AND THEIR INFLUENCE ON RESIDENTIAL DEVELOPMENT 31 (Research Memorandum submitted to Center for Urban and Regional Studies, Institute for Research in Social Science, University of North Carolina, Sept. 21, 1965).

[8] R. W. BAHL, A BLUEGRASS LEAPFROG 18 (1963).

[9] J. E. Smith, *supra* note 2, at 47.

pecuniary and nonpecuniary income, and/or increase the annual pecuniary and non-pecuniary expenses, and/or increase the transfer and transaction costs of selling the land, and/or decrease the estimated future value, and/or increase the rate of return on alternative investments would all tend to encourage the sale of the land by lowering the present value estimate.

In light of the landowner's investment calculus above and the three sets of factors (contextual, property, and landowner characteristics), there are at least three channels through which local governmental policy appears to affect the transition of land: (1) through influencing the landowner's annual income and expenses and thus the profitability of the investment; (2) through influencing the estimated future value of the land and thus the profitability of the investment; and (3) through influencing the present market value of the land relative to the landowner's estimated present value and thus affecting the decision to hold the land for investment or to sell.

Annual expenses are strongly influenced through local taxation policy; in fact, taxes on raw land may often represent the major cost in holding raw land as an investment.[10] Smith found that the cost of taxes more often than not exceeds the current income, even though taxes as a percentage of the market value of the land may be minimal. In addition the impact of taxes is direct; each year the landowner must find the funds to meet this cost. The impact of local policy on income of the landowner is provided through the limitations placed by zoning on the economic use of the property. However, findings from Smith's study suggest that current income considerations are usually not as important as expenses in the landowner's calculus.

The impact of local policy on the estimated future value of the land, however, is less direct than its influence on current income and expenses. The certainty and availability of knowledge of future governmental actions related to spatial extension of public investment, such as highways, water and sewer system, and schools, can have an important stabilizing effect on estimates of future value. Zoning, if stable, can influence estimated future value by its limitation on potential use of the property. But the future value depends on so many other factors that the influence of policy is limited.

Under any given set of contextual and property characteristics influenced by public policy, the characteristics of the owner appear to be important in influencing the transition of a unit of land to urban residential use. There is empirical evidence to support the model's implication that if the landowner has major nonpecuniary motives for holding the land in addition to investment motives, he is less likely to sell simply because he is deriving more annual income from holding than he would be if he was not deriving satisfaction from those nonpecuniary motives.[11] Furthermore, wealthy landowners tend to have high net worth and high liquidity. Both of

---

[10] *Id.* at 104.
[11] *Id.* at 99-100 (table 22).

these facts encourage holding onto the land because of lower rate of return on alternative forms of investment for these people and because they run less risk by holding
the less liquid asset of land than does an owner who does not have other liquid
assets.[12]

The property characteristics will also be important influences on the transition of
land. Annual income, especially from farming, is dependent upon physical property
characteristics such as topography, ground cover, and soil conditions of the land
and structural improvements. The better the land for deriving an annual income,
the higher the present value of the property for the landowner and therefore the less
likely he is to sell. It is also important to note that physical property characteristics
are not easily influenced by local governmental policy. However, the present market
price and expected future market value depend especially on those existing and
expected locational characteristics, such as prestige level of the location, accessibility
(school, employment, shopping, recreation activities), and institutional characteristics,
such as zoning protection, availability of public services, and subdivision regulations,
that might apply to the site. These are affected by present and future government
facilities, services, and regulatory controls. If services are already available to the
site, then the present market value may compare very well with the future expected
market value, and given that the latter would have to be discounted over time this
would encourage earlier completion of the transition to urban residential use.

But the effectiveness of policy as an influence upon the transition of land to
urban use will depend very much on other contextual, property, and decision agent
characteristics. For example, the effectiveness of tax policy will depend on the contextual variable of the general rate of land value appreciation in the area, the spatial
distribution of the decision agent characteristic of income, and importance of nonpecuniary motives for holding land among the landowners. "In areas with very
rapid rates of appreciation, say on the order of 20 percent, only very heavy taxes on
land would eliminate the investment potential" of holding land.[13] Second, the
impact of heavy taxes is less on wealthy landowners because the rate of return on
alternative investments is less. Third, the impact will be less on landowners who
have significant nonpecuniary motives for holding the land in addition to their
pecuniary motives because this intangible current income increases the present value
to the landowner but does not affect market value.

In this section we have discussed the major decision agent in the area of urban
interest, *i.e.*, the area of transition. The factors influencing a landowner's decision
are similar whether the potential buyer is a developer who is actively considering it
for residential development or a speculator who intends to hold the land for future
appreciation of its value. Therefore, whether or not the land advances to the next
state—that of actively being considered for development—depends then not only on

---

[12] *Id.* at 74-78.
[13] *Id.* at 116.

the intention of the landowner to sell but most importantly on the buyer's evaluation of the property specifically as an input into the residential development process. Let us therefore move to the middle stages of the residential development process and to the developer as the major decision maker.

III

THE DEVELOPER'S THREE-STAGE LOCATIONAL DECISION: TO CONSIDER LAND, TO PURCHASE LAND, AND TO DEVELOP LAND FOR RESIDENTIAL USE

The three decisions to be discussed in this section carry the land from the state of urban interest to the state of being physically developed for residential use, state four in figure 1. They will be considered as related subdecisions in one overall locational decision made by what we consider to be the key decision maker in these middle stages of land transition—the residential developer.

In general, a site may pass from the state of urban interest to the state of active consideration for residential development when any one of several agents assumes initiative to contact other agents regarding the possible sale of a tract of land for residential purposes and not merely for further holding in anticipation of capital gain. The developer becomes the key decision maker because basically it is he who must insert the intention to develop the land as a means of profit rather than relying on land value appreciation for capital gain. If the developer feels that a tract may generally fill the specifications for the market he is seeking to meet or that there exists a potential demand for housing appropriate to a specific site called to his attention, and if he can obtain a tentative agreement from the landowner to sell, he then proceeds to the next decision stage in his locational decision process—the land purchase decision. It represents an entrepreneurial locational commitment in the technical production process for manufacturing the new residential housing supply. When the developer decides to purchase a site, he generally is making a commitment not only to an investment in the land but also to the much broader investment in a particular residential development which is to be produced on the site. The land purchase decision is crucial in the spatial pattern of conversion of the land to urban housing. The prior decision to consider the land is anticipatory to this decision; the latter decision to develop the land is anticlimatic to this decision, for the experience in our study area suggests that development typically follows within less than five years and probably in a form not much different than the development programmed at the time of the purchase.[14] Once the land is purchased it is again the developer who is the principal agent in deciding the rate at which the property holdings are to be converted to completed residential packages.

Let us conceptualize a generalized locational decision to which we can relate

[14] S. F. WEISS, J. E. SMITH, E. J. KAISER & K. B. KENNEY, RESIDENTIAL DEVELOPER DECISIONS: A FOCUSED VIEW OF THE URBAN GROWTH PROCESS 58 (Urban Studies Research Monograph, Center for Urban and Regional Studies, Institute for Research in Social Science, University of North Carolina, 1966).

local public policy and the aforementioned three sets of decision factors. The developer arrives at the locational decision by first reaching a very tentative decision to go ahead with development at a specific site subject to further investigation. In commencing this first stage of the three-stage location decision, the developer may follow one of two approaches. In what we call the marketing approach, the developer first identifies a demand for a specific price range of housing. After identifying certain crude site specifications for such housing, he then begins an active search for suitable land. In the other approach, which we call the contact approach, the developer's attention is called to the availability of a tract of land by another agent in the development process, such as a landowner, realtor, or lawyer acting as a broker for a landowner. Upon identifying a suitable housing product for the site, he may ascertain that a demand exists for that housing product. We have found in our empirical work that the generalized approach in the development industry consists of periodic searches superimposed upon random contacts made by other agents.[15] Once the developer makes the tentative decision to go ahead, largely on intuition, he generally obtains a sixty- to ninety-day option, or in some other way comes to a temporary agreement with the landowner which will allow time for investigating the decision before fully committing himself to a purchase of the site.

This most important purchase decision stage actually involves a series of supporting studies and decisions regarding economic feasibility and risk. This stage requires numerous interactions with supporting decision participants in the development process, especially checks with financial intermediaries and public officials. The first order of business is often an economic feasibility study. This study evaluates the profitability of the proposed location in terms of its cost implications (the land engineering study) and its revenue implications (the marketability study). From a land engineering study the developer obtains a feasible plat of lots and street layout, required on-site and off-site improvements, and so on, which enable him to make an estimate of the average developed lot cost. To this estimate of developed lot cost (prorated cost of raw land and estimated physical development costs), he adds overhead costs and a "fair" profit. (Several developers mentioned the specific figure of twenty-five per cent as a desirable markup to cover overhead and fair profit.) In the marketability study, the developer determines, usually intuitively, whether or not there is sufficient demand in terms of annual sales volume for the price range of residential package (house, lot, and location) under consideration. The average lot value is a major output of the marketability study. At this point the developer compares estimated costs and revenues; he compares the minimum acceptable lot value (cost to the developer) to the estimated average lot value (revenue to the developer) to determine the profitability of the site.

This economic feasibility test is tempered by a consideration of investment risks. Some of the more important risks suggested in the interviews are:

---

[15] *Id.* at 31.

1. Risks associated with the calculation of marketability. A striking characteristic of development entrepreneurship is the unsystematic approach to analysis of marketability. The fact component of this analysis is weak. This appears especially true of the controlling facts—those concerning the estimates of the level of market demand, the proper composition of the residential package components of house, lot, physical neighborhood, and location to meet consumer preferences in that market and alternative site availability.[16]

2. Risks associated with land inventory—one risk is not being able to find suitable land when needed. A two- or three-year inventory in each market sector engaged in by the developer was considered reasonable by our sample, while a one-year inventory is minimum. The time is a function of the lag time between land purchase and the finished product being ready for the market. The smaller the inventory the more susceptible the developer is to purchase more marginal sites because of the risk of being without a product to sell at a future date.

   If the land is to be held beyond the time it takes to develop the residential product on the land, then the developer must devote more consideration to the risks of changes in the price of the land and changes in consumer preferences or demand in the market for which the land is being evaluated. In our own empirical work we found that longer term land holding was not common practice. Most developers purchased land for a short-term inventory of suitable land to meet specific markets rather than for long-term speculation in appreciation of land values.

3. Risks associated with local public actions—the "if and when" risks of tax reassessment, annexation, installation of public capital improvements, such as schools, water and sewerage facilities, and highways. Changes in requirements imposed by health, subdivision, and zoning regulations, and so on, are all critical enough to affect profitability for the investment. Several developers in our sample were hurt by these risks. One did not get his land into a school district after he had counted on this. Another was left holding a number of lots unsuitable for septic tanks after the County Health Department stiffened its regulations.

4. Risks associated with obtaining necessary supporting decisions from financial intermediaries. These are critical in the developer's ability to complete the proposed development.

---

[16] This unsystematic approach to decisions by development entrepreneurs appears to be a definite characteristic of the industry. In addition to our interviews, see Wheaton, *Public and Private Agents of Change in Urban Expansion*, in M. WEBBER AND OTHERS, EXPLORATIONS INTO URBAN STRUCTURE 168 (1964); TWIN CITIES METROPOLITAN PLANNING COMM'N, SELECTED DETERMINANTS OF RESIDENTIAL DEVELOPMENT 3 (Background Document No. 1, Series on Determinants of Urban Development, St. Paul, Minn., 1962).

In considering these above risks, it is only reasonable for the developer to attempt to reduce them. In fact, a substantial portion of the developer's entrepreneurial activity and strategy while holding an option is to ascertain and reduce these risks. He will make conservative decisions about the style of house, for example, to avoid risking disapproval of financial intermediaries. He will check his sources of permanent financing and insurers and guarantors of such financing (especially FHA and VA) for their tentative approval of the site and the residential package, but primarily at this time their approval of the price range of the residential package and the lot value. He will also check with public officials about subdivision regulations, zoning changes, school district boundary changes, scheduled public improvements to the site, and so on. And there are numerous other checks to be made in order to line up the affirmative locational decision.[17]

Let us examine the developer's locational decision sequence in the light of the analytical framework shown in figure 2. Again we are hypothesizing that the factors which influence the locational choice are contextual, property, and developer characteristics, and, indirectly, local public policy channeled through these sets of factors.

Again, the influence of local public policy on the residential developer's decision process is channeled primarily through the set of contextual factors and the set of property characteristics. But just as in the other residential decisions, the decision maker's characteristics will affect the reaction of the developer to the other two sets of factors. On the basis of our interviews and our conceptualizations of the decision process, we hypothesize that an influence can be analyzed by examining its effect on the expected costs, the expected revenues, or the risk of the investment.

The effect of contextual, property, and developer characteristics on marketability and revenue tend to dominate costs considerations in our study. If this is true generally, local public policy affecting revenues would tend to have more leverage than policy affecting costs. Property characteristics are key for they provide most of the basis on which the developer estimates costs and marketability of the proposed development. Our interviews indicated the estimated effects of property characteristics on marketability of the residential product far outweigh the estimated effects on cost of producing the product. One reason may be that cost implications for various sites were not quite as uncertain to the developer, nor did they tend to vary as much as marketability effects. In general, the higher the price range, the more important are the estimated marketability effects of the site characteristics as opposed to cost considerations.

Of the property characteristics affecting marketability, locational characteristics are clearly the most important. The frequency of the reply "location, location, location" (to the question about the most important factor in the land purchase decision)

---

[17] For a more detailed list of these checks and studies, see Wheaton, *supra* note 16, at 154-96.

supports this conclusion. And social prestige level of the location is clearly the most important aspect of the locational characteristics. Local public policy may have a substantial effect over a period of time on the accessibility of the site directly through governmental investment policies concerning transportation improvements, school and recreation facilities, and indirectly through zoning for shopping and employment activities. Physical characteristics, such as rolling topography and trees, also influence the amenity value of a site. Institutional characteristics, the most direct reflections of local policy, have some marketability effects. Our study shows that school district lines that tend to reflect differential standards, availability of urban services, and zoning protection appear significant, particularly in higher priced markets.

Despite the greater importance of the estimated marketability effects of site characteristics in our study area, the developer cannot afford to concentrate on marketability at any cost. The locational decision still requires weighing of the costs and thus it is possible for public policy to influence locational decisions by influencing the spatial pattern of land and physical development costs. Again property characteristics can be important, this time in two ways: First, topography, soil conditions, and zoning influence the number of lots derivable from a tract. Second, topography, soil characteristics, subdivision regulations, and zoning influence the costs of providing streets, utilities, and even building construction.

With regard to property characteristics, we have found in our empirical study that subdivision developers have stronger tendencies to locate where water and sewer are available, contiguous to existing development; and more moderate tendencies to locate where zoning protection exists, and where there is higher accessibility to employment areas and where socioeconomic prestige level of the site is higher. The physical characteristics of topography and soil conditions and the accessibility to central business district and schools and nearest major highway do not seem to be as important.[18] Of course, this reflects only one study area with a special set of contextual characteristics which could cause behavior different than would be expected in general or observed in other specific urban areas.

As a contextual factor, public policy can also be a significant variable. It can affect the amount of influence of property characteristics by limiting the general quantity and spatial pattern of urban sites with certain site characteristics, particularly the institutional ones; it can create or remove scarcity of particular property characteristics. For example, it determines the quantity and spatial distribution of the supply of land zoned for a certain minimum lot size. Policy factors may also affect the cost function of the developer directly by establishing a maximum cost for certain production processes. For example, the Greensboro study area has a policy

---

[18] For a detailed analysis leading to this conclusion, see Kaiser, Location Decision Factors in a Producer Model of Residential Development, a paper presented at the Regional Science Ass'n meeting, Philadelphia, Pa., Nov. 12-14, 1965 (revised and expanded, August 1966).

establishing a maximum charge on installation of streets, water, and sanitary sewer within the city limits. This reduced the effective development cost of sites within the city limits which had difficult topographic and soil conditions. It also added a degree of certainty to the developer's estimates of production costs. Thus, by determining the distribution of decision agent characteristics and site characteristics and by helping to set the general atmosphere of the community, the contextual factors can determine the amount of influence of individual decision agent characteristics and site characteristics upon the spatial pattern of locational decisions for urban residential development.

The developer characteristics, such as size of firm, entrepreneurial approach, and nature of the production process used, will affect the locational behavior under similar property and contextual factors. The attitude toward risk aspects of the entrepreneurial approach, and the amount of prefabrication, efficiency in use of equipment, skill in coordinating subdecisions of supporting decision agents will affect the relative attraction of different kinds of sites. In our empirical tests we have found significant differences between the locational decisions of large scale developers (those developing over 100 lots per year) and the locational behavior of smaller scale developers. Large scale developers appear much more sensitive than smaller scale developers to accessibility, to availability of water and sewer, and to zoning protection at all price levels of subdivisions.[19] Since these property characteristics reflect local policy, the findings suggest that policy makers should take into account the proportion of locational decisions made by different types of developers.

IV

THE HOUSEHOLD'S DECISION TO PURCHASE OR RENT

To this point the unit of property under discussion was the entire development project or at least sections of subdivisions which were developed as units in specified periods of time. Upon development into residential packages, the unit of property becomes that which can be associated with an individual dwelling unit. In the case of single-family homes the site is the lot. In the case of multifamily structures, the site becomes whatever private grounds can be associated with each dwelling unit (e.g., garden apartments) plus whatever grounds several dwelling units share in common that is not public property.

This is a significant change in focus. One obvious difference is in the impact of each individual decision, which is now reduced to smaller parcels of urban space. The number of decision makers increases many times and each one's decision has a smaller impact on the total, although in the aggregate this step in the chain of decisions is extremely important. This step determines the nature of the population which will reside in a sector of the community's space. This step, by implication, determines the nature and quantity of demand upon urban services; it establishes linkages, par-

---

[19] Id.

ticularly movement linkages to other spatial, social, and economic sectors of the community. When aggregated, the household locational decisions determine the character of neighborhoods, their viability, and ultimately their renewability and the movement patterns in the urban area.

Let us examine the consumer household's decision as a part of the residential mobility process. The household moves from a former residence to the selected residence in an attempt to fulfill more adequately basic shelter and accessibility needs and to satisfy certain desires with respect to living qualities and social mobility, yet staying within the constraints of a housing budget.

The household's characteristics which appear to be important influences upon residential mobility behavior are categorized into demographic and attitudinal characteristics and previous residential experience.[20] The demographic characteristics of household size, place of work, stage in the family life cycle, and activity pattern determine household preferences for space, facilities, and accessibility in the residential package. The attitudinal characteristics of social mobility aspirations, actual mobility, and life style will determine the livability and prestige preferences governing the selection of a residential place. Household income, of course, is the single biggest factor in the residential budget, but aspirations, stage in the family life cycle, and household size also shape the housing budget to a greater or lesser extent.

The list of property characteristics considered by the predevelopment landowner and developer referred to the land. We must add the characteristics of the capital improvements produced in the development process, for these now become very important in the future transition of the property. Thus, instead of site characteristics we must, at this stage of the chain of events, consider all the characteristics of the residential package consisting of not only the original physical, locational, and institutional characteristics of the site as modified by the developer but also (1) the dwelling unit and other on-site improvements and (2) the social and physical neighborhood created by the development process and the types of households selecting residential packages nearby. The original site characteristics as modified by the developer, and the dwelling unit and other on-site improvements added in the production process, and the neighborhood around the site are inseparable; they are combined into an indivisible package which the household must select on a "take it or leave it" basis. The important characteristics with regard to the dwelling unit include: space, design, tenure (*i.e.*, whether a rental or purchase dwelling unit), equipment, state of repair (if a used unit), or quality of construction (if either new or used unit). The most important characteristics with regard to the site are the locational as they imply: (1) an accessibility to the activity places which the household wishes to utilize, such as school, work place, shopping facilities, and doctor, and (2) a socioeconomic prestige level of the immediate neighborhood.

---

[20] Weiss, Kenney & Steffens, *Consumer Preferences in Residential Location: A Preliminary Investigation of the Home Purchaser Decision*, RESEARCH PREVIEWS, April 1966, at 1.

A number of studies have been done both at the Center and elsewhere which suggest relationships between household characteristics and characteristics of the residential package.[21] Residential experience affects the household's preferences and selection. Previous owners who have lived in the area for a while place emphasis on the social location.[22] This is especially true for families of higher income. Previous renters and households who have not lived long in the area tend to sacrifice both social location and accessibility in favor of "more space for the money."[23] Since non-rooted households tend to maximize cost considerations, they will generally locate in the newer, large-tract subdivisions which are primarily on the outskirts of the urban or metropolitan area. This suggests that fringe areas and large-tract developments play an increasingly important role as reception areas for middle- and upper-income newcomers to the metropolitan area.[24]

Relating local governmental policies to household decisions, we feel that in a private market economy the influence is not easily incorporated into a model. Exceptions are open housing laws which discourage private market discrimination practices and therefore remove constraints which affect the household's locational choice. The limited public intervention indicates that governmental influence over the spatial structure of housing accommodations and populations either will have to be (1) indirectly applied by influencing the developer's choice of residential products to be produced in various locations or (2) applied more directly by influencing the course of change in the residential properties once developed and in this way influencing the future housing characteristics of an area.

As an indirect influence, the effect of policy on landowners and developers can be significant because their decisions precede those of the household in the resi-

---

[21] Reference should be made to the rich literature on residential consumer preferences and residential mobility for the multiplicity of household characteristics (needs, wants, and constraints) which influence the choice of residential location and individual dwelling accommodations. Important references include, among others, Bell, *Social Choice, Life Styles, and Suburban Residence*, in THE SUBURBAN COMMUNITY 225 (M. Dobriner ed. 1958); Foley, Wurster & Smith, *Housing Trends and Related Problems*, in CALIFORNIA HOUSING STUDIES, *supra* note 5, at 57; N. FOOTE, J. ABU-LUGHOD, M. M. FOLEY & L. WINNICK, HOUSING CHOICES AND CONSTRAINTS (1960); W. G. GRIGSBY, HOUSING MARKETS AND PUBLIC POLICY (1963); M. MEYERSON, B. TERRETT & W. L. C. WHEATON, HOUSING, PEOPLE AND CITIES (1962); P. H. ROSSI, WHY FAMILIES MOVE (1955); L. F. SCHNORE, THE URBAN SCENE, especially pt. 4, *The Socioeconomic Status of Cities and Suburbs* 201-41 (1965); and Wilson, *Livability of the City: Attitudes and Urban Development*, in URBAN GROWTH DYNAMICS ch. 11 (F. S. Chapin, Jr. & S. F. Weiss eds. 1962).

For a series of related studies and follow up, see J. B. LANSING, RESIDENTIAL LOCATION AND URBAN MOBILITY: THE SECOND WAVE OF INTERVIEWS (Survey Research Center, Institute for Social Research, University of Michigan, 1966); J. B. LANSING & N. BARTH, RESIDENTIAL LOCATION AND URBAN MOBILITY: A MULTIVARIATE ANALYSIS (Survey Research Center, Institute for Social Research, University of Michigan, 1966); Mueller, *Consumer Aspirations and Housing Demand in the 1960's*, in THE OUTLOOK ON CONSUMER BEHAVIOR 47 (C. Lininger ed. 1964).

[22] L. E. Arminger, Jr., Toward a Model of the Residential Location Decision: A Study of Recent and Prospective Buyers of New and Used Homes, 1966, at 29 (unpublished thesis in University of North Carolina Library).

[23] *Id.* at 98.

[24] *Id.* at 98-99. *See also* GOVERNOR'S ADVISORY COMM'N ON HOUSING PROBLEMS, APPENDIX TO THE REPORT ON HOUSING IN CALIFORNIA 97 (1963).

dential process. The developer determined the supply of new residential packages and made the decisions about on-site and off-site improvements added to the original site characteristics of the property. Especially important were the developer's decisions about the characteristics of the dwelling unit itself, because much of the consumer's housing choice appears to be based on the dwelling unit itself as opposed to the neighborhood and local portion of the residential package.[25]

As a more direct influence, local public policy can affect the course of change in a developed neighborhood through its level of services to the neighborhood, its housing and health codes, and zoning changes in the vicinity. By providing services, protecting the area from incongruous uses and discouraging neglect of the physical improvements, the local government encourages the maintenance of a residential area while opposite policies will encourage deterioration of the physical plant and possible change in the neighborhood composition. But much of the potential for maintenance or deterioration was incorporated in the quality of construction and planning of the original development; and much of the force for change or maintenance is beyond the local public policy in the socioeconomic context of the community which governs the economic vitality of the area, the residential and population trends, federal policy regarding financing for used and new housing, and so on.

More needs to be known about the leverage of local governmental policy to decide whether there is enough flexibility to warrant a strategy of attempting substantial control of residential change after initial development or whether the more appropriate strategy is to adapt governmental policy regarding service levels and so on to the externally controlled change.

V

IMPLICATIONS FOR FUTURE POLICY

The sequence of decisions in the residential development process illustrates the complex interdependent chain-like nature of the process of urban residential change. Our conceptualizations and empirical work thus far suggest that the design of public policy to influence this change must recognize the variety of decisions and decision makers to be involved in the process, the necessity to think in terms of influencing a chain of decisions rather than any single decision or decision maker, and the direct and indirect channels of influence through which local governmental influence can be brought to bear on the process.

For example, the conceptualizations suggest that a taxation policy may encourage some types of landowners to sell but not others, depending upon their wealth and personal motives for holding the land. And a policy that encourages selling may not necessarily lead to urban residential use of the land rather than further speculation unless the site is also profitable for investment in residential development. The

---

[25] N. FOOTE, J. ABU-LUGHOD, M. M. FOLEY & L. WINNICK, *supra* note 21, at 156, 183; and P. H. ROSSI, *supra* note 21, at 154.

conceptualizations and empirical findings suggest that for landowners policies that affect expenses have more leverage than policies affecting current income. The reverse is true for the developers—that is, policies that affect revenues appear more critical to the locational decision of the developer than those which affect costs of development. Our research also gives evidence that decision agent characteristics are significant; for example, large scale developers' locational response to a policy was found to be significantly different from that of smaller developers.

In sum, the research seems to suggest that mixes of policies, rather than single policies, must be designed and/or evaluated—some of which are aimed at land-owners, some at developers, and some at consumer households in already built-in areas. It also suggests that the success of a policy mix in any one sector of the urban region will depend upon the other noncontrollable physical, locational, and institutional property characteristics of the area, socioeconomic interaction, and the community's ad hoc policy course of action. Finally, the effect of a policy mix will also depend upon the characteristics of the key decision agents involved in the residential process—on whom we have focused in this article, and over whom very little direct control is currently, or is likely to be, available. A major aspect of the residential process to which local governmental policy must adapt is the landowner-developer-consumer chain of decision agents who operate in the private market economy.

PUBLIC/PRIVATE APPROACHES TO URBAN MORTGAGE AND HOUSING PROBLEMS

Saul B. Klaman*

I

Introduction: The Problem and the Setting

A. General Approaches

In 1965, the establishment of the Department of Housing and Urban Development gave promise of a new era in urban housing policies and programs. In the preceding three decades or so since the Great Depression, federal intervention in housing and mortgage markets had broadened and deepened—through war and peace, through business expansion and contraction. Now, endowed with cabinet status, federal housing policy-makers were given a voice in the highest councils of government. There could be no doubt of the nation's permanent commitment to housing progress in the setting of an improved urban structure. As Dr. Robert Weaver observed, shortly after his appointment as the first Secretary of HUD: "The national role in urban problem-solving is large and growing."[1]

In 1966, however, the nation's housing and mortgage markets were in disarray. The output of new housing fell to a postwar low. Sales of existing housing dropped to uncommonly low levels. Residential mortgage credit virtually dried up, with net mortgage extensions down forty per cent on a year-to-year basis by year-end. New federal urban revitalization programs were lagging for lack of adequate financing. The national role in urban problem-solving, while undoubtedly large and growing, was only marginally effective in the face of devastating short-run problems.

In 1967, therefore, we have been inundated with proposals to improve the role of government in urban housing and mortgage markets, to make it more effective in short-run as well as long-run urban problem-solving. New federal approaches to long-range urban rebuilding problems, particularly those related to housing for low-income families, have been urged by legislators, planners, and economists alike. And accompanying the new and renewed public approaches, there have been

---

* B.S. 1941, University of Massachusetts; M.A. 1942, Michigan State University; Ph.D. 1961, New York University. Vice President and Chief Economist, National Association of Mutual Savings Banks, since 1966; Director of Research 1959-1966; Economist, 1958-59. Staff Economist, Board of Governors of the Federal Reserve System, 1946-58. Senior Staff Member, Postwar Capital Market Study, National Bureau of Economic Research (1956). Adjunct Professor of Economics and Finance, Bernard Baruch School of Business, City University of New York. Author, THE POSTWAR RESIDENTIAL MORTGAGE MARKET (1961), THE POSTWAR RISE OF MORTGAGE COMPANIES (1959), THE VOLUME OF MORTGAGE DEBT IN THE POSTWAR DECADE (1958).

[1] Address by Secretary Weaver before the National Press Club, Washington, D.C., Feb. 16, 1966.

numerous proposals to improve the efficiency of the private market through structural and institutional changes.

B. A Balanced Perspective

Quite apart from the technical merits of specific approaches to short- and long-run urban problems, it is essential from the policy viewpoint that the relative roles of the public and private sectors be kept in balanced perspective. Federal involvement in the revitalization of our urban environment, in mortgage finance, in housing production and transfer, is clearly great and growing. Private enterprise must surely recognize and accept the key role of government in the building and rebuilding of our urban complex. But government must also appreciate, and indeed welcome, the indispensable role of private enterprise in this gigantic venture.

What is needed, in essence, if we are successfully to revitalize the quality of urban life in America, if we are to find solutions to recurring mortgage and housing problems, is to establish a creative partnership between the private and public sectors of our society. Such a partnership would have its parallel in the "creative federalism" proposed between federal and state and local governments. Such a partnership would seek the realization of broadly accepted public goals through maximum reliance on private means.

It cannot be said, unfortunately, that a well-balanced public/private approach has been characteristic of our urban housing and mortgage programs, policies, and proposals. Among the current maze of mortgage proposals, for example, designed to prevent the recurrence of "another 1966," one can detect efforts to insulate or shelter the flow and terms of housing credit from private market forces, efforts to assure, in a sense, an artificially regulated "ever-normal" flow of funds to finance housing needs. Such an approach is doomed at the outset; it presumes the failure of the private market place.

A balanced approach, as envisioned here, must be based on the fundamental premise that insulation of the mortgage sector from the discipline of the private market is neither practical nor desirable. The mortgage sector must be geared to compete more effectively for scarce funds in the forum of the market place, and to release funds to other sectors when the flow of mortgage credit is excessive relative to basic demands. For the flow of credit to be allocated efficiently among competing private market sectors, however, basic adjustments are needed in public policies and programs—federal, state, and local—which influence mortgage flows and housing activity.

Let me stress at this point that the objective of maximizing the participation of the private sector in the revitalization of our cities, and in the modernization of our mortgage structure, is more than just a basic maxim of a private market system. It is a realistic approach to the massive task involved. It recognizes the practicality of using existing private institutional arrangements, funds, and skills. It recognizes that major reliance on the public sector for needed funds would severely strain the federal budget and administrative structure. The broad, basic goal of public policy in the mortgage and housing area must, therefore, be to encourage and to supplement—not to preempt—the use of private resources.

Against this general policy setting of public/private approaches to urban housing and mortgage problems, the body of this article is divided into two major segments: (1) tentative solutions to recurring short-run mortgage crises; and (2) long-range considerations of federal urban policy.

II

TENTATIVE SOLUTIONS TO RECURRING MORTGAGE CRISES

A. The Problems of Plenitude and Shortage

The 1966 "credit crisis" dramatized the particular vulnerability of the housing and mortgage sectors to cyclical economic change. Earlier periods of credit stringency in the 1950s had also demonstrated, although less dramatically, the inability of real estate market participants to compete for scarce funds. But while the most acute problems in the housing credit area have been associated with painful scarcities of funds, they should not obscure the problems associated with excessive mortgage flows. In fact, during the first half of the 1960s, financial observers were concerned about the deterioration in the quality of housing credit, as mortgage foreclosure rates rose steeply.

In short, the experience of the past decade or so graphically illustrates the unsettling tendency of the residential mortgage sector to swing widely and rapidly from a "plenitude of abundance" to a "plenitude of scarcity." A basic aim of private and public policies, therefore, should be to reduce the volatility of mortgage flows over the business cycle. On balance, this will provide more credit for housing than during alternating periods of feast and famine.

In seeking fundamental solutions, one must identify fundamental causes for the virtual breakdown of the residential mortgage market in 1966, and for the surfeit of mortgage funds in the preceding years of the 1960s. The more immediate and short-run causes lie in the impact of changing business and financial conditions and of government policies. There is no need to provide a detailed chronology of these events. This is available from several other sources. But a brief review will help set the stage for a discussion of the more fundamental, long-run structural problems.

B. The Immediate Factors

The economic environment of the early 1960s was conducive to an excessive flow of mortgage credit relative to basic housing demands. Expansionary monetary policies, relative price and interest rate stability, high and rising employment and incomes, and intensified competition for savings accounts, resulted in record deposit flows at thrift institutions and commercial banks. Because of their restricted loan and investment powers, thrift institutions—particularly savings and loans— channeled their record-breaking saving flows into mortgage markets, even though overall housing demands were relatively sluggish. And commercial banks in this period, faced with the high costs of time deposits in a period of inadequate business loan demand, turned strongly to home mortgage loans (together with municipal securities) as a source of income.

The result was a greater acceptance of marginal credit risks, steadily liberalized mortgage contract terms, excessively high property appraisals, and encouragement of marginal building operations. The quality of credit was clearly being strained. Evidence of deterioration was later apparent in mounting mortgage delinquencies and foreclosures, and in the rising "scheduled items" at several savings and loan associations.[2]

By mid-1965, the situation had changed significantly, however, culminating in the near credit crisis of late 1966. With the nation's physical and human resources virtually fully employed, continued vigorous business expansion put the economy under severe strain. Persistent credit demands from business, governments, and consumers pushed open market interest rates to the highest levels in forty years by late summer of 1966. Of course, this was due in part to the especially restrictive monetary policy stance taken by the Federal Reserve Board. In the absence of adequate fiscal restraints, severe monetary stringency was employed as the only effec- tive anti-inflationary weapon.

In this environment, saving flows fell sharply at thrift institutions, where deposit interest rates were not competitive with open market yields or with special com- mercial bank savings instruments. Savings and loan associations sustained a fifty- seven per cent drop in net saving flows between 1965 and 1966. Their 1966 flow was the smallest in fourteen years and less than the amount of dividends credited to savings accounts. At mutual savings banks, 1966 deposit flows were down twenty- nine per cent from 1965, with the bulk of the gain reflecting the crediting of interest- dividends.

In marked contrast to developments at mortgage-oriented institutions, saving flows into commercial banks held up quite well in 1966, falling only about thirteen per cent from the high 1965 level. The ability of commercial banks to turn over short-term assets quickly, and invest in new high-interest obligations, permitted them to pay attractive rates to depositors. The result was soaring sales of savings cer- tificates and other consumer-type time deposits which substantially offset reduced gains in regular passbook savings, bearing relatively low rates under Regulation Q ceilings.[3] And except for the regulatory roll-back of "consumer C/D" interest

---

[2] Preliminary findings of a National Bureau of Economic Research study on quality of credit (not available for publication at this time) confirm the deterioration in credit quality in the early 1960s.

[3] *See* 12 C.F.R. § 217.6 (Supp. 1966).

rates in September 1966, commercial bank saving flows would undoubtedly have been larger.

All three major deposit-type institutions, of course, were locked in competitive battle with high-flying capital market instruments. These were the immediate cause of the dramatic "disintermediation" of 1966. Individuals channeled a record $11 billion into all types of credit and equity market instruments—more than four times the 1965 volume. They supplied directly almost one-sixth of the nation's total credit demands in 1966, the highest share since 1957, compared with less than four per cent in 1965.

In the face of sharply reduced saving flows, and mounting pressures on earnings and liquidity positions, mortgage-oriented savings institutions drastically cut back their new mortgage activity in 1966. Other credit markets remained well supplied, however, partly because of the direct investment activity of individuals. The severity of the mortgage cutback reflected also the large volume of outstanding mortgage commitments and inventory of "warehoused" mortgage loans over-hanging the market. These technical factors intensified pressures on institutional lenders to curtail new commitments as saving flows turned sharply downward in 1966.

New home mortgage commitment and lending activity was also cut back by life insurance companies in the face of sharply rising bond yields and lucrative returns on income-property loans. Heavy demands for policy loans and reduced home mortgage repayments in the stringent 1966 environment, moreover, reduced cash flows available for home mortgage lending.

All things considered, the immediate factors underlying the 1966 "mortgage crisis" were the unbalanced mix of monetary and fiscal policies, the selective impact of severe financial stringency on mortgage-oriented savings institutions, and the reinforcing influence of technical mortgage market factors. Under these circumstances, curtailed savings growth was quickly translated into sharply reduced mortgage and residential real estate activity. Conversely, in the earlier 1960s when financial ease and relatively low market interest rates stimulated savings growth, mortgage flows soared to excessive levels, relative to housing demand, because savings institutions were limited in their alternative investment opportunities. (The course of these financial developments and their impact on mortgage and housing markets is traced in figure 1.)

C. Structural Problems and Programs

Underlying the immediate causes of recurring "mortgage crises," summarized above, are deep-seated structural problems. And as long as these remain uncorrected, mortgage flows, housing activity, and urban rebuilding will remain susceptible to significant cyclical swings in the changing economic environment. The greater danger in the years ahead, perhaps, is of a sustained shortage, rather than

FIGURE 1

Financial Developments Leading to Mortgage Stringency and
Housing Declines in 1966

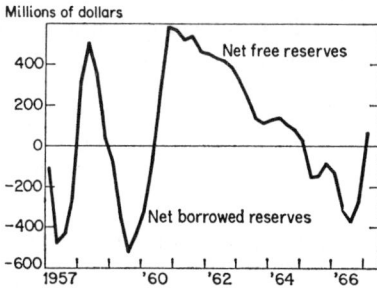

Millions of dollars

Net free reserves

Net borrowed reserves

A. Excessive reliance on monetary
policy to combat inflation in 1966
brought . . .

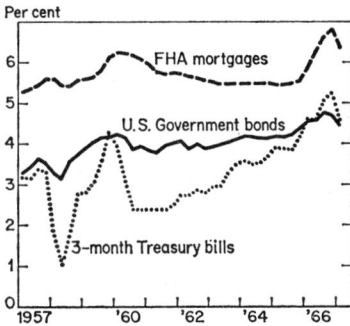

Per cent

FHA mortgages

U.S. Government bonds

3–month Treasury bills

B. Soaring interest rates . . .

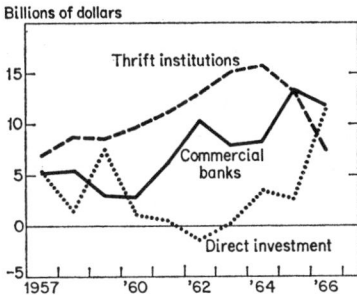

Billions of dollars

Thrift institutions

Commercial banks

Direct investment

C. Massive saving shifts and . . .

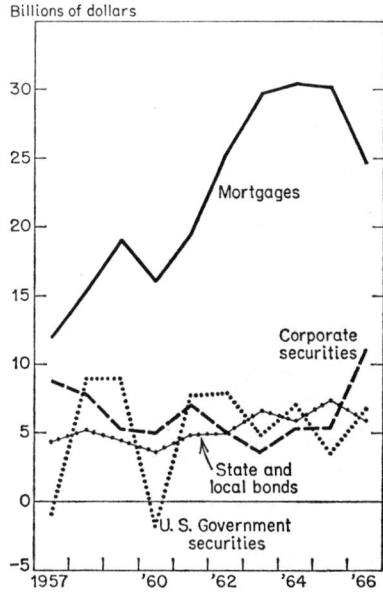

Billions of dollars

Mortgages

Corporate securities

State and local bonds

U. S. Government securities

D. Mortgage flows fell sharply and
corporate and U. S. Government
security issues rose substantially.

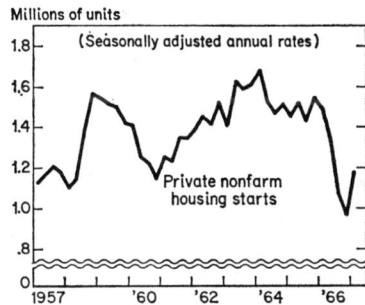

Millions of units

(Seasonally adjusted annual rates)

Private nonfarm housing starts

E. Housing starts declined to a postwar
low.

Source: Nat'l Ass'n of Mutual Savings Banks Ann. Rep. 3, 5 (1967).

plenitude, of housing credit in the face of heavy capital demands for private and public purposes. But whether the long-term trend indicates shortage or adequacy of housing credit, the unsettling effects of cyclical mortgage instability, arising out of structural problems, remain an ever-present danger.

What then are the basic structural problems which adversely affect the flow of residential mortgage credit? In my judgment, they lie in three related areas: (1) the fundamentally changing nature and inadequate structure of savings markets; (2) the cumbersome nature of the mortgage instrument itself; and (3) the unrealistic federal-state regulatory and statutory framework in which the mortgage market functions.

These interrelated problems call for an interrelated, integrated three-part program

(1) to adapt existing mortgage-oriented savings institutions to the changed financial environment,

(2) to tap supplementary sources of mortgage credit through new market instruments, and

(3) to adjust the role of government to the realities of the private market place.

1. *Adapting Savings Institutions*

Any program to strengthen and stabilize the flow of home mortgage credit in the economy must be firmly anchored to the strengthening of mortgage-oriented savings institutions. These institutions are, and will remain, the major suppliers of home mortgage credit. When their inflow of savings is sharply reduced, as in 1966, so also is the flow of home mortgage credit. When their saving inflows are large relative to suitable mortgage outlets, the quality of credit is threatened. Moreover, dislocations generated in one period reinforce the problems of the next.

Improvement in the competitive strength and flexibility of thrift institutions requires the restructuring of both their assets and liabilities. Savings institutions must modify their "borrowing short lending long" policies. They cannot continue, in effect, to promise "instant liquidity" from a basically illiquid balance sheet.

On the liabilities side, therefore, savings institutions must reduce their reliance on the standard passbook savings account to attract funds. They need to supplement these accounts with a variety of higher-yielding saving plans which will limit depositor liquidity, space out depositor claims, and offer higher rates for incremental than for existing savings. Such plans will result in greater flexibility, better control over withdrawals, reduced pressures on earnings, and increased competitive ability to attract savings. Several supplementary savings plans have been developed in recent years and are already in use, but on too limited a basis, both with respect to amount of deposits and number of institutions.

Savings institutions must greatly expand the use, and innovate in the development, of such savings plans as (1) investment-type accounts, including savings certificates, (2) limited withdrawal accounts, requiring sixty to ninety days or more notice, (3) split rate plans with higher rates for long-term accounts, (4) systematic saving plans, with bonuses for regular saving over a period of years, and (5) annuity-type plans pointing toward regular payments in retirement years. In addition, savings institutions must explore the possibilities of issuing debenture-type obligations in the open market to raise funds.

On the assets side of the balance sheet, savings institutions must be permitted broadened loan and investment powers. On the surface, this may appear an anomalous solution to mortgage credit problems, but it is essential to strengthen the structure of the major mortgage credit suppliers. Broadened powers would increase the viability of savings institutions, permit a more rapid adjustment of earnings to rapid interest rate advances, enhance their ability to compete for savings with commercial banks and open market instruments, and hence permit them to meet more effectively basic demands for mortgage credit in the economy. In essence, broadened investment opportunities for savings institutions would mean first, lessened investment risks and increased ability to strengthen long-run earning power and promote thrift continuously. This is so because funds could be allocated more readily among competing investments in accordance with highest yields (consistent with safety and liquidity) while earnings would be more responsive in periods of rapid financial change. These broadened investment opportunities would also mean a more stable flow of mortgage funds over the business cycle. This is so because excessive mortgage credit expansion in periods of relatively low housing demand or rapid savings growth would be avoided, while in other periods, demands for mortgage credit in excess of savings growth could be met by the conversion of short-term loans and other assets into mortgage loans.

These basic facts have been recognized by distinguished observers of the contemporary financial and economic scene. In a recent speech, Federal Reserve Governor Andrew F. Brimmer noted:[4]

> A shift to broader lending capabilities by the savings and loans and savings banks . . . would create more general strength among financial institutions to adjust to monetary stringency and thus help to spread the impact of monetary actions more evenly throughout the financial sector.

And, in their 1967 *Annual Report*, the President's Council of Economic Advisers, recommending federal charters for mutual savings banks, commented:[5]

> While broadened investment privileges of federally chartered mutual savings banks might initially divert some funds from the mortgage market, such chartered banks would improve the efficiency of thrift institutions, strengthen them in competition with banks, and thereby ultimately benefit the mortgage market.

---

[4] Address by Governor Brimmer, Annual Meeting of the Town Hall, Los Angeles, Cal., March 21, 1967.
[5] 1967 COUNCIL OF ECONOMIC ADVISERS ANN. REP., in 1967 ECONOMIC REPORT OF THE PRESIDENT 27, 67.

The tangible advantages of asset flexibility for the mortgage market can be seen clearly in the 1966 experience. Savings banks, with broader powers than savings and loans, were able to channel 108 per cent of their net deposit gains into mortgage loans. This was possible because inadequate deposit flows were supplemented by funds from conversion of other assets and from repayments of non-mortgage loans. Savings and loan associations, however, limited almost entirely to home mortgage lending, were able to channel only eighty-four per cent of their net increase in savings and borrowings into mortgage loans. These developments were explicitly recognized by the Federal Reserve Board, in its 1966 *Annual Report*:[6]

> While reduced net inflows at savings banks led to some reduction in mortgage commitments and acquisitions, these declines were less severe than at savings and loan associations. The ability of the mutual savings banks to better maintain their mortgage acquisitions reflected not only their deposit experience but also their more diversified portfolios, which permitted them to liquidate other securities in order to limit the reduction in their mortgage lending.

Parenthetically, commercial banks placed only thirty-eight per cent of their net savings and time deposit growth into mortgages, reflecting their fundamental orientation towards the business loan sector.

While savings banks do have broader powers than savings and loans, both are quite limited compared with commercial banks. Many savings banks and nearly all savings and loans, for example, are denied the right to make consumer loans. Basic legislation is required to achieve the desired broadening of powers. Such legislation is now at hand in the form of the federal savings bank bill,[7] sponsored by the administration and now before the Congress. This bill authorizes flexible loan and investment powers for federally-chartered savings banks and provides for the conversion of savings and loan associations into federal savings banks. The federal savings bank bill appears to offer a sound and practical route to the achievement of a strengthened mortgage-oriented system of savings institutions.

2. *Supplementary Mortgage Sources Through New Credit Instruments*

If mortgage markets are to function more effectively, additional sources of credit should be developed to supplement flows from traditional lenders, who will remain the major source of funds. This objective will not easily be fulfilled, considering the legally complex, economically cumbersome structure of mortgage finance.

The mortgage instrument reflects the complicated system of real estate transfer and the highly differentiated, localized nature of real estate markets. To be sure, government underwriting, through FHA insurance and VA guarantee, has given the mortgage loan some of the attributes of a modern credit instrument—uniformity

[6] 53 BOARD OF GOVERNORS OF THE FEDERAL RESERVE SYSTEM ANN. REP. 60 (1966).
[7] S. 1955, 90th Cong., 1st Sess. (1967); H.R. 10745, 90th Cong., 1st Sess. (1967).

and transferability. But even so, federally underwritten loans are not readily classifiable or broadly marketable, or unfettered by technical servicing problems.

Nor does legislating some super-secondary market institution into existence to provide "instant liquidity" offer an all-purpose solution to the need for broadened credit sources. Even the multi-billion dollar, government-sponsored, Federal National Mortgage Association (FNMA) severely rationed secondary market transactions in 1966, because of fund limitations.

The difficulties notwithstanding, the advantages of dependable, supplementary sources of mortgage funds in periods of credit stringency are so great that the effort is worth making. Consumers and pension funds, in particular, represent two broad investor groups which could be attracted into mortgage investments if suitable types of credit instruments are developed.

In the case of consumers, there is ample evidence of their willingness to invest directly in capital market instruments when yields are attractive relative to risk and liquidity. As noted previously, consumers invested a record $11 billion in open market securities during 1966, four times the 1965 volume. Needless to say, if part of this large flow could have been attracted into the mortgage sector, the burden of financial stringency would have been more evenly shared, and severe economic dislocations would have been lessened.

But the mortgage instrument and marketing channels are not now geared to attract the sophisticated individual investor. There is need for a security-type mortgage instrument that would be competitive with other capital market securities. In broad terms, such an instrument should be (1) made available in as wide a variety of denominations and maturities as are other open market securities, (2) so designed as to minimize competition with savings deposits and maximize competition with other capital market instruments, and (3) marketed through privately-financed companies, organized perhaps as subsidiaries of financial intermediaries which would purchase mortgages from the intermediaries and, in turn, sell securities to the public backed by these mortgages.

In short, a relatively small-denomination, consumer-type mortgage participation is required that would command public respect and confidence. A repetition of the unhappy investor experience with mortgage guarantee bonds of the 1920s can be avoided. In this regard, one need only note the favorable public reception to participation certificate offerings of FNMA and the Export-Import Bank in recent years. The successful marketing of these instruments, which represent beneficial interests in pools of government-owned assets, including mortgages, strongly suggests that, under the right conditions, consumer response to a mortgage-type security would be favorable.

A similar type of security—but in much larger denominations—could also attract pension funds unwilling to deal in the cumbersome mortgage instrument itself. There is already evidence that a large-denomination trust certificate, secured by a portfolio of federally underwritten mortgages, is being developed by mortgage bankers for purchase by selected pension funds. If this approach proves feasible, it will undoubtedly be more widely adopted.

3. *Adjusting the Role of Government to Market Realities*

Finally, at both the state and federal level, more realistic governmental policies are needed to bring the mortgage market firmly into the twentieth century. Long-standing variations in state mortgage statutes governing foreclosure procedures, redemption periods and "doing business" penalties continue to hamper mortgage market operations. As a practical matter, however, it is probably unrealistic to expect significant improvement in these areas soon.

Shifts in state and federal attitudes toward interest rates, however, are within the realm of possibility. There are at present ten states which impose a six per cent interest rate ceiling on mortgage loans. Such usury laws, enacted years ago, are clearly in need of revision, with the prime rate at this level in 1966 and federal agencies paying as much to borrow. Otherwise, severe dislocations will continue to occur in local mortgage markets, as funds are diverted from low-interest-ceiling states in periods of credit stringency.

The statutory interest rate ceiling on FHA-insured and VA-guaranteed loans is also at six per cent, and rates up to this level are established by administrative action. Discounts from contract rates are permitted, of course, but under such restrictive circumstances that federally underwritten mortgage flows and real estate transactions are, as in 1966, severely affected when the general level of interest rates is high and rising. The economic logic for completely free FHA and VA rates is unassailable, but the political barriers seem equally impenetrable. After years of unsuccessful effort by many groups, I am prepared to concede that a free market rate for FHA and VA loans is probably not attainable in the foreseeable future.

It does seem feasible, however, to achieve greater flexibility of FHA and VA contract interest rates by

(1) requiring the Secretary of Housing and Urban Development to adjust contract interest rates so as to minimize discounts at all times, even to the extent of lifting the contract rate above six per cent when necessary,

(2) modifying the restriction that mortgage discounts cannot be recognized in the price of properties, and

(3) relating FHA and VA mortgage rates to the movement of long-term U.S. Government bond yields.

The last point runs into the difficulty of determining suitable yield spreads, of course, particularly if regional mortgage rate variations are to be taken into account. But the current uniform contract rate allows for no regional variations. The possibility of some increased interest rate flexibility, therefore, even on an imperfect basis, is most appealing.

Among other possible federal policy adjustments, FNMA should not arbitrarily restrict its secondary market purchases on the basis of loan size and date of origination. Such restrictions, in effect, inequitably cut off higher-priced areas from access to FNMA, as well as mortgage holders from selling existing loans to FNMA. In a market economy, price should be more heavily relied on as the basic technique for rationing scarce funds to the market place, and the liquidity needs of lenders should not be so patently ignored. To do otherwise fails to recognize the interrelationship of new and existing house markets, and significantly weakens the role of FNMA as a secondary market facility.

In sum, there is no single dramatic panacea for the problems which periodically beset the mortgage market. A series of basic steps along the lines suggested here seem to encompass a realistic approach—a broad-based attack on a multi-faceted problem, with each segment reinforcing the other. Moreover, it should be emphasized that the overriding goal of policy and programs should be to help the mortgage market function more effectively within the private market place and not to shelter it from the discipline of overall credit availability and price as determined by private market forces.

III

PUBLIC/PRIVATE BALANCE IN URBAN REVITALIZATION

A. The Cost/Benefit Principle

At the outset of this article, it was suggested that effective solutions to urban mortgage and housing problems must rest on the creative partnership of the private and public sectors. In this respect, it was stressed that a basic goal of public policy must be to encourage and to supplement, not to preempt, the use of private resources.

A related principle of sound urban problem-solving, which must be recognized at this point, is the cost/benefit balance in public finance. For this principle to be observed in urban programs, it is clearly necessary for public financial assistance to be openly recognized and disbursed so that costs incurred may be directly measured against benefits achieved.

Unfortunately, this fundamental principle has not always been observed in federal housing policy. Indeed, political expediency or other non-economic criteria have as often dictated policy as long-range criteria of appropriate private/public or cost/ benefit balance. This has meant that the approach of federal housing and urban revitalization programs has not infrequently been piecemeal and uncoordinated. It has meant the accumulation of federal aids, including direct grants, loans, and mortgage insurance, in programs which have tended to supplant, rather than to supplement, private credit. And it has meant that costs have too often been obscured, while concentrating on benefits obtained.

1. *The Submarket Interest Rate Approach: A Violation of Basic Precepts*

One basic approach to housing problems which violates both criteria of maximum private participation and cost/benefit balance is the use of "submarket" interest rates in federally underwritten mortgage lending programs. This approach of making credit available at rates well below the private market is used to subsidize housing costs for low- and middle-income families. It is widely recognized, of course, that such below-market rate loans insured by the Federal Housing Administration and "purchased" by the Federal National Mortgage Association represent a thinly-disguised substitute for direct federal lending.

Admittedly, the submarket rate approach to housing problems is an administratively convenient and politically expedient device to achieve subsidies for families unable to compete in the private market place. But in the long run it is a snare and a delusion. It does not permit the use of private credit, so desperately needed to supplement public funds if low-cost housing programs are to expand significantly. It effectively obscures actual subsidy costs, so necessary to judge the efficiency and usefulness of the program relative to benefits achieved.

I regard the submarket interest rate approach as bad public policy even when associated with direct federal loans. Such loans, sometimes essential to fill a private housing credit gap, ought to be offered at going rates of interest—consistent with federal borrowing costs at least—to borrowers unable, for one or another reason, to secure private funds on competitive terms. Another dimension is added when hidden cost subsidies, as well as direct public credit, are provided through the submarket interest rate technique.

If interest rate subsidies—in addition to public credit—are deemed sound public policy, they should be provided directly and accepted as a measurable social cost. One way of doing this is to have private lenders extend credit at market rates of interest, with the difference between the market rate and subsidized rate to borrowers paid directly to financial institutions by government. In this way, private credit sources would be tapped (reducing the need for public funds) and the actual subsidy costs (interest rate differential) of the program would be directly measurable.

In sum, current submarket interest rate housing programs ought to be gradually eliminated because (1) they preempt rather than supplement the use of private credit, and (2) they obscure actual subsidy costs and thus hinder their measure against benefits achieved.

2. *The Rent Supplement Approach: In Support of Basic Precepts*

In sharp contrast to the below-market rate program, the relatively new rent supplement program directly supports sound basic principles of public policy in urban revitalization. In this program, maximum reliance is placed on the private sector to achieve a desired public objective. The rental housing provided for low-income families is privately built, privately owned, and privately financed, at market prices and interest rates. And, the supplemental rent payments represent subsidy costs openly measurable against benefits received, not obscured through hidden interest-rate subsidies in federal credits.

When the rent supplement program was proposed in 1965, there was at long last implicit federal recognition that both the concept and practicality of the submarket interest rate approach were found wanting. In transmitting the Housing and Urban Development Act of 1965 to the Congress, President Johnson said:[8]

> Up to now Government programs for low- and moderate-income families have concentrated on either direct financing of construction; or on making below-the-market-rate loans to private builders. . . .
>
> . . . .
>
> . . . If [the rent supplement program] works as well as we expect, it should be possible to phase out most of our existing programs of low-interest loans.

The President, in his 1965 message on the central city and its suburbs, also stated: "[W]e must recognize that the benefits of [below-market interest rate programs] are decreasing as the rising costs of Federal borrowing narrows the difference between the interest we ask and that demanded in the private market."[9]

When they were made two years ago, these statements represented, in my judgment, a major step forward in the direction of federal housing policy—a significant turn towards increased reliance on the private sector. I was aware, of course, of the practical problems of discontinuing submarket interest rate programs before the rent supplement and other proposed private/public direct subsidy programs had been proven successful. Now, two years later, I must confess to some disappointment.

The rent supplement program has run into serious congressional obstacles. Its concept is not fully appreciated, its working apparatus considered discouragingly complex. As a result, the program has been operating on minimum funds. Until this program is well funded and given an opportunity to prove its worth, the submarket interest rate program, unfortunately, is likely to remain the basic approach to the low-income housing problem, in violation of fundamental principles of private/public partnership and cost/benefit balance.

B. The Concept and Philosophy of Federal Mortgage Insurance

In the broad range of urban programs, current and proposed, one of those longest in operation stands out as the epitome of the creative partnership between the private and public sectors. I refer, of course, to federal mortgage insurance, established over three decades ago, and operated so successfully through the Federal Housing Administration. With respect to the cost/benefit balance, moreover, the FHA program is entirely self-sustaining through income from insurance premiums. On

---

[8] H.R. Doc. No. 99, 89th Cong., 1st Sess. 7-8 (1965).
[9] *Id.* at 9.

both counts, then, federal mortgage insurance deserves to be the principal credit aid in the revitalization of our cities.

There is a body of private market opinion, however, which disagrees with this view. It holds that for FHA to assume the high risks inherent in urban rebuilding programs is to forsake the basic business principle underlying its creation—the insurance of economically sound residential mortgage credits. In this view, the fundamental concept and philosophy of federal mortgage insurance is violated when FHA moves into areas outside of standard single-family housing and multi-family projects.

This is a rather parochial and short-sighted position to take, however, in a rapidly changing urban scene. It confuses purposes and objectives with specific programs undertaken to attain them. It will be recalled that the FHA was etablished in the depths of the Great Depression (1934) to stimulate the construction of new housing and the repair and modernization of existing housing, in part to provide new employment opportunities. Federal mortgage insurance was the new tool invented to encourage the flow of private credit into markets which, in retrospect, had proven to be excessively risky. The approach was new, daring, and imaginative; the objective was to renew and broaden the residential mortgage market with a viable, modern credit instrument. The cornerstone and prerequisite of the new federal mortgage insurance program was "economic soundness."

In the almost uninterrupted three-decade rise in real estate values which has followed its establishment, FHA has become a resounding business success. Its philosophy, concepts, and objectives have been proven sound. And once proven, they have been embraced by private lenders and investors, now entering markets not earlier dared without federal mortgage insurance.

In today's new urban environment, with its new problems and needs, however, FHA's principal concept and objectives are not well served by continuing to plow old fields, by operating solely in already proven markets, such as single-family suburban housing. Only by pursuing new programs, in fact, does FHA fulfill its original purpose—to open up new markets and opportunities with private resources, which otherwise might be long deferred or developed eventually only with public funds.

In essence, FHA serves its most useful—and originally intended—function when it operates on the frontiers of housing and mortgage markets. It must innovate. It must be cognizant of changing market patterns and unmet needs and, through the insurance technique, channel resources into areas where private industry still fears to tread alone. To follow this course is to break new paths in the original FHA tradition. Not to follow it is to retrogress into a shell of safe, proven markets until the fundamental reason for federal mortgage insurance disappears.

In this frame of reference, no program is better suited to the fulfillment of FHA's basic principles and objectives than the urban revitalization program. And no technique is better suited than federal mortgage insurance—at market rates of interest—to maximize the use of private resources to achieve broadly accepted public goals.

Few tasks have greater economic and social significance than the rebuilding of our urban complex. And few tasks confront private lenders and investors with greater risks in their initial stages of development. These ingredients are tailor-made for the use of federal risk-sharing aids. Once urban rebuilding programs are proven economically sound, the willingness of private industry to participate alone will increase and the need for federal assistance will be reduced.

The acceptance of greater risks inherent in broad new urban programs means, of course, that a larger proportion of the contingent liabilities borne by the federal government through mortgage insurance may ultimately turn into real liabilities. But this is a burden that a federal insurance agency and the American community should be willing to bear, if the objective sought is worth the risk entailed. The logic appears unassailable, then, that federal mortgage insurance ought to be centered on those urban investments which are riskier than alternative private market opportunities but which have a strong long-range base of economic soundness.

C. The Need for a Public/Private Administrative Structure

In concluding this article, I cannot resist the temptation of dusting off an administrative proposal, which I have had occasion to recommend elsewhere. There is a need for a voluntary public/private administrative network—at national, state, and local levels—in which public agencies and private groups jointly plan, develop, and implement programs and policies for urban rebuilding. Such an administrative structure might operate within "Councils of Urban Rebuilding Enterprises" (CURE). This would give specific administrative recognition to the existence of a creative public/private partnership. The existence of CURE, moreover, would recognize that private institutions have more to contribute than money to the massive task of urban revitalization. They have imaginative and technical skills as well.

Such a creative public/private structure is, of course, not an entirely new concept. Similar administrative arrangements have been adopted before at various levels of government and with various degrees of success. There is much that can be learned from the function of these earlier administrative arrangements—both the successful and unsuccessful. The important thing is that through a continuing, cooperative administrative organization, old battle lines between public and private forces might more quickly disintegrate. This, of course, is the essential ingredient to the forging of a meaningful, operative, public/private partnership.

THE INFLUENCE OF MORTGAGE LENDERS ON BUILDING DESIGN

JOHN B. HALPER*

I

WHAT DESIGN AND WHERE?

Driving through a typical American city several years ago, a bank officer and I were visibly depressed by the uniformity and mediocrity of design, as well as the complete void of aesthetic quality in a better than average tract of middle-income homes. Despite the apparent middle-class virtues of shrubbery and lawn maintenance, the appearance of the structures was so appallingly drab that the banker remarked: "Since it seems just as easy to design a good building as a poor one, I always wonder why they don't put a little craftsmanship in them anymore."

I have thought about this observation many times since then, and have reached two basic conclusions: (1) it is easier to design and build the "drabs" only because repetition of the approved formula is both what the building trade feels safe with and what the lenders will knowingly lend against; and (2) since lenders do not insist upon "quality control," much less aesthetic appearance, there is little reason to donate extra effort to the buying public. Quality control is distinct from adherence to specifications, which do not relate to quality in the first place; they merely insure that the building is adequate to endure the life of the mortgage.

A corollary of this is the outright fear many builders have of being original, daring, and producing something for which there is no set lending pattern, that is, no proven yardstick to establish the all important loan-to-value ratio. While these drawbacks in design are largely attributable to timorous lending practices, they have a pervasive effect on borrowers, so that the cycle goes full circle.

A case in point was "The Willows," an attractive type of bee-hive design complex of doctors' offices and labs in Westport, Connecticut. Breaking away from the rectangle or hollow-square design, the architect sought to produce not only a more functional building, but a series of interlocking, or bee-hive, offices with ample and accessible parking space, creating an idea that would fit aesthetically into both landscape and the quasi-rustic locale. Despite the long leases of the doctor-tenants, no insurance company would advance the mortgage funds. Reason: simply no prior experience with such an odd-ball design, no way to compute cubic feet by accepted slide-rule practice, thus no way to measure up the loan.

* B.A. 1946, M.A. 1947, Columbia University; Diploma 1949, *Ecole de Haute Finance,* University of Geneva. President, Halper & Co., Inc., a firm engaged in private mortgage and investment banking and brokerage, headquartered in New York. Mr. Halper served as a correspondent in Switzerland for *Business Week* and other McGraw-Hill publications; in Washington, D.C., for *Congressional Quarterly*; and in New York for *Value Line Investment Survey,* before establishing his own firm in 1964.

The problem was finally settled, if not solved, by bringing in a more flexible New York bank which was sufficiently impressed with the appearance and the endorsement of the tenants to issue the loan, but not at the full amount requested because of the higher "risk" involved in unique construction and design. Needless to say, the next group of doctors desiring to build an office complex turned to a more conventional mold and received a higher loan for their prudence.

While this might demonstrate the force of lenders on design, it is not to imply that all lenders exert a negative influence—merely one heavily coated with conservatism. With regard to shopping centers and major-tenant office buildings, where the national credit rating of the tenant virtually serves as "insurance" for the loan, the most advanced designs in the United States (though not North America) may be seen.[1] But in the field of housing—whether single-family or apartments, Federal Housing Administration (FHA) or conventional—the kindest compliment that can be credited to a lender's influence on the aesthetic continuum is sheer disinterest. That is, he does not actually insist upon square shapes.

Many of the problems arising from this negative influence may be traced directly to FHA codes which, in turn, have produced what is commonly called in the trade either "FHA modern" or "late VA" styles. The blame can be laid squarely on the agency's desire for standardized procedures which allow it to insure mortgages at the lowest common denominator of design and building technique.

For example, the difference between cheap and very good residential construction ranges between $1.25 and $1.50 in cost, approximately a twenty per cent gap. But mortgage lenders make only minor distinctions between good and poor construction. Money is lent on an estimated rent roll; and a cheap speculative building will produce a rent roll very near that of a high quality structure. Tenants, one might assume, will not renew their leases in a shoddy building, but by that time most speculative builders will have taken their accelerated depreciation and sold out for a capital gain. A graphic demonstration of the effect of different cubic foot construction costs for a high-rise in Charlotte, North Carolina, which has 1,000,000 cubic feet (rounded off), is shown in table 1.

Funds received by the builder through the mortgage are the same for all practical purposes in these three cases. Yet the difference between very cheap and good is $250,000. In other words, every cent per cubic foot saved by cost cutting on the quality of construction is a savings of $10,000 for the builder. Thus, in our example, the cost increase between poor quality and good is 18.5 per cent, while the difference between reasonable quality and good is less than seven per cent. Since lenders do not reduce their loans for poorer quality construction by the same percentage ratio as the savings to builders, they indirectly encourage the cheaper construction.

---

[1] Mexico and Brazil are years ahead of the United States in this respect.

TABLE 1

COMPARATIVE CONSTRUCTION COSTS

Construction Quality	Land Cost	Construction Cost	Total
Cheap— $1.25	$100,000	$1,250,000	$1,350,000
Reasonable— $1.40	$100,000	$1,400,000	$1,500,000
Good— $1.50	$100,000	$1,500,000	$1,600,000

In reviewing the role that lending institutions have exerted on building quality, even by default, it would appear at times that they have all but abdicated their influence. Yet that power of influence is maintained as a vast potential, and can be heavily leveraged when mortgage funds are needed and money is tight.

While some helpful hints or suggestions might be made to the prospective borrower during, or after, an inspection of the property site—and when it is often too late to alter architectural design—few aesthetic demands are imposed as a condition precedent to the loan.

In going back through years of requirements on file, I find copious inter-office memoranda from senior fund officials instructing their loan officers or appraisers to double check on zoning, easements, and deed restrictions; off-site requirements, such as utilities, wells, or gas mains; plottage, embankments, and drainage; and even such matters as proximity to odors, smoke, or unusual noise. But seldom is seen a strict pronounciamento to advance or withhold funds because of design or architectural merit, even using such tests as conformity to terrain or use of the building. This critique applies equally to FHA or conventional dwellings, single or multiple. It does not apply to office buildings where, as was pointed out earlier, occupancy by rated tenants permits more advanced, and even highly advanced, design.

Once a loan is committed and the structure is up, the prime interest of both sponsor and lender is merged into one question—will it sell, or rent? All other requirements, or gimmicks, are irrelevant if the result remains empty.

To avoid this catastrophe, sales glamor can often overcome what shoddy, slab construction or poor design imposes. This is especially true if the glamor shows in the right places, such as the building lobby, elevators, kitchens, or terraces. Largely due to the glamor concept, interior decorators have been elevated to new status, while architects have been downgraded. In fact, draftsmen will do, as long as the lending institution has the report of a "supervising architect" to enforce the specifications and codes.

In a high-rise apartment the lobby (or entrance foyers in a garden-type apartment) is the first spot greeting the tenant; and while styles change, the lobby is always in keeping with the current middle-class taste. This calls for an ample thickness of foam in the carpenting, textured or scenic wall paper, and a sufficiency of bronze-lacquer in the chandeliers.

The next eye-catcher is the elevator bank. Self-operated elevators are a must due to prohibitive labor costs (except in very expensive apartments). Regardless of the decor, the elevators are starkly modern because people, as well as lenders, look for the ultra-modern in machinery, despite any clash in decorating styles.

Kitchens are another glamor feature because they make a good selling point, even if they are out of proportion to the rest of the interior composition. Over-sized refrigerators and stoves, relatively speaking, even when there is no separation between kitchen and living room, catch the eye and keep it from wandering elsewhere.

The competitive market, moreover, has created another idiocy—namely the apartment terrace. This is oftentimes little more than a narrow catwalk which more frequently provides neither sunlight nor view, except over a highway or flapping laundry. The concrete shelf is rarely used by the tenant and serves as a thin status symbol. The FHA codes are almost wholly responsible for the balcony disease. The agency has defined a balcony as a room, thus including it in the room count on which funds are allocated. Since balconies cost approximately $850 to $1,000 each, but get an allowance twice that much, builders often thin their equity and install balconies for a higher loan. No wonder FHA projects in northern Alaska have sprouted balconies. Conventional buildings, while not receiving the same monetary blessing, are forced by sheer competition to go along.

We have said relatively little thus far about lenders' influence on single-family homes, and, for that matter, there has been little influence. There are, indeed, definite requirements as to the minimum square feet or number of bathrooms in a fixed-price-range house, but we find a paucity of comment as to design.

A uniquely architected home, for example, in contemporary styling with an abundance of glass panels, open fireplaces, and expanse of redwood deck is not favored by lending institutions just because it may have won a design award or enhances the area. It is more often looked upon as an expression of an individual's idiosyncrasy, on which they are reluctant to advance funds because they are concerned about its resale potential in a stock home market. Thus, penalizing it with a fifty to sixty per cent loan instead of a seventy-five to eighty per cent loan to value (which is the same as cost in this instance), they are exerting the negative influence of keeping imaginative design within bounds. It appears that only the wealthy or the bold, or both, may transgress those bounds.

II

Lenders' Criteria

Some of the larger institutions, such as Equitable Assurance, Mutual Benefit, and Prudential Life Insurance, do indeed make a contributory effort toward the encouragement of good design and quality construction through rigorous adherence to tougher specifications. But since they cannot arbitrarily reject all "poorly designed" residential buildings and remain competitive, they have, by and large, exerted a positive influence by giving preference to well designed structures.

This is particularly applicable to large, expensive edifices where the smaller lenders, such as the local Savings and Loan associations, are forced to withdraw from competitive bidding. In California, for example, where building activity has been intense as well as hectic for two decades, an experienced observer will note that the better-designed, high-unit-cost apartments are almost exclusively backed by top-notch lenders. The reason for this is based on three factors, in order of importance: (1) prestige, which rubs off on the lender; (2) safety of investment in knowing that good design will command occupancy for the life of the loan; and (3) default of competition in the field.

I think this demonstrates, rather than proves, that where there is an election as to which loan to make, the loan will be given to the advanced, though not radical, design. The trouble is that there is frequently no choice to make, since most designs are poor to begin with because there is no insistence upon or premium for them.

Lenders are fully cognizant that an expensive, well-designed, high-unit-cost dwelling creates a more insured long-range security. Against this realization, however, are weighted the business-like exigencies of putting out the least loan amount for the highest return in keeping with the market, as well as the ever present concern about recovery in event of foreclosure. Unfortunately, it is usually the latter consideration which outweighs the former when the decision is close.

III

Borrowers' Reactions

Few things are more sensitive than a borrower seeking money. Sensing that lenders base their outlays on two factors—income from the project and current replacement costs in the area—the borrower has responded to the challenge in a manner to be expected rather than admired. He has jacked up rentals to what he feels the traffic can bear, while reducing maintenance to what the lenders, or tenants, will allow; and he has inflated his construction or land costs so as to arrive at the highest value assignable to his project in order to offset the lender's paring.

While this has been reduced to a mathematical game for both sides, few bonuses are granted the builder who goes out of his way to create something of great merit or which reflects advanced design. Why should he, he reasons, since the real compensation lies elsewhere, and he is rarely in the business for aesthetic satisfaction. Ironically, even to slip into a good design which might cost more is to impose a financial penalty upon himself, because the lender offers no premium.

IV

What Might Be Done

Earlier in this article I referred to the banker who thought well-designed homes might actually cost, size for size, no more than badly designed homes. While this might be true in theory, it cannot be true in today's practice simply because almost all existing patterns, once approved in lending circles, are endlessly and cheaply reproduced. Therefore, a builder, desirous of a larger loan, knows that for every $1.00 spent on space or glamor, he can gain approximately $1.30 in loan value, up to certain limits, of course.

I am sure that the smallish, compact houses built in colonial Williamsburg over two hundred years ago were not only carefully constructed and aesthetically designed by home-grown architects of its day, but that the construction was as inexpensive as a prudent and cash-poor squirearchy could afford. Yet, there is a lasting, good form inherent in the original style, layout, and design which no Levittown has matched. In other words, there was an example of good design of enduring beauty, as inexpensive in its era as some of the future slums we are building today along arterial highways in our expanding "strip" towns.

Since we may conclude that builders will not voluntarily elect to improve residential design—because innovations often work against them—it is left to the major lending institutions to insist upon and reward aesthetically-pleasing residential structures. Imagination and innovation could be encouraged, in fact, by the one thing builders readily understand: monetary inducements.

Each loan application, when it goes before the approving committee, could be granted a premium should the project show design merit over and above its basic loan requirements. So many dollars, or so many percentage points of additional loan, could easily be granted for, say, intricate landscaping, brick lattice work, gas-lit townhouses, arched or recessed doorways, homes staggered on the lots, and all the myriad ideas that could affect the result.

In setting up such a practice, lenders would not only help beautify America and improve the dismal appearance of the high-density sectors of the cities, but also would perform a service to their own self-interest. They would not only forestall future slums, too many of which are now aborning, but also would help insure continued occupancy at stabilized rentals. In turn, this would save the time and expense of foreclosure and forced sale, although that happening is usually remote.

In the few instances where this approach has been taken, such as in Reston, Virginia, it was Gulf Oil Company, rather than a usual lender, that was ready, willing, and able to take the first step. Having proven that good design and land planning is both feasible and fiscally sound, it is also smart business.[2]

It is also one of the major steps that should be undertaken in the private sector of the economy because the government, primarily preoccupied with mass housing as shelter, cannot initiate such a "frill" for fear of criticism. Enlightened self-interest, however, cannot neglect it for long.

V

PRIVATE INVESTMENT IN SLUM IMPROVEMENT

In early 1966 I made the suggestion to Robert C. Wood, Undersecretary of the Department of Housing and Urban Development, that little would be accomplished in slum and ghetto rehabilitation unless some means were agreed upon to induce a massive infusion of private insurance company funds as part of a concerted effort to get the program under way meaningfully.[3] For, in the United States, government programs frequently flounder, even after surviving protracted and crippling legislation, unless they are enthusiastically backed by large segments of private industry and capital. And what is more realistic support than monetary commitments to back slum redevelopment at normal, rather than high risk, rates.

The suggestion carried the point that a consortium of major insurance companies, brought together by the Department and apprised of the magnitude of the problem, would be able to confront the task pragmatically—provided they were given a form of government-backed, FHA-type of loan insurance to offset the added risk.

Insofar as there are almost 350 life insurance companies in the United States, all of whom are capable of making some form of long-term commitments to improve real estate at a reasonable return, perhaps a third of that number could be interested in participating in such a program. If so, that alone would constitute a major breakthrough in steering private capital into ghetto housing. With well over $15 million being channeled from these sources alone into real estate annually, surely it would not be too much to ask that a small portion be syphoned off toward improving the quality of life in the cities.

There is a further suggestion that an insurance industry committee be formed to promote the overall project by recruiting builders who meet tests of adequacy as well as would-be sponsors of low-cost housing. Landholders, agreeing to sell land at less than unconscionable prices, should also be induced to cooperate.

While in practice each participating company would direct its own investments, this would become an excellent opportunity to insist upon good design as an integral

---

[2] Reston has received an infusion of funds because of the vastness of the undertaking.

[3] It has recently been announced that this program, as proposed, has been adopted in principle by the major insurance companies as of September 14, 1967. Insurance lenders, perhaps 98% being life companies, make larger and longer term investments than banks, by and large. Long-term bank commitments come mainly from their pension trusts for which they act as fiduciary trustee, and not for their own account.

part of the loan package. Indeed, it should be a condition precedent to granting the loan, provided there are enough sponsors bidding for the work project.

In fact, my original suggestion to the Department points out that special attention be directed to the creation of "townhouse" type of construction, designed to fit the heavy density pattern of the intra-urban area. Townhouses, as distinct from row houses, can be one of the most aesthetically pleasing architectural forms adaptable for metropolitan environment.[4]

Aside from the excellent townhouse grouping in Southwest Washington, D.C. (recently completed), a historical example may be observed in London as "redeveloped" after the great fire of 1667. Many of its present townhouses were the result of early slum improvement following the fire, and although most of them were replaced during the nineteenth century, the architectural concept remains—along with gardens and trees and walkways built into the center of the square surrounded by relatively low-cost, compact houses, each slightly different but well designed and fitting pleasingly into their "urbascape." In fact, Samuel Pepys tells us that much of the rebuilding effort was directed by the city's insurance underwriters who, in an attempt to reduce their insurance risks, demanded better construction and congestion control. Hence, many of the open squares and crescents, which only later became parks or community gardens.

The same concept, stimulated not by fire this time but by the seething misery of poverty and eruptive violence, should be implemented. But the major theme of this article is that redevelopment without specific attention to well-oriented design of both the dwelling and its surrounding would be nothing more than the heedless creation of future slums within an immediate Kafkaesque nightmare.

If such a program of redevelopment becomes a reality through the auspices of the Department of Housing and Urban Development, and if insurance company lenders do not insist upon and reward aesthetic contributions to design, then both sides will have recommitted so grievous an error as to be downright shameful.

People who work in cities should have a chance not only to live there but also simply to enjoy their homes and surroundings as part of a lasting solution.

---

[4] This was also a part of the suggestion which the writer made to the Department of Housing and Urban Development, Feb. 16, 1966.

HOUSING, THE COMPUTER, AND THE ARCHITECTURAL PROCESS

ARTHUR R. COGSWELL*

INTRODUCTION

So much has been written in recent years about the problems of the poor in America and the way in which these problems reinforce each other, that by now it has almost the ring of a truism to suggest that the needs of the poor are a "system" of needs. Yet it is inescapably so, and any consideration of solutions for one or more of these needs must begin with the fact that the problems faced by the poor are interwoven in a set of complex interrelationships, each supporting and reinforcing the others in their erosion of the energies and opportunities of those unfortunate enough to have been born in poverty.

It accomplishes relatively little to attempt to alleviate in an isolated fashion the effects of any one of the circumstances that surrounds such an individual or such a family. Indeed, it could be anticipated that the relief of one of the multiplicity of restraints surrounding such an individual might only open to him opportunities which would prove quickly to be illusory, with increased frustration and deeper bitterness the sole result.

The effort must begin somewhere, however; and there must be an implicit set of priorities in the situation. It would appear that housing is near the top of this list of priorities. If it is accepted that man is a physical organism, and that the behavior of a physical organism is a response to the conditions of its environment, it is difficult to deny that very thoughtful attention should be given to the enhancement of the quality and character of the physical environment in which we spend our lives, more particularly to the urban housing units which almost overwhelmingly determine the character of the physical surroundings in which most of our people spend most of their days. Winston Churchill said it very simply: "We shape our buildings, and thereafter they shape us."

I

HOUSING ENVIRONMENT AND THE PROBLEMS OF THE POOR

Considered in terms of the physical and emotional needs of the organism that is man, the dwelling units we have shaped might almost be characterized as punitive devices. Indeed, as physical organisms sensitive to and profoundly influenced by their surrounding environment, the human beings living in bad housing which is part of a defunct neighborhood forming a part of a chaotic and ill-functioning city, as most of them are, respond as we might reasonably have predicted them to: they throw up ambition, reject schools, engage in crime, allow their family structures to

---

* A.I.A.; Project Director, North Carolina Fund Low Income Housing Demonstration Project.

dissolve, abjure the values of the general society which we present to them, and when the pressures of frustration mount in the presence of a spark of organization, they riot. If we wish the bulk of our population to become citizens who are both productive economically and sound politically, we must contrive to place them in an environment which will naturally produce such behavior. Better housing conditions and urban design cannot alone produce this result, to paraphrase Secretary Robert Weaver, but neither can these results be obtained without better housing and urban design.

Centuries ago the Roman architect Vitruvius delineated the three principal virtues which any piece of architecture worthy of the name must possess: firmness, commodity, and delight. We can today see much if we attempt to evaluate our housing, our neighborhoods, and our cities in these terms. In an overwhelming number of cases we see that not only are the structures of the neighborhoods and cities neither firm enough to be safe nor commodious enough to be efficiently used, but they are most certainly devoid of any suggestion of delight.

It is difficult to describe good housing without doing it in terms of a neighborhood or larger community, since it is in this context that good housing has meaning. Certain of the new towns being built across the country are examples of well-planned housing arranged in well-planned communities, and what they provide for their inhabitants is a quantum jump in quality of life. Not only are the individual dwelling units light and well ventilated, easy to clean and maintain, satisfactorily equipped in a mechanical sense, efficiently planned to serve the needs of a family with decency and privacy, and possessed of a certain element of delight, but they are arranged in the landscape in meaningful relationship to each other, to the parks, playgrounds, and other green spaces, to neighborhood shopping centers, to recreational and cultural facilities, and to major lines of transportation to work centers and larger metropolitan areas.

The contrast between this and the grimy streets of tenements which crowd our major cities is a bitter one, particularly so when we realize that it is within our capability to do better than we are doing. It is a bitter one when we realize that the conditions implied by this contrast are producing public behavior of the most unhappy and unlawful sort. It is inescapable to the thoughtful observer that the burning, the looting, and the sniping which have occurred during the summer of 1967 are the simple result of a constellation of oppressive conditions, of which bad housing is a part, under which large numbers of our people have been living for over half a century, and with which they have finally become noisily impatient.

II

OBSTACLES TO BETTER HOUSING

It is no small matter to analyze the present housing industry and suggest why it is such a laggard one in terms of technological advance and contribution to the public good, but it is possible to point to a number of factors which are of importance in the situation. Part of the problem lies in the fragmented nature of the building industry and the presence of a multitude of local building codes, most of which are different from any other. These two factors combine to inhibit the efforts of large industrial enterprises which have the financing required to develop industrial processes for producing good housing at minimum cost. In the face of code restrictions which vary from community to community across the country in a thousand ways, enterprises which might otherwise approach the national housing program with some expertise and innovation have held off.

Another item which has inhibited the design and construction of better housing, and particularly home ownership, is the traditional complex of financing and credit practices. Typically, it may take a person of small income several months to obtain a mortgage for the purchase of a small dwelling—if he is successful at all. If his credit background is at all clouded, or if his situation is in any way unorthodox, he will in all probability not obtain the mortgage. Even individuals in the low-income group whose recent credit history is clear, but who have had problems in the past, perhaps in youth, will in most cases be unable to obtain financing for a home. By contrast, financing practices in the mobile home industry are more flexible and resemble more than anything else the practices of the automobile industry. A prospective buyer can obtain financing for a mobile home in a matter of days, if not hours.

An associated problem here is the traditional association of the dwelling with the land upon which it rests. With greater industrialization of the housing industry, and a greater development of the capability of housing to be moved to new sites when local need changes, this indissoluble relationship between house and site may become less important and will lead to the increasing flexibility of financing practices for the small home owner.

This, however, is relative to the single-home market, a market which will inevitably become less and less a factor in the housing industry as time passes. The overwhelming need is for urban housing as the population shifts from a farm culture to an urban one. It is increasingly clear that the obstacles standing in the way of the construction of vastly larger numbers of urban housing units are rooted not only in the use of multiple code forms, in inadequate but traditional practices of land purchase and project financing, and in the failure of local governments to significantly tax undeveloped land as opposed to improved property, but, most importantly, in the failure of our building industry, for whatever reason, to utilize effectively the productive capacity of modern manufacturing techniques in the production of housing. And this failure is due, in turn, not to a lack of will but rather to an incapacity on the part of the designer, the architect, whose role it is to make the decisions that are involved in the assembly of materials and components into a design for a building. Industry has provided the architect in recent years with such an overwhelming multiplicity of materials and products that it is beyond human capacity to keep in mind enough information about performance and cost to choose for the design of a building the one combination of form, site, structure, mechanical equipment, and materials that represents the most satisfactory design for the budget available. It is simply too much for him to be able to judge performance against costs and to explore the complex interplay between all of the possible decisions and subdecisions.

In the absence of reliable facts, it is difficult to make a decision with any real confidence. Most of the decisions involved in designing a building relate to cost in one way or another, and are made with the probable or supposed cost in mind; but no one who has had any contact with the construction industry, however brief or small in scale, has come away from that experience without being made aware of the difficulty of predicting construction costs before the event. This is true of large-scale architectural and engineering projects as well as small, but it is nowhere more serious than in the housing industry. It is true that the housing industry, though of vast size, is a fragmented one with the overwhelming body of construction in the hands of thousands of relatively small construction firms. This has tended to retard innovation in construction practices, with small firms being both unable and uninterested in pioneering efforts aimed at cutting the costs of housing construction. Many other factors as well contribute to the slowness to change expensive and outmoded practices, but none is stronger than the inhibition imposed upon the architectural designer by his inability to predict reliably the costs of construction. This is true even when he is dealing with traditional materials and practices, and the problem is only compounded when he contemplates anything that involves innovation.

Moreover, as has already been mentioned, even when dealing with all of the multitudinous structural, material, mechanical, site-planning, spatial, visual, economic, and countless other considerations in developing a design for a housing project, the architect cannot possibly possess and effectively relate all the information required to enable him to make decisions leading to an optimum design for a given situation. It is simply beyond human capability.

It follows, then, that except by sheer good luck his design will be unnecessarily expensive, and probably less effective functionally than he intended, simply because he was unable to determine accurately which were the best elements to put into it from the standpoint of its own program requirements and budget. The upshot is that because of his lack of information the designer's buildings cost more than they should.

This means that less housing is now being built than the available funds would provide if the process of design were more efficient. The architect is intended to be a problem-solver, but he is woefully inadequate in attempting to solve twentieth century problems with seventeenth century tools.

III

A Computer Approach to Housing Design

In the closing months of 1965, the North Carolina Fund initiated a demonstration project which aimed at the development of an improved cost-analysis tool for the designer of low-income housing. With principal funding in the amount of $160,000 from the U.S. Department of Housing and Urban Development, coupled with $30,000 from the North Carolina Fund, work was begun in Chapel Hill and is scheduled to continue into late 1967. The design system developed is to be field tested with the design and construction of a low-income housing project to be built during 1968.

Known as the Integrated Building Industry System (IBIS), the design tool under development by the North Carolina Fund group does not attempt to change or restructure the basic design procedures traditionally used by the architect; but it does attempt to remove certain obstacles, supplying him with cost and performance information at critical decision stages in his development of a design. While it is true that an architect may, in using the IBIS system, refine a design while seated at a computer console rather than at a drafting table, the difference is more apparent than real. The decision making in which he engages during the development of his design is not changed, but it is materially assisted by the provision of hard information upon which those decisions can be realistically based. It is commonly thought by the layman that it has always been possible for the architect to make realistic design decisions, but this is not the case. Most often, his decisions are made on the basis of his own incomplete experience and written data that may or may not be recent and accurate, in supplement of which he can only employ intuition, imagination, and a certain measure of hope. In witness to the lack of effectiveness of these tools we have only to regard the great numbers of buildings surrounding us which have exceeded their budgets and fulfilled their purposes less than expected.

It is possible that the IBIS system will make a contribution in this area, since it will provide the architect with continuous reports on changes in construction cost resulting from design changes as he is developing his design. He immediately knows, therefore, whether a change he has just made—be it in plan, material, structure, or whatever—resulted in an increase or a decrease in total cost. It is expected that this information will contribute materially to the rationality of the architect's designs.

Briefly stated, the system is used in this fashion:

Step 1—A three dimensional description of the building, interior and exterior, is stored in the machine as a reference base. The machine has already stored a data library consisting of materials, labor, and other costs to be encountered, with a wide range of materials and techniques used in low-income housing construction. These costs are taken from local field experience and are frequently updated.

Step 2—A list of materials and components for the building under analysis is entered by the designer and stored by the machine.

Step 3—The machine compares the three-dimensional description of the building automatically with the outline specifications mentioned above and produces a quantity survey and cost breakdown for the construction of the building.

Step 4—The designer may then modify his building design in dimension, form, material, location on its site, proportion, structure, or any of the other characteristics which he traditionally manipulates in developing an architectural design, and can immediately learn the economic consequences of the design changes as he makes them.

Working as described above, the architect can explore a much wider range of design alternatives than he could possibly do manually. In addition, he can readily learn in which direction lies the most economical and suitable solution for the particular problem at hand.

Working in this fashion, the designer of a low-income housing project can very readily investigate the effects of the major parameters in an architectural problem under analysis. It seems obvious that one of the major uses of the IBIS system will be in permitting a very thorough accelerated analysis of a project. This analysis would be an effective tool in making the very early decisions, such as site selection. Such decisions are frequently made when the general complexion of the project is still rather hazy, although the selection of one site over another may have the most powerful effects upon final construction cost for the project. It would be a very difficult and time-consuming process, for example, to develop a design from a close cost-analysis by conventional methods for each of several available sites, evaluating for each the implications of varying zoning conditions, subsoil conditions, topography, orientation, site size, vehicular and pedestrian access, and land cost, in order to determine which site out of many would permit the most satisfactory housing situation for least cost. As a result, site selection is often made on the basis of incomplete information as to the cost effects of the various options.

All of this could be accomplished rather easily, using the cost-analysis and design system described here. In a short time a design could be developed in its essentials for each site, a design which would approximate the economically optimum solution for that site, taking into account its particular features, so that the net results could be compared for each of the sites under consideration. Selection could then be made on a rational basis, the economic effects of the selection being known in advance.

It is clear that at its present stage of development, IBIS does not achieve the fine resolution required to give cost-analysis on the most particular and detailed aspects of construction cost, such as those that arise from specialized detailing during the preparation of construction drawings. It is equally clear, however, that the system, dealing with a simple building type such as low-income housing, can explore cost alternatives very effectively short of this ultimate stage. It must be remembered that IBIS does not yield a market figure for construction costs. Only the market can do that. Rather, IBIS indicates the *relative* costs of construction alternatives: concrete frame versus bearing walls and open-web joists, for example, or one site layout versus another.

It should be noted, however, that the degree to which IBIS is able to explore the relatively detailed aspects of building design and the costs implied by those considerations exceeds anything currently available to the designer for use on a manual basis. The relative ease with which a great number of design variations can be explored, and the ready facility with which alterations in program requirements or standards can be examined in terms of cost/effectiveness, can be expected to upgrade substantially the quality of the design decisions made by an architect on a low-income housing project.

Indeed, the brief experience designers have had to date with machine-aided cost-analysis suggests very persuasively that the presence of reliable cost information very early in the design stage frees a designer from inhibitions which have heretofore reduced his effectiveness.[1]

The discussion above suggests that major uses for the IBIS system may be found by others than the architectural designer. The capabilities of the system would be of great value to the institutional owner in planning future construction, in choosing sites for this construction, and in project management during the construction process.

The system could also be used by government agencies to evaluate proposed projects for compliance with various standards and planning requirements. Housing projects submitted for approval to the Federal Housing Administration, for example, could be readily and economically checked for the following items:

(1) Compliance with minimum property standards;
(2) Adequacy of mechanical systems;
(3) Compliance with local building code requirements;
(4) Appraisal.

Any checking operation requiring a substantial component of repetitive clerical operations could be adapted for performance by the IBIS system with significant savings not only in manpower but in the very substantial reduction of the required

---

[1] Thomsen, *How High to Rise*, J. AM. INSTITUTE OF ARCHITECTS, April 1965, at 66.

"turn-around" time for approval or disapproval. In many government agencies this would be of great value.

It should be noted here that cost is not the only factor for which a design may be optimized through the use of this system. Equally important might be spatial considerations, function of a particular nature, freedom from maintenance, or any other set of program requirements peculiar to the problem at hand. It is obvious that each building situation is a unique design problem with its own requirements to be resolved. If the significant parameters are more than several, and they almost invariably are, an automated information handling system such as this can be an aid of great value in its solution.

One of the more interesting ways in which the IBIS system could be used is in the cost-analysis of a project under differing code conditions. A project might be analyzed, for example, against the building code of one community and then against the code of one or more others, demonstrating the difference in cost for the same living accommodations imposed by different local building codes. It is possible that the IBIS system would be an effective tool in building code reform.

As implied earlier, the system might also be useful in demonstrating the relationship between costs and standards. It is frequently the case that a very slight increase in construction cost results in a substantial increase in performance or, conversely, that a modest cost saving results in a substantial sacrifice in quality. Using the procedures described here, it would be a relatively simple matter to determine which level of design standards represent the most effective investment for the project at hand.

It has been suggested in this connection that the problems of immediate versus ultimate cost could also be explored with great benefit. For instance, analysis of a particular project might indicate that, in view of limited funds on hand in the face of a great need for housing in a given locality, a design could be developed for minimum first cost which would imply somewhat higher long-term maintenance costs. Thus, in effect, a certain fraction of the total investment over the life of the property could be deferred until a later date and the maintenance costs be taken from the continuing income of the dwelling units.

On the other hand, it might be felt prudent in a particular case to minimize long-term maintenance and accept a greater first cost implied thereby. It is clear that it would be desirable to have both of these factors, minimum first cost and minimum long-term maintenance, taken together in the same project, but it is equally clear that they are almost always mutually exclusive. Some compromise must be struck between the two for each project according to the particular economic circumstances of the situation. What might be a wise choice for one would be imprudent for another. It is possible that the IBIS cost-analysis system would be a useful tool in determining just where the balance should be drawn for individual projects.

The system as herein described has been brought to the point of prototype operation. The programs mentioned are in operation, and the capabilities outlined exist on a program-by-program basis. Work is currently continuing on program linkages and in the simplification of input techniques. Presently required are a number of forms on which the designer enters the design choices and outline specification information. This information must then be placed on punch cards for use with the machine. Several of these forms have now been programmed for use with the IBM 2250 graphic display unit and its associated light pen so that information may be entered with the light pen as a response to a printed question on the scope.

For maximum effectiveness and flexibility, the library of construction costs employed by the system should be frequently updated with data drawn directly from recent field experience by contractors. In the absence of a nationwide data collection network this is clearly impossible. Fortunately, however, the system is able to operate with substantial effectiveness using cost data prepared by professional estimators. It is hoped that in the future a data collection service will evolve, for such a service would permit maximum utilization of the inherent capabilities of the IBIS system.

Obviously the work described here is merely the first step in the development of a comprehensive information-handling system for the construction industry. The programs described here are adequate for dealing with a simple building type, the low-income house. But they should be regarded only as the first imperfect parts of a system that may eventually be expanded to include other building types and provide, quickly and economically, information required by the architect in making design decisions; by the owner in making decisions affecting his current and projected investment; by government agencies acting as evaluator, sponsor or owner; by the contractor who will use the same information for bidding, for scheduling, for ordering materials and managing labor; and for all of these individuals in monitoring the aspects of the construction process with which they are concerned.

IV

EXTENSIONS OF THE COMPUTER APPROACH

The IBIS system as described herein is a very crude and cumbersome instrument, but it is a first step. To achieve maximum usefulness in the future, however, work must be concentrated in several areas. First, the system must develop a capability for suggesting a solution. As presently constituted, it can only wait for the operator to make an intuitive choice when a change is to be made. It would be very useful if the machine were able to survey a set of performance requirements and then select a material, structure, or siting situation or a plan form which best solved the problem at hand and submit this selection for editing by the designer. Only if the machine is given this capability can the architect concentrate again upon his primary function: that of exercising an informed judgment in the organizing of an architectural solution. The machine can perform better than he the trivial operations which currently occupy so much of an architect's time. The checking, catalog searching, ineffective cost estimating, dimensioning, drafting of repetitive detail, and countless other minor clerical tasks occupy the greater part of his time and leave him neither the opportunity nor the energy for concentrating upon the more essential elements of the work at hand.

In addition, the graphic input and output capabilities of the IBIS system should be expanded. The capability of accepting graphic input and of producing output in the form of drawings seems critical for architectural use on a wide scale.

Finally, the scope of the data employed may eventually be extended to include not only cost and performance information but also data reflecting more of the parameters having significant effect upon the construction environment. It is anticipated also that eventually it may be possible to include significant information from the behavioral sciences which bear upon architectural design. At present, research in the behavioral sciences is not so defined as to be of any direct benefit to the designer of low-income housing, and he must rely upon the assistance of knowledgeable consultants in sociology and psychology.

The long-term implications of development such as the one described here are not clear, but they are many. With regard to housing, it is safe to say that the designs which are produced will be less expensive and more functional, as well as more pleasurable to live in. The budgets will be more prudently spent with the result that more amenities will be possible. The architect will find himself less preoccupied with uncertainties as to cost and practicality and will be able to devote a greater portion of his effort to thoughtful consideration of the intangible aspects of design which give meaningful character to a living situation.

On a larger scale there are further implications suggested by this approach to problem solving of a technical sort. It should, for example, be possible to treat problems of larger scale than building design.

If it can be reasonably suggested that the complex needs of the poor form a system, then it can also be stated with some conviction that the resources and capabilities of the various municipal, county, state, federal, and private agencies form a system which can be effectively coordinated for the solution of these needs for the general good.

Currently these resources are poorly coordinated, if at all, in the sense of a total system, and the people are ill served. If the goal of the society can be stated as the continuing improvement in the level of satisfaction of the physical and emotional needs of the people, then it seems prudent to adopt techniques which will permit the effective management of this very complex system for the general benefit.

It is difficult to be very specific about these techniques at present, although rough prototypes do exist which may provide us with some guidance. The procedures being used for the building design cost-analysis described above will perhaps be of some

use; but certainly the most important techniques available to us today in developing a comprehensive management system for the utilization of a state's resources are
those currently in use in large industrial enterprises, particularly those scattered over
a wide geographic area.

A quick look at these management systems convinces us of two things: (1) they
are effective—indeed, the enterprises of which they are part could not operate
effectively without them; and (2) the operations and resources which we wish to
coordinate on a large scale for the public good are neither so dissimilar in character
nor so complex as to be unmanageable by the same methods.

It is possible to imagine that such an effort could lead to the establishment, probably in the office of the state department of administration, of a position occupied by
an individual who would function as a systems coordinator. This person, with a
staff of research associates, would be in daily touch with every aspect of the
operation of the state, the condition of its economy and its commercial structure, the
conditions and trends reported by the social service and welfare agencies, its educational system, health trends and conditions, the state of its agriculture and associated
markets, its relations with various federal programs and agencies, and every other
accessible source of information bearing upon the facilities of the state or the needs of
its people. This information would be constantly maintained and updated in a
computer-based real-time census which would permit the systems coordinator rapidly
to interrogate this data base to recall information required for decision making.

With a much more intimate knowledge of the functioning of the many facilities
operating in the state, both within government and out, than could be maintained
by anyone otherwise occupied in one of the top policy-making positions, and
capable of interrogating a machine-stored data library maintained as a real-time
census, this systems coordinator would be in a position to (1) detect developing
problems before they became serious enough to need crisis treatment, and (2) effectively coordinate whatever resources existed within the state which could appropriately
be brought to bear upon the problem at hand.

For example, if the housing needs of a certain income group began to rise in a
locality where the inventory of available housing was insufficient to satisfy this need,
this fact would immediately be flagged by the information-handling system described
above, and action could be initiated immediately to stimulate new construction of
appropriate housing in that locality. As matters now stand, the housing needs of this
hypothetical group remain unknown until some considerable time after the fact,
when they are made known by some untoward incident which reveals the by then
drastic need. This is inefficient both in terms of the management of available
resources and in terms of the distress to which the people concerned are subjected.
It is particularly bad in terms of business, since a housing market has existed for
some time, undetected and unserved.

CONCLUSION

In summary, it suffices to state that the problem of supplying decent and pleasant housing for a growing population, a population which is increasingly restive and vocal in the presence of intolerable urban housing conditions, is a central one for us today and is very close, indeed, to the heart of the question of the continued successful maintenance of our urban complex and our society as we know it. It is certainly one of the closely-related handful of problems which together define the character of poverty in America today. The decision making tool described in this article is one step toward a more rational utilization of the resources which we have for the easing of one very critical aspect of this complex of problems. It is hoped that field testing will prove its efficacy and permit its wide application, together with the other new techniques springing from other disciplines which will be required in the general effort to lift low-income groups beyond the reach of those corrosive conditions historically associated with the situation of poverty.

MOBILE HOMES—A NEW CHALLENGE

FREDERICK H. BAIR, JR.*

I

INTRODUCTION: THE MOBILE HOME EXPLOSION

In 1936 a newspaper reporter, Howard V. O'Brien, made an extended trip in a primitive trailer, then a novelty, and collected his feature articles into a book.[1] Here are some of his comments:

> The trailer is such a new thing that people are not yet armed against it. It takes them by surprise. It overpowers them. A man may fancy that his home is his castle, but let a trailer appear and his stronghold is like Rome before the Goths.[2]
>
> Life in a trailer is not all play—especially for the women. Food and ice and necessary supplies are not always easily accessible. . . . Fires must be built and ashes disposed of. Toilet arrangements constitute a special problem. Electric light is not always available and oil lamps must be cleaned. Foodstuffs must be bought in small quantities because the space for their storage is rigorously limited.[3]
>
> The trailer is here to stay and it will make many changes in our way of life. Though it is an infant industry now, I believe it will be a giant before long, with great numbers of people employed in servicing it. In the long run, I suspect that it will prove another nail in the coffin of urban congestion. No longer will the city dweller be content with short week-ends trips in a crowded countryside.[4]

From the year 1937 come divergent observations from other sources.

In 1937, Roger Babson predicted that in 20 years more than half of the population of the U.S. would be living in trailers; *The Nation's Business* announced that when trailers became so numerous as to affect the tax structure, tax legislation would be passed which would give conventional housing an edge; and Lewis Mumford decreed that because trailers were small they would never amount to anything.[5]

In 1961, it was noted that the mobile home

makes the most of new design, materials and fabrication techniques. Its wheels remain, but are increasingly vestigial remnants. It arrives at the site fully equipped

* B.S. 1935, University of Chicago. Consultant on urban planning and development regulation, in the firm of Bair and Associates, Auburndale, Fla. Member, American Institute of Planners. Co-author [with Dr. Ernest R. Bartley], MOBILE HOME PARKS AND COMPREHENSIVE COMMUNITY PLANNING (1960); author, REGULATION OF MOBILE HOME SUBDIVISIONS (1961); LOCAL REGULATION OF MOBILE HOME PARKS, TRAVEL TRAILER PARKS AND RELATED FACILITIES (1965). Editor, FLORIDA PLANNING AND DEVELOPMENT (1950-66). Member of the editorial advisory board of ZONING DIGEST (1960-66). Contributor to planning and urban affairs periodicals, and author of books and monographs in the field of planning and zoning.

[1] H. V. O'BRIEN, FOLDING BEDOUINS OR, ADRIFT IN A TRAILER (1936).
[2] *Id.* at 37.
[3] *Id.* at 28.
[4] *Id.* at 105.
[5] Bair, *Trailer Parks*, FLA. PLANNING & DEVELOPMENT, July 1958, at 1.

with furniture and appliances, ready for occupancy as soon as water, sewer and electrical connections are made.

It does not look like a conventional house. It is not built like a conventional house. . . . It is not sold like a conventional house. Its financing, unlike that of the conventional house, includes furniture and all appliances. It frequently does not have the same relationship to the land on which it is located as does the conventional house. And it has not stopped changing.

It continues to get bigger as it moves toward the time when the wheels will come off. Already individual units are moving toward a 600 sq. ft. average, and combinations of elements . . . make possible sizes ranging up to 1,400 sq. ft. and beyond.[6]

And in early 1967, Max S. Wehrly wrote:[7]

The mobile home industry . . . a comparative newcomer to the housing field . . . seems to be in a favorable position to capture an increasing chunk of the market in the lower price range. Particularly promising is the sectional or "doublewide" unit which utilizes the same techniques of factory production developed for the traditional mobile home and, according to House and Home, can meet the $10,000 to $17,000 market, including land.

The doublewide unit is a stranger to wheels except during its journey from factory to site. Two 12-foot wide sections are "slid" onto an already prepared foundation, with or without basement, and permanently joined. The result is a house 24 feet wide, up to 56 or more feet in length, and in most respects indistinguishable from the conventionally built or prefab one-story dwelling.

A. The Branching of the Family Tree

In the past thirty years, the previously dwindling family tree of the covered wagon and gypsy caravan has taken on luxuriant new life, dividing into two main branches. The travel trailer in its most advanced form has become a recreational vehicle for portable temporary housing with mechanical refrigeration, air-conditioning, gas stove, television, bath and flush toilet with sewage holding tank, and hot and cold running water. In early 1967, 625,000 travel trailers were in use; but this number does not include numerous cousins. There were also 360,000 pickup campers (units for mounting on pick-up trucks), 220,000 camping trailers (largely fold-out tents mounted compactly on low trailers), motorized homes (converted trucks or buses or custom-built units), and a growing number of other types including a cross-breed between the travel trailer and the houseboat. Total sales of such units reached 323,500 in 1966, as against 87,500 five years earlier.[8]

As leisure and population increase, the travel trailer and its kin will continue to play a rapidly-growing role in American recreational life, creating minor problems in the planning and regulatory field such as specialized layout of recreational areas

---

[6] AMERICAN SOC'Y OF PLANNING OFFICIALS, REGULATION OF MOBILE HOME SUBDIVISIONS I (ASPO Planning Advisory Service Information Rep. No. 145, 1961).

[7] Wehrly, *The Evolution of the House Trailer*, URBAN LAND, March 1967, at 1, 3-4.

[8] AMERICAN SOC'Y OF PLANNING OFFICIALS, REGULATING STORAGE OF MAJOR RECREATIONAL EQUIPMENT 1-2 (ASPO Planning Advisory Service Information Rep. No. 218, 1967).

and storage when not in use. As related to the main theme of this article, however, the trailer has created one major problem. The split in the family tree some ten or fifteen years ago was not noted by many regulatory bodies, and controls based on the characteristics of the travel trailer—its size, its use, the locational pattern of its parks— are still often employed in regulating the mobile home, which is quite different from the travel trailer.

In the early 1950s, the mobile home began to become large enough and well enough equipped to deserve approval as permanent housing. Since then it has become so large that "mobile" is increasingly a misnomer. Specialized equipment is required for towing units, and moving is expensive. Once the mobile home is moved from the dealer's lot to the location where the customer will use it, there is a fair chance that it will remain there for most of its useful life, being sold to a new occupant on the same site when the original purchaser moves.

The rapid growth of mobile homes in total numbers and in proportion to new housing is traceable to two principle causes. Growth in size and improvements in design and construction have increased and broadened appeal. And there are continuing increases in the size of the age groups to which mobile homes are most attractive—the young marrieds, up to about the time their children enter school, and the retirees.

B. Growth in Size, Improvement in Design

At the beginning of the 1950s, the standard width for mobile homes was eight feet, the average length twenty-seven feet. This meant 216 square feet of floor area, or about the area of the living room in some modern units. Lengths increased steadily, increasing floor area, but until the breakthrough to the ten-foot width in 1954 there were few chances for improvements in design. Bedrooms opening to a longitudinal hall were virtually impossible at eight foot widths, manageable at ten.

By 1961, the ten-wide accounted for 98.5 per cent of production, the eight-wide for only 1.5 per cent. At this point, another breakthrough occurred. Early in 1962, a handful of experimental twelve-wides, double-wides, and expansible units (with telescoping rooms) appeared at the annual national mobile home exposition in Louisville, Kentucky. In 1962, 1.6 per cent of units produced were twelve-wides, with 11.8 per cent expansibles and double-wides.

In the first quarter of 1967, twelve-wides made up 72.3 per cent of production, expansibles and double-wides 7.0 per cent, ten-wides had dropped to 20.1 per cent, and the "standard" eight-wide of only twelve years before accounted for only 0.6 per cent. The average length at the beginning of 1967 was more than double the twenty-seven feet in 1950, at about fifty-six feet. (The largest single category was twelve-wides in the sixty to sixty-four foot class, which made up 34.5 per cent of production.) The average floor area was around seven hundred square feet, more than three times the 1950 figure. Design, construction, furniture, and major appliances were all greatly improved. A very substantial proportion of the units had utility rooms with washing machines and driers, built-in FM and stereo reproduction, and other luxuries which would have been unimaginable a few short years before. But the average retail price of units, including furniture and fixtures, was around $10 per square foot, a little lower than in 1950.[9]

It was not easy to achieve the changes in width. Remodeling assembly lines was expensive. And it was necessary to get changes in state laws relating to highway movement of wide vehicles. Most states now allow twelve feet, subject in many cases to special restrictions, and this is very probably the upper limit.

Added length did not require such radical changes in production methods, and length does not appear to be as important an element in highway safety as width, although here again upper limits appear to have been reached at something over sixty feet.

C. Population and New Housing

Currently, mobile homes appeal particularly to persons in the twenty to twenty-nine and sixty-five to seventy-four age groups. Family-formers setting up housekeeping for the first time like mobile homes because of ease of maintenance, size, financing which packages the unit, major appliances and furniture in one monthly payment, and residual mobility. With the current average of floor space, there is room for one or two small children, although when children reach school age there is now a strong tendency to move to a conventional residence. In the future, increased possibilities for adding components may make "mobile homes" lifetime housing, but this means that they will cease being mobile.

At the other end of the age scale, persons retiring provide a major market. Factors here are the size, easy housekeeping, limited yard to care for, price and space rental within conservative budgets, and the neighborliness and recreational programs and facilities to be found in good parks. The active retirement group will be an even more receptive market as retirement age continues to drop.

The combination of improved units and growth in the two age groups is likely to lead to an even greater upsurge in number of mobile homes than has already taken place. From 1960 through 1966, the twenty to twenty-nine group increased only about 3.6 million. From 1966 to 1970, anticipated increase is 5.5 million as the first wave from the high birth rates following the Second World War comes on. From 1970 to 1980, expected gain will be 9.3 million, to a total of 40.5 million.

Numbers in the sixty-five to seventy-four group are growing more slowly, up only half a million from 1960 to 1966, due to rise another half million by 1970 and then between 1970 and 1980 to increase by about 1.6 million to about 14.5 million. But if earlier retirement is common, about ten million persons in the sixty to sixty-five age

---

[9] F. H. BAIR, JR., MOBILE HOMES AND THE GENERAL HOUSING SUPPLY—PAST, PRESENT AND OUTLOOK I (1967).

bracket in 1980 seem very likely to add considerable strength to the retirement market.[10]

As to the recent mobile home explosion, coming at a time when the prime age groups were increasing relatively slowly, shipments to dealers rose from about 90,000 in 1961 to almost 220,000 in 1966. Combining statistics for mobile homes and other forms of housing, in 1961, mobile homes accounted for 6.2 per cent of all additions to the housing supply, and for 8.7 per cent of private, nonfarm, single-family housing. In 1966, mobile homes made up 14.8 per cent of all new housing, and twenty-two per cent of private, nonfarm, single-family housing.[11]

II

REGULATORY PROBLEMS OUTLINED

With change so rapid and on such a scale, it is not surprising that most state and local regulations have not adjusted to the mobile home. Complicating matters, the mobile home simply does not fit the established regulatory framework.

A (mobile) home is not a house. It is not a building, as the term is often defined.[12] It is only incidentally a vehicle, and may not remain that long. It is not a travel trailer, although its evolution has led to regulation as though it were, with unfortunate results in many instances.

It is usually constructed outside the local jurisdiction, and arrives completed so that it cannot be inspected for conformity with local plumbing, heating, electrical, and structural codes. Moreover, since its structural characteristics and requirements are quite different from housing built on foundations, its construction should be regulated differently.

The mobile home is at present most assuredly a single-family detached residence. But it usually is not permitted on individual lots in zoning districts for single-family detached residences, largely for aesthetic reasons relating to effects on the value of buildings in the neighborhood. Increase in size and exterior appearance of some models is now raising the problem of selection of mobile homes to be admitted to single-family districts. When is "look-alike" enough to qualify? If density is in keeping with basic single-family zoning, should mobile home parks be permitted in single-family districts, given requirements which protect against friction at outer boundaries? In outlying rural and agricultural districts, should the mobile home be permitted as a principal use on an individual lot? As an accessory use?

Where the new mobile home park has current density of six to ten units per acre, it is in an intensity classification rating it with multifamily housing. The fact that

[10] These figures have been rounded from U.S. BUREAU OF THE CENSUS, DEP'T OF COMMERCE, POPULATION ESTIMATES (Current Population Reports, Ser. P-25, No. 359, 1967).

[11] See U.S. DEP'T OF HOUSING AND URBAN DEVELOPMENT, HOUSING STATISTICS (March 1967).

[12] As the 1960 census defined mobile homes, those with additions were counted as conventional single-family housing, so that any analysis of number of units or characteristics of occupants based on the census is seriously defective.

the units are single-family does not matter—most multifamily zoning permits single-family use. And in multifamily districts, the emerging trend toward garden and high-rise apartments using insertable mobile homes (here definitely less mobile after delivery) can be handled through normal zoning methods. But there are some interesting peculiarities in property law and taxation.

The mobile home park has been referred to as a horizontal apartment house.[13] But whether horizontal or vertical, there are differences from other apartment forms. The occupant has full title to the unit, as in the case of condominiums, but unlike the latter, he usually has no common interest in the facilities. In its physical characteristics, the mobile home park is a planned residential development, with common open space, recreation facilities, a community building, and the like. But again, there is no home owners' association with responsibility for maintenance of common facilities, and occupants do not participate in ownership or management.[14]

Then there is the matter of substandard parks and substandard mobile homes. Many of the older parks were built in commercial districts adjacent to highways, because they served travel trailers. Although the travel trailer is different from the mobile home, the "trailer park" has often shifted to long-term residential use by mobile homes. This puts a vulnerable residential use in the wrong place—residential enclaves in commercialized or commercializing districts tend to deteriorate. And a park designed fifteen years ago for travel trailers, or mobile homes no larger than some of the present travel trailers, is now obsolete on lot width, lot depth, and lot area. The eight-wide became ten-wide and then twelve-wide, with extensions and doublewides on hand in increasing numbers. So unless there has been extensive remodeling once or even twice since 1955, the older parks are not only in the wrong place but are likely to be heavily overcrowded.

As to substandard units in or out of parks, the longevity of some of the older mobile homes has been surprising, and there is almost always an occupant for the cheapest housing available. The poorest parks, in location, design, and facilities, tend to attract or retain units which fail to meet even the lowest minimum standards; and rundown residential neighborhoods are frequently spotted with obsolete, dangerous, and unsightly mobile homes. What can be done about these situations?

As to taxes, there is a bewildering variety of local treatments. In some places, the mobile home is taxed as personal property, in some as real estate, in others it is exempt from real or personal property taxes on purchase of a vehicular license, and subject to one or to the other if the owner does not. Where there is homestead exemption, complications may multiply. The mobile home on a foundation (or without

---

[13] *E.g.*, Bair, *supra* note 5, at 2.

[14] In some mobile home *subdivisions*, where lots are sold rather than rented, there is sometimes close conformity with condominium and planned unit development principles, but the number of such subdivisions is small as yet, as is the number of conventional subdivisions for mobile homes in which common facilities are not provided.

foundation) which does (or does not) purchase a vehicular license may (or may not) qualify for homestead exemption on real property tax.

Taxed as personal property, the mobile home is sometimes in an inequitable position because of local tax policies which make most personal property taxes nominal, but place a relatively high assessment on the mobile home. Taxed as real estate, how should it be handled if it is not on its own lot, but on a rented space in a park? (Here the condominium principle offers some help.) Because it *can* be moved, should the park operator be made responsible for collection and payment of taxes on individual units? How should depreciation be computed, and to what lower level?

Taxation as a vehicle (through license fees) has the practical difficulty that the fees do not come directly to the local unit of government; and returns from the state level are often generalized and earmarked for particular purposes. The contribution of the mobile home owner is lost sight of in the general return from vehicular licenses. And the restrictions on purposes for which returns from the state level may be spent do not always fit local budget needs. The only "normal" local tax return comes from the mobile home park itself.

It would be highly optimistic to say that we have adequate responses to all of the challenges offered by the mobile home in its current state, much less to those which appear as the mobile home continues to evolve in different directions— to the immobile unit, the look-alike house, the garden apartment, or high-rise component. But there are some answers which are a vast improvement over most present practice. Here are a few.

III

SOME SUGGESTED SOLUTIONS

One of the most basic requirements for improving the regulatory structure is to make a clear distinction between the mobile home, as a full-scale residence, and temporary portable housing in the form of the travel trailer, the pickup camper, and the like. This distinction should carry through all regulations. The definition should be broad enough to fit present and emerging mobile home forms. The one below is adapted by language in brackets from a recent suggested definition already made obsolescent by the newly-developing interest in use of mobile homes as apartment modules:[15]

> *Mobile home*: A detached single-family dwelling unit [or a dwelling unit for use as a component in a two-family or multifamily structure] with all of the following characteristics:
>
> a. Designed for long-term occupancy, and containing sleeping accommodations, a flush toilet, a tub or shower bath, and kitchen facilities, with plumbing and electrical connections provided for attachment to outside systems.

---

[15] F. H. BAIR, JR., LOCAL REGULATION OF MOBILE HOME PARKS, TRAVEL TRAILER PARKS AND RELATED FACILITIES 12 (1965).

b. Designed to be transported after fabrication on its own wheels, or on flatbed or other trailers or detachable wheels.

c. Arriving at the site where it is to be occupied as a dwelling complete, including major appliances and furniture, and ready for occupancy except for minor and incidental unpacking and assembly operations, location on foundation supports, [integration into a prepared structure] and the like.

To provide for the contingency that furniture may not be included in all mobile homes in the future, perhaps the language at (c) should drop the words "and furniture." The definition should distinguish the mobile home not only from the travel trailer, but from conventional housing and also from the prefabricated house, which may arrive at the site on a trailer but usually requires extensive assembly.

By itself, the travel trailer is relatively easy to define, but a mere travel trailer definition will not do in the regulatory structure, because of other devices being regulated. To simplify matters, regulations involving travel trailers and similar forms might refer to them as recreational "units," defining the term thus: "*Recreational Unit*: A travel trailer, pickup camper, converted bus, tent-trailer, tent, or similar device used for temporary portable housing."[16]

A. State Regulation—Health and Construction

1. *State Health Regulation*

State regulation of health-related aspects of mobile home parks has major advantages. Given state control, substandard facilities cannot develop in local areas having no regulations or regulations which are defective. State regulation assures that the same minimum requirements will apply generally, a matter of substantial importance when the bewildering variety of local standards is considered. (On the matter of sewer, water, and electrical connections, for example, varying specifications for size, location, and connective devices create major problems for park operators, manufacturers, and mobile home occupants. The variation in regulatory requirements is unnecessary in terms of public purposes. Standardized state controls eliminate this problem.)

State regulation of health aspects of mobile home parks also has administrative advantages. County or regional health officers administratively responsible to state boards of health and specialists working directly from state headquarters can usually assure more uniform, and often more expert, application of regulations than can many local jurisdictions.

In some parts of the country, reliance on state regulation would be premature until state controls have been modernized. Some states still fail to distinguish between mobile homes and travel trailers and their parks, with concomitant failure to distinguish between their requirements. Thus, size of individual spaces in what are generically called "trailer parks" or "trailer camps" is adequate for travel trailers but

---

[16] *Id.* at 50.

entirely too small for mobile homes. And some state laws still call generally for facilities needed for travel trailer parks but superfluous in mobile home parks—extensive washroom facilities, laundries, drying yards, and sinks for emptying slop jars are hardly necessary for modern mobile homes with their own baths, washers, and driers.

Many states have updated health regulations to reflect changes. The U.S. Public Health Service has provided guidance in this direction in the form of models which can be adapted for state use or used at the local level.[17] Matters covered in the Public Health Service model for mobile home parks include:

  a. General requirements on condition of soil, ground water, drainage, topography, and surroundings.
  b. Required separation between mobile homes.
  c. Required recreation areas.
  d. Required setbacks, buffer strips, and screening.
  e. Requirements on park street system, including design, width, pavement, grades, and lighting.
  f. Requirements on walkways.
  g. Requirements on off-street parking.
  h. Requirements on mobile home stands.
  i. Water supply.
  j. Sewage disposal.
  k. Electrical distribution system.
  l. Service building and other community service facilities.
  m. Refuse handling.
  n. Insect and rodent control.
  o. Fuel supply and storage.
  p. Fire protection.

To the extent that such matters are handled by state regulation and inspection, localities are freed from responsibilities.

2. State Regulation of Construction

Even more advantageous are state controls of construction of mobile homes, although localities are not helpless without such regulations. As with parks, the principal disadvantage of exclusively local control is that there will be areas where no controls are exercised, in which substandard conditions tend to develop.

[17] U.S. PUBLIC HEALTH SERVICE, DEP'T OF HEALTH, EDUCATION, AND WELFARE, ENVIRONMENTAL HEALTH GUIDE FOR MOBILE HOME PARKS, WITH A RECOMMENDED ORDINANCE (1966); U.S. PUBLIC HEALTH SERVICE, DEP'T OF HEALTH, EDUCATION, AND WELFARE, ENVIRONMENTAL HEALTH GUIDE FOR TRAVEL TRAILER PARKING AREAS, WITH A RECOMMENDED ORDINANCE (1966) (both guides are published by the Mobile Homes Manufacturers Ass'n).

The American Standards Association (ASA) in 1963 formally approved code provision A-119.1, "American Standard for Installation in Mobile Homes of Electrical, Heating and Plumbing Systems," since adopted by the Building Officials Conference of America (BOCA) and the Southern Building Codes Congress. In Kentucky, state law requires that any unit shipped or imported into the state for sale shall conform to this code.[18] In California, the state administers construction codes applicable to mobile homes sold or offered for sale in that state and manufactured after September 1, 1958. These codes give protection roughly equivalent to the ASA code.[19]

The Mobiles Homes Manufacturers Association (MHMA) requires its members to conform to ASA requirements, and each unit must bear a seal certifying to such conformity. This association (which was largely responsible for formulation of the ASA code provisions) has now adopted "Minimum Body and Frame Design and Construction Standards" with January 1, 1968 as the effective date for compliance; and units built under this new code will also bear certification. The MHMA body and frame standards have been submitted to the American Standards Association for approval—and if and as approved will very probably be included in the BOCA and Southern Building Codes.

Requirement for compliance with these or similar codes can be either by the state or by localities. In either case, one of the regulatory problems is solved—how to assure acceptable quality in a dwelling unit constructed outside the local jurisdiction and brought in complete, so that local inspection is impractical.

B. Zoning for Mobile Home Parks

Properly speaking, zoning should concentrate on regulations which vary from district to district. As to mobile homes and their parks, the ordinance should theoretically indicate only which districts will permit them by right or by special exception or other procedure, with requirements calling for varying densities, buffering, access, or other matters in different districts.

Local regulations applying generally to mobile homes and mobile home parks should generally be in codes dealing with similar subject matter (for example, plumbing, heating, electrical, health, and housing) or in a separate body of regulations dealing with mobile homes and mobile home parks. As indicated above, it is advantageous where there are good state regulations to permit them to govern. Certainly where there are good state regulations needless conflicts with local requirements should be avoided.

In practice, zoning for the mobile home and its environment is often loaded with details which belong elsewhere, and quite frequently there are conflicts with state controls or other local regulations with no apparent reason for the difference.

---

[18] KY. REV. STAT. ch. 190, § 190.210(*l*) (Supp. 1966).
[19] CAL. HEALTH & SAFETY CODE § 18371 (West 1964, Supp. 1966). *See* B. HODES & G. ROBERSON, THE LAW OF MOBILE HOMES 6-7 (2d ed. 1964).

1. *Location of Mobile Home Parks*

The mobile home is a residence, and belongs in residential areas, since exposure to commercial or industrial environments is likely to have the same blighting influence as for other forms of housing. Generally, density of a mobile home park is such as to make it appropriate for multiple-family residential districts, although at the low end of the density scale the number of units per acre is in the single-family class. In both cases, *if* there is good design, the mobile home park deserves the same type of density bonuses as planned unit developments in view of the increased utility of common open space.

2. *Minimum Area and Number of Spaces*

To support effective management and a reasonable range of common facilities and services, an adequate economic base is necessary. For this reason, many new ordinances require a minimum tract of eight to ten acres (with dimensional minimums for entrance and other portions) and at least fifty spaces complete and ready for occupancy when the park opens.

3. *Exclusion of Travel Trailers or Limitation on Location*

Late arrivals, early departures, different needs for facilities, and vacation-oriented outlook make travel trailers poor neighbors for mobile homes. Thus, many regulations require mobile home space rentals to be for thirty days or more (a major reversal of older ordinances which limited time of stay) and prohibit travel trailers in mobile home parks.

Under certain circumstances, combinations of mobile home and travel trailer parks may be justified, as for example where a tract has frontage on an important tourist route or is near an outdoor recreation attraction. In such cases, regulations may permit the use of part of the park for travel trailers and the remainder for mobile homes, usually with recreation and service facilities separating the two areas.

4. *Control of Quality of Units*

Although such provisions belong properly in construction and housing codes, zoning is often a vehicle for requirements that mobile homes will not be permitted in parks unless they are certified as meeting the ASA or similar standards as described previously, and there is an emerging tendency to require conformity with occupancy codes. The Public Health Service is currently developing new model occupancy codes for all forms of housing, with a special section on mobile homes which will take account of their design characteristics and the availability of common facilities found in most parks.

5. *Nonresidential Uses Permitted*

Many ordinances permit minor commercial uses in mobile home parks, limiting the area they may occupy and requiring that there shall be no visible evidence of commercial activities from residential areas outside the park. Although this might at first glance appear as allowing spots of commercial development in residential neighborhoods, there are ample precedents in apartment and planned unit development regulations permitting similar convenience establishments. Sales lots are not permitted in connection with parks in most regulations, with the exception of cases where a portion of the tract is in a commercial category allowing such activity.

6. *Buffering*

To provide transitional protection from neighboring property and vice versa, it is common practice in recent ordinances to require that where a park adjoins other residential uses, exterior yards shall have the same dimensions as for front yards in the district involved, regardless of the front, side or rear orientation on the parcel. Some regulations permit fences, walls or vegetative screening of specified kinds and dimensions as a substitute for part of the dimension of the yard; others require such screening in addition to the yard. If carelessly worded, screening requirements can create serious impediments to necessary visibility at intersections of park roadways with bordering public streets.

Some ordinances also require screening where the park adjoins commercial or industrial districts or major streets, in order to protect occupants from potentially adverse effects.

7. *Requirements for Recreational Facilities, Common Open Spaces*

Where state requirements do not cover these matters (and sometimes even where they do), local ordinances often specify that a minimum percentage of the tract or that land with stated minimum dimensions be set aside and improved for community recreation.

FHA's *Minimum Property Standards for Mobile Home Courts,* used extensively as a source for local zoning details or standards for general mobile home ordinances, states concerning size of recreation area: "Not less than 8% of the gross site area shall be devoted to recreational facilities, generally provided in a central location or, in the larger courts, decentralized. Recreation area includes space for community buildings and community use facilities, such as guest parking, adult recreation and child play areas, swimming pools, utilities and drying yards."[20]

8. *Other Details*

Depending on adequacy of coverage of state controls, local zoning or general mobile home park regulation may cover a wide range of other details. In many

---

[20] U.S. FEDERAL HOUSING ADMINISTRATION, MINIMUM PROPERTY STANDARDS FOR MOBILE HOME COURTS § 2414-3.1 (1962).

instances selected portions of FHA's *Minimum Property Standards for Mobile Home Courts* are adopted by reference to minimize bulk of the ordinance. The FHA material is considerably more extensive and specific than the Public Health Service *Environmental Health Guide for Mobile Home Parks* mentioned above.

C. Zoning and Mobile Homes Outside Parks[21]

Outside the park, zoning treatment for the mobile home varies widely, and frequently includes material which is unrelated to the usual purposes of zoning. Mobile homes may be permitted generally as single family dwellings. Sometimes this is intentional; sometimes not. Definitions of single family dwellings which unintentionally fail to distinguish the mobile home from other types have led to difficulties.

Mobile homes distinguished as such may be permitted outside parks in selected single or multifamily districts. Thus in rural areas, mobile homes are occasionally allowed either as principal uses on their own lots or as accessory to agricultural operations. In some areas where guest houses or servants quarters are allowable as accessory to principal permitted residential uses, mobile homes subject to the same limitations (location on the lot and prohibition against rental are often included) may be used for the same purposes.

As a concrete example of zoning language fitting a local circumstance (complete with matter extraneous to zoning), in Carbondale, Illinois it was proposed to permit a mixture of single-family conventional residences and mobile homes in one district. Both mobile homes and conventional dwellings were required to have lots of the same size. Only mobile homes meeting prescribed standards for plumbing, heating, and electrical installations were permitted. Any mobile home moved into the district was required to be supported under all exterior walls by a permanent foundation, and wheels were to be removed. Within six months after location within the district, the mobile home was to be taxed as real property.

What these regulations did was to make it probable that anyone moving into the district with a mobile home would be planning permanent occupancy, to provide protection against the appearance of the exposed undercarriage by requiring the permanent solid foundation, to encourage lowering the unit by requiring the removal of the wheels, and to make tax policy clear. Moreover, removal of the wheels and setting the unit on a foundation made it highly probable that the tax policy would stick. Courts might have some doubts if the wheels remained on the unit and it had no permanent foundation.

Now what about the other situation, where it is proposed to be selective about the type of mobile home to be permitted on its own lot in a single-family neighborhood in which mobile homes generally are not acceptable? Here we enter a grey area in zoning where logic increasingly gives way to prejudice, and where courts

---

[21] Much of this subpart has been adapted from Bair, *Regulation of Mobile Homes, A New Look*, FLA. PLANNING & DEVELOPMENT, June 1963, at 1.

specializing in logic may tear things apart, while those specializing in defending prejudice will give the approach their blessing. What we are seeking is a way to assure that if mobile homes are to be permitted in neighborhoods of conventional single-family residences, they must be sufficiently similar in appearance to pass as conventional single-family residences. So far as we know, no such provisions have as yet been written. Stated briefly, they might be handled as follows:

> Mobile homes will be permitted in the R-1B single-family residential district only
> if they are similar to other residences now existing in the district in dimensions,
> design, and exterior appearance.

This runs into all of the problems of vagueness and lack of standards. Being more specific, the provision might go thus:

> Mobile homes will be permitted in the R-1B district only if the end portions,
> as provided with the delivered unit or added, are at least 20 feet in width, the main
> body of the unit is at least 50 feet in length, the main roof shall be pitched at an
> angle of not less than 30° and the ridge shall be not less than 10 feet from the front
> wall, the unit shall be oriented with its long axis parallel to the street, exterior
> finish shall be of a flat variety, not creating excessive reflection, and colors used shall
> be the same as those generally in use in the neighborhood.

This puts prejudice into more concrete language, and should help to assure that in neighborhoods where major emphasis is on conformity, any mobile homes used as residences will conform. Obviously the provisions have little to do with health or safety or even the general welfare. Perhaps they might be defended on grounds that they protect the "character of the neighborhood." Administrators and courts would be in a far better position to appraise whether a given unit does or does not fit requirements stated in specific terms than regulations which require merely that new houses must look substantially like houses already in the neighborhood. In any event, intelligent courts are likely to ask the penetrating question: "Is the general welfare served by limiting change and forbidding individuals to create new architectural forms?"

There can be little doubt that in many residential areas, typical mobile homes intermingled with conventional residences would have an adverse effect on property values. To the extent that the difference in character is extreme, it seems probable that most courts would uphold exclusion of mobile homes from such neighborhoods. Whether language along the lines indicated above would be acceptable as a guide would depend to a considerable extent on the court involved, but if applied only to mobile homes, and not to other forms of housing it would appear to be inequitable. *Some* language containing workable guidelines is essential, however. To exclude mobile homes built to acceptable standards and indistinguishable in appearance from conventional housing *solely on grounds that they are mobile homes* seems highly arbitrary and unreasonable.

D. Housing Codes

Given adequate control of mobile home parks, there still remains the problem of the substandard mobile home, either in or out of a park. The appropriate regulatory medium here is the housing or occupancy code. As in the case of construction codes, some special tailoring is desirable. The mobile home is still a relatively compact dwelling unit. Its shape and the size and location of its windows tend to give it some advantages over usual conventional housing on the matter of light and air in habitable rooms. Its foundation requirements are different and it has other characteristics which call for some special consideration in regulations.

One point of beginning for regulations of this type is New York State's "Model Housing Code Applicable to One- and Two-Family Dwellings, Multiple Dwellings, Mobile Homes and Mobile Home Courts."[22] The New York codes, for voluntary adoption by local governments, were first produced in 1958. Later it was found that special adaptations were needed for mobile homes and certain other uses, and these were added in the 1960 version. Among other things, there are variations from general residential requirements in habitable space per occupant, ceiling heights, minimum dimensions of habitable rooms and kitchens, glassed areas, foundation, and structural specifications.

Currently, the Public Health Service is preparing model occupancy standards for mobile homes which should prove helpful as a guide for local regulation.

In addition to the observation that occupancy standards for mobile homes should be designed for mobile homes, two other cautionary comments are in order. First, it would be discriminatory to adopt and enforce such standards for mobile homes unless other housing is similarly regulated. And second, the controls should be placed in a housing or occupancy code rather than grafted onto zoning, both in the interest of logical regulatory location and because of the handicap to application created by the special status of nonconformities under zoning.

E. Taxation[23]

In addition to all the complexities as to whether the mobile home is real estate, vehicle or other personal property for tax purposes, there are the problems of how the tax should be collected and distributed and how much the tax should be.

The mobile home is indisputably low-cost housing. As such, even if it is taxed as realty, it does not pay as much as more expensive housing. There are those who argue (and implement their arguments with regulation) that housing in their communities should be kept expensive. To a major extent, this argument is based on tax revenue, although there are strong overtones of social discrimination. Zoning does not estab-

---

[22] 2 NEW YORK STATE DIVISION OF HOUSING, HOUSING CODES—THE KEY TO HOUSING CONSERVATION, MODEL HOUSING CODE APPLICABLE TO ONE- AND TWO-FAMILY DWELLINGS, MULTIPLE DWELLINGS, MOBILE HOMES AND MOBILE HOME COURTS (1960).

[23] A portion of this subpart has been adapted from Bair, *Mobile Homes*, NATION'S CITIES, Aug. 1965, at 18.

lish minimum price of housing directly, but it can have the same effect by requiring large lots and high minimum floor areas.

In the case of mobile homes, exclusion is often based on tax considerations as well as social, and the tax analysis is limited to income, ignoring net profit or loss. If policy stems from prejudice, facts are superfluous. Policy based on facts stands up better in the long run, but requires that the facts be impartially collected and analyzed. These things are usually found to be true when facts are collected:

(1) Single family detached family dwellings produce substantially more students per unit than do other forms of housing. A recent survey in Fairfax County, Virginia, shows 1.08 student per unit in single-family and duplex housing, 0.37 per unit in mobile home parks, 0.21 in garden apartments, and 0.09 in high-rise apartments.

(2) Owner-occupied homes produce a much smaller share of local revenue than is generally realized. Allen Manvel points out: "[O]nly about an eighth of the urban government bill is currently collected in the form of local property taxes on owner-occupied homes."[24]

(3) Balancing local expenditures against revenues per dwelling unit, single-family detached housing is generally found to require greatest subsidy, garden apartments and mobile home parks come closer to paying their own way, and high-density (and particularly high-rise) apartments turn in a substantial surplus.

These three facts are more useful in putting prejudice in its place than in setting policy. They indicate that several standard cliches are wrong, and they point a moral as to what happens if fiscal expediencies of the moment are allowed to set long-range development policy. Starting from accurate premises which have nothing to do with urban purpose, the policy derived from these facts is magnificently logical and ridiculous: *Eliminate single-family detached housing.* It does not amount to much in the revenue picture, it requires excessive subsidies, and it produces too many children.

For tax purposes, a mobile home is what the tax law declares it to be. In Florida, purchase of a vehicular license exempts it from real or personal property taxes. Without the license, it may be taxed as either real or personal property, depending on its location.

In New York, mobile homes have been classified as real property for tax purposes under state law since 1954. Commenting on New York experience, Mary E. Mann, Assistant Counsel, New York State Board of Equalization and Assessment, reflects concern with governmental revenue without analysis of governmental costs:[25]

---

[24] Manvel, *Paying the Urban Bill,* 54 NAT'L CIVIC REV. 16, 18-19 (1965).

[25] Mann, *Assessment and Taxation of Mobile Homes: What is the Town's Best Approach?* N.Y. STATE PLANNING NEWS, March-April 1967, at 4, 12.

Now, the dilemma is that although the intent of the legislature was to provide a means whereby the mobile home would pay "its fair share of local taxes," property taxation does not reflect services rendered by local government. It is an assessment against the market value of the property. . . . As long as the mobile home is cheap housing, its value will never be sufficient to raise an amount of revenue from an ad valorem tax equal to that which may be raised on an average single family dwelling.

The original cost of a new mobile home is rarely that of the average house, and the market value of a used mobile home depreciates each year at least 5% of its original cost. In contrast, in the present state of our economy, other types of real property typically tend to appreciate in value or at least to hold their original value over a long number of years . . . .

A long term approach might be to change the type of tax to one which produces more revenue. For example, California and Colorado . . . impose "in lieu" taxes which are only partly based on value. According to recent studies, these taxes, which are administered by the State, produce more revenue than local ad valorem taxes would have produced.

As a preliminary to discussion of substantial administrative problems with local ad valorem taxation in New York, the Mann paper continues: "The recent California study concluded that 'administratively it does not appear desirable to return the taxation of mobile homes to local governments due to disclosure problems and the like.' "

Another state using a form of "in lieu" taxation is Minnesota. Several features of the Minnesota system are useful solutions to difficult problems—the method of collection, the way in which depreciation is handled, and the manner of distribution of returns.

Under the provisions of Minnesota's mobile home tax law[26] all mobile homes are required to purchase number plates annually on or before January 10 from the secretary of state, paying $3, and, in addition, taxes as indicated below. The listing for taxes and application for registration includes name and address of owner, location, make, model, serial number, length, and weight of the mobile home, and name and number of the school district, the county, and the municipality in which the mobile home is located.

The full and true value of the unit is the suggested factory retail list price. Tax is computed by multiplying the average millage rate of taxes of all counties levied for all purposes and paid during the previous year by a percentage of the full value which declines from ten per cent for a new mobile home to four and a half per cent for a unit six years old or over. Recent figures indicate that a $7,500 mobile home purchased in 1960 (using the 1963 mill rate for an average) would have paid $162.89 in 1960, $73.30 in 1966.[27]

Of the taxes collected, fifty per cent go to the school district, thirty per cent to the

---

[26] MINN. STAT. ANN. §§ 168.011-.012 (1960, Supp. 1966), § 273.13 (1947, Supp. 1966).

[27] MINNESOTA HIGHWAY INTERIM COMMISSION, MOBILE HOMES AND THE MOBILE HOME INDUSTRY 98 (Report of the Highway Interim Comm'n prepared by Consulting Services Corp., 1967).

municipality or township, ten per cent to the county and ten per cent to the State General Revenue Fund.

The results of this approach appear to be generally satisfactory. "Although final judgment is reserved for broader studies to determine, our findings show that revenues from mobile home owners tend to more than compensate for the municipality's cost of services furnished to such residents."[28]

It is interesting to note, however, that even in Minnesota, which seems to have the most equitable and workable approach known to this writer, there is still awareness of possibilities for improvement. The final recommendation on mobile home taxation urges a detailed study to determine disparity between revenues from mobile and stationary homes, suggests analysis to determine practicality of a flexible schedule of fees reflecting individual county mill rates, and concludes: "Such a study should also investigate the workability of taxing mobile homes as realty, as is done in New York."[29]

SUMMARY AND CONCLUSIONS

Mobile homes, the fastest growing segment of the housing industry, are also the most rapidly changing form of housing. Since 1950, growth in size, improvement in design, and control on quality of construction have multiplied the potential market. In the early 1950s, the term "trailer" could be applied indiscriminately to units which might be used for either permanent or vacation housing; there is now a clear break between the increasingly immobile mobile home and the recreational vehicles represented by the travel trailer and its cousins.

Out ahead, several new developments seem likely. Permanently attached wheels will come off most mobile homes. Present manufacturers will use double-wide production and assembly techniques to mass-produce more units indistinguishable in appearance from conventional single-family housing. Units constructed by mobile home assembly techniques will be used in multifamily structures—garden apartments and high rise—and in townhouse forms. Habitat 67, showpiece of the Canadian Centennial Exposition, could well have been built with specially modified mobile homes. The individual apartments are in the mobile home dimensional range.

Thus far, neither conventional construction nor prefabricated conventional housing has been able to produce dwellings furnished and equipped with appliances at anything approaching as low a price as the mobile home, and the difference in cost seems likely to increase rather than diminish. If low-cost housing, with quality assured by construction codes, is a desirable public objective, the mobile home should be encouraged. But *because* it is low-cost housing, and worse—low-cost housing in a form and in locations which do not fit neatly into established taxation patterns—public regulation tends to be either exclusive or repressive.

---

[28] MINNESOTA HIGHWAY INTERIM COMMISSION, REPORT OF THE 1965-66 HIGHWAY INTERIM COMMISSION 25 (1967).
[29] *Id.* at 27.

There is growing need for good mobile home parks and subdivisions, appropriately located in residential environments. Local regulations (backed by state controls) can assure acceptable quality, location, and design. And equitable devices for taxation and other revenue production can assure that the mobile home pays its fair share of governmental costs. Unless local prejudice can be overcome by reason, it seems probable that mounting pressures for areas suitable for mobile home living will lead to increasing activity in the courts.

PERFECTING THE CONDOMINIUM AS A HOUSING TOOL: INNOVATIONS IN TORT LIABILITY AND INSURANCE

Patrick J. Rohan*

Introduction

Housing discussions frequently center around "suburban sprawl" and the city's effort to combat neighborhood decline, originate and maintain low and middle income housing, and meet population pressures with high-rise commercial, apartment, and multipurpose buildings. The condominium concept, virtually unheard of five years ago, may soon see service in all of these areas. Thus, for example, it has been heralded as a means of restoring the amenities of city living, as well as the ideal format for suburban property owner associations. More recently, public officials have begun to explore its potential as a source of "home ownership" for economically deprived families. Whatever the relative merits of these projections, condominiums now constitute a significant percentage of all new housing starts and must figure prominently in the thinking of land planners.

Enabling acts, designed to provide a legislative foundation for the condominium format and to fit it into the existing legal system, have been enacted by the federal government, District of Columbia, and forty-nine states.[1] However, perfection should not be anticipated in such a broad undertaking; drafting flaws are certain to appear as experience is gained with various condominium uses. One such imperfection has recently come to the writer's attention, namely, failure to clarify the unit owner's posture (and that of his household) with respect to tort liability and insurance. What is the nature and extent of the risk assumed as co-owner of the project and its facilities? What policies are available to neutralize this exposure and should protection be purchased on an individual or community basis, or perhaps both? Conversely, is a participant permitted to sue the group (or a fellow unit owner) if negligently harmed? Would such a judgment be covered by a master liability policy? While these and related queries may have been academic in other times and societies, the omnipresence of insurance and today's tort calendars indicate that these questions will press for immediate resolution. As might be anticipated, some unit owners have already fallen on icy, commonly-owned walks or met with other mishaps. Counsel

* B.A. 1954, LL.B. 1956, St. John's University; LL.M. 1957, Harvard University; J.S.D. 1965, Columbia University. Professor of Law, St. John's University. Co-author [with M. A. Reskin], Condominium Law and Practice (1965); Cooperative Housing: Law and Practice (1967); Revision Editor, R. Powell, Real Property.

The writer wishes to acknowledge the research assistance and valuable insights he received from Thomas G. Cody, Esq., of New York.

[1] At this writing, Vermont, the only state without a condominium statute, has an enabling act pending in its legislature.

for insurance carriers grappling with their complaints are finding scant, if any, authority upon which to base an opinion. In the pages which follow, an attempt is made to resolve these uncertainties and to indicate what remedial steps should be taken by the various state legislatures and insurance departments.

I
THE CASE FOR EXPLICIT TREATMENT

Some may object to the assertion that tort liability and insurance should be treated in the enabling legislation (or ancilliary regulations), on the ground that these are matters of detail best left to the individual project's draftsman. While such a laissez-faire attitude currently holds sway, a persuasive case can be made for the proposition that direction, if not uniformity, should be supplied at the legislative or administrative level.

A. The Desideratum of Certainty

Real property laws and procedures have always placed a premium on certainty, for obvious reasons. Condominium projects will have to find that ingredient in either the enabling act or precedents governing concurrent ownership. But condominium statutes are largely silent on tort liability and insurance, and common law treatments are fragmentary at best. Also to be considered is the question whether a condominium statute pre-empts the field, in which event answers would have to be found in oblique legislative passages which were never intended to be controlling. In view of the foregoing, it is doubtful that project draftsmen and attorneys for unit owners can safely state what their clients' rights and obligations are, and what insurance coverage is appropriate. Further, it is not clear that declaration and by-law provisions on this subject would be enforceable. For example, may a project's documentation bar the unit owner's cause of action in negligence or exonerate management for all but willful wrongs? From the long-range viewpoint, uncertainty (or worse, resolution of doubts against the unit owner), might undermine public confidence in condominiums and permanently impair their development. Just such a progression of events led to the demise of syndications as a real estate investment vehicle.

B. The Danger of Improper Insurance Coverage

It is obvious that carriers were not writing liability policies for condominiums (and their constituent owners) prior to 1961, the date of the first legislative activity in the field. Again, no policy then in existence could fit the needs of the condominium, in view of the many uses to which the concept may be put and its peculiar legal structure. Accordingly, it is highly probable that traditional policies will result in duplication of coverage in some instances (as between individual and group insurance), as well as inadequate coverage in others. Similarly, unit and master policies may conflict or bring about troublesome subrogation disputes. A question may also arise as to whether such insurance covers contractual obligations, binding the unit owners to indemnify the board of managers and managing agent. In short, an adequate insurance program is not guaranteed by large premium payments and still larger policy limits. Both condominium unit owners and injured parties would be rendered a disservice if foreseeable risks were not covered, despite sizable premium expenditures. The conclusion appears inescapable that standard condominium liability policies should be drawn up, to provide unit owners with maximum protection for their insurance dollar.

C. The Absence of Litigation and Judgment Execution Guidelines

Several enabling acts contain procedures for processing contractual claims against the condominium association, including detailed steps for collecting these judgments.[2] However, scant attention has been paid to the quantitatively more significant area of tort actions and judgments. In the absence of such directions, counsel for an injured party may take the safest route—that is, serve everyone who might be a necessary or proper party. If this became the practice, any tort claim touching the condominium in any way would result in a suit against the condominium association, the board of managers, managing agent, and all unit owners. Serious problems of title would also ensue, if a judgment resulted in joint and several liability; once docketed, no unit could be sold without placing in escrow the full amount of the judgment, with interest. In a similar vein, what would be the status of unit owners (and of their respective titles), between the time the judgment was rendered and the time the association voted to assess its members to pay it? Many more illustrations may be supplied, but the cited hypotheticals are sufficient to indicate the wisdom of codifying rules governing tort litigation and enforcement of resulting judgments.

D. The Unit Owner as Plaintiff

Perhaps the most troublesome question in this entire area is whether a unit owner may sue a fellow participant or the group itself. Thus, for example, may unit owner *A* sue owner *B* (or the condominium association) in a case where *A* falls over an object left in a common hall by *B*? May *A* sue the group if he is injured in an elevator mishap or through the negligence of maintenance personnel? What if he were injured in a garage or restaurant owned or operated by the association? If *A*'s suit is barred, would the same result be forthcoming in the event a member of *A*'s family (or his servant) met with a similar mishap? If the capacity-to-sue hurdle is overcome, would such judgments be collectible from the association's carrier under the master liability policy, or would this exposure be uninsured?

It cannot be seriously contended that these matters should be worked out on a project-by-project basis, or under the auspices of local carriers. These issues go to the essence of the condominium unit owner's bundle of rights and obligations. Should

---

[2] *E.g.*, N.Y. REAL PROP. LAW § 339-*l* (McKinney Supp. 1967).

there not be a legislative determination as to whom a unit owner may sue in negligence, especially if the conclusion reached is that he cannot sue? Conversely, if such suits are authorized, should there not be a directive as to the contents of master policies in this regard, for the parties most likely to suffer injury in a condominium development are its occupants. There may even be a conflict of interest here. Neither the original draftsman nor insurance carrier will become a unit owner, and both have a motive for keeping insurance costs down: one to minimize carrying charges and sell units, the other to secure the insurance business. Lastly, there is serious question whether private controls along these lines would be against public policy, absent specific legislative sanction. For these reasons, the capacity to sue issue should be resolved authoritatively and on a statewide basis.

II

Unit Owner Liability

A. The Prevailing Pattern

As previously noted, most condominium statutes are silent on the nature and extent of a unit owner's non-contractual liability. Legal observers therefore conclude that, as co-owners, participants would be jointly and severally liable for tortious conduct in connection with the project.[3] Condominium authorities abroad hold to the same view.[4] The full impact of this conclusion is difficult to grasp, until one lists the conceivable sources of liability. A partial list would include:

1. Failure to maintain common elements and appliances—for example, halls, elevators, and boilers;
2. Negligence of maintenance personnel;
3. Failure to keep workmen's compensation in effect on project employees;
4. Failure to supervise pools, playgrounds, and similar areas where children congregate;
5. Violation of statutory duties, such as multiple dwelling laws, building codes, and fire department regulations;
6. Trespass or forcible entry and detainer, where a unit owner (or his lessee) is wrongfully disturbed or dislodged;
7. Automobile accidents involving vehicles owned by the condominium;
8. Products liability, where food, beverages, or detergents are dispensed by vending machines;
9. Injuries suffered in a garage, restaurant, recreation room, health club, or other facility operated by the group;

---

[3] See, e.g., 4 R. Powell, Real Property ¶ 633.25 (1965); Kerr, Condominium—Statutory Implementation, 38 St. John's L. Rev. 1, 17 (1963); Berger, Condominium: Shelter on a Statutory Foundation, 63 Colum. L. Rev. 987, 995 (1963); Comment, Community Apartments: Condominium or Stock Cooperative?, 50 Calif. L. Rev. 299, 312-14 (1962).

[4] See, e.g., A. F. Rath, P. J. Grimes & J. E. Moore, Strata Titles 35-36 (1962); Davis, Condominium and the Strata Titles Act, 9 Can. B.J. 469, 486 (1966).

10. Miscellaneous exposures, such as nuisance, dangerous instrumentalities, non-delegable duties, subrogation, and indemnity agreements.[5]

The foregoing enumeration, which is far from exhaustive, indicates that sources of liability extend far beyond the limits of one's own conduct and care of his unit. While many statutes are worded in terms of delegating maintenance functions to the board of managers or managing agent, it is extremely doubtful that such provisions were intended to free unit owners of the duties which would normally attach to property owners and employers.[6] The same is true of statutes which permit incorporation of the condominium association. Since the corporation would not own the realty, any liability stemming from ownership obligations would not be cut off.[7] Again, courts may regard the corporate entity as a mere device for organizing the condominium's affairs, and not as a party in interest or functioning entity.[8] This conclusion would be reinforced if the corporation were a mere shell, lacking capital or assets of consequence.

B. Miscellaneous Statutory Approaches

A minority of states have sought, with varying degrees of success, to immunize unit owners from all but their fractional share of any tort judgment rendered against the association. The statutes of Alaska[9] and Washington[10] require "all actions relating to the common areas and facilities for damages arising out of tortious conduct" to be brought against the association only. Any judgment obtained becomes a common expense. The Alaska statute explicitly provides that any unit owner may free himself of the lien by paying his proportionate share thereof (as determined by his undivided interest in the common elements). The same thought may be implicit in the portion of the Washington statute which makes tort judgments a common expense.

The Florida[11] and Mississippi[12] enabling acts stipulate that unit owners "have no personal liability for any damages caused by [the association] on or in connection with the use" of common elements. These statutes do provide, however, that a unit owner is liable for injuries occurring within his apartment to the same extent that the owner of a house would be. It is quite probable that these statutes do not completely exonerate the unit owner, and that procedurally a suit would be brought

---

[5] For the insurance coverage designed to meet similar exposures in housing cooperatives, see P. J. ROHAN & M. A. RESKIN, COOPERATIVE HOUSING: LAW AND PRACTICE § 12.02 (1967).

[6] See 4 R. POWELL, supra note 3, ¶¶ 633.24-.25.

[7] It should be noted that most of the enabling acts overcome the association's lack of an insurable interest by specific authorization for it to purchase a master casualty policy.

[8] Cf. Hathway v. Porter Royalty Pool, Inc., 296 Mich. 90, 295 N.W. 571 (1941). One observer, however, has indicated that the condominium "association" may be considered an unincorporated association, with the usual legal consequences flowing from such a desgination. See Kerr, supra note 3, at 41.

[9] ALAS. STAT. § 34.07.260 (Supp. 1966).

[10] WASH. REV. CODE § 64.32.240 (Supp. 1965).

[11] FLA. STAT. ANN. § 711.18 (Supp. 1966).

[12] MISS. CODE ANN. § 896-15 (Supp. 1966).

against the association, which in turn would levy to pay the judgment. Thus viewed, a unit owner's exposure is not non-existent, but limited to the extent of his aliquot share of the levy (including loss of his unit if he does not meet the levy).[13] The Virginia statute,[14] although similar in purpose to the quoted provision, is somewhat obscure. It provides that a unit owner shall not be liable with respect to the negligence of any other co-owner, except insofar as the negligent party is acting for the council of co-owners. This may imply unlimited personal liability for the torts of management personnel. As for torts of single unit owners acting on their own account *but involving common elements or facilities*, the statute may mean there is no liability whatsoever on the part of fellow owners, or merely no liability until a judgment is made a common charge.

The Idaho provision[15] specifies that a unit owner's liability for claims or judgments "arising out of or in connection with the ownership, use, operation or management of the common areas" is limited to the amount of such claim or judgment, times his undivided interest in the project. He may, however, compromise or settle his portion of such claim or judgment without prejudice to the judgment creditor, and without it constituting an admission or evidence against the unit owner. This provision may cause conflict among unit owners if the compromise authority is intended to apply both *before* and after the claim is reduced to a judgment. The Massachusetts provision[16] is unique inasmuch as claims involving the common areas and facilities must be brought against the organization of unit owners, with the resulting judgment constituting a lien on common funds and property (and not on the realty as such). If these assets are insufficient, each unit owner is liable for a sum equal to the balance, times his percentage interest in the common elements. Michigan's enabling act merely provides that "suits against the co-owners shall be in the name of the condominium project."[17] This may mean that unit owners must pay only their aliquot share of an assessment levied to pay a tort judgment. On the other hand, it could be interpreted as a procedural section, akin to that governing actions against partnerships, and not as a bar to unlimited personal liability for each unit owner. The final variation is found in the North Carolina statute[18] to the effect that anyone "claiming damages for injuries without any participation by a unit owner shall first exhaust all available remedies against the Association of Unit Owners prior to proceeding against any unit owner individually." This provision is honey-combed with uncertainty. If a unit owner was personally negligent in connection with common elements or facilities, is the entire section inapplicable or is it only inapplicable to the negligent person? Must a judgment creditor levy

[13] For a more expansive view of the cited Florida statute, see 4 R. POWELL, *supra* note 3, ¶ 633.25. *But see* McCaughan, *The Florida Condominium Act Applied*, 17 U. FLA. L. REV. 1, 18 (1964).
[14] VA. CODE ANN. § 55-79.37(2) (Supp. 1966).
[15] IDAHO CODE ANN. § 55-1515 (Supp. 1965).
[16] MASS. GEN. LAWS ch. 183A, § 13 (Supp. 1966).
[17] MICH. STAT. ANN. § 26.50(22) (Supp. 1965).
[18] N.C. GEN. STAT. § 47A-26 (1966).

execution on the condominium in order to "exhaust" his remedies; and, if so, can a unit owner exonerate himself by paying his aliquot share of the judgment? Once the claimant exhausts his remedies, are all unit owners jointly and severally liable for the unpaid balance?

C. Evaluation of Existing Approaches

Ambiguities inherent in the language of specific statutory provisions have already been noted. In addition, most, if not all, of the cited measures are subject to more general criticisms, a few of which are set out below.

1. *The Type of Actions Covered*

Most of the cited measures apply only to tort claims arising out of management and control of common areas and facilities. This terminology should be replaced by language descriptive of all liabilities arising in connection with the condominium, except those for which an individual is alone responsible. "Ownership and maintenance of common areas" (or equivalent language) may not cover limited common elements—areas or facilities allocated to some but not all unit owners.[19] Again, it may not be broad enough to include such sources of liability as non-delegable duties of property owners, respondeat superior, contractual indemnity claims of management personnel, trespass and forcible detainer, operation of community-owned vehicles, products liability, and injuries suffered by customers of restaurants or other commercial establishments on the premises. Lastly, uncertainty may occur in applying the statutory language in cases where all parts of the property are considered common elements, with the unit owner merely having title to the *space* he occupies.[20]

2. *Notice and Right to Counsel*

None of the statutes specifically provide for service of process upon, or right to counsel for, unit owners.[21] This is so, despite the fact that actions against the association may result in a dollar loss or personal liability to such individuals (as, for ex-

---

[19] *See* Kerr, *supra* note 3, at 27-31.

[20] See 4 R. POWELL, *supra* note 3, ¶¶ 633.19-.29.

[21] Many enabling acts contain a provision modeled upon N.Y. REAL PROP. LAW § 339-dd (McKinney Supp. 1967), which provides as follows:

"Actions may be brought or proceedings instituted by the board of managers in its discretion, on behalf of two or more of the unit owners, as their respective interests may appear, with respect to any cause of action relating to the common elements or more than one unit. Service of process on the unit owners in any action relating to the common elements or more than one unit may be made on the person designated in the declaration to receive service of process."

However, this brief paragraph leaves unresolved most of the questions raised in this paper on the subject of legal representation. For example, may the association's counsel (in all likelihood supplied by its carrier), represent the unit owners on that portion of the plaintiff's demand or settlement offer which exceeds the group's master liability insurance coverage? May counsel for an individual unit owner's insurance carrier also appear? Does a unit owner ever have a right to counsel of his own choosing when the condominium's owners are all made party defendants? *Compare* FLA. STAT. ANN. § 711.12(2) (Supp. 1966), "Service of process upon the association shall not constitute service of process upon any unit owner."

ample, where the master policy is insufficient in amount or does not cover the wrong in question). Moreover, such notification and right to be heard may be a prerequisite to the individual unit owner's claim against his own liability insurance carrier. Finally, lack of these safeguards would result in the anomalous situation that an active tortfeasor joined as a co-defendant would have a right to appear through counsel, whereas unit owners incurring derivative liability would not. Related questions concern the individual unit owner's right to compromise or settle in return for a general release, and the possible applications of res judicata and collateral estoppel.[22]

3. *The Status of the Errant Unit Owner*

None of the statutes clarify the position of the errant unit owner, the individual whose negligent or other tortious conduct led to the plaintiff's injury. It is probable that he may be sued individually or as co-defendant with the association of unit owners; in either case, his personal liability would be obtained. If the plaintiff only elects to sue the association, may the defendant or individual unit owners seek indemnity from the errant unit owner? Would the answer to this question vary with the amount and scope of the master liability policy—that is, with whether the loss was fully covered by insurance?

4. *The Effect of a Unit Owner's Failure to Pay His Aliquot Share of the Judgment*

Most of the cited enactments are unclear on the unit owner's position in the event he pays his aliquot share of the judgment but one or more fellow unit owners do not. If the judgment exceeds the value of the condominium development, or several unit owners do not meet their assessment, the plaintiff's judgment may remain partially unsatisfied. At this juncture, are the unit owners who have already contributed each personally liable for the balance, free of the debt altogether, or liable for a portion of the unpaid balance as re-assessed? If treated like any other common charge, there would be no bar to the unpaid balance being re-assessed.[23]

III

THE UNIT OWNER'S STANDING TO SUE IN TORT

At this juncture the right of the unit owner to sue a fellow unit owner will be considered, followed by an analysis of his right of action, if any, against the association of unit owners. Finally, the rights of household members will be treated. In all three categories, the discussion proceeds on the assumption that the condominium's declaration and by-laws are silent on the subject, or contain restrictions upon suit which are unenforceable under local public policy.

---

[22] Evidentiary questions, such as whether one co-owner's admissions bind the group as an admission against interest, also lurk in the background.

[23] *See* P. J. ROHAN & M. A. RESKIN, CONDOMINIUM: LAW AND PRACTICE § 6.04 (1965). One statute, D.C. CODE ANN. § 5-924(c) (1966), appears to bar such a re-assessment.

A. Actions Between Unit Owners

There does not appear to be any question but that one unit owner can sue another in any case wherein the would-be defendant is the only party liable for the damage suffered. Intra-apartment negligence of a unit owner and trespass are illustrative of such causes of action. A more troublesome question is whether a unit owner may sue a fellow participant when the latter's action gives rise to tort liability on the part of the entire group (including the individual culprit). Thus, for example, may unit owner A sue unit owner B when the evidence discloses that A fell over skates or a milkbox left in a darkened hallway by B? In most states, the absence of legislation on the point would seem to support the view that one unit owner could sue another under these circumstances. In the few states possessing statutory references to the subject, the answer is less clear.[24] These provisions could be interpreted to mean that, in this situation, B could not be sued by anyone—whether or not a unit owner—and that the action would have to be brought against the group (on the ground that maintenance of common elements was at issue). The same legislation could also be read as requiring a plaintiff to elect between a suit against the individual wrongdoer and one against the condominium association. A more plausible interpretation is that such statutes only control liability of the group as co-owners, and that one is free to join the individual wrongdoer and association as co-defendants in a single action (with the judgment binding each defendant jointly and severally). If these statutory hurdles are surmounted, the plaintiff unit owner may possibly be defeated by traditional negligence doctrines such as assumption of risk, contributory negligence and non-delegable duties of landowners. However, the applicability of these defenses would depend upon the facts of the particular case.

B. Actions by a Unit Owner Against the Association

The ability of one unit owner to sue his fellow unit owners as a group will be subject to all of the factors discussed in the preceding paragraph. In addition, there is the more general jurisprudential question whether the condominium enabling act (or the concept itself) abrogates the unit owner's right of action in connection with common areas and facilities. Implication of such a prohibition would reduce insurance premiums and disruptive lawsuits.[25] At the same time, however, hundreds of unit owners (as in a retirement village) would be disenfranchised, perhaps without ever being aware of it. This seems far too serious a step to be founded upon implication. If suit is permitted, traditional tort principles such as non-delegable duties of a landowner, assumption of risk, contributory negligence, and related defenses may bar recovery. If this hurdle is surmounted, a question may arise as to whether the plaintiff must contribute to his own recovery; and here the answer appears to

---

[24] See statutes cited *supra* notes 16-23.

[25] This problem may be minimized through an educational program which brings home to the participants the fact that their premiums rise with the project's loss experience.

be quite clearly affirmative. In the event a master policy were in effect, such a judgment would be covered if the plaintiff were not a named insured or, though a named insured, was nevertheless permitted to recover under the terms of the policy.

C. Actions by Household Members

Much of what has been already stated would govern the rights of members of a unit owner's household, at least to the extent that specific statutory provisions control tort actions against the condominium association in general. An owner's spouse would be in the same position as the unit owner, if the spouse's name appeared on the deed to the unit. Assuming that such is not the case, the troublesome question is whether any disabilities imposed upon a unit owner would be extended to members of his household. Here implication is stretched beyond the breaking point, and no such prohibition against suit could be implied from the existing legislative pattern. In the event the local condominium statute was deemed to bar suits by unit owners against the association, a hybrid situation might arise with respect to a wrongful death action growing out of a unit owner's demise. Here again, however, extension of the disability to the personal representative and next of kin of a unit owner would appear to require specific statutory authority. Query: Whether the "personal application" section of the F.H.A. Model Act and similar statutes would support an extension of a bar to suits to household members and guests?

IV

CONCLUSIONS AND RECOMMENDATIONS

A. The Role of Legislation and Administrative Regulations

Varying legislative approaches are reflected in the condominium enabling acts, ranging from a bare outline of the subject to lengthy, definitive treatments. Similarly, the legislation of any one jurisdiction makes use of multiple drafting techniques. For example, some sections contain hard and fast rules; some sections, legislative judgments which may be altered by agreement; and still others, a mere enumeration of topics to be treated in each project's documentation. To this array may be added the device of entrusting matters of detail to regulations promulgated from time to time by the Attorney General's Office. Some combination of these tools should be brought to bear upon the problems discussed in this paper.

As a minimum, there should be legislative clarification of the condominium's authority to purchase a master liability policy covering every aspect of risk growing out of operation and concurrent ownership of the project. In this connection, it should be noted that most enabling acts contain specific authority for a master casualty policy covering the entire property (including privately owned areas).[26] The absence of an

---

[26] Most carriers have limited the master policy to liability growing out of ownership and maintenance of the common areas and facilities. For a directive to this effect, issued in 1963 by the National Bureau of Casualty Underwriters, see Rohan, *Disruption of the Condominium Venture: The Problems of Casualty Loss and Insurance*, 64 COLUM. L. REV. 1045, 1081 n.229 (1964).

equally broad provision relating to liability insurance may cause some insurance departments or carriers to conclude that similar liability policies lack legislative sanction. Finally, there should be clarification of the unit owner's liability in tort, his capacity to sue, the validity of covenants not to sue, the procedural steps in bringing an action against the association, and the mechanics of levying execution. The overall legislative pattern should be reinforced by formulation of master and unit-owner liability policies by state insurance departments, coupled with a requirement of complete disclosure of the tort and insurance picture in each project's offering plan.

B. Specific Recommendations

1. *Limited Liability Versus Adequate Insurance Coverage*

The principal difficulty in the tort area lies in the fact that each unit owner incurs unlimited liability in his capacity as co-owner of the project (and as employer of its management personnel). Should such a risk be attached to the negligible interest one may have in miles of commonly-owned roads or in multiple high-rise structures? Each unit owner's control over, or right to control, these elements is all but fictional. Moreover, the one exerting control (the managing agent) typically operates under protection of the group's promise to indemnify him in the event he is negligent.[27] In a project of any size, the foregoing arrangement of rights and obligations is difficult to justify. The dilemma posed by the conflicting equities of injured parties and innocent unit owners might be resolved in one of two ways: limited liability for unit owners coupled with mandatory liability insurance coverage, or creation of an adequate, air-tight insurance program. Each solution will be considered in turn.

The limited liability approach has the merit of simplicity and certainty.[28] Moreover, it safeguards the unit owner against unexpected liability through a gap in insurance coverage. Also on the plus side, this approach would place the unit owners on a par with counterparts residing in cooperative housing. In such a venture, liability is centered upon the corporate landowner, with each participant merely running the risk that an uninsured liability would result in loss of the property. Nevertheless, all the factors to be considered in weighing limited liability do not point in a single direction. Thus, if such a limit were decreed, it would be impractical to apply it to large projects and not to small ones. Hence, all condominiums would be given a benefit denied to concurrent owners generally. The cooperative analogy does not meet this objection, because the condominium's common elements are owned individually and not by a corporation. Again, if liability were to be limited, just what acts would be so privileged and where would that limit be drawn. Would the unit owner who caused the common liability be so exempt? Would the unit

---

[27] *See, e.g.*, condominium declarations set forth in P. J. ROHAN & M. A. RESKIN, *supra* note 23, App. C.

[28] Both of these factors would be required to enable a layman to grasp the rights and obligations he is acquiring when he purchases a condominium unit. Complicated liability and insurance provisions would also detract from the condominium's usefulness as a method of supplying home ownership for low income families.

owner's exposure be restricted to loss of his unit or to his pro rata share of the judgment (measured by his undivided interest in the project)? Finally, there would be the problem of fashioning mandatory liability insurance coverage to guarantee that injured members of the public would be fully compensated despite individual liability limitations.

If the limited liability solution is passed over, in favor of increased insurance protection, still other problems must be faced. Is it feasible to write a master policy covering every aspect of unit owner liability in connection with the condominium project, including intra-apartment negligence? If it is possible to draft such a policy, there is the further question whether it is wise to write coverage in this fashion. Should the group pay premiums to cover negligent conduct of individual participants in their own units? Under the prevailing practice, condominiums acquire an "Owner's, Landlord's and Tenant's" policy covering liability arising out of the common elements.[29] Individual unit owners must purchase separate policies to cover negligence dissociated with the property and intra-apartment liability. As previously indicated, however, this two-fold approach to insurance is not tailored to the condominium's needs and may lead to conflicts, excess premiums, or worse, gaps in coverage.

In the writer's view, the best approach to the problem would consist of the following: (1) A statutory requirement that each condominium acquire and keep in force a master liability policy covering all risks faced in common by all condominium unit owners; (2) a provision in the master policy covering the liability of any individual unit owner for acts or omissions in connection with the condominium, including intra-apartment negligence.[30] Premiums for the latter coverage could be allocated to the individual participant to avoid inequities;[31] (3) include the managing agent as an insured party or otherwise cover the unit owners' indemnification agreement; (4) restrict unlimited liability to a unit owner's personal conduct. Where liability is imposed on all unit owners and the insurance in effect is inadequate, limit each participant's liability to his pro rata share of the unpaid judgment (as determined by his undivided interest in the project). In this connection, there should be no additional liability for uncollected portions of the judgment—that is, unpaid segments should not be re-assessed against the remaining unit owners; (5) where the plaintiff complains of negligence giving rise to the liability of all unit owners, suits should be directed against the association and defended by that organiza-

---

[29] For the coverage acquired by individual unit owners, see the directive of the National Bureau of Casualty Underwriters, in Rohan, *supra* note 26.

[30] The condominium's participants share the risk of a member's negligence under a master casualty policy. Are the differences between their casualty and liability problems so great as to preclude common coverage of the latter? If a truly master liability policy cannot be formulated, it may be helpful at least to have the same carrier issue both master and unit liability policies, or to take other steps to avoid troublesome issues of contribution, subrogation, and legal representation.

[31] N.Y. Real Prop. Law § 339-bb (McKinney Supp. 1967) authorizes disproportionate charges to reflect variations in insurance costs as between different units. Query whether this section would have to be enlarged to authorize different charges based on the loss experience of each *owner*?

tion. Notice of the pending litigation should be given to all unit owners; however, the right to participate through counsel should be restricted to cases wherein a unit owner's personal, unlimited liability is sought.[32] Where a unit owner's personal liability is sought in addition to that of the group, the plaintiff should be permitted to join both as party defendants.[33] Thereafter, execution should be allowed against the individual, but limited against the association (to the pro rata levy device discussed above). The levy, of course, should allocate a fraction of the common liability to the unit owner who is personally liable, rather than spreading the liability solely over his fellow unit owners; (6) subrogation of the carrier to claims against individual unit owners should be prohibited.[34]

2. *Capacity to Sue*

Since condominium unit owners will not control common areas in any realistic sense, and in view of the enormous size of these projects (compared to earlier forms of concurrent ownership, including cooperatives), the writer is of the opinion that unit holders should be permitted to sue the group in negligence. Although the participants, as co-owners, are ultimately responsible for the property's condition, they are more akin to proprietary lessees and should be given the same right to sue the organization charged with day-to-day maintenance.[35] Accordingly, it is suggested that the enabling statutes be amended to authorize such suits and to require that the association's liability policies specifically provide coverage for unit owner suits. The mechanics of such a provision could be handled in one of two ways. The legislation could stipulate that a unit owner may sue the association in tort, as if the individual were a member of the public, and that such suits will not be barred on the ground that the plaintiff is a concurrent owner. In the alternative the statute could provide that, for purposes of a suit in tort by a unit owner, the condominium's common elements, facilities, and personnel shall be deemed to be within the exclusive control of the association. Under either approach, the plaintiff would remain subject to the defenses of contributory negligence and assumption of risk (stemming from his conduct and not mere ownership of his interest in the project).

If the position advocated herein is rejected, the legislature may bar unit owner tort suits by a specific provision. It then must decide whether the ban extends to household members, servants, guests, and lessees. A decision must also be reached on how to handle wrongful death actions and minors. A middle-of-the-road position may

---

[32] Attention should also be given to the individual representation question in situations where the plaintiff's demand or settlement offer exceeds the master liability policy.

[33] There is no sound reason for eliminating the personal liability of the individual wrongdoer.

[34] *See* Ellman, *Fundamentals of Condominium and Some Insurance Problems*, 1963 INS. L.J. 733, 738 (1963).

[35] The same factors support the writer's contention that the liability of unit owners in connection with common elements and facilities should be limited. Additional risks, both of injury and of liability, will be present when a condominium consists of mixed units (commercial and residential), bringing more members of the public onto the premises and exposing them (and the unit owners) to greater dangers than those associated with residential uses.

consist of permitting the condominium's documentation to control, through adoption of one of several legislatively approved alternatives. Among the latter might be a limitation upon such suits in the form of: (a) a requirement that all such claims go to arbitration; (b) a ceiling upon recoveries, either in terms of a dollar amount or actual out-of-pocket expenses; or (c) a prohibition against recoveries in excess of the group's liability insurance coverage. If any one or more of these controls are imposed, additional directives would have to be supplied to cover the unit owner's right to sue managerial personnel or the managing agent (to prevent circumvention of the previously imposed restrictions).

Many more questions than answers are supplied in this article. This is to be expected in an area where so little has been written and experience is still limited. It is to be hoped, however, that most of these problems can be resolved through the swift action of legislatures, insurance departments, and interested liability carriers. Otherwise full utilization of the condominium as a housing tool may not be attained.

UNIONS, HOUSING COSTS, AND THE NATIONAL LABOR POLICY

Sylvester Petro*

Introduction

The more one observes the housing industry the more remarkable it seems that there is as much activity as there is, that so many homes are built each year within the reach of persons of modest income, that the houses stand as sturdily as they do, or that they are as comfortable as they are. For no comparable industry is bound as tightly and in as many ways. There are village, town, county, and state boards of various kinds which more often than not impose unnecessary costs and thus tend to put a damper upon building. In larger communities, the village boards expand into multifarious bureaucracies whose regulations and idiosyncracies must be countered in one way or another by the person intent upon filling a piece of empty land with a home or apartment building or other structure. The buyer has his own ideas about what he wants, and when he enters the market for a home he usually prefers something other than a mass-produced edifice as indistinguishable as one among the millions of Chevies which roam the streets.

The tradesmen account by themselves for a number of restrictions. Combine theirs with those of government bureaucracies and the rigidities multiply and expand. Plumbers and electricians and a number of other trades have their unions; they are also licensed trades, licensed by government. Unionization alone, at least in the building industry, involves a significant spectrum of productivity limitations and probably unnecessary cost-increments. Unionization plus governmental licensing strengthens control of labor supply and thus enhances the capacity of building tradesmen and their unions to raise costs above the levels they would reach in genuinely free markets where access is unrestrained.

Any overall study of the factors inhibiting the construction industry and unnecessarily raising its costs must take note, not only of all these influences, but also of the probability that not all the inhibitory, cost-raising elements either can or should be eliminated. In an ideal world without restraints it is possible at least to conceive of houses built in the way that automobiles are now being built, on mass-production lines. One may doubt, however, whether such housing would have the appeal of the kind of housing we are accustomed to, or that it will ever be possible to dispense entirely with town planners, zoning boards, and materials codes.

* A.B. 1943, J.D. 1945, University of Chicago; LL.M. 1950, University of Michigan. Professor of Law, New York University. Member of the Illinois bar. Author, The Labor Policy of the Free Society (1957), The Kohler Strike (1961), The Kingsport Strike (1967). Contributor of labor relations articles to New York University *Annual Survey of American Law* and to numerous legal and general periodicals.

Recognizing that there are limitations to the economies which may be introduced into home construction does not mean that all is well, or even that all is as well as reasonably can be expected. On the contrary, it seems obvious that improvements in the form of removal or reduction of arbitrary and irrational restrictions are possible all along the line. This seems true at least of the aspects of the construction industry with which this article deals.

No one can be sure of the amount which they add to construction costs, but restrictive union practices certainly add something. Moreover, any coercively imposed restriction is from a social point of view both unnecessary and undesirable. A union which prevents nonunion men from practicing a construction trade is getting in the way of the development of the good society; whether the victim is white or black makes not a great deal of difference, for in either case a personal injustice is being done and the cost and therefore the availability of housing are being prejudiced. The conclusion must be the same in regard to the obstacles which unions coercively erect against the introduction of cost-reducing technological advances in home building. Here also the social cost, whatever it may be, is too high.

I do not intend in this article to deal with all the ways in which unions affect construction costs or even with all the forms of restrictionism which they practice. My intention is, first, to sketch generally the economic framework within which unions operate in the construction industry. Then I shall outline the ways in which unions alone, unaided by such controls as licensing laws, seek to gain and maintain control of the labor supply and costs in the industry. Finally, the major portion of the article will explain how the national labor policy as developed by Congress, the National Labor Relations Board, and the Supreme Court is in some ways checking and in other ways encouraging restrictive union practices in construction.

I

ECONOMIC FRAMEWORK OF THE CONSTRUCTION INDUSTRY

When President Lyndon B. Johnson made his Economic Report to the nation on January 26, 1967, according to *The New York Times*, he "tacitly abandoned . . . the Government's fixed standard of 3.2 per cent for noninflationary wage increases, approving settlements somewhat higher."[1] *The Wall Street Journal* indicated that increases gained by the construction unions had steadily exceeded the "Guideposts," that the President's Council of Economic Advisers considered those increases (averaging more than five per cent annually) "inflationary," and that the President's counsel of moderation was addressed as much to the construction unions as to any other group.[2]

Notwithstanding the pleas for restraint, however, wage settlements in the construc-

---

[1] N.Y. Times, Jan. 27, 1967, at 1, col. 8.
[2] Wall Street Journal, Jan. 27, 1967, at 4, cols. 2-3.

tion industry during 1967 have been the highest on record. Victor Riesel reported in his column of May 31, 1967, that bulldozer operators represented by the International Union of Operating Engineers were on strike in Ohio "in a bid for wage hikes which would bring them $500 a week, inclusive of normal overtime pay."[3] Explaining further, Mr. Riesel said:[4]

> The union's "request" was for a pay *raise* of $92 a week for straight time and $121.70 a week with routine overtime. This did not include penalty time, or hazard time or special holiday overtime which sometimes develops when a contractor drives to meet his deadline after acts-of-God delays or, as in this case, the acts of some mighty men. . . . It appears that the Ohio Local . . . is asking for an average of from 46 to 55 percent increase over the current base pay.

While few were as ambitious as the Ohio bulldozer operators, the Bureau of National Affairs reported that construction unions had negotiated in the first half of 1967 average increases of thirty-three cents per hour, more than double the all-industry average of 13.7 cents per hour, and the highest since the Bureau had begun its surveys of wage settlements in 1949.[5] In discussions with homebuilders in Westchester County, New York, I was told repeatedly that wage raises negotiated there would by themselves require price increases of from $500 to $1000 on each home built this year.

In technologically progressive industries, the price-effects of substantial wage increases are softened, if not completely absorbed, by labor-saving machinery, new methods of production, and other cost-reducing devices. The construction industry, however, is apparently reconciled to a constant process of adding increased labor costs immediately to price, even when the demand for housing falls. One columnist,[6] writing in the Spring of 1967, urged prospective homeowners to "buy now," since, she felt, the wage increases recently negotiated by the building trades unions, often extending over three-year periods, could not help boosting housing prices in the years to come. She said: "Even during the worst of the construction slump in 1966, construction cost rose. Homebuilders are openly saying that home prices in 1967 will be at least 5 per cent higher than in 1966, and some put the rise at 10 per cent."[7]

If the building trades unions continue to gain in the future the relatively high wage increases that they have gained in the past, and if those increases are not balanced by increased productivity, housing costs may well climb out of reach of the mass market, perhaps completely out of sight. The result would be a recurrence of the phenomena which have characterized the construction industry so often in the

---

[3] Citizen Register (Ossining, N.Y.), May 31, 1967, at 11, col. 1.
[4] *Id.*
[5] Citizen Register (Ossining, N.Y.), July 21, 1967, at 19, cols. 5-8.
[6] Miss Sylvia Porter, *id.*
[7] *Id.*

past—a falling off of effective demand, leading to a worsening of present housing conditions and to underemployment, not only in the construction industry, but in all the many areas of the economy which prosper when construction activity is high.

U.S. Senator Abraham A. Ribicoff (of Connecticut) was undoubtedly preoccupied with these possibilities when, early in 1967, he urged the Senate to act boldly on construction problems, especially in urban areas.[8]   Among other things, he advocated a ten-year, $50-billion plan to eliminate and rebuild what he estimates at 4.5 million "substandard" housing units that now exist in the nation's metropolitan areas.   He also proposed an "institute for urban development" to examine ways of reducing the costs of housing by improving construction technology.[9]

The problem is evident. Both national housing policies and personal desires for improved housing require that something be done about construction costs and prices.   It is vain to look for miracles. The law of costs applies as rigorously in the construction industry—and to government or social objectives—as it does everywhere else.   Either labor costs are going to have to be checked, or cost-reducing technologies are going to have to be developed and introduced on a large scale into homebuilding as means of keeping increased labor costs from pushing the price of housing out of reach. These are the implications of Senator Ribicoff's recommendations, as they are, indeed, of any serious consideration of current events in the construction industry.

Not long after Senator Ribicoff's speech, however, the Supreme Court of the United States handed down a decision which is likely to lead to the frustration of many technological developments in the construction industry. In the *National Woodwork Manufacturers Association* case,[10] five of the nine Justices took the position that a union had the right to bargain for, and to strike to enforce, a rule against the use of prefinished or pre-assembled products on a construction job. I shall be dealing in detail with this decision later on. Here it is necessary to observe only that generally applauded housing goals are scarcely likely to be realized unless something is done about the ancient Luddite dread of advancing technology—a dread which I intend to demonstrate probably figured much more largely than did legal analysis in the majority opinion in the *National Woodwork* case.

II

Union Control of Labor and Costs

It seems desirable before going into legal analysis to set forth as simply as possible the patterns of conduct and the economic devices which the construction trades unions have developed over the years as means of raising labor costs or prices in the building

---

[8] N.Y. Times, Jan. 24, 1967, at 1, col. 8.
[9] *Id.*
[10] National Woodwork Mfrs. Ass'n v. NLRB, 386 U.S. 612 (1967).

industry. Such an exposition will put our subject in its most relevant context. That context is classic monopoly analysis.[11]

Insofar as it creates a social problem, monopoly must always involve one or another kind of abusive or coercive restriction of alternative sources of supply of the good or service in question. Michelangelo was in a class by himself as a sculptor, and he "monopolized" his own services as such. So long, however, as he refrained from preventing other sculptors from carving he could scarcely be thought of as posing a "monopoly problem" for society. People were free to seek the services of other sculptors without fear of reprisals or of harm from him.

The monopolist who creates a social problem is not content to allow free intercourse between those who demand and others who supply goods or services of the general kind which he supplies. He will probably go for help first to government, the most powerful agency of society, for government is physically capable of barring competition to a degree unequalled by any private agency. Moreover, contrary to frequently heard protestations, governments have historically been friendly to monopoly, and the government of the United States has been in recent years no exception to this historical rule.[12] Thus it is not surprising that the building trades unions, along with others (for example, the maritime unions), have resorted frequently to government as a means of ousting or limiting competition from both nonunion construction workers and competitive products. I refer here to such governmental measures as licensing laws, building codes, and wage determinations under public contracts laws.

Our concern here, however, is with private, nongovernmental practices aimed at eliminating competition from nonunion workers or from products which, by reducing labor costs, are competitive in exactly the same sense, economically, as lower-cost nonunion labor. These practices, which may be called "market controls" for lack of a better term, divide conveniently (though not distinctly) into two categories—namely "predatory practices" (borrowing from the antitrust literature) and "contractual restrictions."

A. Predatory Practices

By predatory practices I mean those coercive or near-coercive activities by means of which the construction unions, along with most other unions, make it physically or economically painful for nonunion labor to compete for jobs, or for builders and contractors to engage or to retain competitive labor. The extreme form of this type of monopolistic restriction is physical violence. A union may assault nonunion workers or sabotage a construction project employing such workers.[13] When it

---

[11] *See generally* L. Von Mises, Human Action 354-76 (1st ed. 1949), for the most definitive monopoly analysis that I have ever encountered, and the one followed in this article.

[12] *See* W. Adams & H. Gray, Monopoly in America: The Government as Promoter (1955).

[13] *See* Gulf Coast Bldg. & Constr. Trades Council v. F. R. Hoar & Son, Inc., 370 F.2d 746 (5th Cir. 1967).

eliminates competition in this fashion, the monopolization is almost as effective as it is when the supremely powerful paraphernalia of government are bent upon denying the public the benefits of competition.

A union may seek to control labor supply and costs less drastically by the activity known as "peaceful stranger picketing." For example, if a carpenter subcontractor employs nonunion men, the Brotherhood of Carpenters may employ one or more persons to patrol the construction project, usually with placards which may say as little as "The Carpenters on This Job are Nonunion Men," or as much as "This Project Is Unfair to Organized Labor; Union Workers Take Note; LABOR SOLIDARITY FOREVER!"[14]

As a general rule, such picketing will tend at least to embarrass operations at the construction site; often it will halt all operations. The Teamsters members who deliver construction materials may refuse to cross the picket line; or members of other construction trades unions employed on the project may refuse to work behind the picket line. In consequence, the builder or the general contractor who has engaged the nonunion carpentry subcontractor is likely to have second thoughts. He may put pressure on the latter to replace his nonunion men with members of the picketing Carpenters, or he may replace him with a unionized carpentry subcontractor.[15] In either case, the nonunion labor will have been ousted, and the Brotherhood of Carpenters will have effectively carried through a monopolistic, competition-excluding operation.

The same result may be and often is produced without picketing. As a member of the local building and construction joint trades council, the Brotherhood of Carpenters may get in touch directly with the appropriate officials of other unions whose members are working on the offending project. This direct contact may, through various channels in each union, possibly with varying degrees of effectiveness, cause either total or fragmentary work stoppages.[16] Similar pressures, leading to similar results, may be imposed in a number of other ways—for example, by means of blacklists or propaganda campaigns addressed to architects, builders, and prospective owners, exhorting them to refrain from dealing with nonunion contractors. Sometimes these campaigns are purly hortatory; at other times, the union will threaten to boycott in turn all who refuse to respond favorably.[17]

There is, of course, a material distinction between the physically violent methods of excluding nonunion labor, on the one hand, and the peaceful picketing, the voluntary cooperation among unions all belonging to the same trades council, and the blacklisting, on the other. The latter contain a consensual element absent in the former. Even when a union pipefitter respects the Carpenters' picket-line because he knows

[14] See Rommel-McFerran Co. v. Local 369, IBEW, 361 F.2d 658 (6th Cir. 1966).
[15] Id.
[16] See Building & Constr. Trades Council of Tampa, 132 N.L.R.B. 1564 (1961).
[17] The classic case was Bossert v. Dhuy, 221 N.Y. 342, 117 N.E. 582 (1917).

that he will be fined by his own union if he crosses it, there is a consensual foundation for his conduct. The fine will normally be based upon provisions in the union constitution or bylaws. Common law theory holds that union membership is a contractual relationship, with the terms of the contract set out in the union constitution and by-laws.[18] If those documents impose a duty upon members to refuse to work on picketed projects, or when so instructed by duly authorized union officials, it is the worker's own membership contract which requires him to quit working, not an external coercive influence. He has agreed to abide by his union's rules.[19]

The analysis is admittedly somewhat attenuated. The pipefitter may himself have joined the union only because, owing to the largely prevalent closed-shop conditions of the construction industry, he could not otherwise have gained employment as a pipefittter. Perhaps, indeed, he joined the union originally under a threat of physical violence. Or perhaps economically and physically coercive activities were inextricably intermingled in the long and complex history of his union's rise to power in the construction industry. For my own part, I consider the latter to be the most generally accurate explanation of the closed-shop conditions which prevail in the building industry.

Difficult or impossible as it may be to disentangle the roles played by physical violence and economic coercion, it will not do to disregard the distinction between them. Our traditions, our legal and economic principles, even our morals have long been shaped and directed along lines based upon the idea that physical violence is unequivocally unacceptable, whereas economic coercion may be tolerated in some cases and forbidden in others. There is a constraining element in almost all contracts; when it becomes strong enough to be called "duress" we sometimes hold that it invalidates the contract. But while the principle is there, the application has always been tricky.[20] As we shall see, this long-run uncertainty with respect to the social acceptability of economically coercive activities probably has more to do with the confusion of present labor relations law than any other single factor.

Although there are many other "predatory" practices, they are all extensions of the kinds we have covered. Thus, if the Carpenters refuse to work on a building because lumber supplies are coming from a nonunion mill, the competition of the nonunion millworkers is as much the target of the union's action as the more direct competition of the nonunion carpenters was in the case we have been considering. There is a tendency to designate a strike against the use of nonunion-made goods as a "product boycott." But whatever it may be called, it is the same case of union labor against nonunion labor that we have been considering all along. Here as there, the Carpenters Brotherhood is pursuing the normal monopolistic objective: exclusion of competition. To say that the case differs because the union carpenters are "only

---

[18] *Cf.* Mayer v. Journeymen Stone-Cutters' Ass'n, 47 N.J. Eq. 519, 20 A. 492 (Ch. 1890).
[19] *Cf.* NLRB v. Allis-Chalmers Mfg. Co., 388 U.S. 175 (1967).
[20] *Cf.* Henningsen v. Bloomfield Motors, Inc., 32 N.J. 358, 161 A.2d 69 (1960).

exercising the right to engage in a primary strike" does not establish much of a distinction. In all these cases the men who refuse to work are exercising what might equally be called a "right to strike." The pipefitter who refuses to work on a job employing nonunion carpenters reflects his own union's conception of where the interests of pipefitters lie. It would be extremely difficult to prove that the competitive effects differ from the one type of competition-ousting work stoppage to the other. If competition is being inhibited in the one, it is being no less inhibited in the other. Once the long step of prohibiting peacefully-conducted boycotts or strikes has been taken, any "line-drawing" among them has to be arbitrary—more so in some cases, less so in others, but still arbitrary in all, from the point of view of competitive effects.

Unionized carpenters may refuse to work because they object to the use of certain products incorporating steps in production which have in the past been done at the construction site. Pre-hung doors present a current example.[21] Historically the process of installing doors in a building has involved a number of construction-site operations, such as cutting the door to size, drilling for handles, fitting hinges, installing the jambs, and so on. Today entirely assembled door-units are available, so that carpenters at the jobsite need only insert the assembled unit between the roughed-in studs. With hourly labor rates as high as they have become, contractors naturally look with interest upon such means of reducing the time of journeymen carpenters on the job. We see here a classic example of the labor-cost-saving technological development, precisely the kind of development which would make it possible to pay construction carpenters higher hourly wages without raising the price of housing beyond the reach of consumers.

If the unionized carpenters refuse to install such pre-fitted doors, is their conduct any different in nature or effect from picketing a project which employs nonunion carpenters? Does it make a difference that the refusal to install pre-fitted doors applies as well to those assembled by union labor as to those assembled by nonunion labor? From the economic point of view it is extremely difficult to identify any significant distinction. The purpose is in any case to eliminate the competition offered by other men seeking to serve the same consumer demand or to fulfill the same productive function. As the consumers' mandatary,[22] directly or indirectly, the contractor who orders the pre-fitted doors, like the contractor who employs nonunion labor, does so because in one way or another he expects his labor costs to be reduced. It must be emphasized that the contractor is interested in total labor costs, which bear no necessary relationship to wage rates. Indeed total labor costs may be lower where higher hourly wage rates are paid; conversely total labor costs may be higher

---

[21] This was the case in National Woodwork Mfrs. Ass'n v. NLRB, 386 U.S. 612 (1967).

[22] *See generally* on the employer as agent for consumers, and on trade unions as organizations likely to abuse both society and nonunion workers, the dissenting opinion of Holmes, C.J., in Plant v. Woods, 176 Mass. 492, 504, 57 N.E. 1011, 1015 (1900).

where wage rates are lower. It is a question of how much production the contractor gets out of each hour's work.

Paradoxically, then, the unionized carpenters at the construction site may refuse to install pre-fitted doors even though the factory work involved in pre-fitting the doors was paid at an hourly rate equal to or even higher than that paid to the construction-site carpenters. But from the point of view of economics, which is to say from the point of view of society and of the consumer, the strike must nevertheless be considered an anticompetitive, cost-raising operation. Moreover, it is anticompetitive and cost-raising in precisely the same way as the other cases we have been considering.

Finally, from the point of view of the striking carpenters themselves their activity may be considered harmful. If the boycott of pre-fitted doors is allowed, and if it works, so too then must other such boycotts be allowed, with the result that the introduction of cost-saving technological developments will be hampered generally. The further consequence must be higher prices for housing and therefore less construction activity and less work for the unionized carpenters themselves.

Thus, it seems accurate to say that "work-preservation" product boycotts and boycotts more directly addressed to the elimination of competitive workers analyze out as substantially identical forms of conduct, regardless of the particular means (assuming only that the means are peaceful) used to effectuate them. Whether the means take the form of picketing, blacklisting, or a direct verbal request for a work stoppage or other kind of refusal to deal, on the one hand; or whether on the other it be a direct work stoppage in the form of a refusal, for example, to install pre-assembled products—in any case, economic pressure is exerted in order to discourage resort to competitive labor. In short, all the "predatory practices" typical of the construction trades unions, with the exception of violent conduct, are mere varieties of the same general species of action, with only insignificant distinctions among them. They all say, in effect: "If you deal with a competitor you will have to do without our services and without the services of unions, contractors, architects, and others who will cooperate with us in denying you their services, too."

B. Contractual Restrictions

By "contractual restrictions" I mean those provisions in collective agreements with either single employers or groups of employers which place a duty upon the employers (a) to insist upon union membership as a condition of employment, or (b) to deal only with other employers approved by the contracting union, or (c) to refrain from specifying products to which the contracting union is opposed. It will be seen immediately that such "contractual restrictions" are the "predatory practices" of the construction unions agreed to in advance.

Thus the agreement requiring union membership as a condition of employment —sometimes referred to as a "union-security" agreement and sometimes as a "compulsory-unionism" agreement—insures in advance that only union members will be employed; or that, if a nonunion man is hired, he will be required to join the union within a specified period if he wishes to be retained. If such an agreement is induced by a strike, a threatened strike, a picket-line, a boycott, or, above all, by violence, its kinship with the "predatory practices" may be seen quickly. Since virtually all compulsory-unionism agreements are induced in one or another such way, there is little practical point in discussing them further. They are monopolistic, competition-excluding devices in precisely the sense in which predatory practices are, to much the same degree, and subject to the same difficult line-drawing problems that exist when-ever an attempt is made to limit peaceful, consensual activities which contain elements of economic coercion.

Agreements requiring the contracting employer to refrain from dealing with certain other employers—often called "hot-cargo" agreements—again rest upon the interest of the contracting union in eliminating cost-reducing competition. More often than not, probably, the target of the "hot-cargo" agreement is a class of firms which the contracting union has tried unsuccessfully to "organize." Failing to organize such firms and thus to control (that is, usually, to raise) their labor costs, the union seeks to eliminate them. A classic example is presented by the Carpenters' drive, now well over a half-century old, to compel lumber mills all over the country to employ only members of the Carpenters Brotherhood.[23]

A variety of the "hot-cargo" contract sometimes referred to as a "product-boycott" calls for somewhat more discussion. In the well-known *Allen Bradley* case,[24] Local 3 of the International Brotherhood of Electrical Workers (IBEW) joined with New York City manufacturers of electrical products and contractors installing such products to prevent the use there of electrical products manufactured elsewhere, even when manufactured by firms employing members of other IBEW local unions. There is no apparent method by means of which the New York City manufacturers, acting alone, could have excluded the competitive products. But if IBEW Local 3 agreed to refuse to allow its members to install them, the exclusion could be accom-plished, since, by one means or another, Local 3 had established closed-shop, monopoly control electrical installation in the city. Representing both construction elec-tricians and employees of the electrical products manufacturers, IBEW Local 3 con-sidered it advantageous to restrict the competition offered even by members of other IBEW locals, for doing so would provide more demand for the services of its own members and in all probability higher pay. Hence IBEW Local 3 agreed with both the manufacturers association and the contractors association to boycott electrical products not manufactured in New York City.

The *Lumber Products Association* case[25] revealed an identical concert of objectives

---

[23] *See* Bossert v. Dhuy, 221 N.Y. 342, 117 N.E. 582 (1917).
[24] Allen Bradley Co. v. Local 3, IBEW, 325 U.S. 797 (1945).
[25] Lumber Products Ass'n v. United States, 144 F.2d 546 (9th Cir. 1944).

and action among millwork producers, construction contractors, and the Brotherhood of Carpenters in the San Francisco area. There the Carpenters agreed to refuse to work with lower-cost lumber products coming from Washington, Oregon, and Wisconsin—where, unlike San Francisco, millwork was produced on a large-scale, rationally-organized, low-cost basis.

The law reports reveal similar arrangements among manufacturers, contractors, and building trades unions in most of the other segments of the construction industry.[26] The basic requirements seem to be closed-shop control by the union involved and a municipality or other geographical area which yields readily to a monopolistic type of enclosure. Political connivance is probably highly important, but the operating mechanism is the union's ability to control all installation of the products in question.

C. Monopoly and the Public Interest

Reviewing the broad spectrum of monopolistic or competition-excluding activities of the construction unions which I have outlined, we may observe that the one feature common to all is the attempt to gain for members of the union involved control of labor functions for which other workers, union and nonunion, are willing to compete. Seeking to gain higher returns for their members, the construction unions know that they must control supply if they are to be successful. They may control supply directly by excluding competitive workers, or indirectly by excluding the products of competitive workers.

To view the situation as one involving a conflict between "labor and capital" or "management and unions" is to misunderstand it. The conflict is between workers, not only fundamentally, but virtually exclusively, with specifically employer-interests involved only marginally and tangentially. From the point of view of the public interest, the basic questions to be asked in formulating legal policy are: How far shall unions be allowed to go in attempting to increase labor costs and consumer prices above the levels they would reach in free markets? What kinds of coercive conduct practiced by unions against nonunion workers and members of other unions should be allowed? Is there any sound public-policy basis for prohibiting some forms of economically coercive, monopolistic conduct while holding privileged other forms which are indistinguishable from the first in terms of economic purpose and effect?

As we review current legal developments we shall see that clear, consistent, and

---

[26] *E.g.*, United States v. Employing Plasterers Ass'n of Chicago, 347 U.S. 186 (1954); Gilmour v. Wood, Wire & Metal Lathers Local 74, 223 F. Supp. 236 (N.D. Ill. 1963); United States v. Hamilton Glass Co., 155 F. Supp. 878 (N.D. Ill. 1957) (glaziers); United States v. Bay Area Painters & Decorators Joint Comm., 49 F. Supp. 733 (N.D. Cal. 1943); United States v. Central Supply Ass'n, 40 F. Supp. 964 (N.D. Ohio 1941), 6 F.R.D. 526 (N.D. Ohio 1947) (plumbers); United States v. Carrozzo, 3 CCH Lab. Cas. ¶ 60,282 (N.D. Ill. 1941), *aff'd per curiam sub nom.*, United States v. Hod Carriers Dist. Council, 313 U.S. 539 (1941) (hod carriers); Building Contractors Employers Ass'n v. Gugliemelli, 128 N.Y.L.J. 59, 22 CCH Lab. Cas. ¶ 67,065 (N.Y. Sup. Ct. 1952) (masons).

coherent thinking along these lines is sadly lacking in some of the relevant legislation and judicial decisions.

III

NATIONAL LABOR POLICY AND RESTRICTIVE UNION PRACTICES

A. Regulation of Predatory Practices

If we turn first to what I have been calling "predatory practices," we find the statutory prescriptions largely consistent but interpretation confused and administration weak. There is no doubt that trade-union violence is as unlawful as any other kind. Besides violating common-law principles and state laws, it also violates section 8(b)(1)(A) of the National Labor Relations Act,[27] which makes it an unfair practice for a union to restrain or coerce employees in the exercise of their right to refrain from joining unions, from bargaining collectively, and from participating in concerted activities.[28] On the other hand, the National Labor Relations Board frequently finds it extraordinarily difficult to attribute to unions the responsibility for violence on picket lines which the unions themselves have set up for the purpose of blocking access to the picketed premises.[29] Moreover, although the Supreme Court has clearly indicated a belief that the Labor Board has power to make unions pay for the harm caused by their violence,[30] the Board continues to insist that it does not have such power.[31] The Board has never ordered a union to compensate employees for the wages they have lost when a violent and obstructive picket line has prevented them from reporting for work. A mere cease-and-desist order after violence has occurred and the dispute has ended carries little deterrent effect. Since the Board imposes no effective deterrent, it may fairly be said that, under the Board's administration, the Taft-Hartley policy against trade-union violence has been less effective than it might have been. If this form of monopolistic union conduct is to be checked, therefore, Congress must specifically provide for appropriate sanctions in future legislation.[32]

Stranger-picketing of a construction project by a union seeking to oust a nonunion subcontractor has long been considered an unfair labor practice. Section 8(b)(4)(A) of the Taft-Hartley Act (which became section 8(b)(4)(B)[33] in 1959, with the passage of the Landrum-Griffin amendments) made it an unfair practice for a union to

---

[27] 29 U.S.C. § 158(b)(1)(A) (1964).

[28] The leading NLRB decision is International Longshoremen's Union, 79 N.L.R.B. 1487 (1948). For a recent case involving violence by a construction union, see Gulf Coast Bldg. & Constr. Trades Council v. F. R. Hoar & Son, Inc., 370 F.2d 746 (5th Cir. 1967).

[29] See, e.g., Retail Store Union, 133 N.L.R.B. 1555 (1961).

[30] See UAW v. Russell, 356 U.S. 634 (1958), especially where, speaking for the Court, Justice Burton said of a person who had lost wages as a result of union violence, "We assume, for the purpose of the argument, that the Board would have had authority to award back pay to Russell." Id. at 641.

[31] The leading Board decision is United Furniture Workers, 84 N.L.R.B. 563 (1949).

[32] See generally S. PETRO, HOW THE NLRB CAN STOP UNION VIOLENCE (Labor Policy Ass'n, 1958), for a more extended critique of the Board's policy on violence.

[33] 29 U.S.C. § 158(b)(4)(B) (1964).

induce a work stoppage where an object was forcing or requiring one employer to cease doing business with another. Picketing of a construction project on which a nonunion subcontractor is engaged falls comfortably within the prohibition: the immediate object is to induce or encourage workers in the other trades to cease working till the nonunion subcontractor is dismissed, and thus the requisite objective of fracturing a business relationship may also readily be inferred. Over contentions that such picketing is simply "primary"action—not a "secondary boycott"—the Supreme Court of the United States held in the *Denver* case, as early as 1951, that a plain violation of the statute was involved.[34]

In the years since the Taft-Hartley Act was passed, and since the *Denver* case was decided, the Labor Board has found numerous loopholes in the proscriptions of section 8(b)(4). These loopholes have acquired such exotic names as "roving situs," "common situs," "allies," "primary action," and so on.[35] Upon occasion, as we shall see, a construction union manages to slide through one or another of these loopholes by fitting its violation of the Act precisely into the requisite mold. But employers are often astute to checkmate such conduct by appropriate adjustments of the construction project.

Comprehensive treatment of all the moves and countermoves occasioned by the Labor Board's jurisprudence would take much more time and space than are available here. We shall have to content ourselves with one example. The Labor Board's "roving situs" doctrine holds that where the employer with whom a union is disputing has no fixed situs which may be picketed "satisfactorily," the union may follow the "situs" till it comes to rest somewhere, and picket it there.[36] Translated into realistic language, what this means is that the Board gives unions a privilege to picket the employer at the location where the picketing is likely to do the union the most good and the employer and his nonunion employees the most harm. Thus, if the Teamsters wish to compel unionization of truckdrivers who do not themselves wish to join, it will do the union little good to picket the owner of the trucks at his home terminal; picketing there will impose no coercive pressure upon either the owner or his employees. Accordingly the Board holds, under what are called the "Moore-Drydock Rules,"[37] that in a roving situs situation the union may picket the trucks or other such "situs" at the terminal points where they come into contact with someone who, by respecting the picket line, will put pressure on the recalcitrant employer and employees to accept and recognize the union. It is necessary, however, for the union to hold its mouth just right if it wishes the cover of the "Moore-Drydock Rules." It must identify the roving situs as the sole object of the picketing

---

[34] NLRB v. Denver Bldg. & Constr. Trades Council, 341 U.S. 675 (1951).

[35] *See generally* S. PETRO, HOW THE NLRB REPEALED TAFT-HARTLEY (Labor Policy Ass'n, 1958), for an extended review of the Board's doctrines.

[36] The leading Board decision is Teamsters Local 807, 87 N.L.R.B. 502 (1949).

[37] Sailors' Union of the Pacific, 92 N.L.R.B. 547 (1950).

and disavow any suggestion that the dispute is with the employer located at the picketing site.[38]

Probably because the construction unions rarely are interested in organizing the nonunion employees of offending subcontractors—their interest lying mainly instead in replacing the nonunion subcontractor with a unionized one—the "roving situs" loophole has never been a comfortable fit for them. The United States Court of Appeals for the Sixth Circuit has indeed recently affirmed a Board finding that a construction union had availed itself properly of the "Moore-Drydock Rules."[39] But the loophole will not often be useful if employers continue to establish "separate gates" for the employees of nonunion subcontractors on construction projects. When such separate gates are used, the union must picket only there; and of course picketing so confined will not act as a signal to workers in the other trades.[40]

The efficacy of stranger picketing as a means of restricting competition from nonunion workers has been substantially reduced since the enactment of the Landrum-Griffin Law in 1959, and particularly of section 8(b)(7).[41] That provision outlaws stranger picketing for recognition or organizational purposes where (a) the employer is lawfully recognizing another union, or (b) an election has been held among the picketed employees within the preceding year, or (c) in any event for more than thirty days without seeking an election. The last subdivision is qualified by a proviso which exculpates picketing designed solely to inform the public of the existence of a labor dispute, providing such picketing does not have the effect of inducing a work stoppage. Only last year, the Ninth Circuit upheld the Board in finding that the Carpenters violated section 8(b)(4), despite the fact that the picketing placards at a construction project were "Directed to Consumers Only."[42] The picketing having induced a pipefitter to walk off the job, the probability is that it would also have been held a violation of section 8(b)(7) had the complaint been framed in terms of that section.

It may be concluded from the foregoing review that the various statutory restrictions upon peaceful but coercive union methods of ousting nonunion labor are being applied with some consistency. A decision handed down on June 30, 1967, suggests that the Labor Board may be inclined to apply the law in the future with even more regard for congressional intent. The case involved picketing of a construction project by the Sheet Metal Workers Union as a means of ousting a nonunion subcontractor.[43] Cooperating with the Sheet Metal Workers, the Bricklayers' business agent instructed union bricklayers to respect the picket line. When some refused

[38] Id. at 549.
[39] Rommel-McFerran Co. v. Local 369, IBEW, 361 F.2d 658 (6th Cir. 1966).
[40] See Orange Belt Dist. Council of Painters v. NLRB, 361 F.2d 70 (D.C. Cir. 1966); Building & Constr. Trades Council of New Orleans, 155 N.L.R.B. 319 (1965).
[41] 29 U.S.C. § 158(b)(7) (1964).
[42] NLRB v. Carpenters Local 550, 367 F.2d 953 (9th Cir. 1966).
[43] Bricklayers Local 2, 166 N.L.R.B. No. 26 (1967).

to do so, the Bricklayers Union fined them $25 each. In a 2-1 decision, with Member Brown dissenting, the Labor Board ruled the act of fining disobedient members amounted in itself to the inducement or encouragement of a work stoppage prohibited by section 8(b)(4)—and ordered the Bricklayers to make restitution of the amounts of the fines. Member Brown's dissent was only to the restitution order, which he thought exceeded the Board's powers. But since the Act empowers the Board to issue any affirmative order reasonably calculated to remedy unfair practices and to effectuate the policies of the Act,[44] it would seem that the restitution order lay well within the Board's powers. Perhaps, now that the Board has issued a money order in a section 8(b)(4) case it will reconsider its anomalous opinion that it is without power to make compensatory money awards in cases in which unions have caused wage losses by violent conduct.

So far as peaceful economic coercion by construction unions is concerned, the pressing need now is for speedy, consistent, and vigorous enforcement of the substantive law. On the assumption that peaceful anticompetitive conduct is a fit subject for government regulation, the statute and to a lesser degree the substantive interpretations are comprehensive and coherent. If enforcement were improved, the prospects of keeping the monopolistic tendencies of the construction industries under control would be much brighter than they are. Quite possibly, completely effective enforcement of the competitive policies of the Labor Relations Act will never come so long as the Labor Board has a virtual monopoly of enforcement, for many builders and contractors will yield to unlawful union demands merely because it is so complicated and takes so long to get relief via the Labor Board's processes.[45] If the Norris-LaGuardia Act[46] were repealed, or even if it were only amended to permit direct suits for injunctive relief against union unfair practices, it seems fairly predictable that the resistance of builders and contractors would grow—and that the present highly monopolistic control over the labor market exerted by the construction unions would be brought down to tolerable proportions.

B. Regulation of Contractual Restrictions

1. The Closed Shop

It is a matter of common gossip in the trade that, the Taft-Hartley Act to the contrary notwithstanding, closed shop conditions largely prevail in the construction industry. The act itself prohibits the closed shop and all other contractual arrange-

---

[44] § 10(c), 29 U.S.C. § 160(c) (1964). *See generally* S. PETRO, *supra* note 32; Note, *Back Pay Awards Against Unions Under the LMRA,* 51 COLUM. L. REV. 508 (1951).

[45] *See* NLRB v. Lexington Elec. Prods. Co., 283 F.2d 54 (3d Cir. 1960), where the Board imposed a heavy penalty on an employer for participating in an unlawful compulsory-unionism agreement, despite the fact that the employer resisted till he learned that the Board would not take action against the union's unlawful pressures.

[46] 29 U.S.C. §§ 101-15 (1964). This Act, generally speaking, virtually erases the power of the federal courts to grant injunctive relief in labor disputes where the petitioner is a private party.

ments which require union membership as a hiring condition.[47]   Generally speaking, majority unions may negotiate for only such compulsory-unionism agreements as require union membership after employment has begun, although in section 8(f) the act permits construction unions to negotiate such contracts even before they have established majority status.

For a certain period beginning during the Eisenhower administration, the Labor Board had been holding that hiring through unions violated the act even though the unions undertook contractually to refer union and nonunion men indiscriminately for employment.[48]   However, the rule is now different.   Unions may now bargain and even strike to gain administrative control of the hiring process unless the contractual proposal on its face provides for discrimination in favor of union members.[49]   As Judge Bell put it in a recent decision, "No doubt union membership will be encouraged under the arrangement, indeed it may be a boon to the union; nevertheless such an arrangement does not constitute compulsory unionism so long as the arrangement is not employed in a discriminatory manner."[50]

The prevalence of closed shop conditions in the construction industry undoubtedly traces in part to such restrictive interpretation of the national policy against compulsory unionism.   Beyond much question, moreover, hiring through unions in the construction trades rests to some extent on valid economic grounds: it is simply most convenient and even most economic in some cases to rely upon unions and their hiring halls for competent journeymen.   But to a substantial extent, probably, contractors yield to effective closed shop conditions because the construction unions are in a position to hurt them badly if they resist, and because the law affords no speedy and effective protection to a resisting employer.[51]   Injunctive relief in state courts—even in states which have right-to-work-laws—is barred by the pre-emption doctrine;[52] and it is barred in the federal courts by the Norris-LaGuardia Act.[53]   The employer confronted by a union demand for effective closed shop conditions must either yield or rely upon the long, drawn-out processes of the Labor Board.   When it finally comes, the relief afforded by the Board is too little, and much too late.[54]

Considerable publicity has been directed in recent years to the tendency among construction unions to deny admission to members of minority groups, and it is widely

---

[47] §§ 8(a)(3), (b)(2), 29 U.S.C. §§ 158(a)(3), (b)(2) (1964), permit a modified type of "union-shop" agreement under which union membership of a highly limited type may be required after a person has been hired.
[48] See NLRB v. H. K. Ferguson Co., 337 F.2d 205 (5th Cir. 1964).
[49] The basic Supreme Court decisions were: Local 60, Carpenters v. NLRB, 365 U.S. 651 (1961); Local 357, Teamsters v. NLRB, 365 U.S. 667 (1961); NLRB v. News Syndicate Co., 365 U.S. 695 (1961).
[50] NLRB v. Houston Chapter, Associated Gen. Contractors, 349 F.2d 449, 453 (5th Cir. 1965).
[51] See, e.g., NLRB v. Lexington Elec. Prods. Co., 283 F.2d 54 (3d Cir. 1960).
[52] Local 438, Construction & Gen. Laborers' Union v. Curry, 371 U.S. 542 (1963); Local 429, IBEW v. Farnsworth & Chambers Co., 353 U.S. 969 (1957).   Compare Retail Clerks, Local 1625 v. Schermerhorn, 373 U.S. 746 (1963).
[53] 29 U.S.C. §§ 101-15 (1964).
[54] See NLRB v. Lexington Elec. Prods. Co., 283 F.2d 54 (3d Cir. 1960); Note, supra note 44.

recognized that this denial of membership amounts to a denial of employment. Certainly the ambitions of Negroes for social and economic advancement would be helped along if they had easier access to the skilled trades, for such has been the path of progress in the case of members of many other minority groups. Moreover, general consumer interests would be well served if the severe shortages which have prevailed in the skilled trades for many years could be eased.

The case for breaking down the closed shop conditions of the building industry is thus a particularly strong one. Whether or not such conditions can ever be removed completely, one may doubt—especially since, as has been noted, they rest to some extent on valid economic grounds. But if all forms of compulsory unionism were unequivocally outlawed, and if employers were granted direct access to the courts for relief from union pressures, the chances are good that entry into the skilled trades would be facilitated for members of minority groups, and that labor market conditions in the construction industry would thus be eased. Undoubtedly wage rates would remain high; they are bound to be so as long as our government continues its inflationary course. But the upward pressures would be bound to diminish; construction costs, it may be hoped, would quit climbing so steeply; the industry might enjoy a steadier future than its boom-and-bust past; and the consumer would certainly be better off.

2. "Hot Cargo" Contracts

Congress has long been preoccupied with union conduct aimed at restricting employer access to competitive labor and product markets and has prohibited it in the strongest and plainest terms. Yet the Labor Board and the Supreme Court of the United States have established monopolistic privileges for trade unions of the precise kind which Congress has condemned. Despite the most unequivocal congressional expression of intent to outlaw "hot cargo" contracts, the Labor Board and the Court have held that they are lawful where designed to preserve for the participating union's members the kinds of work that they have traditionally performed. These decisions are likely to have antisocial consequences throughout the economy. But their impact will be especially costly in the construction industry, where technological progress has been delayed so long and is so pressingly needed.

Before reviewing the authorities, let us briefly inspect the statutory scheme. Twenty years ago, in enacting the Taft-Hartley Act by overwhelming majorities in both the House and the Senate, Congress demonstrated a clear intent to prohibit unions from dictating or even attempting to dictate the relations which employers might form with other persons, whether workers or other businessmen. The principal measure was section 8(b)(4).[55] That section made it an unfair practice for a union to induce or encourage a work stoppage where "an object" was forcing or requiring any person to "cease using, selling, handling, transporting, or otherwise

[55] Ch. 120, § 101, 61 Stat. 141 (1947), *as amended,* 29 U.S.C. §§ 158(b)(4)(A), (B) (1964).

dealing in the products of any other producer, processor, or manufacturer, or to cease doing business with any other person."

There would seem to be little question that a faithful application of the literal meaning and the spirit of the foregoing language should have led to the effective prohibition of any attempt to negotiate for, to enter into, or to enforce a "hot cargo" contract. For the essence of such contracts is that they require employers to cease dealing with other employers or in their products. Moreover, a "hot cargo" clause, like every other bargaining objective of a union, is secured by either a strike or a threatened strike. Employers have a common law right to deal or not to deal with other employers as they wish. They do not need a collective agreement in order either to establish or to exercise that right. The collective agreement can only take it away; can only involve a concession by the employer to the union. Like every other concession, it is yielded because the employer would rather yield than take a strike. Thus, negotiating for a "hot cargo" contract would seem clearly to involve a violation of section 8(b)(4).

Moreover, the contract itself, once entered, would seem equally to violate the section. This conclusion follows because, once negotiated, the contract is itself a continuous inducement to a work stoppage whenever the employer deals with, or in the products of, the employer proscribed by the contract. The statute does not exclude contracts from the category of prohibited inducements. It outlaws inducements without qualification. To hold that the contract does not amount to the kind of inducement prohibited by the statute would be to hold that a private contract supersedes a congressionally declared policy—something which the Labor Board has consistently denied in all cases except those involving "hot cargo" agreements.[56]

Finally, if due respect is to be accorded to statutory language, it would seem that an actual work stoppage occasioned by the employer's flouting the "hot cargo" clause should be held a violation of section 8(b)(4). For a work stoppage induced by the employer's doing business with some other person falls squarely within the language of section 8(b)(4); hence it could be exonerated only on the theory that the contract negated the statute. But that theory must be rejected on the ground stated above.

Notwithstanding the strength and the clarity of the foregoing analysis, the Labor Board held for some time that a union did not violate section 8(b)(4) either in negotiating for, or entering, or even in striking to enforce a "hot cargo" contract.[57] Later the Board held that while the contract was in itself unobjectionable, a strike to

---

[56] National Licorice Co. v. NLRB, 309 U.S. 350 (1940); Utility Workers v. Consolidated Edison Co., 309 U.S. 261 (1940); cf. Garner v. Teamsters Local 776, 346 U.S. 485 (1953); Wallace Corp. v. NLRB, 323 U.S. 248 (1944); Sun Ship Employees Ass'n v. NLRB, 139 F.2d 744 (3d Cir. 1943); NLRB v. General Motors Corp., 116 F.2d 306 (7th Cir. 1940).

[57] Local 135, Teamsters, 105 N.L.R.B. 740 (1953); Teamsters, Local 294, 87 N.L.R.B. 972 (1949), enforced, Rabouin v. NLRB, 195 F.2d 906 (2d Cir. 1952) (L. Hand, J., dissenting). See generally S. PETRO, supra note 35, at 103-07, for a detailed review of the NLRB's views of the legality of "hot cargo" action.

enforce it constituted a violation of section 8(b)(4).[58] Still later, the Board came to the conclusion that a "hot cargo" clause was itself unlawful in the trucking industry, on the theory that common carriers have a duty to serve all without discrimination.[59]

The Board's middle position received the approval of the Supreme Court in 1958, in the *Sand Door* case.[60] There the Court held that while the contract itself was lawful, the union could not enforce it by calling a work stoppage when the employer departed from the agreement. Incidentally, the contract in *Sand Door* provided that "workmen shall not be required to handle nonunion material." Nevertheless the general contractors involved in the case ordered doors from the Sand Door & Plywood Company, a nonunion firm. On orders from the business agent of the Brotherhood of Carpenters, the carpenters refused to install the doors.

Sand Door was much in the minds of Congressmen in 1959, when they were considering the proposals which were to become the Landrum-Griffin Law.[61] They were concerned especially with the Court's holding that the contract was in itself lawful. This holding, they felt, exposed employers to legal actions for breach of contract. Obviously wishing to make completely effective the Taft-Hartley policy which the Board and the Supreme Court had in part frustrated, they enacted measures which explicitly outlawed union pressures designed to impose "hot-cargo" agreements, as well as the agreements themselves. Landrum-Griffin also continued in section 8(b)(4)(B) the stautory language which the Supreme Court had applied in *Sand Door* to outlaw work stoppages enforcing "hot cargo" clauses. The new provisions are found in sections 8(b)(4)(i) and (ii)(A) and 8(e).[62]

The former makes it an unfair practice for a union to induce or encourage any kind of a work stoppage or to "threaten, coerce, or restrain" any person where an object is to force or require him to enter into any agreement prohibited by section 8(e). Section 8(e) in turn provides as follows:

> It shall be an unfair labor practice for any labor organization and any employer to enter into any contract or agreement, express or implied, whereby such employer ceases or refrains or agrees to cease or refrain from handling, using, selling, transporting or otherwise dealing in any of the products of any other employer, or to cease doing business with any other person, and any contract or agreement entered into heretofore or hereafter containing such an agreement shall be to such extent unenforcible and void . . . .

The section contains three provisos, two entirely negating the Act's boycott proscriptions in the garment industry, and one fragmentarily modifying the section 8(e) boycott proscriptions in the construction industry. The latter provides that

---

[58] Teamsters Local 554, 110 N.L.R.B. 1769, (1965); Marie T. Reilly, 110 N.L.R.B. 1742 (1954).
[59] Local 728, Teamsters, 119 N.L.R.B. 339 (1957).
[60] Local 1976, Carpenters v. NLRB, 357 U.S. 93 (1958).
[61] *See* National Woodwork Mfrs. Ass'n v. NLRB, 386 U.S. 612, 634-44 (1967).
[62] 29 U.S.C. §§ 158(b)(4)(i), (ii)(A), 158(e) (1964).

nothing in this subsection (e) shall apply to an agreement between a labor organization and an employer in the construction industry relating to the contracting or
subcontracting of work to be done at the site of the construction, alteration, paint-
ing, or repair of a building, structure, or other work.

Read sensibly in connection with the enacting clause, this proviso would privilege,
say, the Carpenters Brotherhood in negotiating an agreement establishing its jurisdiction over given work at the construction site. For example, the Carpenters might
insist that installing wallboard should be a function for carpenters rather than lathers.
The emphasis in the proviso on construction-site work and its silence with respect to
the product boycotts prohibited by both section 8(b)(4) and the enacting clause of
section 8(e) have clear import. They necessarily imply that Congress apparently intended by the enacting clause of section 8(e) to keep construction unions from
interfering with the employer's choice of product, while permitting them to attempt
to induce construction contractors to allocate work at the building site in certain
ways. Thus, in our example, the carpenter would not be permitted to exclude the
wallboard itself, although they could lawfully bargain for the job of installing it.
This interpretation fits smoothly and well with other congressional policies applicable
in the construction industry. For example, in section 10(k) of the Act, Congress has
encouraged the development of private arbitration techniques for the settlement of
jurisdictional disputes.[63] The construction-site work proviso reflects the same desire
to promote consensual work-allocations in the building industry.

Notwithstanding the tolerably simple and clear intent of section 8(b)(4)(A) and
section 8(e) thus revealed, the Labor Board—and more recently the Supreme Court,
too—have already managed to confuse its meaning and sharply to reduce its effectiveness. The Board has been holding that construction unions may strike in order
to secure "hot cargo" clauses, if the clauses bear any relationship to work which has
ever been done at the construction site.[64] The theory is that if certain work has
been done at the site in the past, an agreement forestalling the use of products incorporating that work comes within the privilege established by the construction-site
provision.[65]

The Board's theory is carried through with some coherence. For example, it
holds that if a contractor is bound by specifications calling for the use of certain
products, a union may not lawfully refuse to install those products even though they
incorporate work historically done at construction sites.[66] Again, the Board withholds

---

[63] Cf. Carey v. Westinghouse Elec. Corp., 375 U.S. 261 (1964); NLRB v. Radio Engineers, Local
1212, 364 U.S. 573 (1961); Local 68, Wood, Wire & Metal Lathers, 142 N.L.R.B. 1073 (1963).

[64] For a clear account of the Board's position, see NLRB v. Muskegon Bricklayers Local 5, 55 CCH Lab.
Cas. ¶ 11,996 (6th Cir. 1967). See also NLRB v. IBEW, Local 683, 359 F.2d 385 (6th Cir. 1966); NLRB
v. Local 217, Plumbers, 361 F.2d 160 (1st Cir. 1966).

[65] But not if the agreement reserves the right to cease work if any nonunion workers, regardless of
craft, are employed. Cf. NLRB v. Muskegon Bricklayers Local 5, 55 CCH Lab. Cas. ¶ 11,996 (6th Cir.
1967).

[66] See National Woodwork Mfrs. Ass'n v. NLRB, 386 U.S. 612, 615-16 nn.2 & 3 (1967).

approval from "hot cargo" clauses addressed expressly to nonunion-made products as such. In short, the Board holds consistently that "hot cargo" clauses are valid only when they are narrowly and essentially confined to preserving work under the contractor's control that has traditionally been done at the job-site.

In his opinion for the bare majority which upheld the Board's decision in the *National Woodwork* case, Mr. Justice Brennan adopted a far more complex and far less acceptable mode of analysis. While bowing frequently to the primacy of congressional intent and to the necessity of applying the "spirit" of statutes,[67] what he actually did amounted to a thorough flouting of both.

National Woodwork is the case involving a refusal by union carpenters to install pre-assembled doors. The Carpenters Brotherhood had negotiated a collective agreement with a contractor's association. Rule seventeen of the agreement provided that no member of the Brotherhood would "handle . . . any doors . . . which have been fitted prior to being furnished on the job."[68] Rule seventeen also prohibited nonunion-made materials, but the Labor Board held that the bocyott of nonunion materials was an unfair practice, and the union did not appeal that holding, so it did not figure in the Supreme Court's opinion.[69]

Although Mr. Justice Brennan did not concede that section 8(e) was unambiguous, he said that even if it were clear on its face the Court would still be obliged to apply it consistently with the "spirit" of the legislation.[70] He then proceeded to develop what Mr. Justice Stewart, dissenting, called a "protracted review of legislative and decisional history in an effort to show that the clear words of the statute should be disregarded in these cases."[71]

In support of his conclusion that sections 8(b)(4)(B) and 8(e) were not intended to outlaw "work-preservation" product boycotts, Mr. Justice Brennan did cover considerable ground. The basic framework of his analysis, however, is astonishingly simple, once uncovered. His syllogism runs as follows: Congress intended to forbid secondary boycotts; work-preservation product boycotts are primary in character; hence they are not prohibited.

Some ten years ago I wrote a long, exhaustively-documented technical monograph demonstrating that the "primary-secondary" dichotomy was a pure figment of the Labor Board's imagination, bearing no relationship to the objectives of Congress as set out in either the Taft-Hartley Act or its legislative history.[72] Moreover, the weight of authority in the federal courts, till the Supreme Court imposed the Board's dichotomy

---

[67] *E.g., id.* at 619, 644.

[68] *Id.* at 615 n.2.

[69] *Id.* at 616 n.3.

[70] *Id.* at 619.

[71] *Id.* at 650.

[72] S. PETRO, *supra* note 35, especially at 35-49, 71-110, where the legislative history of the Taft-Hartley Act is comprehensively reviewed in order to demonstrate that neither it nor the statutory language supported the "primary-secondary" dichotomy.

on them,[73] was of the same opinion. For example, the Ninth Circuit said that "the statute . . . does not use the terms 'hot cargo,' 'picketing the product,' or 'secondary boycott.' It broadly sweeps within its prohibition an entire pattern of industrial warfare deemed by Congress to be harmful to the public interest."[74] Writing for the Second Circuit, Judge Augustus Hand said that "it seems idle . . . to argue that only such 'secondary boycotts' as were unlawful at common law, or under the law of some particular state fall within the prohibitions of [section 8(b)(4)]."[75] The Fifth Circuit perhaps put the weakness of the "primary-secondary" dichotomy in the clearest form when it said:[76]

> The statute clearly provides a remedy for the type of conduct engaged in by the union, without resort to any distinction between primary and secondary activities. If the union's activities come within the language of the statute, they constitute an unfair labor practice, regardless of whether they might have been considered a true "secondary boycott" under the old common law or any of the modern and popular theories.

In the face of the foregoing it is extremely difficult to accept Justice Brennan's assertion that "judicial decisions interpreting the broad language of § 8(b)(4)(A) of the Taft-Hartley Act uniformly [sic] limited its application to such 'secondary' situations";[77] or to accept his reference to "the scholarly acceptance of this primary-secondary dichotomy."[78]

In an attempt to demonstrate that section 8(b)(4) of the Taft-Hartley Act was totally preoccupied with "secondary" conduct, Justice Brennan argued that sub-division (B) thereof dealt with a situation where pressure was brought upon one employer to force another to recognize an uncertified union; that subdivision (C) forbade one union to induce a work stoppage in order to compel recognition by an employer who was dealing with another, certified, union; and that subdivision (D) prohibited work stoppages designed to compel an employer to assign to the strikers work which he had already assigned to members of another union.[79]

All these subdivisions, said Brennan, were "limited to protecting employers in the position of neutrals between contending parties."[80] Or again: "The central theme pervading these provisions of protection for the neutral employer confirms the assurance of those sponsoring the section that in subsection (A) Congress likewise

---

[73] Principally in NLRB v. International Rice Milling Co., 341 U.S. 665 (1951).

[74] Printing Union, Local 388 v. LeBaron, 171 F.2d 331, 334 (9th Cir. 1948).

[75] NLRB v. Wine Workers Union, Local 1, 178 F.2d 584, 587 (2d Cir. 1949).

[76] International Rice Milling Co. v. NLRB, 183 F.2d 21, 26 (5th Cir. 1950), rev'd, 341 U.S. 665 (1951).

[77] 386 U.S. at 626. Justice Stewart's dissenting opinion accepts Justice Brennan's version of the "primary-secondary" dichotomy but feels that the Carpenters' boycott of pre-assembled doors is a violation of § 8(e), anyway. Id. at 651-52.

[78] Id. at 626 n.16.

[79] Id. at 625-26.

[80] Id. at 625.

meant to protect the employer only from union pressures designed to involve him in disputes not his own."[81]

The subdivisions cited by Justice Brennan are far from establishing his conclusion. It must be noted in the first place that Justice Brennan left out a significant feature of section 8(b)(4)(A). That section includes a clause which makes it an unfair practice for a union to strike where an object is forcing or requiring "any employer or self-employed person to join any labor or employer organization." Quite obviously, under any presently prevailing concept of the "secondary boycott," such a strike would not be considered "secondary." This clause of section 8(b)(4)(A) discloses the basic weakness of Justice Brennan's analysis. It is too bad he did not notice its existence.

However, the analysis is insupportable anyway, and section 8(b)(4)(D)—when presented fully—quite adequately reveals the shortcomings of his analysis. Subdivision (D) does not limit itself to work assignment disputes between contending unions, as Justice Brennan apparently believed. On the contrary, it forbids a union to strike for jobs, not only when those jobs are being filled by members of another union—but also when the jobs have been assigned unilaterally by the employer to nonunion men. The full relevant text makes it unlawful for a union to force or require "any employer to assign particular work to employees in a particular labor organization or in a particular trade, craft, or class rather than to employees in another labor organization *or in another trade, craft, or class.*"[82]

When the full text of subdivision (D) is considered, it becomes apparent that the provision does not bespeak, as Justice Brennan believes, a congressional concern confined to "neutral" employers.[83] The employer who assigns to nonunion men jobs which unions wish to take for their own members is not a "neutral" in any intelligible sense of that term. He is as direct a participant in the dispute as anyone else. His decision, his work assignment, is what the union objects to.

The employer who assigns union-claimed work to nonunion men stands with

---

[81] *Id.* at 625-26.

[82] 29 U.S.C. § 158(b)(4)(D) (1964). (Emphasis added.) The description of § 8(b)(4)(D) carried in 3 CCH LAB. L. REP. ¶ 5230 is revealing. It says:

"The term 'jurisdictional strike' is commonly applied to work-assignment disputes of the kind covered by Section 8(b)(4)(D), since they often arise as a result of rival unions' conflicting claims to particular work, and since only strikes or inducement of work stoppages were forbidden methods of coercing work assignments before the 1959 amendments. However, the coverage of Section 8(b)(4)(D) is much broader than the conduct involved in a traditional jurisdictional strike. It also covers situations involving only a single union, when that union seeks to compel assignment to its members of work being performed by an employer's unorganized employees. . . . Both primary and secondary activities are included in Section 8(b)(4)(D)'s ban . . . ."

Cases agreeing with this comment and holding that the section applies to both "primary" and "secondary" action are: Dooley v. Local 107, Teamsters, 39 CCH Lab. Cas. ¶ 66,288 (D. Del. 1960); Local 450, Operating Engineers v. Elliott, 256 F.2d 630 (5th Cir. 1958); ILA Local 1351, 108 N.L.R.B. 712 (1954). For decisions holding that § 8(b)(4)(D) is not violated where the dispute is between a union and nonunion employees despite the plain language of the section—see Schauffler v. Local 1291, Longshoremen, 292 F.2d 182 (3d Cir. 1961); Cuneo v. Local 472, Hod Carriers, 175 F. Supp. 131 (D.N.J. 1959).

[83] 386 U.S. at 622.

respect to the union in precisely the same relationship as the contractor who orders products to which a construction union is opposed. He has chosen to contract with someone else in a way which reduces the amount of work controlled by the union. The fact that subdivision (D) forbids unions to interfere in the work assignments made by employers refutes Justice Brennan's theory that section 8(b)(4) is concerned only to protect "neutrals," as well as his theory that in section 8(b)(4) Congress was interested in limiting only "secondary boycotts." It would seem to establish a fatal defect in his conclusion that a work-preservation boycott should not be held unlawful despite the plain prohibition of the statute, because it is "primary" action.

In reaching his conclusion, Justice Brennan was compelled to grapple with the fact that Congress had been dramatically intent upon outlawing the kind of union conduct revealed in the *Allen Bradley* case.[84] There, it will be remembered, Local 3 of the International Brotherhood of Electrical Workers had joined with New York City manufacturers and contractors to bar electrical products manufactured outside the City. The Supreme Court had held that it would have exonerated the boycott but for the fact that the union had combined with employer groups to effectuate it. This qualification disturbed Congress. In passing the Taft-Hartley Act, therefore, Congress made explicit its intention to outlaw such boycotts even where they were conceived and effectuated by unions acting alone.[85] Since the boycott in *National Woodwork* strongly resembled the *Allen Bradley* boycott, and since the *Allen Bradley* boycott admittedly fell within the words and the "spirit" of the statute, it was incumbent upon Justice Brennan to distinguish the cases. This he did by asserting that the *Allen Bradley* boycott was designed to increase the work governed by Local 3, while the Carpenters in *National Woodwork* were intent upon preserving work that they had done in the past: "[T]he boycott in *Allen Bradley* was carried on not as a shield to preserve the jobs of Local 3 members, traditionally a primary labor activity, but as a sword, to reach out and monopolize all the manufacturing tasks for Local 3 members."[86]

Here too it is possible that Justice Brennan had not got the facts quite straight. In his dissenting opinion, Justice Stewart pointed out that:

> Just as in the case before us, the union [in *Allen Bradley*] enforced the product boycott to protect the work opportunities of its members. . . .[87]
>
> . . . .
>
> . . . [I]t is misleading to state that the union in *Allen Bradley* used the product boycott as a "sword." The record in that case establishes that the boycott was undertaken for the defensive purpose of restoring job opportunities lost in the depression. Moreover, the Court is unable to cite anything in *Allen Bradley*, or in the Taft-Hartley Act and its legislative history, to support a distinction in

---

[84] Allen Bradley Co. v. Local 3, IBEW, 325 U.S. 797 (1945).
[85] *See, e.g.,* the comments of Senators Ball, Taft, and Ellender, quoted in 386 U.S. at 629-39, 630 n.18, 655.
[86] *Id.* at 630.
[87] *Id.* at 653.

the applicability of § 8(b)(4) based on the origin of the job opportunities sought to be preserved by a product boycott. The Court creates its sword and shield distinction out of thin air; nothing could more clearly indicate that the Court is simply substituting its own concepts of desirable labor policy for the scheme enacted by Congress.[88]

After distinguishing *Allen Bradley* on the basis of the "sword-shield" metaphor, Justice Brennan reverted briefly to textual analysis of section 8(e). Although unable to demonstrate that the enacting language of the section fails to proscribe "work-preservation" product boycotts, he nevertheless insisted that such boycotts are excluded because they are "primary" and because Congress "meant that both §§ 8(e) and 8(b)(4)(B) reach only secondary pressures."[89] According to Justice Brennan, this assertion followed from the necessary implications of the construction-site proviso. That proviso makes sense, he said, only if section 8(e) is preoccupied with "secondary" conduct. Otherwise,

> the construction industry proviso, which permits "hot cargo" agreements only for jobsite work, would have the curious and unsupported result of allowing the construction worker to make agreements preserving his traditional tasks against jobsite prefabrication and subcontracting but not against nonjobsite prefabrication and subcontracting.[90]

This language seems unnecessarily difficult and opaque. It is anomalous to speak, in the context of the language of section 8(e), of "jobsite prefabrication." The term "prefabrication" is normally and naturally used in connection with articles or products which come to the jobsite in "prefabricated" or "pre-assembled" form. If Justice Brennan had used language in the normal way, the difficulty he posed would have disappeared. As shown above, there is nothing at all anomalous, perplexing, or contradictory in the relationship of the enacting language of section 8(e) and the jobsite proviso, when the words used are given their normal meaning. Summed up, the enacting language says: no product boycotts; and the proviso says: the work of installing products at the construction site is subject to agreement between union and contractor. Once this clear and simple relationship between the enacting language and the proviso is seen, the difficulty disappears; the "primary-secondary dichotomy" so heavily emphasized by Justice Brennan is seen as a gratuitous irrelevancy; and any doubts concerning the illegality of the Carpenters' boycott of the nonjobsite pre-hung doors are easily resolved.[91]

It is possible that Justice Brennan's difficulty traced, fundamentally, to his having moved in a circle. Perhaps he began his analysis with the assumption that the jobsite proviso was designed to permit construction unions to negotiate with respect

---

[88] *Id.* at 657-58.

[89] *Id.* at 638.

[90] *Id.*

[91] As Justice Stewart put it, "The Union's boycott of the prefitted doors clearly falls within the express terms of the federal labor law . . . ." *Id.* at 650 (dissenting opinion).

to any kind of work which might conceivably be done at the construction site. But such an assumption is impermissible; for the language of section 8(e) and the relationship between that language and the construction-site proviso preclude it. The basic language prohibits without exception all product boycotts. It is possible for a proviso to negate an enacting section. But in order to do so, the language adopted must fit the purpose. For example, had the proviso repeated the language of the enacting section either in terms or in substance, and then said that it was inapplicable in the construction industry, one might rationally conclude that the intent of Congress was to permit the construction unions to negotiate with respect to any kind of work which might conceivably be done at the construction site. But the jobsite-work proviso does not purport to negate the whole of section 8(e); it carves out a portion of the prohibition.

The point is best made, perhaps, by observing the difference between the construction-site proviso and the adjacent proviso, which does in fact and obvious language entirely negate the applicability of section 8(e)—and of section 8(b)(4)(B)—to the garment industry. While the construction-site proviso confines itself to "work to be done at the site of the construction," the garment-industry proviso goes the whole way. It states that

> for the purposes of this subsection (e) and section 8(b)(4)(B) the terms "any employer", "any person engaged in commerce or an industry affecting commerce", and "any person" when used in relation to the terms "any other producer, processor, or manufacturer", "any other employer", or "any other person" shall not include persons in the relation of a jobber, manufacturer, contractor, or subcontractor working on the goods or premises of the jobber or manufacturer or performing parts of an integrated process of production in the apparel and clothing industry.

Justice Brennan indicated a belief that the garment-industry proviso sustained his conclusion.[92] But its effect, quite clearly, is the precise contrary. In drafting that proviso, Congress demonstrated its capacity to negate section 8(e) in an industry in which it wished to do so. The sharp distinction in its approach to the construction industry establishes an intention to provide there only a fragmentary exclusion from the reach of section 8(e). The only fragmentary exclusion which carries an intelligible content is the one which distinguishes between products and work done at the construction site. The House Conference Report demonstrates that Congress had no doubts about that:[93]

> It should be particularly noted that the proviso relates only and exclusively to the contracting or subcontracting of work to be done at the site of the construction. The proviso does not exempt from section 8(e) agreements relating to supplies or

---

[92] Id. at 637-38.

[93] H.R. REP. No. 1147, 86th Cong., 1st Sess. 39 (1959), quoted by Mr. Justice Stewart, 386 U.S. at 661-62.

other products or materials shipped or otherwise transported to and delivered on the site of the construction.

Grappling with Justice Brennan's rationale, dissenting Justice Stewart (and with him Justices Black, Clark, and Douglas) recognized that the majority opinion had been guilty of assuming the answer to the question posed by the case. Justice Stewart said:[94]

> The Court indeed recognizes that the . . . proviso does not immunize product boycotts . . . . By a curious inversion of logic, the Court purports to deduce from this fact the proposition that product boycotts are not covered by § 8(e). But if § 8(e) and its legislative history are approached without preconceptions, it is evident that Congress intended to bar the use of any provisions in a collective agreement to authorize the product boycott involved in the case before us.

After covering the statute and its legislative history, Justice Brennan sought support for his conclusion in the *Fibreboard* case,[95] an earlier ruling to the effect that an employer must in certain circumstances bargain over subcontracting. "It would . . . be incongruous," he said, "to interpret § 8(e) to invalidate clauses over which the parties may be mandated to bargain and which have been successfully incorporated through collective bargaining in many of this Nation's major labor agreements."[96]

Justice Brennan was correct in detecting the existence of an incongruity, but not in identifying it. The *Fibreboard* decision is itself an anomaly which cannot be squared with either the collective-bargaining policies of the National Labor Relations Act or its policies against union control of jobs. The Act requires collective bargaining over "wages, hours, and other terms and conditions of employment."[97] Subcontracting does not fit comfortably into any of these categories. An employer's decision to subcontract an operation, like a decision to substitute machinery for men—indeed, like every decision to buy rather than make—is likely to affect the availability of work in his own operation; but so too, for that matter, is a decision on plant location, choice of product, or even price of product. The point is that affecting the availability of work is by no means the same thing as establishing wages, hours, or other terms of employment—the subject-matter of compulsory collective bargaining. To observe that much collective bargaining concerns itself with subcontracting is not to establish that activity as a compulsory bargaining subject.

Again, compelling employers to bargain over subcontracting clearly flouted the mandate of section 8(e) as well as other congressional proscriptions of job-controlling activities by unions. As we have seen, congressional measures against such job-control are scattered throughout the statute. For example, section 8(b)(2) makes it an unfair practice for a union to acquire closed-shop control or even merely to attempt to

---

[94] 386 U.S. at 662.
[95] Fibreboard Paper Prods. Corp. v. NLRB, 379 U.S. 203 (1964).
[96] 386 U.S. at 643.
[97] § 8(d), 29 U.S.C. § 158(d) (1964).

achieve it.[98] Section 8(b)(4) proscribes union efforts to dictate the parties with whom an employer may deal. And section 8(b)(4)(D) makes it an unfair practice for a union to use pressure as a means of securing for its members work which an employer is assigning to others.

Properly understood, the *Fibreboard* principle undercuts these statutory policies by encouraging unions to exercise the kind of job-control that so many statutory measures were intended to discourage. Since the principle is not itself based on any necessary implication of the statutory language, the *Fibreboard* decision must be viewed as another example of the Court's rejecting congressional policy in favor of its own.

Perhaps because of these apparent inconsistencies between the policies of the Act and the decision in *Fibreboard*, the Court was very careful there in limiting the reach of its decision. As Justice Stewart noted in his *National Woodwork* dissent,[99] the *Fibreboard* Court did not intend to establish any broad principle. On the contrary, it said:[100]

> The Company's decision to contract out the maintenance work did not alter the Company's basic operation. The maintenance work still had to be performed in the plant. . . . [T]he Company merely replaced existing employees with those of an independent contractor to do the same work under similar conditions of employment. Therefore, to require the employer to bargain about the matter would not significantly abridge his freedom to manage the business.

Justice Stewart's comment on the use of *Fibreboard* as a basis for the decision in *National Woodwork* seems definitive to me. He said:[101]

> An employer's decision as to the products he wishes to buy presents entirely different issues. That decision has traditionally been regarded as one within management's discretion, and *Fibreboard* does not indicate that it is a mandatory subject of collective bargaining, much less a permissible basis for a product boycott made illegal by federal labor law.

CONCLUSION

The majority opinion in *National Woodwork* is so strained and artificial that it cannot be regarded as a seriously intended piece of statutory analysis. In the circumstances, one must "look to the equities"; one must search for the policy considerations which animated the majority. These are not hard to find. Justice Brennan speaks much of "onrushing technological change," of the "significant and difficult problems" posed by such change, and of his expectation that any congressional intent to preclude union resistance to such change "be preceded by extensive congressional

---

[98] The language of § 8(b)(2) is very broad: "It shall be an unfair labor practice for a labor organization . . . to cause or to attempt to cause an employer to discriminate against an employee in violation of subsection (a)(3) . . . ."

[99] 386 U.S. at 662-63.

[100] 379 U.S. at 213.

[101] 386 U.S. at 663.

study and debate, and consideration of voluminous economic, scientific, and statistical data."[102] A similar preoccupation is evident in the opinion of Justice Harlan, whose concurrence was vital to the majority. In his brief concurring opinion, Justice Harlan made room to say:[103]

> Especially at a time when Congress is continuing to explore methods for meeting the economic problems increasingly arising in this technological age from scientific advances, this Court should not take such a step until Congress has made unmistakably clear that it wishes wholly to exclude collective bargaining as one avenue of approach to solutions in this elusive aspect of our economy.

Anyone with a minimum understanding of conditions in the construction industry must have difficulty believing that such fears of technological displacement had a rightful, or even sensible, role to play in the decision in *National Woodwork*. One of the most profound problems of the industry is posed by the paucity of technological development which has occurred there, and references to "onrushing technological change" are incongruous, if not downright funny. Equally significant, the construction industry has been suffering a severe labor shortage, especially in the skilled trades, for many years. Speaking recently with carpenters in Chicago, I heard everywhere that they have more work than they can handle. Many told me that they stop working when they have earned $400 in a week because they wish to keep their taxes down. Contractors who try to get too many hours from their carpenters only lose them to those who are willing to accept fewer hours of work.

I have dwelt at length on the *National Woodwork* case because of the attitude it reveals and because of the problems which that attitude poses for any legislative program designed to limit the capacity of the construction unions to rig costs and prices. The various provisions of the National Labor Relations Act which I have reviewed in this article, take them all in all, constitute a strong, clear, and coherent design for the confinement of monopolistic union practices. Notwithstanding that fact, the administration of the law by the National Labor Relations Board generally, and by the Supreme Court all too frequently, has left unions with substantially the control over labor supply and costs that they had before the Taft-Hartley Act was passed. Possibly, indeed, their control has increased in the years since 1947.

Perhaps it is time, then, to abandon the attempt to control the peacefully exerted economic pressures of trade unions. Or perhaps it is time for Congress to take from the Labor Board the virtual monopoly which it has had in administering the National Labor Relations Act, and to permit aggrieved parties to go directly to court for relief. Appropriate modification of the Norris-LaGuardia Act would be needed. It is long overdue.

Ending on an optimistic note, I should like to remind the reader once again of the

---

[102] *Id.* at 640.
[103] *Id.* at 650.

"lineup" in the *National Woodwork* case. Only a bare majority could be mustered in support of the decision. Four Justices saw with Justice Holmes that "much trouble is made by substituting other phrases assumed to be equivalent, which then are reasoned from as if they were in the Act." Those four Justices were willing to apply Congress's law as it was written, even though the result would have been to limit the socially exploitative activities of trade unions, those favorites who have so often been the objects of the whole Court's tenderest solicitude. There is ground here for the hope, first, that the Court may one day come firmly to the conclusion that it is best all round to leave the basic policy-making to Congress; and second, that the whole Court may one day agree—with Congress, the dissenters in *National Woodwork*, and the universal opinion of economists—that monopolistic conduct is no more in the general interest when trade unions engage in it than it is when bureaucrats or businessmen are involved.

SLUM HOUSING: A FUNCTIONAL ANALYSIS

GEORGE STERNLIEB*

INTRODUCTION

A sharp division is opening in the ranks of American social activists between the institutionalists and what may be termed the "marketers." The axiomatic role of present housing policy as a social input similarly is under challenge. Congress reflects this uncertainty on optimum action for the future.

The institutionalists are those individuals who, harking back to the lesson of the 1930s, believe in the disposition of social welfare funds through channels clearly defined and structured by the government. There is a strong acceptance by them of certain given tools and values: external guidance of the poor reflected in strong advocacy of public housing, efforts to strengthen the ministrations of the welfare worker, and so on.

The marketers, at least in the socially activist area, are much newer and harder to describe. Essentially they are united in believing that the poor should have greater options—for example, that social welfare funds should be utilized directly to enhance the buying power of the underprivileged, without an intervening structuring of the disposition of these funds. The use of guaranteed incomes in some form is a frequently advocated instrument. Inadequacies of housing are seen as reconcilable by giving the poor more money—and permitting them at their option to buy better shelter.

Obviously, the dichotomy indicated above does not do justice to the broad range of in-between belief, of tools such as rent subsidies which are usable by either group, and of the diversity of consumers to be serviced by the low-end housing market. Accepting these strictures, however, I am still impressed by the speed with which the concept of bringing the poor into the market mechanisms, as against direct governmental servicing of their needs, has progressed.

In substantial part this change in attitude mirrors the change in the perspective given the problems of the poor. A very short time ago, for example, the expression "urban problems" would have been used in place of "problems of the poor." In part this would have been a euphemism—in part, however, it mirrored the confusion in thinking and motivation prevalent at the time.

There has been a confusion between efforts at rehabilitating the city on the one hand, and helping people who happen to be presently concentrated within cities, on the other.

* A.B. 1950, Brooklyn College; M.B.A. 1953, D.B.A. 1962, Harvard University. Professor, Graduate School of Business Administration, Rutgers—The State University. Author, THE FUTURE OF THE DOWNTOWN DEPARTMENT STORE (1962); THE TENEMENT LANDLORD (1966); SOCIAL NEEDS AND SOCIAL RESOURCES (1967).

I

THE NEGRO IN THE CITY

A. "If There Were No Negroes"

"If there were no Negroes, the city would be . . . ." Any of a number of "good" things are proposed by all too many people of the United States as a function of this introductory clause. The sins of the city: its decay, its lack of relevance to the current folkways of middle class America, and not infrequently all of its problems generally, are seen as a function of the change in the racial mixture which has taken place in this last generation. I would suggest that this is romantic hogwash. The city is an antiquated form of social organization; its social and economic relevance to the growth frontiers of American society are and have been increasingly tenuous over a lengthy period of years.

The inadequacies of municipal government, revealed strikingly by the series of riots which seems to be a commonplace of every summer, are neither new nor unique. It is not that municipal government is less adequate; to the contrary, a good case can be made for its being much more adequate than was true historically. It is rather that the realities of the city simply cannot provide the standard of living and amenities which the new focal points of American civilization—the new cities, the suburbs—hold out as a measuring stick of adequacy.

B. Black Power Romanticism

The efforts of Black Power advocates, in this context, can similarly be seen as completely anachronistic in aspiration; the city which they attempt to secure is a bankrupt entity.[1] It is bankrupt not merely in answers, but in its capacity to deliver the improved standard of living which is the universal of American middle class aspiration levels. The "trauma" of the city have been with us probably since its inception.

The city is falling into discard, not because its population distribution has been altered, but rather because the world around the city, the competition faced by the city as an organization, has changed. It is competition, rather than decline in the absolute level of service, that has altered its role. Any efforts at changing this situation must take this basic premise into account. Unfortunately, this has not been the case. Past governmental policy in the city was substantially one, at least initially, of rebuilding some conceived of Golden Age in the past.

The city must be made a way station toward middle class America for the new immigrants, just as it was for older groups. It is as a means to an end that the city and its housing is to be utilized, rather than as an end in itself.

---

[1] A clear case in point is the effort to secure Negro ownership of the traditional central core small stores in the face of the discount house and supermarket.

II

Using the Slums

The very slums of the city provide a potential takeoff place in this regard, if we can move toward owner residence. This can provide a key element in the development of capital accumulation for the core dweller.

If a gross oversimplification may be permitted, the problem of the slums is one both of plumbing and morale. It has largely been viewed in the past as consisting solely of the plumbing. This is not to denigrate the latter; the provision of appropriate housing amenities is certainly an essential step toward improving the outlook and aspiration level of slum dwellers. However, the morale problem cannot be cured merely by providing these physical amenities.

The present market situation is one of virtual stagnation in the hard core slum areas. The combination of risk, decreasing profitability, and loss of potential for capital gains has substantially restricted the kinds of professional owners who are willing to invest in slum properties. It takes a pretty hard-shelled individual to become a professional nonresident owner of slum property, given present societal attitude. And this is not an individual who is easily influenced to invest his money unless an appropriate return can be secured. Given the relative weakness of the slum apartment market, the professional landlord has been faced with the choice of basically two alternatives: to stand pat and not increase his investment, or to attempt to improve his parcel in order to secure higher rentals.

The pattern that we have seen in our studies indicates that the choice has usually been the former. The observer cannot fail to be struck by the "heads we win, tails you lose" nature of this phenomenon. When the apartment market is very strong the landlord need not improve; when the apartment market is very weak the landlord fears for his investment and does not improve.[2]

III

What Is, or Should Be, Public Policy Toward Slums and Slum Dwellers?

The goal of government policy towards the slums must have as its primary aim the improvement of the morale of the inhabitants thereof: tax policy, code enforcement policy, financing aid, municipal service policy, all of these must be viewed within the context of the overall objective.

The community must face the realities of the slum situation fairly, without self-deception or romanticism, and at the same time move for change. Let us review the slum conditions as they exist.

1. In Northern industrial cities, the overwhelming majority of hard core slum

---

[2] *See generally* G. Sternlieb, The Tenement Landlord (1966); J. Meyer, H. Schwartz *et al.*, Economic Description of the Real Estate Market on the Lower East Side of New York (1967).

area residents are Negroes. The decreasing number of whites are typically an elderly remnant of earlier immigrations.

2. There is little evidence of a substantial return of the white middle class to the slum areas of the city.

3. The bulk of slum tenements are owned by absentee white owners. These owners are not merely absentee from the slums per se, they are also absentee, at least as residents, from the city in which they own property.

4. The single most basic variable which accounts for variations in the maintenance of slum properties is the factor of ownership. Good parcel maintenance typically is a function of resident ownership.

5. Subject to major programs of land clearance for the purposes of urban renewal or highway construction or both, a population vacuum is developing in the slums. The tidal wave of southern Negro migration, has slowed down and is substantially bypassing some of the northern cities which were its traditional goal. With a virtual stability in Puerto Rican migrant population size, there is no new depressed group on the horizon to fill the older slums.

6. While this population decrease makes the problem of relocation much simpler, it also tends to limit the landlords' capacity and will to improve parcels.

7. Given a substantial dependence upon land taxes in the face of increased demands upon the municipality for services, taxes have become a major inhibitor of entrepreneurial activity in the central city. Particularly in terms of the uncertainty which surround their administration, current municipal tax policies are leading to further degeneration of the slums.

8. The relationship of client and patron, which plays a dominant role in the dealings between government, both municipal and federal, and the poor population of the slums, is deleterious to the morale of the individuals concerned.

IV

BOOSTING THE PROPORTION OF RESIDENT LANDLORDS IN SLUM TENEMENTS

There is no question of the significance of local landlord residence, particularly of single parcel landlords, in ensuring proper maintenance of slum tenements. Given the priority accorded by multiple-parcel owners to tenant problems and the lack of feeling on this score by resident landlords,[3] the latter's good record in maintenance is most significant. It is the resident landlord, and only the resident landlord, who is in a position to properly screen and supervise his tenantry. No oneshot wave of maintenance and a paint-up, sweep-up campaign, can provide the day-to-day maintenance which is required in slum areas. This can only be accomplished by a resident landlord. The record of these landlords as we have noted in our studies is such as to inspire confidence in their future behavior on this score.

---

[3] When asked to rank his problems, the resident landlord cites tenants as minor. The absentee owner, however, puts tenant problems in first place.

By making it feasible for more residents to become owners, we further encourage the development of local leadership which is so sorely lacking in most slums. The role of resident owners as guides and creators of life patterns for the youth of the slums to follow is clearly evident. Most important of all, we can encourage the growth of capital accumulation which is an essential of social mobility within our society.

A. Financing

How could this type of development be stimulated? There are several prime requirements. The first of these, obviously, is financing help. The term of mortgages is much more significant from a cash flow point-of-view than are interest rates. For example, a mortgage at six per cent which is written for a fifteen year period involves less cash flow than an equivalent size mortgage for a ten year period at 3½ per cent. Given the dearth of available financing which is currently the case in the slums, there is obviously no alternative but to provide something in the way of long-term FHA-guaranteed mortgages for slum tenement purchases by residents. The analogy with the early Homestead Act springs readily to mind.[4] In that case government lands were provided to those who would live on them, at relatively reasonable rates and with liberal financing. The same thing must be done in the slums.

B. Advisory Services

Financing, however, is merely one of the several steps which is required. The relatively innocent new resident buyers of slum tenements are frequently victimized by a variety of home improvement services. Thus, a moneylender, interviewed by the writer, pointed to the fact that commonly, when he has to repossess a parcel, the typical cause is that the owner has burdened the parcel with two, three, or more home improvement loans. Just as the Agriculture Department provides a variety of advisory services for the farmer, so the city or the federal government, or both, must provide equivalent advisory services for the new home owner in the slum areas. These advisors must be competent not merely in home improvements, but also in financing and appraising parcels. It would seem entirely possible that among the ranks of senior savings and loan people, as well, possibly, as within the ranks of the present FHA personnel, such individuals could be found. Technical competence, however, must be linked with a basic sympathy with the aspiration level of the now owner and with none of the *deux ex machina* attitude that so often exists in government relations with the poor.

C. Tax Policy

The question of tax policy is a most significant one on this score, as it is with respect to the general problem of slums. It may well behoove the city to continue

---

[4] Ch. 75, 12 Stat. 392 (1862).

its policy of full assessment based upon market values. Obviously, where broad-based taxation is available on a basis other than land, it may reduce some of the strain. Reassessment policy, however, must be more clearly defined than is presently the case. The landlord should have no reason to fear city reassessment as a result of a new coat of paint.

It is essential that the city not merely adopt a more reasonable attitude toward taxation, but also sell the facts of this attitude to those who may be influenced by misconceptions as to its reality. In addition, in the long run it may very well pay the city to provide the equivalent of homestead rebates for resident landlords. This is a format (which will be recognized by those who are familiar, for example, with tax policy in a city such as Miami Beach) in which the homesteader—*i.e.,* the resident landlord—receives either a reduction or a rebate in his real estate taxes. This might well be coupled with a stipulation that the rebate be employed in the improvement of the parcel in question. The area of uncertainty and suspicion which surrounds current taxing procedures must be clarified. Its existence clearly inhibits improvements.

D. Municipal Services

There seems to be ample evidence that the level of municipal services required by the slum areas is higher than that required by nonslum equivalent areas. At the same time, there is reason to believe that the actual delivery level of these services is reversed, with poorer areas being slighted.

Every effort must be made by the city to provide an optimum level of services within the slums. Such functions as police protection, street lighting, parking restrictions, garbage collection, and a host of others could be named here. Not least among these is the question of educational facilities. While this is a subject whose depth is beyond the scope of this article, it can not be omitted. Without substantial efforts on all of these fronts, the efforts at utilizing the slum as ladders toward upward mobility will fail.

E. Code Enforcement

Parallel with all of the above suggestions is the requirement that code enforcement be made much more rigorous. But, prior to this, there is required a much more adequate definition of just what the code should be. Adequate insect and rodent control, plumbing that works, paint, and general cleanliness may be much more significant to the inhabitants of a tenement, both physically and spiritually, than the existence of central heat or plaster walls. Whether the studs used in a repair are sixteen inches on center or are twenty inches on center may be completely irrelevant to a tenant. A building which is completely satisfactory on the basis of existing codes may be completely unsatisfactory in terms of its effect upon its occupants.

Code enforcement, therefore, must require a much more subjective approach than has heretofore been the case. This is particularly the case with those buildings in the hands of landlords who cannot afford repairs. In those cases, it may be necessary to work out a long term plan of rehabilitating the parcel in question—with major emphasis being given to the paint and cleanliness functions, those most easily encompassed by "sweat equity." Good maintenance and resident landlordism are much more significant than mechanical adherence to a mechanical code.

V

The Future of the Hard Core Slum

I would seriously question the potential of hard core slum areas for rehabilitation. Given the relatively loose housing market, which presently exists in many center cities, the bulldozer approach to such hard core areas would seem to be the only answer. This should not wait upon redevelopers. The existence of such hard core blight drags down the neighborhoods peripheral to it.[5]

The loss of tax revenue to the municipality through this process of demolition must be accepted as surgery essential to preserve the surrounding areas from the spread of deep-seated blight. Obviously, the scale of this blight will require considerable discretion on the part of municipal authorities on the phasing and speed of demolition. Given the present functioning of the market, as has earlier been indicated, we cannot depend upon private enterprise to remove no longer useable buildings.

There is some question in my mind as to whether a change in tax policy to encourage demolition might not be in order. The city's need for more open space, and the potential of already assembled and cleared substantial size tracts in encouraging further development, must be depended upon to generate future use for the areas in question. Their maintenance by the city, given the facts of alternative housing availability, cannot be justified upon tax income reasons alone.

VI

Conclusion: No False Romanticism

The self-help capacity of the poor is limited. Some resident landlords are elderly, others are uneducated, and some lack an appropriate aspiration level. The fact remains, however, that as a group, they are presently the best landlords in the slums, and provide probably the major hope for better maintenance in the future. It will require a talented and understanding guidance operation to help generate landlord enthusiasm, while restraining over-expenditure. The problems here should

---

[5] Current gross vacancy rates, for example, in the twenty-five core census tracts of Newark are on the order of 10% in the midst of a tight housing market. This incongruity is a function of the lack of desirability of core vacancies. In the seventy-five tracts outside the core, the vacancy rate is under 4%. G. Sternlieb *et al.*, Vacancy Rate Analysis (in preparation).

not be underestimated. It is essential if this operation is to be truly successful, particularly from a morale standpoint, and also from the standpoint of securing long-run improvement, that the advisory service be a guide and an inspiration, not a directorate.

The present and future strains on the municipality's budget, coupled with limited increases in revenue, will make it most difficult to pay for the services that are required. The alternative, however, of increasing degeneration is all too clear-cut. From a fiscal point of view, the program outlined above is a most burdensome one; this point should not be evaded. There is no other answer, however, from the city's standpoint.

Tax policy must be directed toward aiding the good landlord and penalizing those owners who do not properly maintain their properties. A tax policy based on sales value can easily have the reverse effect. The potential of homestead exemption, of rigorous code enforcement, and of self-help stimulating devices must be rigorously exploited.

There is a well-founded fear on the part of the tenantry that rehabilitation leads to rent increases. This must be accepted as a fact of the market. Although tax policy can somewhat relieve this factor, particularly when coupled with more adequate financing, this fact should be faced. The potential of rent subsidies for the under-incomed, with which they can afford better rents, is clear-cut here. The reward in terms of the aspiration level and general morale of the slum dweller will, I think, outweigh the cost. This is particularly true when the cost/benefits are contrasted with those of institutionalized public housing.

The key to improving the slums from a "people" point of view is the creation of a resident responsible middle class within those areas—not a middle class which while physically in the area does not belong to it, as is the case with the efforts to create new middle class housing within slum areas cleared by urban renewal. This has no organic unity with the tenements per se and can only provide frustration, rather than leadership and emulation. These goals can best be accomplished and living conditions within the slum areas most enhanced, by increasing the number of owner residents of slum tenements. This will require a highly coordinated effort in terms of tax policy, financing help, code enforcement, and advisory services. The rewards of a successful program are very great. The cost of present policies are equally evident.

GOVERNMENT AND SLUM HOUSING: SOME GENERAL CONSIDERATIONS

LAWRENCE M. FRIEDMAN*

Housing was a latecomer to the federal trough. The federal government historically made war, killed Indians, gave away land, tried cases, raised taxes, regulated business, and appropriated money. It hardly ever built houses, except for itself, its soldiers, and its prisoners. But in the last generation or so, the federal government has begun to make up for lost time. It has begun building and financing houses. The Wagner Housing Act, enacted in 1937,[1] was only a first step. The federal housing effort now has a cabinet department of its own—a status higher than that of food and drugs, the Army, and social security, all of which have to be content with representation at the sub-cabinet level. The new status is evidence of a new emphasis—or at least evidence of a nagging feeling in society that something is wrong and that something must be done. Specifically, what is wrong is the slums.

It is still a question, however, whether the main federal effort in housing will go toward slum housing or toward something else. In the 1930s stress was placed on housing the lower working class. In the 1940s defense workers and veterans were the prime beneficiaries of federal action. In the 1950s emphasis was placed on middleincome housing in the suburbs, and upper-income housing in the renewed urban core. Only in the 1960s does it seem even possible that the desperate urban poor will move to the center of the stage. And even that is an open question.

Government emphasis (and money) is never a matter of whim. It is a matter of cash and of votes; of letters from home addressed to Congress; of riots and lawsuits and pressures. Concrete social forces have determined why government has done what it has done in the field of housing. Concrete social forces have similarly determined why it has not done the things that have not yet been done. This short overview will discuss the federal effort to eliminate the slums and provide decent homes for the poorest of the poor, in terms of the social forces that have made the job so far so hard. Clearly the slums have not been eliminated. Clearly many of the poor remain locked in their ghettos, in dark, dank, overcrowded rooms. Clearly, the situation is unhappy. Can we shed any light on the causes and cures?

I

SLUM HOUSING: THE PROBLEM

It is natural for people to think of problems in absolute terms. Most people

---

* A.B. 1948, J.D. 1951, LL.M. 1953, University of Chicago. Professor of Law, University of Wisconsin. Author, CONTRACT LAW IN AMERICA (1965); GOVERNMENT AND SLUM HOUSING: A CENTURY OF FRUSTRATION (in press, 1967). The author's current research on housing and social legislation is supported by the Institute for Research on Poverty at the University of Wisconsin.

[1] United States Housing Act of 1937, ch. 896, 50 Stat. 888.

believe that air pollution, the population explosion, the gold flow, and increasing crime rates are threats to humanity in an objectively measurable sense. Yet it is important to note that a problem is also—and primarily—a state of mind. A problem is a situation that worries some segment of the population. If there is no worry, there is no problem. The air remains polluted, but there is no pressure for political and social action. A "problem" exists, then, only to the extent it is so perceived. Otherwise, it is like the noise of a tree falling in an empty forest.

There is no question, at least not now, that slum housing is a problem. Three groups of people see it that way. One group is composed of some of the people who live in the slums. Another is composed of some outsiders. The third is made up of some elected and appointed government officials. But each group sees the problem in a very different light.

The person who lives in the slums, if he thinks of his housing condition as a problem, feels his situation as a personal trouble. It is a deficiency in his own standard of living, a source of discomfort, stigma, and pain. The outsider cannot see slum housing in this way: his own house is in order. His perception of the slum housing problem, then, cannot be the same as that of the poor themselves. The outsider may have, instead of a perception of a problem, a perception of an *interest*. Some people have a direct, material stake in government housing programs. Among these are manufacturers of building supplies and labor unions whose members are bricklayers and masons. Similarly, cement companies have a direct interest in the federal highway program. This kind of interest has played an important and pervasive role in the history of Government's housing effort. Building-trade unions, for example, lobbied vigorously for passage of the New Deal public housing law.[2] Landlords with vacant apartments in marginal neighborhoods welcome the new leasing program[3] with open arms, since it promises to put federal rent money in their pockets.

Most people, however, lack strong material interests in any particular item of legislation. Slum housing affects them only obliquely. Many people do feel that slum housing is a threat, not to them individually and directly, but indirectly, because it is a threat to the collectivity of which they are a part. One might call this the *social* interest. In a way it differs from direct interests only in degree. The citizen may oppose air pollution because a factory next door is pouring malodorous smoke in his window, or because the air in a city he likes to visit is slightly brown and acrid in the gills. Both problems affect him, but in different ways. Vast numbers of people feel a social interest in a wide range of problems.

The first laws that had anything whatsoever to do with slum housing were fire laws.[4] Fires can begin in the slums and spread to the better parts of town. They endangered some people directly, but many more indirectly. It has always been easy to

---

[2] T. McDonnell, The Wagner Housing Act 116-23 (1957).
[3] 42 U.S.C. § 1421b (Supp. II, 1965-66).
[4] *E.g.*, Act of May 3, 1895, ch. 355, [1895] Wis. Laws 719.

denounce the slums, not for any welfare motive or motive of heart, but because the slum threatens the safety of his city. Similarly, the slums have been called a social danger because they are alleged to breed crime, socialism, boss-rule, or disease. Jacob Riis told the world that the tenements were "hot-beds of the epidemics that carry death to rich and poor alike; the nurseries of pauperism and crime," which bred "a scum of . . . human wrecks . . . [and] maintain a standing army of ten thousand tramps."[5] The Boston Anti-Tenement House League helped induce Massachusetts to enact a law "to Prevent the Manufacture and Sale of Clothing Made in Unhealthy Places."[6] The idea was that in tenement sweatshops, dread germs were transmitted to the clothes. These germs spread sickness to the people who bought and wore the clothes. Any reader can think of pungent contemporary examples—appeals to reform the slums in order to roll back Communism or achieve some other social result.

Finally, there is pure disinterest—the *reform* motivation. Some people have worked to improve the life of the poor for no outward reasons of personal or social gain. Conscience and conviction have been powerful engines of social change. The history of housing legislation has been full of individual heroes—men like Jacob Riis, or Lawrence Veiller, who was the soul and spirit behind the New York Tenement House Law of 1907.[7] Reformers cannot, as a general rule, induce people to betray what they consider their direct individual interests. But they can persuade people where their indirect, social interests lie. Hence reformers have been enormously important, as catalysts and propagandists.

What is the interest of government? There are, to be sure, bureaucratic interests. Department heads will fight tooth and nail to get a program into their bailiwick rather than someone else's. They will lobby for programs that strengthen their position or aggrandize their empire. But in general, the governmental interest is quite different from the nongovernmental interest. Abstractly stated, it is the interest in satisfying the most outside demands at the least possible cost to itself.

The governmental interest is worth dwelling on. In some ways, it is the critical interest. The subject matter of this article is a body of law: enacted programs of government. But government is not usually an initiator; it reacts. It responds to demands made upon it. These demands are evoked by other people with interests, direct or indirect, in situations which appear to the demandants as problems. Government responds; but it filters demands through the special needs of government as an institution or a system. The basic need is for equilibrium, for balance, for stability. It is a need to respond while incurring as little cost as possible, and running as few risks as possible. Now cost is not meant in a narrow literal sense. Losing an election is a cost to a Congressman or President, indeed, the highest cost of all. Some responses to demands call for costs in the obvious monetary sense. If a program

---

[5] J. Riis, How the Other Half Lives 3 (1906).

[6] Act of May 28, 1891, ch. 357, [1891] Mass. Acts & Resolves 922.

[7] *See generally* R. Lubove, The Progressives and the Slums (1962).

promises to be expensive, taxes may have to be raised. Or alternative programs may have to be foregone. But these may cause grumbling, disturbances, angry letters, threats to withhold votes and contributions, or even riots in extreme cases. The ideal program would be one that pleased everybody. Such programs, needless to say, are few and far between. All others involve a measure of cost.

The remarks above are elementary and perhaps hardly worth the mention. But the course of housing history makes no rational sense from any other point of view. The history of housing legislation, all in all, makes no ethical sense, no economic sense, no social sense. But it makes sense in terms of the system needs of political bodies. Yet this dimension is frequently ignored. The rise of a federal housing program is often taken to be a sign that good is finally prevailing over evil. Social scientists have discarded as useless the notion of progress—a one-line movement of society from the bad to the good. But the concept of progress hangs on in the folk mind with an iron grip. Ideas of good and bad are valuable, even necessary. They tell us what to work for. But they are very bad at explaining the past. The past is best accounted for by rigorous search for direct and indirect interests, among the relevant actors, and by careful consideration of the governmental interest. Government, after all, is a crucial player in the game. Government, the body that makes and enforces law, is a vast institution; and it is made up of ordinary men. To assume that these men are inclined to maximize responses at minimum cost, is to assume only that they are terribly human. This primitive assumption brings light into fields of great darkness.

II

ON MAJORITY RULE

Political life, in this country, follows roughly the principle of majority rule. This principle, baldly stated, is very abstract. But one can draw several corollaries from it. First, it is clear that government will ordinarily serve majority interests, not minority interests, when the two are sharply defined, and in conflict. Often enough, the two are sharply defined, and do conflict. And government sides with the loudest and most numerous voice.

In the United States, there is a huge middle class. It outnumbers by far both the rich and the poor. Hence there is a deeply ingrained, inverterate slippage of poverty programs into middle class programs. The American public housing movement itself provides one long verification of this statement. America never had any public housing to speak of until the period just after the First World War, when a few sporadic programs were launched in the states.[8] Massachusetts and North Dakota (an unlikely pair) were among the pioneering states. Both programs, however, were

---

[8] During the First World War, the federal government began a program to house workers in shipyards and defense industries. After the war, the program was quickly dismantled. Act of March 1, 1918, ch. 19, 40 Stat. 438; Act of May 16, 1918, ch. 74, 40 Stat. 550; Act of July 19, 1919, ch. 24, 41 Stat. 224. *See generally* R. FISHER, TWENTY YEARS OF PUBLIC HOUSING 74-79 (1959).

profoundly different from public housing as it developed in the 1950s and 1960s. Neither was really interested in the bottom level poor. These programs were rather geared toward the lower middle class. Massachusetts's plan was explicitly designed for "mechanics, laborers, wage-earners."[9] The houses were to be small suburban cottages. The North Dakota Experiment (1919-1923) called for the construction of homes, financed by state funds, to be sold to residents of the state.[10] Its main interest was in the simple farmer—though not the tenant farmer or the migrant farm worker. Neither plan succeeded, but not because they aimed at the wrong level of society, politically speaking.[11]

New Deal public housing was of course a more radical program. But it turned out to be politically feasible only during a period in which millions of the former middle class had lost their jobs but not their political voices. This was the unique situation in the days of the great depression. Vast numbers of Americans had become much poorer than they were. Yet in culture and habit, they were still members of the middle class.[12] These fallen members of the middle class were to be the prime beneficiaries of public housing. They were the depression equivalent of the honest farmers and sturdy mechanics of the North Dakota and Massachusetts experiments. Hence, although public housing tenants had to be poor, they could not be too poor. They had to be able to pay the rent. The rent was heavily subsidized—but it was not by any means free. Those who could not pay it, and those who were deficient in good character, were not to be let in.[13]

And even at that, the heyday of public housing lasted only so long as the depression lasted. Its momentum was swept away during the Second World War. It was only natural to expend wartime and immediate post-war energy on defense workers and veterans.[14] Afterwards, the major effort went into assuring middle-class migration into the suburbs. Public housing became a feeble program starved for funds. New public construction was and is lucky if it equals two per cent of private housing starts.[15] Congress during the 1950s came close to killing public housing altogether. The effect of public housing is cumulative, of course. More than 2,000,000 people live in public housing. They are oddly distributed, however. Almost a quarter of them are tenants of the New York City Housing Authority.

---

[9] Act of May 25, 1917, ch. 310, [1917] Mass. Gen. Acts 317.

[10] Act of Feb. 25, 1919, ch. 150, [1919] N.D. Laws 210.

[11] See generally D. SCHAFFTER, STATE HOUSING AGENCIES 9-33, 552-67 (1942); Robinson, Public Housing in Massachusetts, 18 B.U.L. REV. 83 (1938).

[12] See generally Friedman, Public Housing and the Poor: An Overview, in THE LAW OF THE POOR 318 (J. tenBroek ed. 1966).

[13] It is still possible to be too poor for public housing. But the rock-bottom poor are generally on welfare, and their rent payments are taken care of by welfare agencies. In 1949, the federal statute was specifically amended to provide that no one was to be excluded from public housing solely because he was on welfare. Housing Act of 1949, ch. 338, § 301, 63 Stat. 423. This proviso is no longer part of the federal statute but in practice welfare families are freely admitted to public housing.

[14] E.g., Veterans' Emergency Housing Act of 1946, ch. 268, 60 Stat. 207.

[15] See 18 HHFA ANN. REP. 386 (1964).

And however one counts the poor, public housing has not been an impressive effort at housing the indigent. Public housing may not be worth doing at all. But this halfway effort is hard to justify on any theory. It is not hard to explain, however. The political zest of politicians for programs is a function of the payoff to them in honor or votes. Even the housing reformers found public housing disgusting by the late 1950s;[16] and the right wing, especially the real estate right, was paranoid on the subject. The only flicker of enthusiasm for the program at this low point in public housing's career was generated by programs to house the elderly. Some cities which had no interest in the usual sort of public housing mounted substantial plans for housing the elderly. A high percentage of current housing effort is going into this program.[17] The program is eminently worthwhile. But so are others which are death at the box office—such as anything which even smacks of racial integration in the suburbs and in the solid middle class areas. Or any infusions of the welfare poor middle class neighborhoods.

In fact, the enthusiasm for housing the elderly is best explained on political grounds. The elderly are the last remaining pool of predominantly white, culturally middle class poor. They tend to be docile. They tend to be grateful. They create no problems of management and no problems of discipline. Except when afflicted with the forgetfulness of age, they pay their rent on time. They do not overload the schools, since they have no children. And they can conveniently be housed in big towers in the central cities.

Race was mentioned, somewhat offhandedly, in the last paragraph. It deserves a more pointed treatment. The decline in the fortunes of public housing has gone hand in hand with the rise in the percentage of Negroes in public housing. Public housing in the big cities is central city housing; and the central cities are now pre-dominantly Negro ghettoes. The process has been going on for a long time, but since the end of the Second World War it has vastly accelerated. Public housing in Washington, D.C., is virtually all Negro. Chicago and St. Louis have some whites in public housing, but not many. In some other cities the percentage of Negroes rises to seventy, eighty, and ninety per cent or more. At the end of 1965, every single tenant in Philadelphia's Raymond Rosen Apartments was Negro. This project had 1,122 dwelling units.[18] The reader does not have to be told what happens to public support of public housing if public housing means Negro ghettoes. Instead of the angry marginal whites of the New Deal period, public housing in the big cities is more and more the home of the most despised and dispossessed group in America: the urban, problem-family Negro. The more this happens, the more others abandon public housing—physically, by moving out, and politically, by despising it. The worst

---

[16] *E.g.*, Bauer, *The Dreary Deadlock of Public Housing*, ARCHITECTURAL FORUM, May 1957, at 140.

[17] *See* Friedman, *supra* note 12, at 329.

[18] U.S. DEP'T OF HOUSING AND URBAN DEVELOPMENT, LOW-RENT PROJECT DIRECTORY 30 (Dec. 3, 1965).

thing about big-city public housing is not that it is shoddy and dreary.[19] The worst thing is that it is despicable to live there, and that degraded, hopeless people, the victims of weakness, fate, and prejudice, make their homes there. And the more this is true, the more the white community reacts with hostility. The very mention of public housing in the suburbs or in middle class areas is political death. Mayor Lindsay of New York seems to have the courage to speak the truth; and to demand that public housing be scattered throughout the city. But he may not have the power to carry this program out. Government must follow its line of least resistance, at least as a general rule. It must follow the will of the majority. And the will of the majority is that public housing stay put in its ghetto.

The story of public housing, then, in sum, indicates the desperate straits of a program that cannot, will not, or does not accommodate middle class interests. Another good example of the same process is the fate of Aid for Dependent Children. This too began as a kind of middle class program—for unfortunate but respectable widows. When, through demographic and economic change, it became a program primarily (or at least notoriously) for Negro women with big broods of illegitimate children, the program became unpopular to the point of crisis. It is still subject to constant congressional and local sniping.[20]

Government, moreover, is constantly seeking new ways to help those who are politically grateful and who count. The much touted rent supplement is a case in point.[21] As originally proposed, this was a program to benefit the lower middle class—the "rich poor" as they were called. Congress refused and restricted the program to the public housing poor. One cannot identify either side as the champions of the social underdog. That Congress is not is suggested by the fact that the right wing was as eager to restrict the scope of the rent supplement to the public housing poor as anyone. Not that the right was deaf to the entreaties of the middle class. But the spectre which haunts the right is government "competition" with private industry. Congress has been exceedingly careful—paranoid may be the better word—on this subject. One example is the provision of the federal public housing law which requires a twenty per cent gap between the "upper rental limits for admission to . . . low-rent housing and the lowest rents at which private enterprise unaided by public subsidy is providing . . . a substantial supply of decent, safe, and sanitary housing."[22] The rent supplement, as originally proposed, raised the fear that government might invade a private market. This the right could not abide.

For some, keeping government out of competition is a matter of economic and social principle. It is a principle which has been used to justify letting

---

[19] As if Americans had such elevated aesthetic taste! As if Levittown or the average luxury apartment were any prettier.

[20] See generally on the history of this program, W. BELL, AID TO DEPENDENT CHILDREN (1965); G. STEINER, SOCIAL INSECURITY, THE POLITICS OF WELFARE 113 (1966).

[21] See generally Krier, The Rent Supplement Program of 1965: Out of the Ghetto, Into the . . . ?, 19 STAN. L. REV. 555 (1967).

[22] 42 U.S.C. § 1415(7)(b)(ii) (1964).

people die of malnutrition rather than have the state intervene, as if the poor were Hindu mystics starving to death for a higher cause. Fortunately, for most people, laissez faire is not a sacred principle at all. It is merely an aspect of selfishness. A selfish man is not as dangerous as an ideolog; he can always be bribed. The same real estate interests who fought public housing tooth and nail have, in some cities, eagerly welcomed a 1965 program under which housing authorities lease private apartments and homes.[23] The program sops up nagging vacancies and gives long-term leases to landlords, with a government guarantee of the rent. It stays away from low-vacancy cities. Hence it has been, so far, highly acceptable to landlords and brokers.

The administration originally proposed a rent supplement for the "rich poor." Yet it fought hard for the congressional plan, which benefits only the public housing poor. The fight has been hard. The rent supplement has been killed at least twice. Both times the White House brought it back to life by mouth-to-mouth breathing. It seemed finally, irrevocably dead, when the summer riots of 1967 brought it back to life (along with the now famous rat control bill). Yet the altruism of the administration is rendered doubtful by their original conception; and by their willingness to fight for a rent supplement—of any kind. One suspects that the administration felt it had to have a housing program, politically speaking—almost any one would do—and a rent supplement was part of this program. And the rent supplement (in its 1965 version) was likely to make jobs, house old people, and please religious and charitable organizations.

It is a hopeful sign that everybody, even arch-conservatives, seems to think a housing program is either desirable or inevitable. Hence, "alternatives" to present programs have proliferated, with constant new ideas trotted out by this side or that. There is the Percy plan, for example, which stresses Americanism and owning-your-own-home.[24] It has a quaintly archaic ring. What this plan has in mind seems to be a neat little village of bungalows, inhabited by the honest (but low-paid) working class. Its relevance to the big-city slums is minimal.

III

ON THE POLITICAL ECONOMY OF WELFARE

The second corollary of our general proposition is that government will seek the line of financial least resistance. Costly programs mean taxes and taxes are unpopular. Or they mean foregoing genuinely popular programs. Hence direct government expenditures on housing for the poor are not as attractive as expenditures which stimulate or force somebody else to spend their money. Consequently, the history of government and housing is a long tale of attempts at stimulation and force.

---

[23] 42 U.S.C. § 1421b (Supp. II, 1965-66). A study of the the program by L. Friedman and J. Krier will be published in a forthcoming issue of the *Pennsylvania Law Review*.

[24] S. 1952, 90th Cong., 1st Sess. (1967). There is also a Kennedy plan: S. 2088, 90th Cong., 1st Sess. (1967); S. 2100, 90th Cong., 1st Sess. (1967).

Force is the older technique, and therefore deserves earlier mention. The first important slum control laws were the tenement house laws. Modern housing codes differ from these in a number of technical respects, but in essence, they are their lineal descendants. The first notable tenement house law was passed in New York in 1867, shortly after a venomous cholera epidemic.[25] Much more influential was the law of 1901, which was imitated in Connecticut, New Jersey, and Wisconsin.[26] Modern housing codes, essentially, are products of the urban redevelopment and renewal laws. To qualify for federal gold, communities must have a "workable program." Among the prerequisites of such a program is a housing code.[27] This is reason enough to explain the great rush to enact these codes. They have multiplied ten-fold or more in the last fifteen years.

Housing codes vary a great deal. But the general idea is everywhere the same. The law sets up minimum standards of decency and maintenance. Overcrowding is prohibited. Sanitary conditions are insisted upon. Houses must be kept in good repair. It is obvious to the naked eye that vast tracts in New York, Chicago, and other major cities could not possibly stand in conformity with any but the most minimal type of code. Everyone knows that the Negro ghettoes are overcrowded and that conditions in many of the tenements are appalling. Enforcement of the codes, then, is something less than perfect. The same was true of their ancestors, the tenement house laws.

Law enforcement is never a simple matter; and the likelihood of enforcement is different in different cities. A good deal depends upon the resources put into enforcement. Obviously, if the call for enforcement comes only from the minority poor, no one will listen. But apart from this an essential vice gnaws at the heart of these laws. It is that the job is basically too big for punitive sanctions to work. The punitive aspects of housing laws consist not so much in the fact that criminal penalties are appended to them (though they are), as in the fact that the social burdens under these laws are distributed in such a lop-sided way. Everyone admits it would take billions of dollars to clear the slums or upgrade them and give every American a decent home. Yet if the housing codes were perfectly enforced, every American *would* have a minimally decent home. This means that the codes in essence demand that landlords expend billions of dollars improving their property. But where are those billions to come from? Not from government, which offers only to pay the policeman and the inspector, but from the landlords themselves.

[25] Act of May 14, 1867, ch. 908, [1867] N.Y. Laws 2265. *See generally* C. ROSENBERG, THE CHOLERA YEARS 175-234 (1962).

[26] Act of June 29, 1905, ch. 178, [1905] Conn. Laws 376; Act of March 25, 1904, ch. 61, [1904] N.J. Laws 96; Act of April 12, 1901, ch. 334, [1901] N.Y. Laws 889; Act of June 21, 1907, ch. 269, [1907] Wis. Laws 910. *See generally* R. LUBOVE, *supra* note 7, on the background of the New York law; Friedman & Spector, *Tenement House Legislation in Wisconsin: Reform and Reaction*, 9 AM. J. LEGAL HIST. 41 (1965), on the background of the Wisconsin law.

[27] 42 U.S.C. § 1451 (1964, Supp. II, 1965-66). *See generally* Guandolo, *Housing Codes in Urban Renewal*, 25 GEO. WASH. L. REV. 1 (1956); Note, *Enforcement of Municipal Housing Codes*, 78 HARV. L. REV. 801 (1965).

The only way to justify *exclusive* use of housing codes in the attack on the slums would be to assume, as so many are willing to assume, that landlords are heartless monsters reaping enormous, clandestine profits out of the misery of their tenants' lives. There is some evidence that these profits are mythical—at least as a general rule.[28] No one is certain. What seems likely is that the more dilapidated the building, the lower the profits. It is, however, inconsistent to argue that slum houses are gold mines, and then to worry (as the administration and most housing experts worry) about the difficulties of stimulating investment in low-income housing. Orthodox economists might point out that if housing the poor were truly a gold mine, capital would rush into the market. As a matter of fact, slum housing is a poor business from a number of aspects. It is a high risk, low prestige operation. Apartment houses in the slums need careful management and constant attention to be profitable. Respectable capital is leery of this kind of business. What moves in is uninformed capital, marginal operators—and the disreputable.

But the tenement house laws and housing codes have helped *create* a climate inimical to normal, respectable investment. These laws have helped create the unscrupulous landlord. They have invited evasion or corruption of formal enactments. And they have done so at least in part because the punitive approach is so cheap and so easy for the government. Passing a housing code calls for the most minimal sort of public investment. Yet it satisfies the outcry to do something about the slums. It names a scapegoat (the landlord), and dumps upon him the whole cost of renovating the national stock of housing. When he fails to respond, government increases its posture of indignation. It authorizes rent strikes, passes receivership laws, and fulminates about taking the profit out of the slums.[29] The same philosophy lies behind the recent antirioting laws. Congress was faced with demands to do something about big-city riots. Any real program would have been costly and controversial. Congress found it cheap and convenient to name a scapegoat instead and pass a law thundering empty words against the scapegoat. Not a penny had to be appropriated, not a tax dollar raised. Nobody was offended, except the radical fringe.

Government has often hit upon an analogous pseudo-solution to the problem of housing integration. Here government faces a real dilemma. Negroes demand integrated housing. Many white liberals agree, with varying passion and commitment. Other whites violently disagree, particularly small householders in the suburbs and in urban ethnic enclaves. From the standpoint of government, the best solution is to place an ordinance or statute on the books which proclaims the right of Negroes to live everywhere; and to do nothing further. Actually, the form of these ordinances repre-

---

[28] *See* W. Klein, Let in the Sun 141-68, 173-74 (1964); Sporn, *Empirical Studies in the Economics of Slum Ownership*, 36 Land Econ. 333 (1960). A superb treatment is G. Sternlieb, The Tenement Landlord (1966), a recent study of the situation in Newark.

[29] *See* L. Friedman, Government and Slum Housing: A Century of Frustration, ch. 2 (in press, 1967).

sents a quite typical compromise. Those in favor are not strong enough to ram through fair housing laws which really sting; those against are not strong enough to block passage. The compromise takes the form of a ringing symbolic declaration, coupled with flabby enforcement provisions. When these laws fail to be enforced (as is usually the case) the liberals cry out for more teeth.

Yet one wonders if the teeth could really bite. The opposition is numerous and feels the problem deeply. Particularly under these circumstances, the punitive approach is likely to fail. It satisfies only the natural timidity of government. The path followed is much like that of the tenement house laws. First, there is a search for a scapegoat. He is easy to find. The Southern Yahoo, the Polish factory worker, the suburban Bircher—these will do nicely. To castigate these people may be good for the soul and for the adrenalin; it does not integrate a city. To move men and change institutions usually requires more than symbols; it requires the input of actual resources. Those who oppose integration are not merely bigots; they are also frightened men. They are afraid that their property values will decline, that their schools will deteriorate, that police and fire protection will vanish, that crime will rise in their neighborhoods. They feel, in other words, that integration will impose heavy costs on them. They see nobody willing to help them absorb these costs. Government offers preachments and punishments. Politically speaking, a perceived cost is as good as a real cost. Hence, even if the famous decline in property values is illusory, that people believe in it is important. The white opposition to integration will continue to avoid, evade, and frustrate racial integration, as long as they feel that they are asked to bear heavy and unnecessary costs—at no gain to them in any way.

Stimulation has been as popular a device for government as punishment. The idea is to sow seed money, which will induce the private sector to invest heavily in low-income property. Even before the federal seed money days, many hoped that philanthropists, out of the goodness of their hearts, would solve the slum problem by building model tenements to house the poor. The model tenement movement dates from the middle of the nineteenth century. The philanthropists who built model houses were genuinely animated by a desire to solve pressing problems of society. Perhaps they also wished to demonstrate that respectable private business had both the conscience and the means to do what government could not and would not achieve. Unfortunately, the demonstration failed. Some projects were outright failures; others avoided housing the poorest of the poor, choosing instead to benefit the lower middle class and the honest workman. And volume never lived up to expectations. Capital simply did not flow in any great quantity into the slums.[30]

It became clear that kindhearted millionaires could not, unaided, clear the slums.

---

[30] *See generally* on the model tenement house movement, *id.* ch. 3; 2 J. FORD, SLUMS AND HOUSING 572-90, 671-701 (1936); E. WOOD, THE HOUSING OF THE UNSKILLED WAGE EARNER 91-132 (1919). A fascinating case-study is Bremner, *The Big Flat: History of a New York Tenement House*, 64 AM. HIST. REV. 54 (1958).

Gingerly, government tried modest subsidies—the right of eminent domain, tax exemption provisions.[31]

Gradually the incentives have diversified and expanded. Government has become fonder and fonder of the idea, or hope, that private enterprise would rescue it from its housing dilemma. Housing and Urban Development has become an empire of little gimmicks and bailiwicks, programs and subprograms, a bewildering, baffling congeries of devices, many of them motivated by the hope that the market can somehow be galvanized cheaply into life. The government will lend money at below-market interest, it will guarantee mortgages, it will subsidize "demonstrations," it will support planning and research, it will encourage tearing down and building up—constantly in search of a key that will magically open a wonderful door of investment. It was recently announced, with trumpets and sennets, from the highest pinnacles in Washington that insurance companies were prepared to invest a billion dollars in the slums.[32] This development fulfilled so many administration dreams. It met, in part, the demand that something be done about the slums. And it did so at no cost to government, other than the trifling expense of flattering and cajoling executives into taking this step. Moreover, investment by this industry might very well stimulate even more investments by others. Fresh investment in housing in slum areas, by insurance companies, philanthropists, the Roman Catholic church, and whoever else has resources and willingness, is of course very welcome—provided always that demolition, relocation, and rehabilitation are carried on with due attention to human values. But may one be permitted a note of skepticism? Past experience, if it is any guide at all, tells us that private investment is unlikely to make more than a beginning of the job. Low-rent housing must show a profit to attract anyone but philanthropists. And philanthropists are not rich enough, or are too fickle, to mount a sustained attack on the problem. The private effort, then, tends to falter, at which point heavier and heavier subsidies are needed. But it was such subsidies that government wished to avoid in the first place.

CONCLUSION

Is there any hope that the poor will be decently housed? At first glance, there seems to be little ground for optimism. All indications are that the problem requires massive public investment. All the political lessons are that this investment is currently impossible. Billions can be voted for defense and for war; even a pittance for domestic programs requires Herculean battle.

---

[31] Act of May 10, 1926, ch. 823, [1926] N.Y. Laws 1507. See generally L. PINK, THE NEW DAY IN HOUSING 105-14 (1928).

[32] N.Y. Times, Sept. 14, 1967, at 1, col. 1 (city ed.). Earlier, President Johnson had "ordered the Department of Housing and Urban Development . . . to undertake a pilot program aimed at drawing private resources into public housing . . . [to] involve private developers in not only the construction but also the management of . . . projects." N.Y. Times, Aug. 18, 1967, at 1, col. 2. Such a program would cut criticisms as well as costs.

Technological breakthrough might act as *deus ex machina*. After all, even the poorest enjoy some amenities of life unthinkable for the rich a century ago. Television is an example. In America, millions of relatively poor people can afford at least a beaten-up nag of a car. This gives freedom, mobility, a chance of change the peasants of India or the textile workers of Victorian England could hardly have dreamt of. Will technology find a way to mass-produce housing for the poor? Some miracle of engineering or science is bound to occur. Experiments in "instant rehabilitation" of slum houses suggest that this is more than a dream.

Technology, however, is no accident. It depends on brute social facts. Innovation flows where it is wanted; it flows where minds and resources have been invested. One can be relatively certain of technological improvement in an industry or field if there is the social will for improvement, a market for the improved product, and investment in research and development. Clearly, there is a market for cheap housing. But there would also be a market for a $100 new car. The bigger and more lucrative market is the middle class market. The technological hope is tied in with the political and social dilemma of slum housing, and welfare in general. Moreover, technological breakthrough will follow, not precede, massive social investment.

Another possibility is political. The punitive aspects of housing laws were explained, in part, as attempts by government to satisfy maximum demands at minimum price. But some of the classic solutions and responses have begun to pall. They are not working. Demands are not being satisfied. Unrest seems to be growing. Profoundly disturbing riots occurred in big cities in the summer of 1967. Both Negroes and whites appear to have grown more intransigent. Negro militancy means that a new set of demands, stemming from a group that could once be ignored, must now be taken into account. The price of law and order has gone up sharply. Much more output must be allotted by government to the urban poor, if tranquility is to be preserved. And yet the new output—interracial housing, for example—evokes rage and even bloodshed in white communities. It may be that there are no cheap solutions left. The rational course of action may be a difficult and costly one. Investment in slum housing may have to be tripled, quadrupled, to satisfy demands of Negroes and the poor. At the same time, white opposition may have to be bought off, too, by heavy investment in the needs of middle class whites—perhaps with better police protection, schools, street lighting, fire-fighting service. Perhaps bold new devices will have to be tried—price-supports for the little frame houses on the ghetto fringe, to lay the haunting fear of "loss of property values" finally to rest. It is not bigotry but fact that neighhorhoods decay when they become Negro ghettoes. The bigotry consists of the belief that race causes the decay. That the schools deteriorate, that the police stop policing, that the quality of municipal services go down, that buildings become crowded—these are facts, not bigotry. They cannot be met with exhortations. Its costs money to demonstrate that an interracial neighborhood can be a sound, stable neighborhood. It costs money—not fair housing laws or speeches. But the politics of urban unrest may eventually drive the country to the point of willingness to spend. And, ultimately, integration and achievement of housing goals means massive public building or subsidizing—scattered housing, suburban housing, vest-pocket housing, not high-rise ghettoes near downtown.

Success in this venture is far from certain. In theory, there is a rational solution to every social problem. But an elementary glance at human history shows that the rational solution is not always reached. History is a long dismal tale of wars, disorders, rebellions. It is full of examples of societies that failed to adapt, societies that never found a way to the optimal solution of their problems. The same may be true of urban problems of the United States, and particularly problems of slum housing and the ghetto. Riots, for example, may result not in increased investment but in increased race-hate and increased repression.

As a first step, however, the problem must be stripped of cant, hypocrisy, and obstructive indignation. It has to be seen in all its political, economic, and social complexity. The futility of cheap minimal solutions must become apparent. Only then is there hope of clearing the slums and housing all the people in decent comfort.

Part II

The Federal Role

FOREWORD

The first part of this two-issue symposium on Housing has pointed out many of the major problems that must be confronted and solved before the nation's housing needs can be met.[1] This issue discusses the institutions and programs that constitute the federal government's response to these needs.

Housing problems are far from static. In fact, daily they become more acute as (1) new family formations attributable to the post-World War II "baby boom" in particular, and rising population in general, create enormous pressure for new dwelling units; and (2) the continuing urbanization of the nation's population is reflected in rising population densities in the core areas of our major cities, accelerating the decay of their aging multi-family residences. Additional dimensions of complexity are provided by the fact that, for both urban and rural dwellers, housing deficiencies correlate closely with low income levels, inferior employment and educational opportunities, and, frequently, racial discrimination. These socioeconomic complexities compound the difficulty of achieving the national goal of standard housing for every citizen at a price that he can afford.

In some instances, solutions to housing problems must be sought at the state and local levels. More often, however, adequate solutions will require federal participation of various types. The optimum form and scope of this federal participation are subjects of continuing public debate, which reflects basic disagreement concerning both the permissible objectives of federal assistance and the means by which it can legitimately be implemented. Typically, advocates of a federal role subordinate to and supportive of private housing markets are deployed against proponents of federal programs of greater magnitude. Within the Congress, this unresolved controversy provides one explanation for the Executive's inability to mobilize sustained legislative support for the creation and funding of new housing assistance programs.

The federal programs more specifically oriented to housing[2] have shown, over the years, not only a great increase in number but also a broadening in approach. Among the earliest federal activities which directly concerned housing was the drafting of model zoning, subdivision control, and planning legislation for enactment

---

[1] Other symposia on these problems that have appeared in this publication are *Low-Cost Housing and Slum Clearance*, 1 LAW & CONTEMP. PROB. 135-256 (1934); *Housing*, 12 *id.* at 1-205 (1947); *Land Planning in a Democracy*, 20 *id.* at 197-350 (1955); *Urban Housing and Planning*, 20 *id.* at 351-529 (1955); *Urban Renewal, Part I*, 25 *id.* at 631-812 (1960); *Urban Renewal, Part II*, 26 *id.* at 1-171 (1961).

[2] Of course, federal influence on housing is not limited to programs chiefly designed for that purpose. For example, defense policy affects the availability of men, material, and financing for housing construction. Similarly, federal fiscal and monetary decisions concerning balance of payments, rediscount rate, and the like, help determine how many units of housing will be built at a particular time. Federal labor policy may affect construction costs and techniques. Prevailing wage, equal employment opportunity, payment and performance bond, and other requirements applicable to federal and federally-assisted construction tend to influence what housing is built and by which developers.

by state legislatures.[3] Then, during the Depression, the Federal Housing Administration (FHA) was created by the Housing Act of 1934[4] to lure private investment funds into the housing market at a time when many home owners were facing foreclosure. In addition to the funds (and the possibilities of home ownership) it made available, the FHA also had a significant impact on financing and construction practices. For example, developers were required to meet design specifications in order to qualify for FHA financing. In addition, many municipalities conformed their land use controls to the stricter FHA requirements.

A few years after the federal government began assisting private investment in home mortgages, it entered the field of public housing. Local housing authorities have served as the vehicle for this program. These authorities, with the backing of a federal annual contributions contract, could borrow the funds for construction of public housing projects in the private market. Since the obligations of the local housing authorities enjoy certain exemptions and immunities from taxation, they have been attractive to investors. Just as many local ordinances were drafted or revised with an eye to FHA requirements, so also state legislation in the field of public housing was drafted in a way that would enable local projects to qualify for federal contributions.

The federal government originally entered urban renewal chiefly as a means for meeting national housing needs.[5] The original urban renewal legislation contained no "non-residential exception."[6] Just as in the case of public housing, the form of state urban renewal enabling legislation was affected by the desire to qualify for federal grants.

In connection with urban renewal, public housing, and certain FHA programs, Congress introduced in 1954 the requirement of a local "workable program."[7] By means of this requirement, municipalities were placed under heavy pressure to prepare a comprehensive community plan, make a neighborhood analysis of blight, and adopt adequate codes and ordinances.

Since that time federal housing programs have displayed increased emphasis on comprehensive community planning. In urban renewal, local public agencies were encouraged to develop "general neighborhood renewal plans"; and, more recently, funds have been made available for localities to prepare community renewal plans. To some extent, the Model Cities legislation[8] may be viewed as a further step in

[3] The Department of Commerce proposed certain Model Acts. See C. HAAR, LAND-USE PLANNING (1959).

[4] National Housing Act, ch. 847, 48 Stat. 1246 (1934).

[5] Urban renewal was authorized by the Housing Act of 1949, ch. 338 63 Stat. 413. Furnishing employment, as well as adequate housing, may also have been a legislative objective. See generally Foard & Fefferman, Federal Urban Renewal Legislation, 25 LAW & CONTEMP. PROB. 635 (1960).

[6] Foard & Fefferman, supra note 5, at 657. The project had to be "predominantly residential." A variety of factors have influenced the creation of the "nonresidential exception." Among them was the belief that the entire living environment of the community should be renewed and that redevelopment which was limited to residential areas would not be fully successful. Id. at 662-72.

[7] Housing Act of 1954, ch. 649, § 303, 68 Stat. 623. See generally Rhyne, The Workable Program—A Challenge for Community Improvement, 25 LAW & CONTEMP. PROB. 635 (1960). In Mr. Rhyne's view, the "workable program" requirement "marks a milestone in federal-city relations." Id. at 688.

[8] 42 U.S.C. §§ 1453, 3301-13 (Supp. II, 1965-66). See generally Taylor & Williams, Housing in Model Cities, in this symposium, pp. 397-408.

this same direction; and the creation of a Department of Housing and Urban Development embodies the same assumption that housing needs should be met as part of a comprehensive, and well-planned, program of community development.

The federal efforts to provide adequate housing have also been characterized by increasing emphasis on conservation and rehabilitation. The change in nomenclature from "urban redevelopment" to "urban renewal" was part of this trend, as was the "workable program" requirement of adequate codes and ordinances.[9] Federal funds are now available on a matching basis to help expand local inspection and code enforcement efforts. Loans and grants are available to individuals for rehabilitation purposes in urban renewal projects. Housing projects are being rehabilitated by their owners for lease or sale to local housing authorities.

In connection with federal housing programs, a variety of relationships have been developed with local agencies. To a considerable extent the federal government has underwritten local efforts—by loans, grants, annual contributions contracts, tax exclusions, and payments in lieu of taxes.[10] Obviously, the power of the purse has been used to provide considerable, and often detailed, guidance to the municipalities— for example, as to the wording and enforcement of housing and occupancy codes. Through the "workable program" requirement and otherwise, this federal influence has been pervasive at the local level.

With respect to the private sector, federal programs have moved towards creation of a more effective partnership in meeting housing needs: (1) Through expansion of FHA programs, private developers are being induced to provide housing for low- and middle-income groups that were previously neglected. (2) By reason of the federal income tax exclusion with respect to interest on municipal obligations, public housing and urban renewal projects have been financed, for the most part, by loans from private investors, rather than by direct federal loans.[11] (3) In urban renewal, local eminent domain powers are invoked, with federal financial backing, to assemble property which, under restrictions contained in the urban renewal plan, will be disposed of to private redevelopers; these redevelopers may, in turn, finance their construction of new housing with section 220 loans, payable over long terms at low interest rates, guaranteed by FHA, and backed by the Federal National Mortgage Association. (4) In public housing, this partnership has been marked by the development of the Turnkey principle—which is now being extended from construction to management.[12] (5) Another spectacular example is the rent supplement, which is made available to low-income tenants in private housing projects.[13]

---

[9] This requirement was a main impetus for the adoption of housing and occupancy codes in a number of cities. These codes, of course, were not limited in applicability to the particular area of an urban renewal project.

[10] The payment in lieu of taxes (PILOT), which has been used in connection with public housing, has been rceommended by some in connection with other federal activities or programs which immunize considerable property from local or state taxes.

[11] The availability of the federal loan or grant is itself the chief security for the obligations issued by the local housing authority or local public agency.

[12] Federal contributions for public housing can also be made available in connection with the leasing of units from private landlords.

[13] The National Association of Homebuilders was among the groups that seemed to favor rent supplements. Interestingly, in 1937, when public housing legislation was being considered, the Chamber

In dealing with the private sector, federal housing programs have recognized the acceptability of the profit motive. Although a nonprofit sponsor can obtain a larger loan (percentagewise) for construction of a below-market-interest-rate 221(d)(3) project, a limited distribution sponsor is also permissible. The developer who sells a Turnkey project to a local housing authority is not subject to the limitations on profit provided by competitive bidding or cost certification.[14] And perhaps the most powerful incentive for development of new housing, both federally-assisted and "conventional," has been provided by the availability of accelerated depreciation.

In addition to participation by local officialdom and by private business in the effort to enlarge the inventory of adequate housing, the federal government is also seeking to enlist citizen participation, especially by those who are receiving special benefits from federal assistance. The "workable program" requires citizen participation, and has led to the creation of local citizens' advisory groups. In connection with antipoverty programs of the Office of Economic Opportunity, local organizations have been formed to represent the indigent, or in which the indigent have a substantial voice; these organizations have frequently been active in negotiations or consultations with local housing authorities and urban renewal agencies. The Turnkey III program contemplates that families in public housing projects will obtain a "sweat equity" through maintenance of their units, and through this equity will ultimately be able to obtain home ownership. The federal programs which seek to facilitate home ownership are predicated to some extent on the assumption that a person with an equity in his home will be more strongly motivated to maintain it properly than would a mere tenant.

By now, however, it is clear that neither federal programs nor private market forces have sufficed to meet the nation's ever-increasing housing needs. Several pending legislative proposals envisage an extension of federal programs to foster a more meaningful partnership with private capital in housing construction and rehabilitation.[15] It is to be hoped that, when domestic problems can again command serious attention in Congress and at the highest levels of the Executive, new proposals for federal action to meet the developing housing crisis will receive the consideration they deserve.

Meanwhile, as the development of the Turnkey program attests, considerable progress can also be made through legitimate innovation in the administration of existing federal laws. It is, perhaps, in this regard that lawyers can make a unique contribution to federal efforts to provide adequate housing for every American.

Robinson O. Everett.
John D. Johnston, Jr.

---

of Commerce favored rent supplements in preference to public housing. *See* Note, *Government Housing Assistance to the Poor*, 76 Yale L.J. 508 (1967).

[14] Cost certification is necessary in some instances when the developer does not carry through the project but sells the land and his plans to the local housing authority.

[15] Senator Robert Kennedy and Senator Percy, among others, have made far-reaching proposals for new federal programs.

THE DEPARTMENT OF HOUSING AND URBAN DEVELOPMENT—BUILDING A NEW FEDERAL DEPARTMENT

Introduction

When Robert C. Weaver was sworn into office on January 18, 1966, as the nation's first Secretary of Housing and Urban Development (HUD), he undertook the most ambitious and dramatic revamping attempted by any Cabinet department in recent years.

The act which created the Department[1] elevated to Cabinet rank the Housing and Home Finance Agency (HHFA), which he had headed for five years as Administrator, and endowed it with a political fulcrum lacking in the old agency. But this was far more than a pro forma merger of related functions and programs under a newly-created Cabinet member. The Act characterized in broad terms the role of the Department and the Secretary in relation to other federal agencies and other levels of government; and it vested in the Secretary full powers to integrate and administer the expanded programs and activities of the Department.

At the signing ceremony creating the new Department, President Johnson described it as "a very new and needed instrument to serve all the people of America."

"We are taking the first step," he said, "toward organizing our system for a more rational response to the pressing challenge of urban life."

In the main, organization of the Department was left to the discretion of the Secretary. Only these two major organizational changes were spelled out in the bill:

1. The Act specified that there shall be within the Department a Federal Housing Administration headed by one of the Assistant Secretaries, who would also be the Federal Housing Commissioner.[2]

2. The Act transferred intact to the new department the former agency's mixed-ownership corporation, the Federal National Mortgage Association, with the Secretary as chairman of its board of directors.[3]

These two provisions signified the beginning of many changes to come in the Department. But these and other revisions during the past year should not obscure the fact that there were also significant changes in the fifteen-year evolution of its predecessor.

At the time HHFA assumed departmental status as HUD it had become one of

---

* Assistant Secretary for Administration, Department of Housing and Urban Development.
[1] Department of Housing and Urban Development Act, 42 U.S.C. §§ 3531-37 (Supp. II, 1965-66).
[2] § 4(a), 42 U.S.C. § 3533(a) (Supp. II, 1965-66).
[3] § 5(b), 42 U.S.C. § 3534(b) (Supp. II, 1965-66).

the most complex agencies in the executive branch. In fact, the Secretary's Organization Order No. 1 assigned responsibility within the Department for some fifty-five enumerated programs and activities. And its financial involvement had reached $73 billion as of June 30, 1965, the closest date to the establishment of the Department for which the figures were compiled.

This statistic indicates that the HHFA was a very different agency from the one established by Reorganization Plan No. 3 of 1947.[4] Under that plan HHFA was strictly a housing agency, consisting of three principal constituents, the Federal Housing Administration, the Home Loan Bank Board, and the Public Housing Administration. Starting with the Great Depression, and spurred by President Roosevelt, a great deal had been done by way of public-assisted housing at the federal level, and it was clear that, so far as the federal government was concerned, public housing was here to stay. The note of urban development, however, was yet the echo of a distant horn.

The first major chord in the new theme was struck in the Housing Act of 1949.[5] In title I of that Act Congress recognized that public housing in and by itself was not an effective vehicle for slum clearance—one of its principal stated purposes in 1937. In the 1949 Act the Congress embraced a new concept—not only clearance of slum areas, but their redevelopment in accordance with a plan developed by the community itself. To protect the displaced, the Congress required that a relocation program be developed to make available decent, safe, and sanitary housing. To assure an overall improvement in housing, the Act also required that the area be predominantly residential either before or after its clearance and redevelopment.

Thus, while the focus was still on housing, the Agency was precipitated abruptly into a new and broader dimension—the orderly development and redevelopment of communities in accordance with locally conceived plans and objectives. A number of important steps were taken, both administratively and by congressional action, to channel the Agency's programs in the area of urban planning, including grants for sewers, schools and hospitals, loans and grants for community facilities, grants for open space land, loans and grants to assist mass transportation, and urban beautification.

At the same time the Agency's housing responsibilities were growing and diversifying. They included the college housing loan program, the manufacture of housing, supervision of the Federal National Mortgage Association, loans for prefabricated housing, mortgage insurance programs for housing in urban renewal areas, housing credit for small and remote communities, housing for the elderly and the handicapped.

Thus it is fair to say that when Congress established the new Department in 1965, the HHFA was already deeply involved in the problems of both housing and urban development.

---

[4] 61 Stat. 954 (1947).

[5] Ch. 338, 63 Stat. 413 (codified in scattered sections of 12, 42 U.S.C.).

I

THEORY OF THE NEW ORGANIZATION

It became clear to the new Department that its greatest challenge lay in the area of congestion in the cities, with its growing list of critical urban ills—substandard housing, inadequate schools, overcrowded hospitals, welfare loads, malnutrition, unemployment, pollution of air and water, insufficient recreational facilities, and the tremendous upsurge of crime and delinquency in the streets. What was needed— and obviously lacking in the past—was a comprehensive and realistic urban policy, linking together administratively the many urban aid programs and envisaging the city in terms of total urban development, sociological as well as physical.

The knottiest problem in approaching the organization of the new Department was to determine the most effective method in which to group its manifold programs and activities to respond to these urban needs. Of the various available alternatives, the one selected was the grouping of functions and programs in such a manner that the organization format itself would tend to compel problems to be resolved in the context of other, related problems—regardless of historical program distinctions or past organizational separation. The Congress implicitly espoused this approach in the departmental act, when it gave separate organizational recognition to "programs relating to the private mortgage market."[6]

Taking this as the first, a second grouping of functions was put together dealing essentially with the problems of the central city. This included, for instance, urban renewal, public housing, aids to the provision of neighborhood centers and similar facilities, and the provision of open space and beautification in densely built-up central areas. Also placed here was the focal point for dealing with the relocation problems of urban families.

A third such grouping was made up of functions and programs dealing with metropolitan areas and the urbanizing countryside. It included such programs as grants for preservation of open space as urbanization spills outward; assistance for area-wide planning; grants for water and sewer development, geared to the concept of developing area-wide systems; aids for urban mass transportation; and assistance in advance planning for, and acquisition of land for future, public need.

A fourth grouping brought together the Department's demonstration programs such as Model Cities, and the wholly new and developmental work in the area of intergovernmental relations—the search for more effective means of coordination within and among the federal, state, metropolitan and municipal levels of government.[7]

The Department was now organized on a basis which would enable Secretary

---

[6] § 4(a), 42 U.S.C. § 3533(a) (Supp. II, 1965-66).

[7] New as it is, the organization of the Department is understandably still in a state of growth and change. Pending legislation (H.R. 8068, 90th Cong., 1st Sess. (1967) and S. 1445, 90th Cong., 1st Sess. (1967)) requests congressional authorization of an additional Assistant Secretary to handle research, engineering, and urban technology.

Weaver to harness all its resources effectively and efficiently. Five semi-autonomous units were melded into a single cohesive Department, with all authority given by statute to the Secretary.

This organizational approach would be open to the charge of over-simplification if it had been based on the assumption that these were neat, self-contained packages. It was not. It recognized that the problems of the central city are different from those of the urbanizing fringe, and are more closely interrelated with each other than with those of the urbanizing fringe. But it also recognized that none of these problems can be wholly isolated from any other.

Thus, for example, most public housing is located in central cities, but some is not. There is, indeed, no generally acceptable or applicable definition of the term "central city." Incorporated limits grow progressively less meaningful as urban population and attitudes outgrow established political jurisdictions. Urban transportation systems, while they are organic functions of whole regional economic areas, strike into the heart of the central city with profound effects on housing, commerce, land values, and an infinite variety of other municipal concerns. These considerations were fully recognized in the organizational approach.

This organizational thesis had a most interesting consequence in the role established for the Assistant Secretaries within the Department. The current concept in public administration is that a top official should occupy either a line role or a staff role. He either occupies a position in the line of command, receiving authority from his superior and conveying it to his subordinates, or he stands aside from the command chain as one who analyzes problems, accumulates information, and advises or proposes.

When it came to the concrete problem of organizing the Department, however, this conventional solution proved inadequate. What was needed was a senior representative of the Secretary who was concerned *both* with effective program execution and with the Department-wide interrelationships exemplified earlier.

Again, the Congress itself took the lead when it stipulated that one Assistant Secretary should be at once the Federal Housing Commissioner and the Secretary's principal adviser in connection with programs related to the private mortgage market—thus by law enjoining him to perform a mixed line and staff function. The solution adopted on a Department-wide basis followed this congressional concept. An Assistant Secretary was given overall leadership and command responsibility for each of the four functional areas briefly summarized above; at the same time, the Assistant Secretaries *collectively* were given the responsibility of serving, in the Secretary's words, as his "general staff for the management of the Department." Sitting in this capacity, they are not expected to be simply advocates or spokesmen for the programs under their direction, but jointly to review, evaluate and contribute to the Department's approach to its entire mission.

The five Assistant Secretaries operate as a closely knit team. Frequently they meet together in their homes to review the Department's basic policy objectives in the interest of making the Department function more efficiently.

A Budget Review Committee consisting of the Assistant Secretaries and Deputy Under Secretary meets regularly, with Under Secretary Robert Wood serving as chairman, to compare respective programs and recommend to the Secretary its collective judgment on the allocation of departmental resources.

A Deputy Under Secretary for Policy Analysis and Program Evaluation performs the function of comparing programs, sharpening policy objectives and reviewing the extent to which the Department carries out those objectives.

In addition there was a major consolidation of the administrative functions of the Department. In personnel, accounting, audit, general services and budget, the responsibility for establishing department-wide policies and standards and for carrying out operations on a centralized basis for most of the activities of the Department was consolidated at the departmental level under the Assistant Secretary for Administration.

II

Strengthening the Field

Equally important was the approach taken to organization of the Department's facilities in the field. Here again the principle adopted as a guide was the effort to get individual decisions concerted with other related decisions affecting the same community—regardless of program lines. In order to accomplish this, four major changes were made:

1. The regional administrators who head the Department's seven regional offices were made the representatives of and the spokesmen for the Department as a whole in their respective geographic areas.

2. The regional administrators report directly to the Secretary as line managers directly responsible for the programs developing in their jurisdictions.

3. The formerly separate regional offices for the public housing program and for FHA multifamily housing programs were physically and organizationally merged into the regional offices of the Department. Exempted from this change, for obvious practical reasons, was the function of the FHA state and local insuring offices in connection with insurance of mortgages on one to four family homes.

4. A new coordinative function was established directly under the regional administrator to assure common assumptions and common policies on programs which have an impact in a particular community. As the Secretary described the intent of this new arrangement:[8]

> Thus, any project originating in any of these programs will be fed through a
> central review point which will check out and bring to light its relationships to

[8] *Hearings on the Independent Offices and Department of Housing and Urban Development Appropriations for 1968 before the Subcomm. on Independent Offices and Department of Housing and Urban Development of the House Comm. on Appropriations,* 90th Cong., 1st Sess., pt. 3, at 7 (1967).

or its significance for other programs being carried out in the same community; its relationship to the workable program of the community; how it stacks up in terms of the latest information available to the Department on market conditions in the area; how it fits in with local planning for the development of the area as a whole; and whether the community has realistically identified and made sound provision for the relocation problems which its proposed project or projects will bring about.

As more strength is added to the regions, the Department is now proceeding to the next step of delegating more responsibility to them—a task not without its difficulties and stumbling blocks. The process of decentralization does not lend itself automatically to all programs. As a general rule, established programs with well-drawn policy and procedures guidelines can be delegated to the field, while authority over new programs often must be reserved to Washington because of their precedent-setting character.

With respect to a given program, however, it is not simply a question of whether all the decision making process rests in Washington or whether it should be delegated to the field. Most programs involve a number of different elements, ranging from the initial application for a planning grant, through the planning phase, and the award and implementation of the program itself.

Within a particular program some of these elements may be decentralized; and, with the passage of time, more of them will generally lend themselves to decentralization. The Model Cities program is one example of a new and precedent-setting undertaking in which project approvals must be made in Washington. But the regional offices are heavily involved in the project review process, and will administer this program together with the field representatives of other departments that are also heavily involved.

These arrangements mean that communities participating in HUD programs can be served more directly and efficiently. A central point of contact has been established in the field for local agencies and officials, cutting the time and distance between the need for action and the decision to act.

III

INTERDEPARTMENTAL COOPERATION AND INTERGOVERNMENTAL RELATIONS

The departmental act specifies that the Secretary shall "exercise leadership at the direction of the President in coordinating Federal activities affecting housing and urban development."[9] He is also directed to "encourage comprehensive planning by the State aud [sic] local governments with a view to coordinating Federal, State, and local urban and community development activities."[10] In brief, HUD was created to help give form and substance to President Johnson's concept of "creative fed-

---

[9] § 3(b), 42 U.S.C. § 3532(b) (Supp. II, 1965-66).
[10] Id.

eralism"—a concept in which the resources of all three levels of government are focused on solving major problems.

The importance of this approach was recognized at the Assistant Secretary level, and a premium was placed on acquiring new methods and techniques to achieve greater cooperation among federal agencies and with other government bodies.

In the past, many types of machinery were tried, one of which was the standing interdepartmental committee. This, in my opinion, has been unsatisfactory. Standing committees waste time and delay decisions. After a while most permanent committees tend to deteriorate and become of limited use. The Department is now developing less formal and more flexible links with the other chains of government through informal working groups and task forces which have limited objectives and operate for a prescribed time.

Under the so-called "Convenor Order,"[11] the Secretary is authorized to convene meetings of Departments and agencies having responsibilities related to common problems. Thus, the order is a significant document and a meaningful instrument in getting people and institutions to work together with common policies and common goals.

The Model Cities program offers a workable illustration of how the Department is attempting to develop effective ways to draw together the right people at the right time to deal with specific problems or policy issues. Applications for Model Cities planning grants have been filed by almost 200 local communities. These are reviewed in the field on an inter-agency basis by the four principal agencies involved —HUD, Health, Education and Welfare, the Office of Equal Opportunity (OEO), and the Department of Labor—plus the Community Relations Service of the Justice Department and the Economic Development Administration of the Commerce Department.

Reports on the capabilities of the applicant cities are sent by the field to a Review Committee in Washington headed by Assistant Secretary Ralph Taylor of HUD and consisting of representatives from the principal agencies, and the other two agencies if they are involved. The Review Committee in turn recommends the cities to be selected by Secretary Weaver for Model City planning grants. Each agency must administer its own component of the program, but in a manner which would preserve the overall integrity and character of the program.

IV

CONSIDERING THE HUMAN FACTOR

In seeking to mesh social and economic factors with the physical elements of urban development, the human factor has not been neglected. For example, there is today a far greater emphasis on the rehabilitation of existing neighborhoods and individual buildings, as opposed to the former practice of clearing areas with bull-

---

[11] Exec. Order No. 11,297, 3 C.F.R. 141 (Comp. 1966).

dozers to make way for new projects. Special units have been established at head-quarters and in each regional office to reduce to a minimum the problem of reloca-tion in cases where people must be moved even temporarily because of federal projects. The Department is also working far more closely in this area with people-oriented agencies such as the Department of Health, Education and Welfare, the Department of Labor, and the Office of Economic Opportunity.

V

RESEARCH NEEDS

While progress has been made on many fronts, one of the areas in which we have been lagging is research. It seems a curious thing that there has never been a coordinated, concentrated research program focused on housing and urban prob-lems. Sporadic investigations have been undertaken, of course, by universities and foundations, and the federal government has made some contribution. But these have been isolated and topical efforts—often valuable in themselves, but not con-stituting a plan or scheme of orderly investigation. As the Secretary testified to the House Committee on Appropriations:[12]

> In our view, this is a major area of neglect. Sophisticated research techniques and a close working partnership between the Federal Government and private in-dustry, universities, and private research foundations have yielded spectacular results in agriculture, in public health, in space exploration, and in many other areas. It is sad but true that nothing even remotely comparable exists to investi-gate and throw light on the problems that plague our cities and the people who live in them.

As this is written, the probability seems good that there will be made available for the first time a substantial appropriation for research in housing and urban technology. This will be a major step toward the realization of the aims for which the Department was established.

Such an appropriation will bring into meaningful focus two responsibilities of the Secretary as set forth in the basic act: first, to conduct studies of problems of housing and urban technology; second, to conduct a clearinghouse service to make such information available to all levels of government—federal, state, metropolitan and local. The format and mechanics of such a service remain to be worked out. But whatever the mechanics, we have the right to feel hopeful that we are entering a period when decisions of public policy in the field of urban affairs can be made on the basis of better information and understanding.

Toward that objective, an Office of Urban Technology was recently established in HUD, and President Johnson has sought congressional authorization to expand the Office under an Assistant Secretary. It is the hope of the Department that many of the methods and techniques developed in the aerospace and defense areas can be adapted for the improvement of the urban environment.

---

[12] *Hearings, supra* note 8, at 4.

VI

New Legislation Accelerates Department's Efforts

As we continued the Department's building program, several new pieces of legislation gave new thrust and direction to HUD's efforts to achieve greater coordination among programs with an urban impact.

One of these was the rent supplement program for low income families, authorized by the Housing and Urban Development Act of 1965.[13] The act also authorized rehabilitation grants to the owner-occupants of homes in urban renewal areas and federally-assisted code enforcement areas, and a new program of FHA mortgage insurance for the purchase of homes by veterans.

The Demonstration Cities and Metropolitan Development Act of 1966[14] authorized supplemental grants where development in metropolitan areas is being carried out in accordance with metropolitan planning and programming; grants to states to help finance urban information and technical services to small communities; and broadened the mortgage insurance program for land development to provide insured mortgage financing for new communities. The Secretary was also authorized to carry out a comprehensive program of studies of urban environment factors.

VII

The Department Now Fully Organized

The foregoing steps which have taken place during the past year add up to a precedent-setting reorganization both in headquarters and the field. During this same period the Department also has endeavored to provide a new emphasis on meshing economic, social and physical planning in relation to urban problems. Plans have been developed for a diversified research program, and a whole new approach to federal grants-in-aid administration has been undertaken through the Model Cities program.

The massive shifts of functions and staff required to accomplish these objectives have been completed. We believe the Department is now organized on a basis which better enables it to develop and initiate major new programs, as well as increasing the effectiveness of existing programs.

This does not mean, of course, that the Department has perfected its organization procedures and techniques. HUD is still going through its shakedown period, and many procedures must be adjusted to the new organization. A major effort has been launched to speed up the processing of grants through a Joint Administrative Task Force consisting of representatives from HUD, HEW, OEO, and Labor.

Although we want to further strengthen the Department, I believe HUD has now emerged as a vital reality and a major factor in the contemporary American scene.

---

[13] 12 U.S.C. § 1701s (Supp. II, 1965-66).
[14] Pub. L. No. 89-754, 80 Stat. 1255 (codified in scattered sections of 11, 12, 15, 16, 40, 42 U.S.C.).

THE IMPACT OF FISCAL AND MONETARY POLICY ON THE HOUSING MARKET*

Thomas H. Naylor†

I

STRUCTURE OF THE HOUSING MARKET

When one speaks of the "housing market" he is in reality referring to four inter-related submarkets: (1) newly constructed single-family houses not yet sold or occupied, (2) new rental units, (3) previously occupied units being offered for resale, and (4) previously occupied units offered for rent.[1] In this article we shall focus our attention on new housing, submarkets (1) and (2), but we shall by no means ignore the influence of previously occupied resale and rental units on purchases of new housing.

Since World War II expenditures for the purchase of new housing have been estimated to be about four per cent of Gross National Product (GNP). If one includes expenditures for equipment, furnishings, services, and so on which accompany the purchase of new housing, then the broader class of expenditures for new housing approaches twelve per cent of the GNP.[2]

Three different groups of individuals make decisions to construct new houses: (1) individuals who contract for or build a house for their own use, (2) builders who start houses that they expect to sell to new owner-occupiers, and (3) builders who start rental units. Although the percentages of new housing starts in these three groups vary widely from month to month, in the early 1960s the market was roughly divided one-quarter, one-half, and one-quarter respectively.[3] In analyzing the structure of the housing market, we shall concentrate on the decisions by builders to start construction on houses for sale or rental. We will not consider separately decision by individuals to build for their own use. We shall assume that individuals who build for their own use have the same impact on the market as builders and developers.

To facilitate our analysis of the housing market we shall make use of the flow

* This article is based on research supported by National Science Foundation Grant GS-1104.

† B.S. 1958, Millsaps College; B.S. 1959, Columbia University; M.B.A. 1961, Indiana University; Ph.D. 1964, Tulane University. Associate Professor of Economics, Duke University. Co-author, [with E. T. Byrne] LINEAR PROGRAMMING (1963); [with J. L. Balintfy, D. S. Burdick, & K. Chu] COMPUTER SIMULATION TECHNIQUES (1966); Editor, THE IMPACT OF THE COMPUTER ON SOCIETY (1967). Contributor to journals in the fields of economics, management science, and computer science.

[1] Maisel, *A Theory of Fluctuations in Residential Construction Starts*, 53 AM. ECON. REV. 359, 367 (1963).

[2] W. J. FRAZER & W. P. YOHE, MONEY AND BANKING 404 (1966).

[3] Maisel, *Nonbusiness Construction*, in THE BROOKINGS QUARTERLY ECONOMETRIC MODEL OF THE UNITED STATES 185 (1965).

FIGURE 1

FLOW CHART OF CONSTRUCTION IN THE HOUSING MARKET

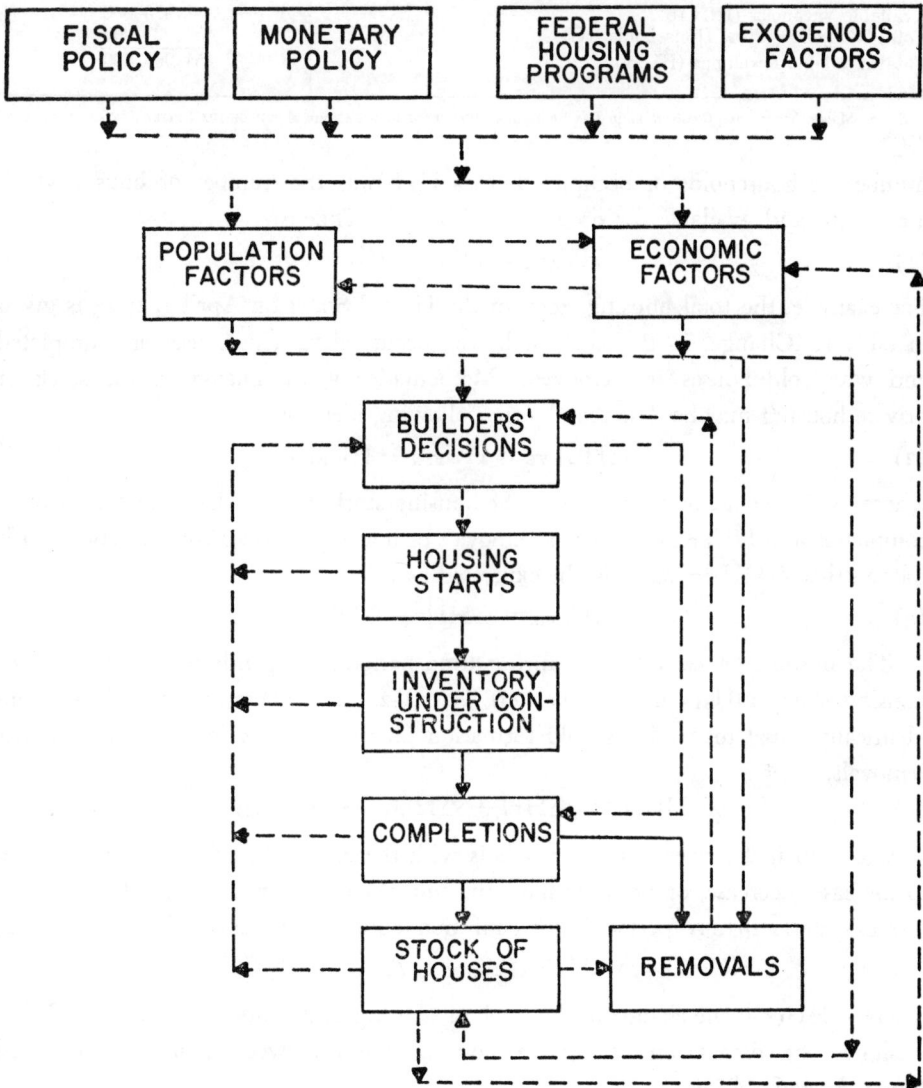

chart in figure 1. The broken lines in figure 1 denote informational flows and the solid lines denote construction flows. Central to our flow chart of the housing market is the builder. He must continuously make two different types of decisions: (1) how many private housing units should be constructed and (2) what should be the size, quality, and value of each housing unit?

At any given point in time the stock of private dwellings HU_{AVL} is equal to the

TABLE 1

Total Housing Stock in the United States on April 1, 1960

Available Vacancies (HUvac)	1,975,000
Total Occupied = Total Households (HH)	53,021,000
Total Available Dwellings (HUavl)	54,966,000

Source: Maisel, *Nonbusiness Construction*, in The Brookings Quarterly Econometric Model of the United States, ch. 6, at 190 (1965).

number of households or occupied houses HH plus the number of houses which are vacant and available for occupancy HU_{VAC}.[4] That is,

$$(1) \qquad HU_{AVL} = HH + HU_{VAC}$$

For example, the total housing stock in the United States on April 1, 1960, is given in table 1. Changes in the stock of houses occur when new houses are completed and when old houses are removed. Mathematically, the change in the stock of private housing may be described by the following identity,

$$(2) \qquad \triangle HU_{AVL} = HU_{FIN} - HU_{REM}$$

where $\triangle HU_{AVL}$ denotes a change in the housing stock, HU_{FIN} denotes housing units completed, and HU_{REM} denotes net removals of housing units. From equation (1) it follows that $\triangle HU_{AVL}$ may also be expressed as

$$(3) \qquad \triangle HU_{AVL} = \triangle HH + \triangle HU_{VAC}$$

The number of completions during time period T depends on the number of housing starts HU_{STS} in time periods T-1, T-2, etc. Therefore, completions are identically equal to net household formation plus the change in vacancies and net removals,

$$(4) \qquad HU_{FIN} = \triangle HH + \triangle HU_{VAC} + HU_{REM}$$

Our principal concern in this article is with the process by which builders decide to increase, decrease, or hold constant the number of housing starts. The level of housing starts in any period is by definition equal to the sum of four variables,

$$(5) \qquad HU_{STS} = \triangle HH + HU_{REM} + \triangle HU_{VAC} + \triangle HU_{UC}$$

where $\triangle HU_{UC}$ is the change in the stock of housing units under construction. Table 2 shows the disposition of private housing starts between April 1, 1950 and March 31, 1960.

Suppose that the housing market is in equilibrium at the beginning of planning period T. Builders start exactly enough houses to maintain a constant stock of housing units under construction. Completions are exactly equal to increases in the demand for housing (household formation plus removals),

$$(6) \qquad HU_{FIN} = \triangle HH + HU_{REM}$$

In attempting to decide how many houses to construct during planning period

---

[4] Throughout this article we use notation developed by Sherman J. Maisel.

TABLE 2

Disposition of Total Estimated Starts of Private Housing Units in the United States April 1, 1950 to March 31, 1960

Net Additions to Households ($\triangle$HH).........................	9,645,000
Net Removals (HU$_{\text{REM}}$).........................	2,833,000
Increase in Available Vacant Units ($\triangle$HU$_{\text{VAC}}$)................	1,245,000
Change in Inventory under Construction ($\triangle$HU$_{\text{UC}}$).............	−37,000
Total Private Housing Starts (HU$_{\text{STS}}$).......................	13,686,000

Source: Maisel, *A Theory of Fluctuations in Residential Construction Starts,* 53 AM. ECON. REV. 359, 361 (1963).

T, builders estimate the change in the actual number of new dwelling units coming into the market during planning period T. That is, builders make conjectures about the magnitude of changes in the stock of houses as a result of completions during period T. The number of completions in period T depends upon (1) the number of starts in preceding periods, (2) the amount of resources committed by the builders to the completion process in period T, and (3) exogenous factors such as weather, strikes, and so on, which are beyond the control of builders. Builders also make conjectures about the change in the demand for housing ($\triangle$HH + HU$_{\text{REM}}$) during planning period T. If builders conjecture that the increase in aggregate demand for housing during the planning period is likely to exceed the number of completions during that period, then conjectured profits will be relatively high and builders will increase the number of housing starts and increase the rate at which houses under construction are completed. On the other hand, if builders conjecture that completions will outrun the rate at which housing demand increases, vacancies will build up, conjectured profits will decline, and builders will cut back on housing starts and slow down completions. Builders are continuously making new conjectures about the housing market in the light of additional information which becomes available to them. Housing starts and completions are in turn continuously adjusted to reflect these changes in the builders' forecasts about the future.

What are some of the factors that cause builders to adjust the number of housing starts and the rate at which they employ resources to complete houses? Grebler and Maisel have developed a partial list of factors which affect builders' decisions about housing starts:[5]

1. Changes in population
   a. Increase in population
   b. Changes in the age-sex composition
   c. Changes in the number, type, and size of households
   d. Internal migration and immigration

[5] Grebler & Maisel, *Determinants of Residential Construction,* in COMMISSION ON MONEY AND CREDIT, IMPACTS OF MONETARY POLICY 476-77 (1963).

2. Changes in income and employment
   a. Total disposable personal income: past, current, expected
   b. Income distribution
   c. Employment and unemployment
3. Consumer asset holdings and their distribution, especially liquid assets and equities in existing houses
4. Changes in the prices of housing
   a. The price elasticity of housing relative to other prices
   b. The shape of the construction supply and cost curves
5. Relationship between occupancy costs and prices of dwellings
   a. Credit availability and the cost of credit
   b. Real estate taxes and operating expenses
   c. Depreciation
   d. Imputed costs of equity funds
6. Consumer tastes and preferences
7. Net replacement demand for dwelling units demolished or otherwise removed from the inventory less net conversions and mergers of existing units.
8. Conditions in the existing housing supply
   a. Utilization of the housing inventory
      (1) Vacancies
      (2) Intensity of occupancy
   b. Prices and rents for existing dwelling units
   c. Quality, location
9. Reaction to changes in demand
   a. Builders' organization and profit expectations
   b. Investors' organization and profit expectations
   c. Market structure and market information

We have condensed these nine factors into three general categories in figure 1: population factors, economic factors, and housing market factors. Each of these three factors is simultaneously determined by four variables: governmental fiscal policies, governmental monetary policies, federal housing programs, and exogenous variables such as weather, individual tastes, wars, and strikes, to mention only a few. In the remainder of this article we shall give particular attention to the impact of fiscal and monetary policies on the housing market.

II

BEHAVIOR OF THE HOUSING MARKET IN THE 1960s

Housing production as measured by housing starts "has earned the dubious distinction of ranking among the most cyclically volatile industries."[6] During the

---

[6] Maisel, *supra* note 1, at 359.

postwar years prior to 1960 housing starts tended to rise sharply during recessions and during the early stages of recovery periods, reaching a peak about six months after the low point in general business activity. Throughout the remaining period of expanded business activity housing starts would continue to decline, thus providing a constraint on other expansive forces at work in the economy.

FIGURE 2
PRIVATE NONFARM HOUSING STARTS

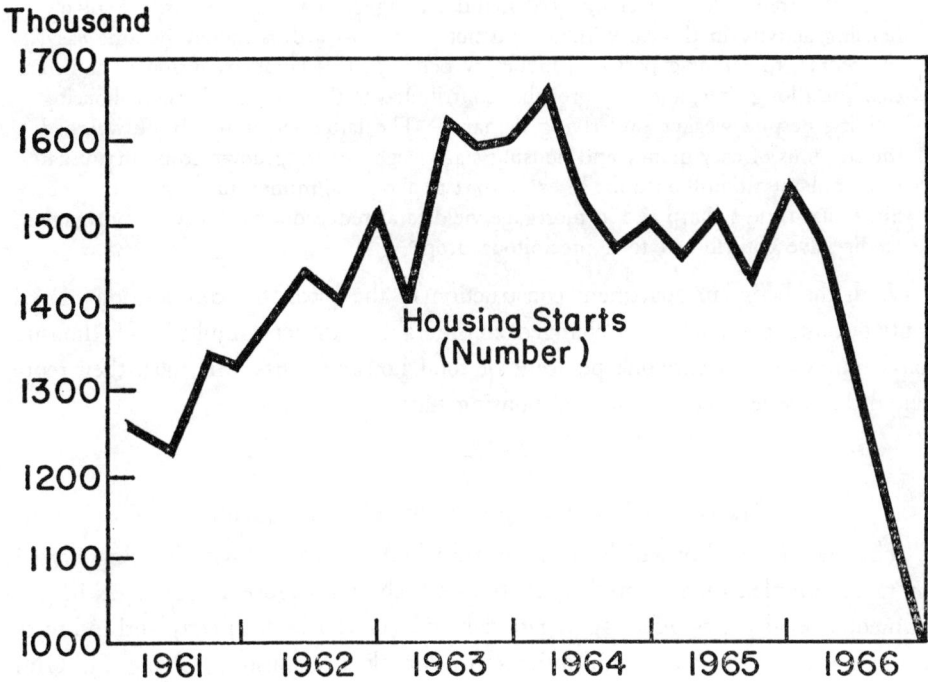

Source: U.S. DEP'T OF COMMERCE.

During the 1960s the U.S. economy has been characterized by a period of record expansion which began in early 1961 and continued through the end of 1966. Housing starts during this period have behaved in a manner which differs significantly from the pattern established in the earlier postwar years. (See figure 2.) There was no obvious upturn in housing starts prior to the beginning of the recovery period in 1961. The subsequent upswing in housing starts was quite mild, lasting only three years and reaching a peak in 1964. Although the economy as a whole was continuing to expand in late 1966, housing starts dropped to an annual rate of 1.0 million units in the fourth quarter of 1966.

What caused the disappearance of the vitality which housing starts had displayed in the 1950s?

In previous cycles, housing had frequently moved contra-cyclically, rising in recession years because of low interest rates and abundant credit and then being choked off in recovery as rising demand for credit raised rates and shut off the flow of funds. While interest rates remained stable and funds were readily available, housing nevertheless responded only sluggishly and peaked out in early 1964.[7]

Alhough no precise reason can be given for the relatively sluggish performance of the housing market in the 1960s, a partial explanation may be a decline in the underlying demand for housing in the 1960s.

With the tremendous blacklog of demand having been worked off in the 1950's, housing activity in the early 1960's did not surge forward as money became easy. In contrast to earlier experience, monetary policy in this latest expansion remained easy for a long time, and this probably contributed to the prolonged rise in housing activity, despite weaker underlying demand. The latter factor finally outweighed the stimulus of easy money and housing starts began drifting down from an annual rate of about 1.6 million units in early 1964 to about 1.5 million units in early 1966. Since that time a sharp rise in mortgage yields and reduced availability of mortgage credit have contributed to a precipitous drop.[8]

With the boom in apartment construction in the 1960s, the composition of residential construction has also changed considerably. In 1960, multi-family housing starts represented twenty-one per cent of total housing starts. In 1963, they represented thirty-seven per cent of total housing starts.

III

IMPACT OF FISCAL POLICY ON THE HOUSING MARKET

The line of causality which links governmental fiscal policy with housing starts is far more complex than is implied by the flow chart in figure 1. Changes in governmental fiscal policy affect aggregate demand (GNP) both directly and indirectly through a series of complex multiplier and feedback mechanisms. Changes in GNP may, in turn, affect disposable personal income, income distribution, employment, price levels, and so forth. Housing starts are sensitive in varying degrees to each of these economic parameters.

In general, two different types of fiscal policy instruments are available to the federal government—*revenue policies* and *expenditure policies.* Revenue policies or tax policies are those policies which determine: (1) personal income tax rates, (2) corporate profit tax rates, (3) indirect business (excise) tax rates, and (4) contributions to social insurance (social security and Medicare). Conventional wisdom (macroeconomic theory) postulates that for given federal expenditure patterns, an increase (decrease) in tax rates will lead to a decrease (increase) in GNP. A decrease (increase) in GNP will indirectly affect housing starts by inducing changes in the intermediate economic variables (disposable income, employment, prices, and so on)

---

[7] FEDERAL RESERVE BANK OF RICHMOND ANN. REP. 8 (1966).
[8] *Id.* at 26.

listed above. These economic factors may also affect certain demographic variables which tend to influence housing starts.

Alternatively, governmental policy makers may also affect GNP by increasing or decreasing governmental expenditures in the form of (1) transfer payments or (2) purchases of goods and services. Transfer payments include payments to individuals in the form of social security benefits, Medicare benefits, unemployment compensation, and so on. For given tax rates, an increase (decrease) in government spending will usually lead to an increase (decrease) in GNP. As mentioned before, a change in GNP may trigger a change in housing starts.

Although there is general agreement among economists that governmental fiscal policy has substantially influenced the U.S. economy during the expansion period of the 1960s, it is difficult to say to what extent fiscal policy affected the housing market. During the 1961-1966 expansion three types of governmental expenditures grew rapidly: expenditures for defense, expenditures for social security and older welfare programs, and expenditures for new welfare programs. On the revenue side, two innovations appeared during the 1960s. First, two important measures were introduced specifically to reduce business taxes. These included liberalized depreciation allowances and a seven per cent investment tax credit. Second, there was a major reduction in personal and corporate income taxes in 1964 at a time when business was expanding and the budget was still showing a sizable deficit. Deficits in the federal cash budget were registered in every quarter but two during this period and usually ranged well over $1 billion. The expansionary effect of these deficits was especially important as is evidenced by the fact that GNP increased by nearly fifty per cent during this period. However, in late 1965 and early 1966, as the economy began to approach full employment, these deficits generated strong inflationary pressures.

On the basis of this brief sketch of some of the major developments in governmental fiscal policy in the 1960s and on the basis of a cursory glance at the time path of housing starts during this period (figure 2), one can conclude that the relationship between fiscal policy and the housing market is somewhat less than straightforward. While the U.S. economy was responding vigorously to expansionary fiscal policies, the housing market demonstrated, at best, a "mixed" performance. It is virtually impossible to say anything meaningful about the relationship between fiscal policy and the housing market without resorting to sophisticated econometric models. In the following section we shall describe the results of several simulation experiments with alternative fiscal and monetary policies in which an econometric model was used to evaluate the impact of these policies on the housing market.

IV

IMPACT OF MONETARY POLICY ON THE HOUSING MARKET

In grossly simplified terms, the purpose of monetary policies administered by the Federal Reserve Board is to influence the supply of money in the U.S. economy.

Policies which tend to increase the supply of money available in the economy will lead to reductions in interest rates. Lower interest rates stimulate consumption and investment. Increased consumption and investment mean higher aggregate demand as well as increased personal income and employment. In terms of the housing market, lower interest rates imply lower credit costs; and, in theory, lower credit costs should stimulate the demand for housing.

> In assessing the probable effects of interest rate changes on consumers' demand for credit for housing expenditures, however, it is important to recognize a purely numerical phenomenon. Aside from net income tax advantages associated with various amounts of interest payments, the mere fact that the typical mortgagor makes constant monthly payments on a very long-term mortgage means (1) that small changes in contractual interest rates have relatively little effect on the monthly payment (2) that, in turn, this latter change itself is likely to have only a small direct effect on consumers' demand for credit.[9]

As was the case with fiscal policies, the line of causality and functional relationships between monetary policy changes and the behavior of the housing market are extremely complex. Hypotheses concerning the nature of these relationships require extensive testing and verification before one can attach operational significance to them.

Three major policy instruments are available to the Federal Reserve: (1) the open market purchase and sale of U.S. Government securities, (2) changes in the reserve requirements of member banks, and (3) changes in the discount rate, i.e., the interest rate charged to member banks by the Federal Reserve. The terms "tight money" and "easy money" are sometimes used to differentiate among alternative monetary policies. A "tight money" policy is one which tends to restrict the supply of money by (1) the sale of government securities, (2) raising reserve requirements, and (3) increasing the discount rate. "Easy money" policies are characterized by (1) the purchase of government securities, (2) decreased reserve requirements, and (3) lower discount rates.

Needless to say, one should proceed with extreme caution in advocating a particular monetary policy to achieve a specific goal in terms of interest rates, price levels, personal income, or employment. The pioneering work of Frank De Leeuw[10] and others at the Federal Reserve Board represents an initial attempt to quantify the effects of monetary policy on U.S. financial markets. De Leeuw's model has also been used as a sector of *The Brookings Quarterly Econometric Model of the United States* thus providing a linkage between monetary policy and the behavior of the entire U.S. economy. Unfortunately, it is impossible to adequately describe these two models and spell out their relationship to the housing market within the constraints imposed on the length of this article.

---

[9] W. J. FRAZER & W. P. YOHE, *supra* note 2, at 406.

[10] De Leeuw, *A Model of Financial Behavior*, in THE BROOKINGS QUARTERLY ECONOMETRIC MODEL OF THE UNITED STATES 465-530 (1965).

During the expansion period of the 1960s, monetary policy can be briefly summarized as follows: Between 1960 and 1963 the Federal Reserve followed an active "easy money" policy. In early 1963 the Federal Reserve began moving toward a policy of "restrained ease" which continued through 1964. In late 1964 the economy began showing signs of overheating. Beginning in 1965 the Federal Reserve moved further in the direction of "tight money." By 1966 a "tight money" policy was being pursued vigorously.

Turning to the relationship between monetary policy and housing starts, we observe in figure 2 that during the period of "easy money," when interests rates were relatively low and credit was readily available, housing starts increased in number. However, when the Federal Reserve turned to a "tight money" policy, housing starts reached a peak and turned downward at a rapid rate. By the spring of 1966 there was a severe squeeze on the market for mortgage funds. The situation had become so acute for potential home builders or buyers and for the construction industry that the Federal Reserve put into effect several special measures designed to channel additional funds into the mortage market.

Perhaps the most promising attempt to date to evaluate the impact of monetary (and fiscal) policies on the housing market is the paper by Gary Fromm entitled "An Evaluation of Monetary Policy Instruments."[11] Fromm uses *The Brookings Quarterly Econometric Model of the United States* and computer simulation techniques to evaluate four different monetary actions and two fiscal policy alternatives.[12] The version of the Brookings Model used by Fromm consists of 176 simultaneous equations. The financial sector of the model numbers over thirty equations. Of particular interest to us is the fourteen-equation nonbusiness construction model developed by Sherman J. Maisel which is contained within the complete Brookings Model. Maisel's model relates nonfarm residential construction to a number of variables including: (1) a housing cost index; (2) housing starts in periods T, T-1, and T-2; (3) total available housing; (4) the implicit price deflator for nonfarm construction; and (5) the implicit price deflator for GNP. The model also includes an equation which expresses housing starts as a function of: (1) changes in the number of households; (2) net removals of housing; (3) vacant available housing in period T-1; (4) the rent component of the consumer price index in period T-1; (5) average market yield of three-month U.S. Treasury bills; and (6) housing starts in periods T-1 and T-3.

In Fromm's simulation experiments the discount rate, average reserve ratios required against demand and time deposits, and the unborrowed reserves of member banks (controlled by Federal Reserve open market operations) were treated as mone-

---

[11] Presented at the annual meeting of the Econometric Society, San Francisco, December 29, 1966.

[12] Computer simulation is defined as a numerical technique for conducting experiments on a digital computer with a mathematical model describing an economic system. *See* T. H. NAYLOR, J. L. BALINTFY, D. S. BURDICK & K. CHU, COMPUTER SIMULATION TECHNIQUES (1966).

tary policy instruments. Given the structural coefficients of the equations of the Brookings Model and certain other exogenous variables (*i.e.*, population and governmental expenditures), then the model determines the values of the endogenous variables which describe the system. Six separate simulations were run. The simulations included four different monetary policy changes and two different fiscal policy changes. The monetary policy changes were: (1) a cut in the discount rate, (2) a reduction in the time deposits reserve requirements, (3) a reduction in the demand deposits reserve requirements, and (4) an increase in unborrowed reserves (open market operations). The fiscal policy changes were: (1) an increase in government durables purchases and (2) a reduction in personal federal income tax rates. In each simulation, all other parameters and exogenous variables remained unchanged. A control simulation was also run. All of the simulations were for the mid-1960 through 1962 recession period (seven quarters). The control simulation represents an approximation to the actual behavior of the economy during the 1960-62 period. The simulations provide some indication of events that might have taken place had the above monetary and fiscal policy changes been instituted at the end of the second-quarter of 1960.

The two fiscal policy changes had relatively little impact on nonfarm residential construction. Of the four monetary policy changes, the reduction in the demand deposits reserve requirements and the increase in unborrowed reserves stimulated nonfarm residential construction by the greatest amount over the seven-quarter period. The cut in the discount rate had the greatest sustaining effect on the housing market. For all of the policies, with the exception of the discount rate reduction, the impact on business plant and equipment investment is greater than the impact on nonfarm residential construction. This implies that the responsiveness (elasticities) of business investment to changes in interest rates and income are greater than the responsiveness of nonfarm residential construction to changes in interest rates and income.

V

THE IMPACT OF FEDERAL HOUSING PROGRAMS ON THE HOUSING MARKET

In addition to fiscal and monetary policies, the housing market is also affected by a number of governmental housing programs. These programs include:

1. Veterans Administration
2. Department of Housing and Urban Development
   a. Federal National Mortgage Association
   b. Public Housing Administration
   c. Federal Housing Administration
3. Home Loan Bank Board

The principal aim of the Veterans Administration (VA) and the Federal Housing Administration (FHA) is to make available credit for home purchases by insuring the lenders of funds against loss. The Veterans Administration guarantees at no cost a portion of the value of loans to eligible veterans, thus eliminating or greatly reducing the usual cash down payment for the purchase of a home. The federal housing program is an insurance program under which approved lenders are insured for the full amount of their mortgage loans in return for a premium paid by the home owner. "One of the effects of the VA- and FHA-underwritten mortgages, however, has been to cause housing expenditures to vary, at times, counter to the short cycle of income, output, and employment."[13] The objective of the Federal National Mortgage Association ("Fannie Mae") is to increase the liquidity of government-insured mortgages (VA and FHA) by providing a secondary market facility to widen the market for government-insured mortgages. The Federal Home Loan Bank Board, a part of the Home Loan Banking System, provides credit to home financing institutions. The Public Housing Administration has focused its attention on the development of low-rent housing facilities for lower-income families. What effects have these programs had on the housing market?

> Considerable literature exists on the effects of Federal housing programs on the composition of residential construction and on short term fluctuations. Most of it is of the verbal-qualitative type. With one exception, the statistical-econometric models at best concern themselves with the effects of changes in credit conditions generally, without attempting to examine and quantify the component sources of such changes. The long-run impact on the level of construction has had relatively little attention. Yet, whether the extensive housing aids offered by the Federal Government have helped raise the level of new construction or accelerate the growth of the housing sector would seem to be a strategic question.[14]

Although the average yield on FHA- and VA-home mortgage loans would appear to be seemingly obvious credit variables in evaluating the impact of federal housing programs on the housing market, because of intricacies in the mortgage market (*e.g.*, discounting) they are, in fact, poor measures of the cost of credit. In concluding his econometric study of the housing market, Maisel stated:

> Because credit is an important government policy variable, significant changes in past relationships may occur which must be considered in analysis and forecasting. Clearly, if the Federal Reserve succeeds in breaking past relationships between the Treasury bill rate and the availability and cost of credit, . . . [housing starts] will be affected. Even more important may be the changing policies of the Federal National Mortgage Association. In this study [Maisel's study], FNMA intervention in the credit market appeared significant on theoretical grounds, and nearly so on a statistical basis. However, since FNMA action was closely related in time to interest rate movements, it did little to increase our sta-

---

[13] W. J. FRAZER & W. P. YOHE, *supra* note 2, at 408.
[14] Grebler & Maisel, *supra* note 5, at 584.

tistical explanation of past movements. Even though this collinearity did result in insignificant [regression] coefficients . . . [in an equation relating FNMA policy to housing starts], it seems logical to assign direct governmental intervention of this type a good deal of weight, even if only subjectively.[15]

VI

SUMMARY

We have outlined a number of possible relationships between fiscal and monetary policy, as well as federal housing programs, and the housing market. Although a large number of empirical studies of the housing market have been conducted, none of these studies has as its principal aim the delineation of relationships between fiscal and monetary policy (and governmental housing programs) and the housing market. The major conclusion of this study is, therefore, that there is considerable need for an econometric model of the housing market which includes as instrumental variables (1) fiscal policy instruments (2) monetary policy instruments, and (3) federal housing program instruments. Until such a model is constructed, generalizations about the relationship between these policy instruments and the behavior of the housing market can at best be termed "speculative."

---

[15] Maisel, *supra* note 1, at 378.

HOUSING IN MODEL CITIES

H. Ralph Taylor* and George A. Williams, Jr.†

Introduction

The Model Cities Program, authorized by title I of the Demonstration Cities and Metropolitan Development Act of 1966,[1] is a unique new federal program designed to bring to bear a variety of resources—public and private—in a comprehensive and coordinated attack on social, economic, and physical problems in large slum and blighted neighborhoods. It calls for focusing and interrelating all relevant existing federal grant-in-aid programs in a single area and for developing and testing out new and innovative approaches which cannot be financed under existing grant-in-aid programs.

Because it is a new concept and its potential is untried, the Model Cities Program is a demonstration program, to be carried out in a limited number of cities offering the best potential for achieving program objectives. It is hoped that through the solutions developed and demonstrated by participating cities, other cities may be able to cope more successfully with their urban problems.

The objective of the Model Cities Program can best be summarized as the elimination of opportunity-denying circumstances. The program calls for a locally developed plan to eliminate the blockages which prevent residents of slum and blighted areas from obtaining such things as decent housing, good jobs, and quality education. The specific objectives each local program is expected to meet are

> to rebuild or revitalize large slum and blighted areas; to expand housing, job, and income opportunities; to reduce dependence on welfare payments; to improve educational facilities and programs; to combat disease and ill health, to reduce the incidence of crime and delinquency; to enhance recreational and cultural opportunities; to establish better access between homes and jobs; and generally to improve living conditions for the people who live in such areas . . . .[2]

A major component of most, if not all, local programs will be directed at the problems of housing. Not only will much of the housing in the neighborhoods in which the program will operate be of poor quality, but in many instances it will be overcrowded or too expensive for its occupants in that the rental represents a dis-

* A.B. 1939, M.A. (Public Administration) 1947, Harvard University; M.A. (Government) 1946, Louisiana State University. Assistant Secretary for Demonstrations and Intergovernmental Relations, Department of Housing and Urban Development.

† B.S. 1949, University of Utah; LL.B. 1956, LL.M. 1963, Harvard University. Deputy Director for Program Operations and Technical Assistance in the Model Cities Administration, Department of Housing and Urban Development.

[1] 42 U.S.C. §§ 1453, 3301-13 (Supp. II, 1965-66).
[2] § 101, 42 U.S.C. § 3301 (Supp. II, 1965-66).

proportionate share of the occupants' limited income and impairs their ability to obtain adequate food, clothing, and other essentials.

Before discussing the specific approach to housing taken by the Model Cities legislation, some of the novel features of the program which influence that approach should be explained. As a federal grant-in-aid program the Model Cities Program is unique in a number of respects:

(1) It builds on activities financed under the other grant-in-aid programs and is designed to encourage the coordinated use of these other grant-in-aid programs. The supplementary financing provided by the program provides a powerful incentive to local concentration and coordination of federal grant-in-aid programs because it is based upon the non-federal contribution made to those federal grant-in-aid programs which the city includes and coordinates through its comprehensive plan.

(2) The statutory criteria which local programs are required to meet leave wide latitude for the local design of programs to meet unique situations. The statute provides that a comprehensive city demonstration program is eligible for assistance if

> the program is of sufficient magnitude to make a substantial impact on the physical and social problems and to remove or arrest blight and decay in entire sections or neighborhoods; to contribute to the sound development of the entire city; to make marked progress in reducing social and educational disadvantages, ill health, underemployment, and enforced idleness; and to provide educational, health, and social services necessary to serve the poor and disadvantaged in the area, widespread citizen participation in the program, maximum opportunities for employing residents of the area in all phases of the program, and enlarged opportunities for work and training;
>
> the program, including rebuilding or restoration, will contribute to a well-balanced city with a substantial increase in the supply of standard housing of low and moderate cost, maximum opportunities in the choice of housing accommodations for all citizens of all income levels, adequate public facilities (including those needed for education, health and social services, transportation, and recreation), commercial facilities adequate to serve the residential areas, and ease of access between the residential areas and centers of employment . . . .[3]

These criteria are to be applied administratively as performance standards rather than specification standards which in effect dictate program content. Detailed regulations or manuals which specify in considerable particular what can and cannot be done have not and will not be developed.

(3) The supplementary funds are not narrowly restricted in their use by tight legislative or administrative requirements. They are "unearmarked," problem-solving funds. Cities are responsible for assessing and analyzing the problems and designing their own programmatic response. Any locally proposed use of supplementary grant funds which offers promise of achieving solution of physical, social, or economic problems of the area is a permissible use.

---

[3] §§ 103(a)(2)-(3), 42 U.S.C. §§ 3303(a)(2)-(3) (Supp. II, 1965-66).

These unique features mean that there will be considerable variation in the approach taken to solve housing problems. No two local programs will be alike. Each program will be responding to somewhat different problems and circumstances and each program in its solution of those problems will respond differently to the opportunity to innovate and experiment. Nevertheless, each local program will be responding to the same statutory performance standards and, therefore, certain characteristics common to many of the local programs are likely to emerge.

I

The Housing Emphasis

The emphasis of the Model Cities Program is on people. This emphasis, as it relates to housing, means that the focus will be on meeting the housing needs of the residents of the area in which the program operates and not on the physical condition of existing housing in the area per se. Of course, improvement of the quality of existing housing will be an important means of meeting those needs but it is only one means. The statute calls for a substantial increase in the supply of low- and moderate-income standard housing and for maximum opportunities in the choice of housing for all citizens of all income levels;[4] thus the local housing effort must also include measures to add to the existing housing stock through new construction and to increase the availability of the existing stock to all groups.

II

Housing Supply

A frequently-voiced criticism of the urban renewal program is that in eliminating slums and blight it has decreased the supply of low- and moderate-income housing, either by razing such housing or pricing it out of the reach of low- and moderate-income households through rehabilitation. This criticism is inaccurate in that it views the urban renewal program in isolation and fails to take into account that urban renewal is only one of a number of interrelated federally-assisted efforts to improve the quality of the physical environment. The impact of urban renewal should properly be considered in conjunction with the impact of the low-rent public housing program, the rent supplement program, and the moderate-income private housing (section 221(d)(3)) program. It may be true, however, that in a specific situation in a specific locality a decrease of the supply of low- and moderate-income housing resulting from the renewal activity has not been offset by an increase through the various federally-assisted housing programs. The Model Cities legislation is intended to avoid such a result. The statute requires a proper relationship between urban renewal activity and those programs which are designed to increase the supply of low- and moderate-income housing. While calling for a local program

---

[4] § 103(a)(3), 42 U.S.C. § 3303(a)(3) (Supp. II, 1965-66).

which will remove or arrest blight and decay[5] (urban renewal being the principal tool), it also calls for a program that will "contribute to a well-balanced city with substantial increase in the supply of standard housing of low and moderate cost."[6]

What is expected of localities in this regard? How much new construction will satisfy the statutory requirement of "substantial increase"? The quantity to be added will depend upon the needs of the people in the target area for such housing and upon the extent to which those needs can be met by the existing housing stock. Obviously the quantity needed in a community with a seven per cent vacancy rate in low- and moderate-cost standard housing is less than one with a two per cent vacancy rate. The quantity to be added to the supply must also be viewed against the dynamics of the particular housing markets involved. How many units and in what price ranges are currently being added by ongoing public programs and private market activities? How many units and in what range are being eliminated from the supply by various public actions (e.g., highway construction, urban renewal, and code enforcement) and by private demolitions?

The Model Cities Program *Guide*, which provides administrative interpretation to the statutory requirements, states the requirement this way:

> The program should add to the overall supply of low- and moderate-income housing, not decrease it. The needed increase in the housing supply should be based on the number of people in the model neighborhood area and in the city as a whole living in substandard housing, in overcrowded housing or in standard housing at higher prices than they can reasonably afford (based on expenditures for housing of more than 20 or 25 percent of income, dependent on family size and other factors). The program should increase the supply of standard low- and moderate-cost housing in the model neighborhood area, or elsewhere in the city and metropolitan area, by an amount sufficient to meet the need for such housing by neighborhood residents. It should do so without adversely affecting other low- and moderate-income families outside the model neighborhood area, which would occur if relocated households were moved into areas in which existing housing is in short supply. If such housing is in short supply the program should also add to the total supply of low- and moderate-income housing over and above the amount needed to provide all area residents with standard housing at rents they can afford.
>
> While the community-wide need for low- and moderate-income housing may be greater than can be met through the Model Cities Program alone, there should be an awareness of the magnitude of the shortage of standard housing of low- and moderate-cost and a program should be developed to overcome such shortages. As a first step, an estimate of housing needs should be developed showing the gains projected, losses, and gaps in housing for the city as a whole. Programs can then be shaped in terms of overall needs.[7]

General estimates of city-wide housing needs and of the effective demand for various kinds of housing are being developed with more and more sophistication in

---

[5] § 103(a)(2), 42 U.S.C. § 3303(a)(2) (Supp. II, 1965-66).

[6] § 103(a)(3), 42 U.S.C. § 3303(a)(3) (Supp. II, 1965-66).

[7] U.S. DEP'T OF HOUSING AND URBAN DEVELOPMENT, IMPROVING THE QUALITY OF URBAN LIFE, A PROGRAM GUIDE TO MODEL NEIGHBORHOODS IN DEMONSTRATION CITIES 15 (1966).

various community renewal programs around the country. They are also being included with increasing frequency in community-wide general plans for physical improvement. In the absence of such existing estimates of community-wide housing needs and effective demand, the local staff planning the Model Cities program will be expected to develop its own general community-wide estimates in addition to the specific needs and effective demand of the residents of the neighborhoods on which the program is focused. This will indicate the total dimensions of the housing problem against which the locality's effort under the Model Cities program can be measured.

III

HOUSING CHOICE

The statute also provides that the program contribute "maximum opportunities in the choice of housing accommodations for all citizens of all income levels."[8] Opportunity in the choice of housing is dependent on whether there is a sufficient vacancy rate for standard units of various sizes and prices to allow for the exercise of choice, whether such housing is located outside slum or deteriorating areas, and whether existing housing is available to all residents of the city. A Model Cities program must, therefore, be concerned not only with the sufficiency of the supply of housing, but also with the location of that supply and its availability to all citizens of all income levels.

A. Location

To provide an adequate range of choice in the city the program should contribute to the provision of a reasonable mix of various housing types and price levels in various parts of the city. It should not result in intensifying the concentration of lower-cost housing of a particular price level in slum or deteriorating areas of the city. Therefore, the location of various kinds of new housing will be an important consideration. This will particularly be so with respect to new low- and moderate-income housing being provided as a relocation resource. The Model Cities effort to avoid perpetuation of concentration of low-income housing in one area is reinforced by new Public Housing regulations stipulating that any proposal to locate housing only in areas of racial concentration will be prima facie unacceptable.[9] All this adds up to a broad HUD program to prevent federal assistance to housing from being used to solidify ghetto housing patterns. These measures may not affect the patterns of discrimination by which suburbs exclude minority persons and they do not necessarily require the opening of all parts of the city itself to minority persons. But if a city is to take advantage of substantial federal housing assistance it will have to give minority persons the chance to live outside the ghetto.

---

[8] § 103(a)(3), 42 U.S.C. § 3303(a)(3) (Supp. II, 1965-66).
[9] U.S. HOUSING ASSISTANCE ADMINISTRATION, DEP'T OF HOUSING AND URBAN DEVELOPMENT, LOW RENT HOUSING MANUAL § 205.1, at 7 (1967).

Another dimension of the locational aspects of housing choice relates to the location of housing units offered as relocation resources to households displaced by the program. The requirement of maximum opportunities in the choice of housing accommodations means that relocatees must be given a reasonable opportunity to relocate in housing at rents or prices they can reasonably afford in areas free of blight. This adds to the usual relocation requirements in federal programs. Under the urban renewal program, for example, relocation housing must be decent, safe, and sanitary, and the neighborhood in which the relocation housing is located must be "not generally less desirable in regard to public utilities and public and commercial facilities"[10] and "reasonably accessible to their places of employment."[11] This means that present relocation requirements may be met by providing relocation housing which itself is standard but which is located in a blighted neighborhood, if the former neighborhood was itself blighted.[12] Under Model Cities Program requirements a relocatee must have a real option to select housing in a neighborhood that represents an improvement in the quality of his surrounding physical environment.

B. Availability

With respect to making the existing supply available to all citizens of all income levels, there are a variety of ways in which a Model Cities program could meet the performance standard of providing "maximum opportunities" in the choice of housing accommodations. One way would be through enforcement of an open occupancy ordinance. However, such an ordinance is not a requirement for carrying out a program. The original proposal for using the Model Cities legislation as an aggressive instrument to compel open occupancy was specifically deleted by the Congress. Nevertheless, existing legal requirements and regulations applying to various program components will continue to apply. Thus, any relocation of families and persons will be subject to existing relocation policies and the housing which is to be relied on as a relocation resource must be housing which is available on a non-discriminatory basis.

In addition, the housing that is developed in order to comply with the statutory requirement of a "substantial increase in the supply of standard housing of low- and moderate-cost" will most likely be federally-aided housing, and therefore subject to

---

[10] *Id.* at 12.

[11] *Id.*

[12] The area should not, however, be subject to serious hazards or nuisances or in an area scheduled for major clearance activity in the near future to be eligible for relocation adjustment payments. U.S. Urban Renewal Administration, Housing and Home Finance Agency, Local Public Agency Letter No. 321, at 4 (Jan. 13, 1965). Localities are advised that relocation standards "should not contemplate the use of a dwelling unit for rehousing if it is in a neighborhood that is officially programmed for clearance action in the near future." HHFA, Urban Renewal Administration, Determining Local Relocation Standards, Technical Guide No. 9 (1961).

requirements of title VI of the Civil Rights Act of 1964[13] and the Executive Order on Housing.[14]

These considerations aside, the legislation affords the locality a wide degree of latitude as to the manner in which it will provide "maximum opportunities in the choice of housing accommodations for all citizens of all income levels." The statute contemplates imaginative measures for maximizing choice, and open occupancy laws are only one method. Alternatively, a locality might, for example, undertake such activities as the establishment of housing information services geared to meet house-hunting needs of minority families, cooperative arrangements with private fair housing organizations, or an education program designed to assure full compliance with various legal requirements such as the Civil Rights Act of 1964 and the Execu-tive Order on Housing.

IV

Comprehensive Housing Development

The Model Cities Program adds a new dimension to local governmental concern for housing. In meeting the housing requirements of the statute many participating cities will be developing a comprehensive approach to housing development directly tied to implementation, and will be tying together the efforts of a variety of govern-mental agencies and the efforts of private housing developers and sponsors into a unique public-private housing development effort.

This effort can be seen as the next logical step in the growing concern for housing on the part of municipal government. Local government involvement in housing began in the last century with the regulation of construction by ordinance to protect public health, safety, and welfare. In the 1930s the concern was extended to direct public ownership of housing for low-income households. With the urban renewal program came governmental involvement in large scale elimination of substandard housing and in marketing land, temporarily in public ownership, for a variety of re-uses, including housing. This marketing process involved localities in considera-tion of questions of housing market demand and community needs for various kinds of housing.

Over the years, concern for quality of the existing stock of housing has increased. The 1940s and 1950s saw the development of housing codes providing for standards applicable to existing housing. Under the prodding of the workable program re-quirements[15] local code enforcement agencies have begun to develop far-reaching

---

[13] 42 U.S.C. §§ 2000d to 2000d-4 (1964).

[14] Exec. Order No. 11,063, 3 C.F.R. 261 (Supp. 1962), 42 U.S.C. § 1982 (1964).

[15] Section 101(c) of the Housing Act of 1949 provides:

"Commencing three years after the date of enactment of the Housing Act of 1964, no workable program shall be certified or re-certified unless (A) the locality has had in effect, for at least six months prior to such certification or re-certification, a minimum standards housing code, related but not limited to health, sanitation, and occupancy requirements, which is deemed adequate

programs for maintaining the quality of housing. The increasing emphasis placed on rehabilitation in the urban renewal program has involved local government, through the local public agencies administering the urban renewal program, in the provision of assistance to homeowners in obtaining financing and contractor services and, with the advent of section 312 rehabilitation loans,[16] with the actual making of loans.

The enactment of low- and moderate-income private housing programs in recent years has begun to involve local government in the active promotion of private residential construction; in many instances, local urban renewal agencies are employing staff to encourage and assist non-profit sponsors of $221(d)(3)$[17] and rent supplement housing[18] in renewal areas. Finally, city planning efforts, particularly in the development plans, have become increasingly concerned with housing and particularly with an appraisal of the community-wide need for housing of various types and income ranges.

Taken together, these efforts amount to a broad involvement of local government in many different aspects of housing. However, these various housing activities are still by and large disparate. They tend to be undertaken as separate, discrete efforts by a variety of different agencies and not as a part of a total comprehensive program. What is needed in many localities is a pulling together of all the various efforts directed at the quantity and quality of new and existing housing into a comprehensive and coordinated housing development program, and the construction of an implementing mechanism by which estimates of overall housing needs can be translated into actual construction of housing units meeting those needs.

The Model Cities Program is calculated to achieve such a result. The Model Cities planning process will require the locality to set housing goals relative to the number of units of various types and prices to be added to the supply, and to determine how the goals are to be achieved and by whom. In order to provide the administrative machinery to carry out the program on a consolidated and coordinated basis as required by the statute,[18a] the Model Cities agency overseeing the carrying out of the housing program will be tying together the efforts of private housing sponsors and builders of low- and moderate-income housing, the city planning department, code enforcement agencies, the public housing authority, and the urban renewal agency.

The private sector will be responsible for a large portion of the task of meeting the housing goals, yet the local government will have overall responsibility for seeing that the goals are met. This means that municipal government must take affirmative steps to work with private enterprise in meeting housing needs. Such steps could

---

by the Administrator, and (B) the Administrator is satisfied that the locality is carrying out an effective program of enforcement to achieve compliance with such housing code."
42 U.S.C. § 1451(c) (Supp. II, 1965-66).

[16] Housing Act of 1964, § 312, 42 U.S.C. § 1452b (1964, Supp. II, 1965-66).

[17] National Housing Act § 221(d)(3), 12 U.S.C. § 1715*l*(d)(3) (Supp. II, 1965-66).

[18] Housing and Urban Development Act of 1965, 12 U.S.C. § 1701s (Supp. II, 1965-66).

[18a] § 103(a)(4), 42 U.S.C. § 3303(a)(4) (Supp. II, 1965-66).

include activities designed to develop competent non-profit sponsors of low- and moderate-income housing. Provision of "seed money" and continuing technical assistance might be an appropriate use of supplementary funds. Analysis of the factors inhibiting construction activity and efforts to remove unnecessary blockages would also be required; appraisal and possible modification of building codes, zoning ordinances, and taxation policies would be an essential part of this effort.

V

IMPACT ON REHABILITATION

The Model Cities Program expands the emphasis already being given to rehabilitation in the urban renewal program. The Model Cities Program *Guide* provides: "The overall emphasis of the physical improvement activity in the Demonstration Cities Program is on rehabilitation. Therefore, as a general rule, model neighborhood areas should contain substantial numbers of residential buildings that can be rehabilitated."[19] Since each local program will be operating in large areas of the city containing as much as ten per cent of the total population, rehabilitation activity will be undertaken at a scale which should materially quicken the development of the much-needed rehabilitation industry in the United States. Rehabilitation can proceed at a volume at which significant reductions in costs can be realized, since there will be a market sufficiently extensive to attract the development and utilization of new materials and construction techniques.

A major concern of most local programs will be on how to bring rehabilitated housing within the financial means of low- and moderate-income households. Utilization of the whole array of federal rehabilitation tools—section 23 low rent housing in rehabiliated private accommodations,[20] section 221(d)(3)[21] and rent supplement financing[22] of rehabilitated housing, section 312 three per cent rehabilitation loans,[23] and section 115 rehabilitation grants[24]—are anticipated. In addition, the imaginative use of Model Cities supplementary funds to achieve results which cannot be achieved under existing programs is expected. The flexibility permitted in the use of supplementary grant funds can result in their being used to solve problems which presently inhibit rehabilitation activity. For example, the present rehabilitation grant provided under section 115 of the Housing Act of 1949 is limited to $1500. This is not always sufficient to permit the low-income elderly homeowner to meet the cost of rehabilitation. The Model Cities supplementary grant funds could be used in a number of ways to solve this problem: an additional rehabilitation grant payment might be provided; a loan with interest and amortization provisions scaled to the owner's ability to pay and secured by a lien payable on resale at the owner's

---

[19] U.S. DEP'T OF HOUSING AND URBAN DEVELOPMENT, *supra* note 7, at 6.

[20] 42 U.S.C. § 1421b (Supp. II, 1965-66).

[21] 12 U.S.C. § 1715*l*(d)(3) (Supp. II, 1965-66).

[22] 12 U.S.C. § 1710s (Supp. II, 1965-66).

[23] Housing Act of 1964, § 312, 42 U.S.C. § 1452b (1964, Supp. II, 1965-66).

[24] 42 U.S.C. § 1466 (Supp. II, 1965-66).

death might be used; or the housing unit might be purchased by a non-profit corporation which would rehabilitate it and then lease it back to the former owner for life.

Supplementary funds can also be used in other ways to make rehabilitation "feasible." Owners of substandard buildings, faced with the expense of bringing property up to rehabilitation standards and without the prospect of attracting higher income groups of tenants, may not find rehabilitation "economically feasible." Absent the ability to charge higher rents, rehabilitation is economically feasible only if it will result in an increase in the capitalized value of the property by (1) improving the occupancy rate, (2) decreasing maintenance and operating expenses, (3) extending the economic life of the building, or (4) reducing risk of ownership and thereby reducing the required rate of return on investment.[25]

However, economic feasibility in the sense used here is feasibility from the private owner's point of view: will the increase in net income as a result of rehabilitation be worth the cost of rehabilitation? But from the standpoint of the public interest, economic feasibility should be measured against the alternative cost of providing needed housing through new construction. In terms of public investment it may be less costly to absorb some of the cost of rehabilitation of existing housing than to provide a standard unit for low- and moderate-income occupancy through new construction. Therefore, there may be sound reason to provide public subsidy of that portion of the cost of rehabilitation which will make the remaining portion "economically feasible" from the private investor's point of view. This is precisely what could be done by employing section 107 of the Housing Act of 1949[26] to write down the cost of existing property in need of rehabilitation for low- and moderate-income housing. Here the cost of acquired property is written down to a price which, with the addition of the cost of rehabilitation, can be supported by rents that can reasonably be afforded by low- and moderate-income families.

The emphasis placed on rehabilitation in the Model Cities Program, plus the requirement of a substantial increase in the supply of standard units of low- and moderate-cost, is likely to result in a significant increase in the utilization of section 107. It is also likely to result in utilization of the supplementary funds to absorb some of the cost of rehabilitation. One technique would be to use supplementary funds as working capital for a non-profit corporation which would buy substandard housing, rehabilitate it and resell it at a price which would be supported by low- and moderate-income rents. There are many others. The possible uses of the supplementary funds are limited only by the nature of the housing problems in the locality and the ingenuity of local officials. Whatever offers promise of solving a housing problem would be an appropriate expenditure of supplementary funds.

---

[25] Jarchaw, *Feasibility of Property Rehabilitation Financing Under FHA Section 220*, in RESIDENTIAL REHABILITATION (M. McFarland & W. Vivrett eds. 1966).

[26] 42 U.S.C. § 1457 (1964).

VI

HOUSING COSTS

The Model Cities legislation envisions experiments to make new housing available to low- and moderate-income households through a variety of subsidy techniques, from straight "front-end" subsidy of a portion of the capital cost of housing to various devices to subsidize a portion of the cost of taxes and interest. It is hoped that supplementary funds will also be used to test a variety of techniques to achieve homeownership by lower-income families.

The program should also stimulate efforts to reduce the cost of construction. The statute requires that the local program make maximum use of new and improved technology, including cost-reduction techniques.[27] In their applications for planning grants applicants are asked to specify the steps which are to be taken to implement this provision. It is hoped that communities participating in the program will experiment in various new and innovative techniques to lower the cost of housing.

The statute also provides that substantive local laws, regulations, and other requirements must be consistent with the objectives of the program.[28] Here cities will be expected to examine building, housing and zoning regulations to assure that they do not unnecessarily impede the use of materials, methods and technical innovations that could lead to lower cost construction.

VII

OTHER IMPACTS OF THE PROGRAM ON HOUSING

The Model Cities Program is expected to have indirect impact on housing through the activities to be carried out in the fields of health, education, employment and social services. The following examples are but random illustrations.

A basic thrust of the program is to enhance job skills and job opportunities; as this is done—as incomes rise—so will the effective demand for standard non-assisted housing.

In the program, public assistance activities will be linked to physical development activities, thus bringing into public focus the fact that in many cases payments sustain slums and that the shelter component of welfare allowances is too low to permit the recipient to live in standard housing. A number of localities are expected to work on this problem with state agencies and their state legislatures.

The Model Cities statute calls for citizen participation in all phases of the program.[29] One of the benefits of total involvement in community building, in which the

---

[27] Demonstration Cities and Metropolitan Development Act of 1966, § 103(b)(3)(C), 42 U.S.C. § 3303(b)(3)(C) (Supp. II, 1965-66).
[28] § 103(a)(4), 42 U.S.C. § 3303(a)(4) (Supp. II, 1965-66).
[29] § 103(a)(2), 42 U.S.C. § 3303(a)(2) (Supp. II, 1965-66).

residents—owners and tenants—have both a stake and a voice, is expected to be an increased respect for property and desire to maintain it.

The Model Cities legislation calls for provision of "social services necessary to serve the poor and disadvantaged in the area."[30] It is anticipated that a number of such services provided through local community action agencies will be directed to housing problems. These services might include such things as the provision of housing advisors to help citizens work for better housing conditions through landlord-tenant discussions, and legal services to provide representation of the interests of low-income tenants. The concentrated focus on the needs of the poor and disadvantaged should give impetus to new and imaginative shaping of the law to better meet those needs. Experiments with new kinds of legislation such as rent escrow, the use of receiverships and provisions to ferret out true owners of slum property would be appropriate.

Conclusion

The Model Cities Program will not provide all the answers to housing problems—there is still far too much we need to learn in order to reach the goal of "a decent home and a suitable living environment for every American family." But it will provide a fertile testing ground for experimentation and innovation, and through the emphasis given to housing and through the freedom allowed in the use of funds a significant advance can be made toward that goal.

---

[30] Id.

COOPERATIVE SELF-HELP HOUSING

Tom L. Davis*

Too many people in our country are badly housed. According to the 1960 census, 10.6 million units of the available 58.3 million housing units were considered substandard. In urban areas there were 4.3 million substandard units; 4.8 million substandard units were in rural nonfarm communities, and on rural farms there were 1.5 million such units.[1] Except where aided by grants or subsidies, the poor of the nation are found in substandard housing.

I

The Problem—Substandard Housing and the Poor

There are approximately 35 million poor persons in the nation.[2] Generally, they are not organized politically, economically, or socially. If employed, they are found most often in jobs without the protection and benefit of union organization or minimum wage law. Lower income and poor families tend to have more children than other income groups. This boosts their family needs beyond their capabilities and pyramids their problems. Due to their economic isolation or segregation from the mainstream of American "know-how" culture, they are not aware of scientific achievements and the available methods of family planning and birth control. Culturally segregated in the crowded city or culturally isolated in the rural areas, there is little opportunity for the poor to be part of, or proud of, the accomplishments of this country in any field of endeavor. Until recently the dialogue between the poor and the rest of the population of the nation has been practically nonexistent. Tom Sawyer and Huckleberry Finn for the new generation of Americans are dead. The Prince and the Pauper do not speak the same language. The lack of communication and understanding between the two groups is analogous to the situation existing in France prior to the French Revolution. The average suburbanite making his way between his home "styled for gracious living" and his job in the city rarely sees the poor and is as unconcerned as the members of the court of Louis XVI making their trips between Versailles and the fashionable shops of Paris. The saving grace and moral difference between the times is the aroused concern of the educational,

* A.B. 1946, LL.B. 1941, University of Texas. Chief Counsel, Cooperative and Special Programs Section, Office of the General Counsel, Federal Housing Administration, Department of Housing and Urban Development.

The ideas and views expressed in this article are those of the author and do not represent the views and policy of the Federal Housing Administration or the Department of Housing and Urban Development.

[1] Hearings on the Federal Role in Urban Affairs Before the Subcomm. on Executive Reorganization of the Senate Comm. on Government Operations, 89th Cong., 2d Sess., pt. 1, at 147 (1966) [hereinafter cited as 1966 Hearings].

[2] See, e.g., 1966 Hearings, pt. 2, at 460; M. Harrington, The Other America 182 (1962).

social, religious, business, labor, and political leaders of the nation with the problems of the poor. Enlightened leaders are aware that riots and violence against property are the harvest of generations of neglect and that the resources of a nation are dependent upon the productivity and cultural ties of its people.

In order to eliminate substandard housing, the nation would have to invest over $30 billion.[3] It has been suggested that the rapidity of the implementation of a housing program of such magnitude is dependent upon economic conditions and that during inflationary periods the effectiveness of a subsidized housing program for the poor, due to rising costs, would be diminished. Conversely, when there is slack in the economy, the tempo of such a housing program could be accelerated with gains and benefits not only to the reduction of substandard housing but to the increase in economic activity in the nation.[4] While this is economic theory, ironically it is not applied to the interstate highway construction program for which, as a people, we are spending $30 billion at a rate of $4.4 billion per year in federal grants, nor to the space program costing over $5 billion a year.[5] The crisis of the poor cannot be treated solely with words and phrases. Treatment will require reallocation of dollars, employment and use of skilled technicians, and the elimination of political obstacles. In the dialogue relating to the needs of the nation, housing and other human necessities deserve first class priority.

II

A Solution—Cooperative Self-Help Housing

It is apparent that the cost of a subsidized housing program for the poor can be reduced by the value of self-help labor contributed by the future owners or occupants and that at any given time in the economy the use of self-help would result in more housing being built at reduced costs. A program involving self-help can be persuasive politically and can achieve many moral objectives.

The following short-run priorities[6] would result in maximum immediate benefits to the poor:

(1) Through planned parenthood, help the poor control the size of their families. This objective can be achieved at a negligible cost to the nation and would, of course, in the long run be of great assistance in achieving the other priorities.

(2) Expand assistance to poor children and create jobs for their parents.

(3) Create subsidized standard housing for the working poor.

---

[3] S. Levitan, Programs in Aid of the Poor 57 (1965). (This work also appears as exhibit 42 of *1966 Hearings*, pt. 2, at 459.)

[4] *Id.*

[5] 113 Cong. Rec. H4799 (daily ed. April 27, 1967) (1967 National Housing Conference Legislative Resolutions, introduced for the Record by Congressman Patman).

[6] *See* S. Levitan, *supra* note 3, at 49-58.

It is significant that each of the above short-run priorities contains elements of self-help which can be a part of, and furthered by, an effective self-help housing program.

A. The Need for Organization

In order for any area or locality to have an effective self-help housing program for the poor, there must be either a private or a public self-help housing organization which has a profound belief in self-help and which is able to provide the proper administration and support to the self-help housing specialialists who will select and work with the families who are to provide the labor.

In any given community the self-help housing sponsor would have to deal with the following principal preconstruction problems:

(1) Obtaining a working arrangement with the affected labor unions so that self-help labor by the prospective occupants will be accepted by the unions and will not be a cause for labor difficulties and delays during the construction period;

(2) Selecting and obtaining a site in the community for the new construction or the rehabilitation of existing housing;

(3) Selecting the construction foreman, the group social worker, and any other self-help specialists who may be needed for the project;

(4) Establishing criteria for the selection of self-help families, including a determination of the type, amount, and scheduling of self-help;

(5) Arranging for preparation of building or rehabilitation plans;

(6) Obtaining financing for the project; and

(7) Organizing and staffing the self-help cooperative or condominium association pending the transfer of memberships or title to the self-help families.

B. Cooperative and Condominium Ownership

In urban areas—city or suburb—the cooperative and condominium forms of ownership are particularly well-designed to further the aims of a self-help housing program, which include the development of individual self-esteem and pride inherent in home ownership as well as creating group and community spirit. These two forms of ownership are also adaptable and can be used in the development of detached, semi-detached, and row housing, as well as high-rise.

Under the cooperative form of ownership, a corporation owns the housing and each member owns stock in the corporation which entitles him to live in a unit after the execution of an occupancy agreement. One mortgage covers the entire project, and the members pay carrying charges under their occupancy agreements to the corporation. The corporation is responsible for all of the expenses of the project including taxes and mortgage payments. Each member occupant has an equal vote in electing the board of directors, but the carrying charges are established generally on the basis of unit size.

Under condominium ownership, fee simple title to a dwelling unit as well as specified undivided interest in the common areas and facilities is vested in each condominium owner. Each unit and its specified undivided interest are covered by a mortgage. Mortgage payments and taxes for the unit and its undivided interest are the responsibility of the individual unit owner. All of the units and their undivided interests are subject to a recorded plan of condominium ownership which restricts the use of the property and provides for the creation of an association of owners, consisting of all of the unit owners, which has through its board of directors the authority to assess each of the units for its share of the expenses relating to the common expenses of the association. The assessments as well as the voting rights in the association are established as a percentage of the value of the dwelling unit to the entire project.

Both cooperative and condominium ownership may include commercial as well as community facilities, and the leasing and use of same would be the responsibility of the board of directors of the cooperative or of the condominium. Both forms of ownership provide incentive to the owners and ample opportunity for them to develop personal and group abilities through cooperative and democratic processes. When combined with a self-help program, the participants would acquire technical knowledge and skills resulting in the creation of pride in the individual and the family through a feeling that they have learned something, perfected something, created something through their own abilities working with representatives of society who are interested in entering into a relationship with them for the development of their environment.

Legally, if desired, the cooperative and condominum forms of ownership are useful devices to restrict resale of the units to specified income groups. Such restrictions on resale could be included in the cooperative charter or by-laws, or in the condominium plan of ownership. Consequently, a self-help housing program using the cooperative or condominium form of ownership, which is subsidized either by public or private means, has a ready answer to any opposition or criticism that the housing could be acquired for speculative purposes.

If the self-help housing organization is properly based in the community, the cooperative and condominium forms of ownership would also permit the construction and use of any commercial and community facilities associated with the development on a cooperative basis. For example, with respect to commercial facilities, the housing cooperative could lease them to cooperative business ventures—groceries, drug stores, cafeterias, bakeries. In addition to the rental income received by the cooperative housing corporation from the enterprises, the sponsoring self-help organization could, with the approval of the community authorities, initiate these cooperative businesses with the dual purpose of their being used as training institutions for the residents of the area, who would be given the first opportunity for employment training, as well as affording all area residents lower prices for the goods and services provided on a cooperative basis. In some instances, the self-help sponsoring organization might be able to initiate the leasing of space from the cooperative or condominium housing owner by the city for the purpose of installing public health sub-stations, branch libraries, employment offices, and nurseries, thereby affording income to the housing cooperative or condominium, achieving the availability of public services to all residents of the area, and if an arrangement is made with the community, providing an opportunity and a place for training and employment of the low income people of the area in these particular fields. Whenever such cooperative or condominium housing for the poor can be located near other income group housing, both will reap benefits. For example, the middle or higher income housing occupants can be a source of employment for the residents of the low income project, who can carry forward cooperative principles they have learned by forming a cooperatively-operated enterprise to furnish domestic and similar services. Likewise, in a community development area where the sponsoring self-help organization can encourage the inclusion of special type housing such as nursing homes, hospitals, and elderly housing, the sponsor can increase its effectiveness by working out an employment training program which will provide jobs for the low income residents of the area and also provide the institutions with much needed services from a readily available labor source.

C. Individual Participation

Where self-help is used to build cooperative and condominium housing, the sponsoring agency should have an agreement with each self-help participant as to the type and amount of self-help labor required. The agreement should specifically provide that membership in the cooperative or title to the condominium unit will not be transferred to the participant until the required amount of labor has been completed. Such agreement may also provide for the transfer of the participant's rights to another self-help family which is willing and able to complete the self-help contract in the event the original participant is unable to complete. Prior to the commencement of construction and the execution of the self-help contracts, there should be sufficient meetings with the self-help families, the social worker, and the construction foreman so that each participant and his family will know exactly what will be expected of them. The final selection of families to be involved should come after these explanatory meetings. It is recommended for cooperative and condominium housing that teams of workers will be formed and that work will be carried out on a project construction basis rather than on an individual home basis. When the project is completed, each family will draw lots for the particular type and size of unit for which it is eligible.

There are several advantages in utilizing a team system for working on all of the houses rather than each individual family working exclusively on its own house. The construction foreman can teach the unskilled participants on a group basis and does not have to separately instruct each family. As the group progresses from house to house, the foreman will not have to supervise as closely since the repetition of the same scheduled work on each house will increase the skill of the team's performance, and as a result, the foreman can devote his time to a new team which will be scheduled to perform another stage of construction. Team building also encourages exchange of ideas within the group and offers an opportunity to learn from each other's abilities and errors. Finally, there is no temptation to give more effort and skill to any one house since no particular house has been assigned to any participant during construction.

D. Financing

Section 212 of the National Housing Act, with certain exceptions, provides that in all FHA multifamily housing projects prevailing wages established by the Department of Labor must be paid.[7] Accordingly, unless this section is amended, prevailing wages must be paid to laborers building any section 213[8] cooperative or any section 234[9] condominium project; and self-help or donated labor by low income families would not be possible. However, this requirement for prevailing wages would not apply to self-help or donated labor in a section 221(d)(3)[10] low and moderate income cooperative project where members of the cooperative are not otherwise employed in the construction of the project and voluntarily donate their services without compensation. Therefore, the principles of self-help and donated labor are available to cooperatives for low income groups under section 221(d)(3).

Assuming that the restrictions imposed by prevailing wages under the National Housing Act can be relaxed, the FHA mortgage insurance programs for sections 213 cooperatives and section 234 condominiums could serve as financing vehicles for a self-help housing program. However, in order to reach low income groups, even with the use of self-help equity, it may be necessary for some form of subsidy to be available. There could be, for example, a combination of a FHA-insured mortgage covering the project at market rate interest and a grant, either from public or private sources. The grant would permit the FHA-insured mortgage to be in a lower amount with resulting lower monthly payments by the low income cooperator or condominium unit owner. This procedure would parallel one used now by FHA and the Department of Health, Education, and Welfare involving nonprofit nursing homes which are financed by a combination of a Hill-Burton federal grant and a

[7] 12 U.S.C. § 1715c(a) (Supp. II, 1965-66).
[8] 12 U.S.C. § 1715e (1964, Supp. II, 1965-66).
[9] 12 U.S.C. § 1715y (1964, Supp. II, 1965-66).
[10] 12 U.S.C. § 1715l (Supp. II, 1965-66).

FHA-insured mortgage. Forms of subsidy, such as low interest rates, for condomium individual mortgages would require legislative changes to the National Housing Act.

Great strides have been made in housing the middle income group. In the heat of political debate or in the meticulous listing of his mortgage interest on his income tax return, the typical middle or upper income home owner would look askance at any person who might suggest that he is enjoying the benefit of a federal subsidy by reason of the interest deduction in determining the amount of his income tax. It has been estimated that in 1962, federal subsidies by reason of interest tax deductions to homeowners in the upper twenty per cent of income distribution amounted to $1.7 billion as compared to $820 million of federal subsidies for poor people.[11]

In view of the great shortage of standard housing for the low income group, new avenues of federal revenue may need exploration. In inflationary times, when the government has so many top priorities—foreign and domestic—there may be some economic merit in suggesting that expenditures for luxury housing result in the channeling of goods and services away from housing for the low income group. The analogy can be drawn that taxes on nonessentials, such as furs, perfumes, and other luxury items, may be extended in the form of a federal transfer tax to luxury homes and apartments. The objective of the tax would be not only to produce revenue but also to direct goods, services, and money to housing for which there is a greater need. Since such a tax would fall primarily on the upper income group rather than on the middle income group, it might receive the support of the majority of the people. Alternatively, the amount of deductible mortgage interest for income tax purposes could be limited as in the case of charitable contributions and medical expenses, thereby increasing federal income tax revenue. The limitation on deductible mortgage interest could be set at a figure which would generally not affect the middle income home or apartment owners.

CONCLUSION

The use of self-help in the construction of cooperative and condominium housing should be explored as one of the methods of achieving home ownership for the low income group in the United States. Self-help has been successfully used in undeveloped countries[12] and is receiving additional interest in the United States.[13]

---

[11] S. LEVITAN, *supra* note 3, at 40.

[12] *See* DEPARTMENT OF ECONOMIC AND SOCIAL AFFAIRS, UNITED NATIONS, MANUAL ON SELF-HELP HOUSING, U.N. DOC. ST/SOA/53 (1964); INTER-AMERICAN HOUSING AND PLANNING CENTER (BOGOTÁ), PAN AMERICAN UNION, SELF-HELP HOUSING GUIDE (1962).

[13] *See* 113 CONG. REC. S3769 (daily ed. March 14, 1967) (The War on Poverty—message from the President); *1966 Hearings*, pt. 1, at 38 (statement of Senator Robert Kennedy); 113 CONG. REC. H99 (daily ed. Jan. 11, 1967) (remarks of Congressman Widnall concerning the Percy Home Ownership Plan); Blackburn, *Citizen Participation*, 20 J. HOUSING 440 (1963), describing the Flanner Homes self-help project in Indianapolis.

REHABILITATION OF HOUSING: FEDERAL PROGRAMS AND PRIVATE ENTERPRISE

Bernard E. Loshbough*

Introduction

A basic fact of life for millions of people, particularly for those trapped in urban ghettos, is the need for adequate housing at a price they can afford to pay. The attack on the problem, until recent years, has centered on the tearing down of large areas of obsolescent, deteriorated housing, with the consequent dislocation of large numbers of people, which in turn has led to overcrowding and accelerated decay elsewhere.

More recently, industry and government people concerned with housing have been suggesting, and in some cases probing, another approach to the problem. This is to develop techniques for large-scale rehabilitation of basically sound but aging existing structures. The best estimates indicate that there are at least 5,000,000 substandard houses in the blighted areas of U.S. cities that are capable of rehabilitation.[1]

Obviously, from the public point of view, a massive effort is needed to transform this potential into reality within a reasonably short period of time. This calls for teamwork between the public and private sectors.

ACTION-Housing[2] has formulated and is presenting to industry and government a thoroughly researched proposal directed at achieving a major breakthrough in the mass rehabilitation of housing. This new concept is based, in part, on this private, nonprofit civic organization's experience in renovating a group of twenty-two single-family, two-story attached, sixty-year-old houses in an aging Pittsburgh neighborhood. It has been prepared after a series of consultation conferences with industry's foremost administrators and research heads, and government leaders in housing.

The proposal, which will be explained in detail later in this article, calls for private enterprise to take the initiative in forming a new, broadly-based corporation which, in cooperation with government, would bring about housing modernization on a sizable scale, with particular attention to the needs of families of low and moderate income.

Others have expressed themselves as thinking along similar, if not precisely the same, lines. They include the President of the United States, several U.S. Senators of both parties, and chief executive officers of some of the nation's largest corporations and financial institutions. In April 1967, Senator Charles H. Percy, addressing the thirty-sixth annual meeting of the National Housing Conference, observed:[3]

---

* Executive Director, ACTION-Housing, Inc.

[1] *E.g., Finding a Profit in Slum Streets*, Bus. Week, Feb. 4, 1967, at 52.

[2] Allegheny Council to Improve Our Neighborhoods, Pittsburgh, Pennsylvania.

[3] Address by Senator Percy before the National Housing Conference, Washington, D.C., April 10, 1967.

All the programs which encourage home ownership—whether it be a single-family home, row house, a share in a housing cooperative, or an apartment in one of the newer condominiums—are aimed at those families of middle or upper income. Those who may well need home ownership and profit from it most have been left out.

I am convinced that if home ownership, in its various forms, can be made a realistic possibility to the poor but aspiring family, they will surmount that motivation barrier and strive to achieve the economic security that can make ownership a reality for them.

The Senator, who is a member of the Senate's Banking and Currency Committee, urged the creation of a federally-sponsored National Home Ownership Foundation, to give technical assistance and make loans to local organizations conducting programs to help lower income families own their own homes or apartments. "Its purpose would be to mobilize the enormous resources of the non-government sector behind a national effort to expand home ownership opportunities for all Americans,"[4] he said.

While the Senator's program has areas of similarity, it differs from ACTION-Housing's private enterprise proposal, which concentrates on rehabilitation and would encompass rental as well as sales housing for families of low and moderate income. Senator Percy also proposed a program for increasing the supply of qualified housing specialists, which is one of the recommendations of the ACTION-Housing proposal, and establishing a fund to provide "seed money" to local nonprofit housing sponsors, which ACTION-Housing has performed on a smaller scale at the local level with its private enterprise Development Fund since 1959.

It is evident that today both private enterprise and government, at the federal, state, and local levels, have become increasingly aware of the potential of a program of mass housing rehabilitation to answer the housing needs of urban families of moderate income, thus leading to the revitalizing of the declining neighborhoods of our cities.

Before expanding on ACTION-Housing's proposal to bring this about, it is important to the purpose of this article to recount the federal role in housing rehabilitation in the past.

I

The Federal Role in Housing Rehabilitation

A. Background

The depression inspired early federal ventures into residential rehabilitation. In 1933, the Home Owners' Loan Corporation (HOLC) was authorized to make loans to save the homes of families whose mortgages had been foreclosed as a result of the depression.[5] An offshoot of this program resulted when the HOLC began making

---

[4] *Id.*

[5] Home Owners' Loan Act of 1933, ch. 64, 48 Stat. 128.

loans for the modernization and improvement of residential properties.[6]   And in 1934, title I of the National Housing Act authorized the Federal Housing Administration (FHA) to insure loans made by private lending institutions for the purpose of financing alterations, repairs, and improvements upon real property.[7]

The importance of these two programs (HOLC and FHA) lies in the recognition of residential rehabilitation as a concept, rather than in the method in which it was handled.   The aid was not confined specifically to older cities, urban areas, declining neighborhoods, and so on, but instead the loans went to property owners regardless of area.   The primary criterion was financial distress of the borrower rather than the condition of the structure in which he lived.   There was no plan or scheme to fit the rehabilitation effort into a broader concept of community planning.

A series of reports and studies published between 1940 and 1950 indicated the necessity for approaching housing rehabilitation on a neighborhood basis, with reference to the framework of the whole community.   This approach was adopted in the Housing Act of 1949,[8] the principal law authorizing federal assistance to slum clearance and urban renewal.   Under this act a series of federal financial aids to encourage rehabilitation and conservation of existing residential properties in deteriorating urban neighborhoods were sponsored.   However, it was not until 1954 that these tools were organized into a comprehensive effort.

A brief summary of the housing acts of 1954 through 1965 reveals an evolution in federal efforts to provide meaningful legislation to assist revitalization of the urban housing supply.

B. The Housing Act of 1954[9]

In 1953, President Eisenhower appointed a committee to undertake a re-evaluation of the federal government's housing policies and programs.   Largely through the efforts of James Rouse, a Baltimore mortgage banker, the committee recommended that the federal government (1) provide assistance to help communities attack the slum problem and urban decay, (2) provide federal loans and grants to communities for such purposes, and (3) extend the long-term FHA mortgage insurance into older communities to facilitate liberal financing to build and rehabilitate dwelling units for sale and rent.[10]

These recommendations were enacted into law in the Housing Act of 1954.   The Act broadened the provisions of title I to authorize federal assistance for prevention

---

[6] See generally RESIDENTIAL REHABILITATION (M. C. McFarland & W. K. Vivrett eds. 1966).

[7] Ch. 847, § 2, 48 Stat. 1246 (1934), as amended, 12 U.S.C. § 1703 (1964, Supp. II, 1965-66).

[8] Ch. 338, 63 Stat. 413 (codified in scattered sections of 12, 42 U.S.C.).

[9] Ch. 649, 68 Stat. 590 (codified in scattered sections of 12, 18, 20, 31, 40, 42 U.S.C.).

[10] See THE PRESIDENT'S ADVISORY COMMITTEE ON GOVERNMENT HOUSING POLICIES AND PROGRAMS, RECOMMENDATIONS ON GOVERNMENT HOUSING POLICIES AND PROGRAMS (Report to the President of the United States, 1953).

of the spread of slums and urban blight through the rehabilitation and conservation
of blighted and deteriorated areas.

C. The Housing Act of 1956[11]

The Housing Act of 1956 further liberalized title I of the Housing Act of 1949.
It included, among other changes, a provision for the allocation of federal advances
for the preparation of General Neighborhood Renewal Plans (GNRP). The
GNRP was simply the designation of larger urban areas into combination urban
renewal, rehabilitation, and conservation plans, but it was a significant step away
from the total clearance approach. The first signs of neighborhood rehabilitation
efforts began to work as federal policy. The campaign to encourage private rehabilitation of structures as part of a total neighborhood approach became an integral part
of every urban renewal effort under the General Neighborhood Renewal Plan.

D. The Housing Act of 1959[12]

An expansion of the General Neighborhood Renewal Plan idea into a total community approach was an important aspect of the Housing Act of 1959. New provisions for federal grants to Community Renewal Programs were liberalized under
title I. Under this title, grants for the preparation or completion of Community
Renewal Plans (CRPs) were authorized. The CRPs generally included, but were
not limited to (1) identification of slum areas or blighted, deteriorated or deteriorating areas in the community, and (2) the measurement of the nature and degree of
blight and blighting factors within such areas.

The desirability of a closely-integrated community renewal effort with comprehensive planning was recognized as an integral part of the 1959 Housing Act, for it
made an attempt to combine good planning practice with common sense.

E. The Housing Act of 1961[13]

In 1961 the need for a continued effort to maintain and improve the existing supply
of urban housing was as great as, if not greater than, it was at the time of the
passage of the Housing Act of 1954. In 1961, President Kennedy reaffirmed federal
policy with regard to rehabilitation and conservation, and Congress passed the
Housing Act of 1961. Once again title I of the Act was amended to include, among
other provisions, authorization for local urban renewal agencies to carry out rehabilitation demonstrations in urban renewal areas.

This addition to title I was an important step in the process. For years the question
of feasibility had been ignored. That is, was it feasible to rehabilitate and conserve
older residential structures in certain urban areas? Improvement of the physical
environment alone obviously was not enough in many run-down sections. Educa-

---

[11] Ch. 1029, 70 Stat. 1091 (codified in scattered sections of 12, 40, 42 U.S.C.).
[12] Pub. L. No. 86-372, 73 Stat. 654 (codified in scattered sections of 12, 40, 42 U.S.C.).
[13] Pub. L. No. 87-70, 75 Stat. 149 (codified in scattered sections of 12, 15, 40, 42 U.S.C.).

tion, health, opportunities for employment, a sense of civic responsibility—all these and other human factors were involved. It makes no sense to rehabilitate houses when the people themselves are deprived, hopeless, and apathetic.

The Housing Act of 1961 did not change the basic concept of residential rehabilitation, but it did add further legislative tools designed to make the program more effective. These were (1) liberalizing of FHA programs which were to be used to finance rehabilitation, (2) authorizing FHA to insure below-market interest rate loans used for rehabilitation carried out by nonprofit, limited dividend, or cooperative organizations, (3) insuring supplementary rehabilitation loans under section 220(h)[14] based on any type of security acceptable to the FHA Commissioner, including second mortgage, and (4) calculating loan amounts for rehabilitation based on the value of existing property plus the cost of repairs.

F. The Housing Act of 1964[15]

The passage of the Housing Act of 1964 was a reaffirmation of national policy with another attempt to strengthen the Act of 1961. Implementation of the legislative tools was still the critical question. However, some redefinition was added to increase the use of federal financial aid for home improvement loans in urban renewal and code enforcement areas. Thus the presumed purpose of section 220(h)[16] was to aid in the elimination of slums and blighted conditions and the prevention of the deterioration of residential properties by supplementing the insurance of mortgages.

To be eligible for insurance under section 220(h) of this housing act, the mortgaged property had to be located in the area of a slum clearance and urban redevelopment project covered by the Housing Act of 1949 and subsequent amendments. The improvements in section 220(h) provided for further assistance in the conservation, improvement, repair, and rehabilitation of property located in the area of an urban renewal project, or in an area in which a program of concentrated code enforcement activities was being carried out. This expansion of powers also has permitted the authorization of loans and terms under a broader commitment basis, including advances during the construction or improvement period made by institutions on and after the enactment of the Housing Act of 1961.

G. The Housing and Urban Development Act of 1965[17]

Until the Housing and Urban Development Act of 1965, the majority of moderate income housing attempted to be built, rehabilitated, or conserved with the help of federal assistance in deteriorating urban areas was accomplished under sections 220 and 221 of the National Housing Act as amended through 1964.[18] The Act of 1965

---

[14] Pub. L. No. 87-70, § 102(a), 75 Stat. 154, *as amended*, 12 U.S.C. § 1715k(h) (1964, Supp. II, 1965-66).

[15] Pub. L. No. 88-560, 78 Stat. 769 (codified in scattered sections of 12, 15, 20, 38, 40, 42 U.S.C.).

[16] 12 U.S.C. § 1715k(h) (1964), *as amended*, (Supp. II, 1965-66).

[17] Pub. L. No. 89-117, 79 Stat. 451 (codified in scattered sections of 12, 15, 20, 38, 40, 42, 49 U.S.C.).

[18] 12 U.S.C. §§ 1715k, 1715*l* (1964), *as amended*, (Supp. II, 1965-66).

made significant strides toward providing housing for low and moderate income families.

The Act continued the moderate income housing provisions of the 1961 Act and reduced the below-market interest rate to three per cent to assure lower rents. In addition, it provided a series of special provisions for disadvantaged persons which included:

(1) Authorization of the newly established Federal Department of Housing and Urban Development (HUD) to undertake a program of rent supplements to serve people who are in need of housing and are in the lower income range—eligible to receive public housing.

(2) Extension of the FHA section 221 programs.

(3) Section 115 rehabilitation grants to homeowners in urban renewal areas, enabling low-income homeowners whose dwellings are required by an urban renewal plan to be rehabilitated to improve their homes, and to remain in them, rather than be compelled to leave. These grants may go up to $1,500 for families whose incomes do not exceed $3,000 yearly, or a lower amount, based on the need of homeowners with higher than $3,000 per year income.[19]

(4) Section 312 rehabilitation loans for owners of properties in title I urban renewal projects or section 117 code enforcement areas. More restrictive in nature, these loans are not to exceed $10,000 or an additional $4,500 in high cost areas. These loans are limited to rehabilitation, and the cost may not exceed the cost of rehabilitation added to the amount of the existing debt secured by the property. The sum of the section 312 loan and any remaining debt may not be more than $30,000 for a single-family residence, $32,500 for a two- or three-family residence, and $37,500 for a four-family residence.[20]

The section 312 loans are liberal with regard to financing. Whenever the principal and interest payments for a 312 loan and the mortgage payments (principal and interest) exceed twenty per cent of the applicant's total income, the applicant is eligible for refinancing.

The principal purpose of the amendments to the section 220 terms was to remove obstacles which restricted the use of FHA section 220 programs as they apply to non-occupant owners, particularly in urban renewal areas.

Non-occupant mortgagors of one- to eleven-unit residential rental housing would be entitled to a larger loan amount more consistent with those on larger multi-family structures. The amendments would also include refinancing to permit existing indebtedness for improvement of the property to be included in the computation

[19] U.S. Urban Renewal Administration, Housing and Home Finance Agency, Local Public Agency Letter No. 342 (Aug. 1965).

[20] U.S. Urban Renewal Administration, Housing and Home Finance Agency, Local Public Agency Letter Nos. 3707, 335, 340, 341 (Sept., June, Aug. 1965).

of the amount of a mortgage, whether or not the indebtedness secured by the property was included in the insured mortgage.

Under the 1965 Act, with funding in 1966, an experimental program in home ownership has been launched under section 221(h).[21] It provides for the sale of new or rehabilitated houses to persons of low and moderate income at below-market interest rate mortgages (three per cent), if the buyer meets all the family composition and annual income requirements necessary for section 221(d)(3)[22] rental families. However, the funds allocated for section 221(h) are minimal—not exceeding $20 million.

Thus far we have seen the "premise" of federal legislation in the recognition of the need for financial tools to assist urban areas in the rehabilitation of residential structures. Also traced has been the steady progression of these tools from their earlier development to the present comprehensive laws which are attempting to deal with the problems of (1) conserving the nation's urban housing supply, (2) providing housing for families of low and middle income, and (3) erasing the present signs and causes of blight in urban areas.

II

PROBLEMS IN THE USE OF FEDERAL PROGRAMS

Federal recognition of the problems of residential rehabilitation and conservation has been progressive, but not all that has been proposed has been achieved. Many of the difficulties in the use of the federal tools can be attributed to the complexities of dealing with civic and private institutions, people, and ideas. These major drawbacks require explanation and amplification.

A major difficulty arises in the area of code standards and enforcement. One of the most crucial steps in the systematic achieving of neighborhood rehabilitation is the establishment of rehabilitation standards that are in accordance with present or proposed re-use plans. This critical aspect, which bears directly on the feasibility of using federal financing, is a program in and of itself. Trained personnel are needed who are familiar with codes, construction, and financing, for value judgments have to be made both for the property owner and the community as a whole. What will it take in terms of rehabilitation dollars to balance the old with the proposed new; will repair be more predominant than replacement on an item-by-item basis; and what best combination of detailed standards will provide decent, sanitary, and safe housing? All of these factors in the final analysis will determine whether or not the use of the federal financial aid is feasible.

Just as the establishment of code standards is a crucial step, so is the interpretation and enforcement of the code standards. The interpretation by local FHA insuring

---

[21] 12 U.S.C. § 1715*l*(h) (Supp. II, 1965-66).
[22] 12 U.S.C. § 1715*l*(d)(3) (Supp. II, 1965-66).

offices of urban renewal and FHA code requirements has presented, and still presents, a major stumbling block in the effective rehabilitation and conservation of existing residential structures through the use of federal resources. All too often the local, urban renewal and federal standards are at odds. What might be acceptable property standards under an urban renewal plan might be unacceptable to the FHA-insuring office for loan purposes, and vice versa.

To correct this problem the Federal Housing Administration has recently established "minimum property standards" for urban renewal rehabilitation.[23] These standards now provide a national basis for standards used in rehabilitation projects located in urban renewal areas for residential structures containing one through eleven units. The determination on the part of the government to add flexibility where it previously was non-existent can be seen in the development of these standards. On the one hand, there is the establishment of a minimum level below which FHA insurance will not be provided; on the other hand, the standards are interpreted as suggestions for which no mandatory level is established. Thus, while guaranteeing items pertaining to safety and sanitation, flexibility is built in to help establish feasibility.

Obviously, the effectiveness of a housing code depends upon its contents and its enforcement. Adequate standards must be implemented with firm and vigorous enforcement. In many cities the enforcement of housing codes has been replete with difficulties—lack of sufficient funds and staff, the dispersion of inspection responsibilities among several bureaus or departments, the handling of inspections on a complaint rather than area basis, the ineffectiveness of court action, and the lack of adequate relocation resources to back up vigorous enforcement.

The importance of housing codes is stressed in an integral part of the Housing Act of 1949 as amended. The Act provides that no contract shall be entered into for any capital grant or loans for urban renewal, nor any mortgage insured under sections 220 or 221 of the National Housing Act, and no annual contributions or capital grant contracts for public housing shall be entered into, unless there is presented to the Administrator of the FHA by the locality a workable program of the community for utilizing private and public resources to eliminate present slums and prevent their spread in the future.[24]

Another hindrance to the effective use of federal financial aids is the procedure required by local lending institutions and FHA to process an application for use of funds to promote rehabilitation. This tedious and complicated procedure is confusing to the majority of homeowners and developers. The process is not a simplified one and requires the time of specialists. Most homeowners are not familiar with the procedure and lack the expertise to accomplish it. Most lending institutions would prefer not to get involved because of time-money factors. Larger developers hire

---

[23] U.S. FEDERAL HOUSING ADMINISTRATION, DEP'T OF HOUSING AND URBAN DEVELOPMENT, MINIMUM PROPERTY STANDARDS FOR URBAN RENEWAL REHABILITATION (1966).

[24] § 101(c), 42 U.S.C. § 1451(c) (Supp. II, 1965-66).

specialists but pass the cost on to the subsequent user, thus raising costs and obviating the use of the rehabilitated units for the low- and middle-income users.

III

THE ACTION-HOUSING PROPOSAL

In spite of these problems, many of the best brains of industry and government have nevertheless come to the conclusion that the most feasible way to eradicate blight in our cities is to rehabilitate, on a large scale, existing deteriorating but structurally sound housing, particularly for families of low and moderate income. This calls for teamwork between the public and private sectors. The tools are available, as provided by the federal legislation. There is a profit incentive as well as a civic motive for private industry. The need is for a catalyst to join all forces.

Pittsburgh's ACTION-Housing, Inc., is advancing such a proposal to top industry administrators and research heads and government representatives concerned with housing. The proposal recommends that private enterprise organize and operate a new profit-making development corporation to conduct full-scale modernization of deteriorating urban housing, initially in the Pittsburgh metropolitan area, in cooperation with the local, state, and federal agencies. It suggests very close interaction between private enterprise and the public sectors in carrying out the program.

Here Pittsburgh has an opportunity to lead the nation in providing a creative and effective solution to a troublesome public problem. The most likely source for this kind of effort is the private sector, particularly our large corporate entities with their tremendous resources in human talent, technological know-how, financial strength, and problem-solving capabilities.

The motivation for involvement in this effort may vary from one company to another. It may be enlightened self-interest for those that have a direct stake in the general community environment, or the acceptance of the challenge of civic responsibility, or direct commercial interest in terms of enlarging the market for products and services in the housing field. These are opportunities for business to demonstrate what it can achieve through the appropriate application of its capabilities in an area of broad public concern.

The profit motivation for those companies whose capabilities mesh with the commercial opportunities inherent in this field should not be de-emphasized. To be perfectly pragmatic, in the long run this motivation offers the most potent stimulant for action on a massive scale. After all, our profit-motivated system has proven itself to be the most prolific provider for human needs and wants yet known to man.

What is called for, then, is a mechanism which can successfully blend all of these motivations into a single concerted attack on the problem of mass housing rehabilitation and at the same time provide a laboratory for experimentation in this field through which individual companies can gain experience and confidence, and ultimately, hopefully, proliferate this effort on an ever-expanding scale. This is really what the ACTION-Housing proposal is all about.

A. Summary

This proposal recommends the formation of a new corporation, capitalized at $3 million to $4 million, to engage in the rehabilitation of structurally sound but deteriorating housing in the Pittsburgh metropolitan area, on a profit-motivated basis, in cooperation with the local, state, and federal agencies. Participating companies would commit to purchase common stocks or debentures. Policy would be established by a board of their selection. Professional staff and management personnel would be provided by the newly-created company. The Pittsburgh demonstration by the proposed Allegheny Housing Rehabilitation Corporation (AHRCO) would, when experience has proven it successful, constitute a prototype which could be repeated in many cities throughout the nation.

B. Details of the Proposal

Allegheny County contains 503,000 dwelling units, of which it is estimated approximately 90,000 need and are susceptible of rehabilitation. Of these, 40,000 are in the City of Pittsburgh. A total of approximately 17,000 dwelling units in the City and County are beyond restoration and should be demolished.

Total clearance and redevelopment of the area in which the 90,000 units are located is monetarily and otherwise not feasible. Public housing in Pittsburgh has averaged less than 325 units per year in the last thirty years, although the rate has increased in the last few years to about 430. At this rate, including consideration of private building and rehabilitation, Allegheny County's inventory of substandard housing will increase.

As a demonstration, ACTION-Housing, Inc., undertook in 1966 the rehabilitation of twenty-two row houses on Cora Street in the Homewood-Brushton area of Pittsburgh. ACTION-Housing acquired the properties for about $4,000 each and expended approximately $6,000 additional per unit to provide good housing for twenty-two families in that neighborhood at a rental only slightly higher than previous payments.

Construction work was performed by a private contractor; interim financing was provided under a participation agreement by the Mellon National Bank and Trust Company and the Development Fund of ACTION-Housing, Inc. The permanent mortgage financing was obtained from the federal government under its below-market interest rate program (section 221(d)(3) of the National Housing Act), which provides three per cent funds and up to a forty year mortgage term for 100 per cent of the total costs where the mortgagor is a nonprofit corporation like ACTION-Housing, Inc. Limited dividend corporations could secure a mortgage for ninety per cent of the total costs.

The Cora Street rehabilitation has had a distinct advantage in being located in a neighborhood which has a strongly structured Citizens Renewal Council, a pioneer urban extension group which ACTION-Housing helped to organize and has given professional guidance to for seven years. The Council has leadership and participation by neighborhood people, as well as backing by the major industries and merchants of the neighborhood. When the Cora Street project was first publicly announced, the then president of the Council said: "The modernization of whole sections of basically sound housing will provide the visible evidence of change that should inspire us all."[25]

Although Cora Street has demonstrated obstacles and need for changes in procedures, the following conclusions were reached:

(1) Such work is feasible and provides a good end-result for tenants of low and moderate income without major dislocation. Tenants are happy with the housing.

(2) A reasonable profit is available to developers, subject to normal business risks, and to persons providing services (*e.g.*, architect, contractor, lender, attorney, realtor).

(3) This form of private enterprise development provides advantages in cost, markets, and time over new construction and other current housing programs.

(4) Major expansion of this concept requires substantial capital and private enterprise production techniques and purchasing power.

(5) Such an undertaking provides an immense sociological benefit to older neighborhoods in decaying urban communities—an urgent necessity in halting further deterioration and social strife.

Major capital, private enterprise methods, and the affirmative cooperation of federal, state, and local governments are essential to provide quantity rehabilitation for impact upon Allegheny County communities.

Secretary Robert C. Weaver has signed an agreement between ACTION-Housing and the Department of Housing and Urban Development concerning the proposed pilot rehabilitation project in Pittsburgh. For its participation in the plan, the federal government offers financial resources, technical advice, streamlined Federal Housing Administration processing, and an array of programs through which most families of low and moderate income can qualify for the housing.

Philip N. Brownstein, Assistant Secretary and Federal Housing Administration Commissioner, sees the ACTION-Housing proposal as using five major program concepts, and possibly a sixth. They are, in his words:[26]

---

[25] News Release, ACTION-Housing, Inc., Aug. 1, 1966.

[26] Address by Mr. Brownstein, typed copy issued by the U.S. Federal Housing Administration, Dep't of Housing and Urban Development, June 20, 1967.

(1) Through Federal support of the Urban Renewal Program, we can have price write-downs to keep some rents within the means of the families to be served. This is for properties in urban renewal areas.

(2) and (3) For low-income families, there is a choice between the public housing lease approach or the much maligned and little understood rent supplement program. For the first, the landlord would be the public housing authority, and the second would be privately owned by a nonprofit organization or limited-dividend corporation with the government making a contribution toward the rent in each case.

(4) The proposition also calls for the use of a program to bring home ownership to low-income families through the use of below market interest rate funds.

(5) Another possibility is the turnkey approach to public housing, in which a private builder sells the finished product to the public housing authority.

(6) Still another program uses the below-market interest rate approach to provide rental units for families of modest means.

In a June 7, 1967, letter of transmittal concerning the agreement with ACTION-Housing, Secretary Weaver emphasized the importance of involving minority group members in the construction. He offered a three-point program of goals to be developed with the contractors and the unions, at the local level:[27]

1. Where qualified minority group journeymen and apprentices are available in the Pittsburgh area and individual unions are not now "open," those unions should guarantee that a maximum number of such persons will be employed in the rehabilitation work.
2. Where minority group members lack the needed skills, a training program should be developed—jointly by management and labor—to provide them with the skills needed for employment in the construction industry.
3. The creation of a special category of workmen—known perhaps as "rehabilitation specialists"—should be explored with the unions and the Department of Labor. These specialists would cut across jurisdictional lines and would facilitate the utilization of minority group workers in rehabilitation projects.

Secretary Weaver made the point that involvement of minority workmen will serve many purposes which transcend compliance with the law. He feels that such involvement of minority workmen will enhance the initial reception and ultimate acceptance of the program by the indigenous community and "a reduction of inter-group tension is bound to result in Pittsburgh if a forthright attempt is made to end discrimination in the building trades."[28]

The agreement with the Department of Housing and Urban Development was announced at a dinner for 167 outstanding leaders of the Pittsburgh area, and elsewhere, to launch the Allegheny Housing Rehabilitation Corporation. At the dinner, held June 20, 1967, Anthony J. Furlan, President of the Pittsburgh Building Trades Council, spoke briefly but to the point in pledging the support of unions. He said:

[27] Agreement between ACTION-Housing, Inc. and the Department of Housing and Urban Development, June 7, 1967.
[28] Id.

"We are going to hire members of minority groups to do construction work and cross jurisdictional lines with composite work crews."[29] This statement was applauded as a most significant breakthrough.

The City of Pittsburgh promised every effort to implement the development of the undertaking. There were meetings with the City Solicitor, the Director of Public Safety, the Executive Director of the Planning Department, the Superintendent of the Bureau of Building Inspection, the Mayor's Executive Secretary, and members of their staffs. Joseph M. Barr, Mayor of Pittsburgh, reported in writing:[30]

> As a result of these discussions, there was agreement that the proposals for major rehabilitation of neighborhood housing for low and moderate income families warrant modifications of our building and zoning codes to effect the objectives of the rehabilitation program.
>
> I am therefore planning to submit to City Council a series of recommendations amending these codes to facilitate large-scale rehabilitation of housing financed through special federal mortgage assistance for low and moderate income families.
>
> These changes will include the redefining of work permitted under rehabilitation standards in the building code and modification of the zoning code to permit rehabilitation for non-conforming uses. I am convinced that effective housing rehabilitation is the key to making new federal programs like Model Cities succeed in Pittsburgh, without the large-scale clearance, dislocation of families, and neighborhood disruption associated with the normal urban renewal process.

The support for AHRCO of the U.S. Departments of Housing and Urban Development and Labor and the City of Pittsburgh having been cited, it is pertinent to record the response of one of the leading business executives of the nation—James F. Oates, Jr., Chairman of the Board of the Equitable Life Assurance Society. In a recent letter to Richard K. Mellon, Mr. Oates said:[31]

> The Society is very much interested in the ACTION-Housing proposal for the creation of the Allegheny Housing Rehabilitation Corporation. We are prepared to consider becoming an active participant in this proposal. . . . We compliment you on the excellent approach you are taking to solve this most important challenge to our urban existence.

C. AHRCO: Its Modus Operandi

A preliminary survey by qualified appraisers has indicated that sufficient housing might be acquired in the open market to initiate a major rehabilitation program in the Pittsburgh area. Continuation of the program over an extended period will require close cooperation of the Urban Redevelopment Authority. As the program progresses, high annual rates of acquisition will force the market up, but the Urban Redevelopment Authority, by providing necessary "write-downs" where required, can

---

[29] Address by Mr. Furlan before the presentation dinner for the proposed Allegheny Housing Rehabilitation Corporation, Pittsburgh, Pa., June 20, 1967.

[30] Letter from Mayor Joseph M. Barr to ACTION-Housing, Inc., June 15, 1967.

[31] Letter from James F. Oates, Jr., to Richard K. Mellon, June 7, 1967.

control this cost factor. This cooperation would make it possible for AHRCO to rehabilitate old housing for families of low and moderate income at a monthly cost they could afford to pay.

The Allegheny Housing Rehabilitation Corporation would acquire housing units, arrange for interim financing, secure architectural services, and perform or contract for their rehabilitation. Completed units could be sold to eligible nonprofit corporations, limited dividend entities, cooperatives, or individuals, approved by FHA and eligible for the special assistance mortgage programs available under existing housing acts. An alternative approach is the sale of units to public housing agencies under the so-called turnkey program. AHRCO also would have the option of retaining units for long-range investment.

Inasmuch as no housing rehabilitation industry exists today, major development effort will be required of material suppliers, architects, contractors, and labor. New materials, methods of work, material application, construction systems, training programs for business and labor, and financing are indicated for long-term success of a major housing rehabilitation program.

D. Recommendation

It is recommended that the major Pittsburgh-based companies and others, to the extent that they are interested in housing rehabilitation, form an operating company (AHRCO) capitalized at $3 million to $4 million for the purpose of buying structurally sound but substandard housing principally in, but not limited to, Allegheny County, then rehabilitating and selling, or holding and renting it.

The level of financing suggested is believed to be sufficient to build up to and sustain a rate of 1,000 housing units annually, provided that housing units are turned over in about one year. Based on the assumptions shown in the exhibits attached as an appendix to this article, cash flow would be sufficient in the fifth year after formation to commence payment of dividends.

It is also recommended that a nonprofit research organization be formed to which AHRCO would subscribe ten per cent of its gross profits. The research company, with grants from foundations, governments, and AHRCO, would sponsor research on construction—methods and materials—application problems requiring solution.

Upon acceptance in principle of this proposal by a sufficient number of companies, ACTION-Housing will undertake to form a shareholder's committee to draw up the required agreements for formation and financing the proposed operating company (AHRCO). After formation of the company, ACTION-Housing, Inc. would be retained by it in a consulting capacity.

Final determination of staff, rate of growth, and volume of business, will be determined by the board of directors of the new company. A series of exhibits which illustrate how the company might be organized and operated is included in the appendix.

The structure of the AHRCO proposal indicates that no financial losses would be incurred by the group of companies subscribing to the development corporation. We believe there would be a profit from the sale of houses. A huge rehabilitation market does exist, and there is an exciting opportunity and challenge to develop it on a profit-motivated basis. Profit is not the primary incentive, however, nor is the sale of products.

The major corporations whose interest has been kindled by the proposal see their real benefits as rebuilding and enhancement of the total environment of American cities, where most of them are located and where most of their employees live and work. An enlightened self-interest, if you will.

In the words of J. Stanley Purnell, ACTION-Housing's Chairman of the Board and President:[32]

> Mass rehabilitation of existing housing for families of low and and moderate income has been caught in an economic stranglehold. It has been scattered, haphazard, and on too limited a scale to be significant.
>
> Can it be that we, a nation of builders, have not learned the economics of rebuilding? Or how to develop and adapt space-age construction systems and technologies to housing rehabilitation?
>
> This presents an opportunity for private enterprise to take the lead. It can in cooperation with government, using all the federal tools available, create a new profit-motivated industry. At the same time it would fulfill a well-documented social and physical need.

E. Proposed Federal Legislation

Two prominent U.S. Senators, one Democrat and one Republican, are presenting in the Senate major proposals for providing more and better low-cost housing, through a partnership between private enterprise and government. The AHRCO proposal has been designed to conduct large-scale housing rehabilitation for families of moderate income—between $4,000 and $9,000. It assumes that some form of federal subsidy is required to house very low income families.

New York's Senator Robert F. Kennedy has a plan,[33] based partly on experience in a program initiated six months ago in the Bedford-Stuyvesant section of Brooklyn, to achieve two objectives through a combination of tax incentives, low-interest mortgages, and other devices. The first objective is low-cost housing for the poor, and the second is a substantial return on investment for private entrepreneurs who build such housing.

The Kennedy plan suggests the construction or rehabilitation of 300,000 to 400,000 low-cost housing units over the next seven years, and postulates the possibility of rents no greater than $100 a month and some as low as $73 a month in all of these

---

[32] ACTION-HOUSING, INC., PROPOSAL FOR THE CREATION OF THE ALLEGHENY HOUSING REHABILITATION CORPORATION 6 (1967).

[33] S. 2088, 90th Cong., 1st Sess. (1967); S. 2100, 90th Cong., 1st Sess. (1967).

units. The assumption is that, following the yardstick of a twenty-five per cent expenditure of monthly income on rent, such rentals would be within the range of families with an annual income of between $3,500 and $4,800 annually.

Low, federally subsidized mortgages are called for by the Kennedy plan to keep rents down. The builder agreeing to construct low-cost units in a declining urban neighborhood would receive mortgage insurance of up to eighty per cent of the cost of the project, amortized over fifty years at a rate of two per cent annually.

The investor would have to contract to build or rehabilitate at least 100 units whose rentals would be fixed by the federal government, and agree to meet basic standards of design and maintenance. He would accept a basic, direct return on his equity of only three per cent. However, there would be tax incentives, a primary one being an "investment credit." This would call for a scale of credits ranging from three per cent for the person who invests $200,000 in a project—the "credit" being $6,000—to twenty-two per cent for the person or company who invests 100 per cent, one who builds a project entirely with his own cash. The plan also calls for accelerated depreciation, as low as ten years for investors who put up the full cost of the project.

There is an overall promise of a net return for investors who build low-rent housing of between thirteen and fifteen per cent.

The Republican bill to provide home ownership for the poor,[34] developed and sponsored by Senator Charles H. Percy of Illinois, has been outlined earlier in this article. Senator Percy attended the dinner meeting in Pittsburgh on June 20, 1967, to launch the AHRCO proposal. It is worth noting that that meeting was co-hosted by the following seven executives of Pittsburgh-based corporations: L. B. Worthington, President, United States Steel Corporation; John D. Harper, President, Aluminum Company of America; D. C. Burnham, President, Westinghouse Electric Corporation; F. L. Byrom, President, Koppers Company, Inc.; R. F. Barker, President, PPG Industries; R. E. Seymour, President, Peoples Natural Gas Company; Philip A. Fleger, President, Duquesne Light Company. Richard K. Mellon, President of T. Mellon & Sons, hosted a reception before the dinner. Top management of more than forty national corporations, FHA Commissioner Brownstein, and other government officials at federal, state, and local levels, were present. Support for the concept was advanced by Pennsylvania's Governor Raymond P. Shafer, Senators Joseph S. Clark and Hugh Scott, and others.

Senator Percy took back to Washington a documentary film relating the Cora Street experience, for presentation in the Senate auditorium. In the *Congressional Record* of June 23, 1967, wherein the entire AHRCO proposal is published,[35] Senator Percy related his reactions to the proposal, of which the following is an excerpt:[36]

[34] S. 1592, 90th Cong., 1st Sess. (1967).
[35] 113 CONG. REC. S8811 (daily ed. June 23, 1967).
[36] *Id.* at S8810.

Nowhere . . . do I know of such a comprehensive, well-conceived attack on slum housing and community problems, nor have I ever seen such a concerted effort by every sector of the community to build a better city. Again, the city that turned blight into the golden triangle is truly showing the way in this vital area.

There are those who scoff at such ventures. There are those who say that business and labor and Government can never reach a smooth, effective, working agreement to achieve such lofty goals. I invite those people to go to Pittsburgh, as I did, and see for themselves.

The problem of large-scale housing rehabilitation has existed and been defined and redefined for generations. Today the tools and knowledge are available to solve it, and it seems evident that the AHRCO proposal could bring about such rehabilitated housing for families of moderate income, and even families of low income if rent supplement money is available. Legislation such as that being introduced by Senators Percy and Kennedy, if enacted, apparently would help make it possible to provide both new and rehabilitated housing for more families of low income through a joint venture of private and public enterprise with private industry taking the leadership.

* * *

APPENDIX

MODEL HOUSING REHABILITATION CORPORATION

exhibit no. 1

organization chart

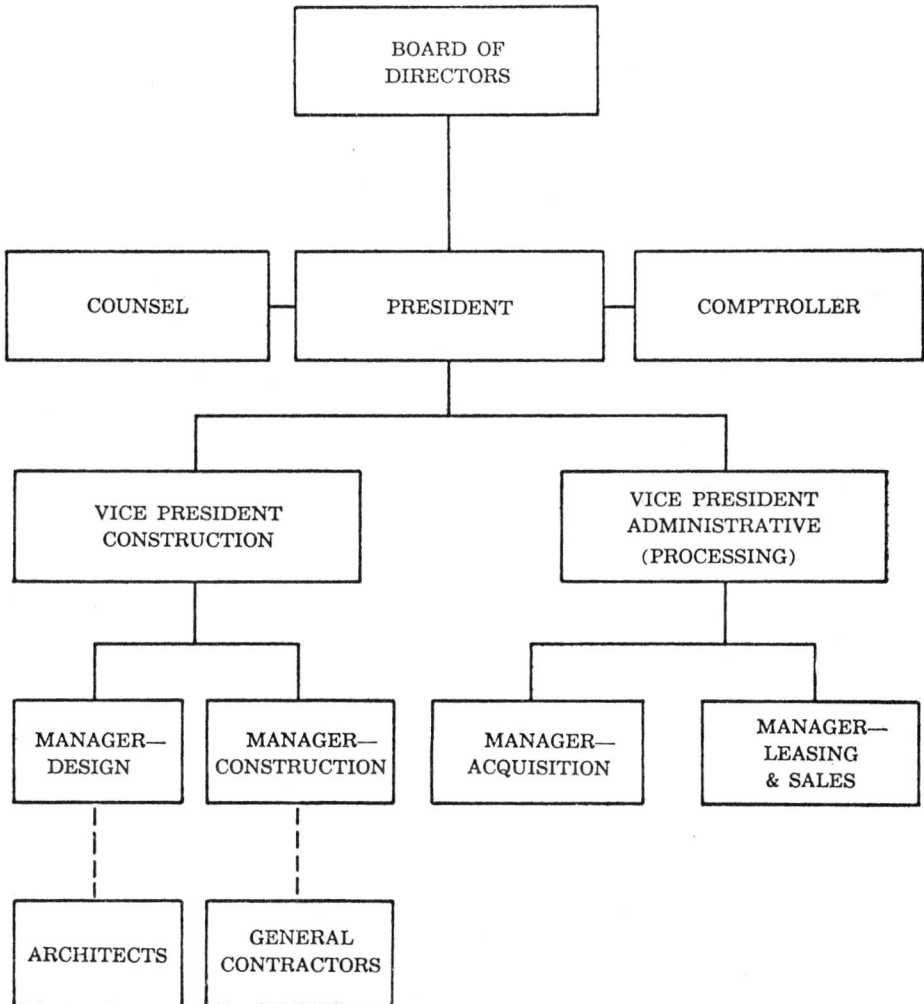

exhibit no. 2   ESTIMATED ANNUAL BUDGET—OPERATING COMPANY

I. Personnel
   A. President $ 35,000

   B. Vice Presidents...................................1 at $24,000

                                              1 at 20,000   44,000

   C. Attorney   18,000

   D. Comptroller   18,000

   E. Managers
        Construction.. 18,000
        Design.. 15,000
        Acquisition... 14,000
        Leasing & Sales.................................... 14,000   61,000

   F. Clerical
        Secretaries/Typists
        (6 at $6,000)....................................... 36,000
        Clerks
        (6 at $6,000)....................................... 36,000   72,000

   G. Engineers, Draftsmen, Job Superintendents,
        Construction Analysts/Inspectors
        (2 at $12,000)...................................... 24,000
        (2 at $10,000)...................................... 20,000
        Draftsmen
        (4 at $8,000)....................................... 32,000
        Engineer.. 12,000   88,000

                               SUB-TOTAL $ 336,000

   H. Fringes @ 15%   50,000

               TOTAL — EMPLOYMENT COSTS $ 386,000

II. Office Expenses
        Rent..$18,000
        Communications...................................... 6,000
        Printing & Supplies..... 8,000
        Transportation & Trips............................. 10,000
        Furniture/Fixtures................................. 10,000 $ 52,000

III. Purchased Services
        Legal...$20,000
        Audit.. 12,000
        Consultant... 20,000 $ 52,000

                               SUB-TOTAL $ 490,000

        Contingencies   10,000

                                  TOTAL $ 500,000

exhibit no. 3

WORKING CAPITAL REQUIREMENTS – 1,000 UNITS ANNUALLY

Estimated Acquisition Costs	$ 4,000,000
(@ $4,000 each)	
Less: Initial Mortgage Loan (60%)	2,400,000
Cash Requirements for Acquisition	$ 1,600,000
Rehabilitation Cost.....................................$ 6,000,000	
Less: Construction Loan.................................. 5,000,000	
Balance:	1,000,000
Plus: General Overhead	500,000
TOTAL	$ 3,100,000

exhibit no. 4

HYPOTHETICAL CASE ANALYSIS – 100% LOAN
(Line of Credit Financing)

1. Acquisition Costs		$ 4,000
2. Improvement Costs		6,000
(a) Labor and Materials....................................$ 5,450		
(b) Subcontractors Costs and P & O.........................	550	
3. Carrying and Financing Charges		600
(a) Interest (12 mos. at 6% x $6,000 avg.)....................	180	
(b) Taxes and Insurance...................................	150	
(c) FHA - FNMA..	200	
(d) Title and Recording...................................	50	
(e) Miscellaneous..	20	
4. Miscellaneous Costs		400
(a) Contingencies (Construction)...........................	300	
(b) Promotion and Leasing................................	50	
(c) Transfer Costs..	50	
TOTAL COSTS		$ 11,000
5. Estimated Sales Price		12,100
6. Less Total Costs		11,000
7. Gross Profit		$ 1,100
8. Less:		600
(a) General Overhead.....................................	500	
(b) Reserves..	50	
(c) R & D Commitment....................................	50	
NET PROFIT		$ 500

**exhibit
no. 5**

LIMITATIONS AND ADVANTAGES OF REHABILITATION
CONSTRUCTION AND OWNERSHIP
($12,100 UNIT)

I. Construction
  1. Gross Profit/Overhead Allowance
     (10% x Gross Costs)... $ 1,100.00
  2. Estimated Net Profit (before taxes)............................ 500.00*

II. Ownership
  1. Annual Maximum Allowable Dividend
     (6% x 11.11% x $10,900 mortgage)............................ 72.60
  2. Potential Maximum Surplus Accumulation
     (7% vacancy factor @ $100 mo. rent) 84.00
  3. Estimated Amortization
     (1.3% x $10,900 — 1st year)................................. 141.70
  4. Replacement Reserves (estimated)............................. 35.00
  5. Depreciation (non-component) — 1st year
     a. Straight-line
        (2½% x $10,900) — $272.50
     b. Double-declining —   545.00
  6. Possible Tax Result (1st year)
     a. Income (Items #1,3,4)................................. 249.30
     b. Depreciation (s/l).................................... 272.50
     c. Depreciation (d/d)................................... 545.00
     d. Tax Loss (s/l)....................................... (23.20)
     e. Tax Loss (d/d)....................................... (295.70)
     f. Tax Free Cash Flow................................... 72.60

III. Sale After Ownership (1 year)
  1. Recovery — Profit/Overhead Allowance........................ 1,100.00
  2. Amortization... 141.70
  3. Reserves.. 35.00
                                    TOTAL $ 1,276.70**

*Subject to rate of annual production and initial costs (See Exhibit No. 8)
**Plus: Cumulative Tax Benefits

exhibit no. 6

RELATIONSHIP OF INCOME, RENT AND COSTS
(FHA 221 (d) (3) BMIR PROGRAM — PITTSBURGH — MARCH 1967)

Persons Per Family	Unit Size (Bedrooms)	Maximum Annual Income	Maximum* Monthly Rent	Probable Maximum Unit Cost
2	1-2	$5,950	$ 99.50	$10,500
3	2	7,000	117.00	12,500
4	2-3	7,000	117.00	12,500
5	3	8,050	134.50	14,500
6	3-4	8,050	134.50	14,500
7+	4	9,100	151.67	16,500

*20% of income

exhibit no. 7

SUMMARY CORA STREET, PITTSBURGH, PA.
(PER FHA COMMITMENT)

Number of Units.. 22
Acquisition Cost...$ 87,000

Improvement Costs:
    Construction................................$ 117,900
    Carrying Costs.............................. 2,700
    Architect's Fees............................. 5,500
    Other Fees/Costs.......................... 16,200

Total: All Costs...$ 229,300
    Mortgage... 228,000
    Cash Equity... 1,300

Time Elements:
    Acquisition/Mortgage Processing — 8 months
    Construction — 8 months
    Leasing (During Construction)

Leasing Data and Status:
    Pre-Acquisition Rents........................$ 60-65
    Plus Utilities............................... 25-25
                           $ 85-90 Month
Post Improvement
    Rents (average)
    (Utilities, Decorating, and Repairs.
    Management & Reserves incl.)..............$ 96 Month

Mortgage Terms:
    Amount per unit — $10,200
    Term — 38 years, 7 months
    Interest (During Construction) — 5½%
           (After Completion) — 3%

PROJECTED CASH FLOW

exhibit no. 8

ITEM	1st 6 months	1st Year (250 Units)	2nd Year (500 Units)	3rd Year (750 Units)	4th Year (1000 Units)	5th Year (1000 Units)	6th Year (1000 Units)
General Overhead.............	$ 150,000	$ 300,000	$ 500,000	$ 500,000	$ 500,000	$ 500,000	$ 500,000
Advanced Acquisition Funds (@ $1,600 per unit).........		400,000	800,000	1,200,000	1,600,000	1,600,000	1,600,000
Advanced Improvement Funds (@ $1,000 per unit).........		250,000	500,000	750,000	1,000,000	1,000,000	1,000,000
Total............	$ 150,000	$ 950,000	$ 1,800,000	$ 2,450,000	$ 3,100,000	$ 3,100,000	$ 3,100,000
Less Return of:		(125 Units)	(375 Units)	(625 Units)	(875 Units)	(1000 Units)	(1000 Units)
General Overhead Allowance (incl. L/O @ $500 per unit).....	$	$ (1) 62,500	$ (2) 187,500	$ (2) 312,500	$ (2) 437,500	$ (2) 500,000	$ (2) 500,000
Advanced Acquisition Funds........		(1) 200,000	(2) 600,000	(2) 1,000,000	(2) 1,400,000	(2) 1,600,000	(2) 1,600,000
Advanced Improvement Funds......		(1) 125,000	(2) 375,000	(2) 625,000	(2) 875,000	(2) 1,000,000	(2) 1,000,000
Profit and Reserves Allowance (@ $600 per unit) (4).........		(3)	(3) 75,000	(3) 225,000	(3) 375,000	(3) 525,000	(3) 600,000
Total............	$ ---	$ 387,500	$ 1,237,500	$ 2,162,500	$ 3,087,500	$ 3,625,000	$ 3,700,000
Annual Difference.............	$ (150,000)	$ (562,500)	$ (562,500)	$ (287,050)	$ (12,500)	$ 525,000	$ 600,000
Cumulative Difference............	$ (150,000)	$ (712,500)	$ (1,275,000)	$ (1,562,500)	$ (1,575,000)	$ (1,050,000)	$ (450,000)

NOTES: (1)   50% completion — current year
        (2)   50% completion — current year; balance of units from prior year
        (3)   Sale of units completed in prior year
        (4)   Exclusive of accumulations and/or depreciation benefits during ownership

FHA AND FNMA ASSISTANCE FOR MULTIFAMILY HOUSING*

B. T. FITZPATRICK†

INTRODUCTION

When the Federal Housing Administration (FHA) was established in 1934, its area of concern was mortgage financing in connection with single family, owner occupied homes. In 1938 FHA was given its first legislative authorization to assist in financing multifamily housing through the enactment of section 207 of the National Housing Act, as amended.[1] However, FHA was not a significant factor in this segment of the homebuilding industry until the Congress, by the enactment of section 608 in 1942,[2] granted it further authorization to assist multifamily housing during the Second World War. Thereafter, because multifamily housing was becoming an increasingly important means of meeting our total housing needs, Congress has, over the years, added a large number of new FHA authorizations to assist in enlarging the annual volume of needed multifamily housing. These new authorizations include cooperative and condominium housing, urban renewal housing, housing for families of low and moderate income, and housing for elderly persons.

These new multifamily housing programs have vastly increased the scope of FHA's responsibilities. Especially when combined with some of the special assistance powers of the Federal National Mortgage Association (FNMA), the FHA now has the powers to be a dynamic and potent influence in the field of multifamily housing production. The need for a future total annual housing production which is far in excess of our best previous production is well established; a much greater percentage of such total housing production must consist of planned, multifamily housing projects. This is an absolute requirement for the success of any real national effort toward marked improvement of our urban areas. Any evaluation of FHA's pro-

* This article was prepared prior to March 1967 and does not seek to review developments since that time.

† A.B. 1930, Dartmouth College; LL.B. 1933, Harvard University. Member of the District of Columbia and Hawaii bars; Counsellor-at-Law, in private practice since 1955. Deputy Administrator and General Counsel, Housing and Home Finance Agency, 1947-1955; General Counsel and Associate General Counsel, National Housing Agency, 1942-1947; Counsel, Public Housing Administration and United States Housing Authority, 1938-1942; Vice Chairman and Director, Defense Homes Corporation 1946-47; Vice Chairman and Director, Federal National Mortgage Association, 1950-1955. Author, THE PRIVATE REDEVELOPER IN THE URBAN RENEWAL PROGRAM (1959), CONTRACT DISPOSITION PROBLEMS IN URBAN RENEWAL (1961), THE ROLE OF THE REDEVELOPER IN URBAN RENEWAL (1961), THE GOALS OF OUR NATIONAL HOUSING POLICIES (1961), ASSISTANCE FOR COLLEGES AND UNIVERSITIES LOCATED IN OR NEAR URBAN RENEWAL AREAS (1961), FHA PROGRAMS FOR LOW INCOME FAMILIES (1965).

The author wishes to express his grateful appreciation to William S. Tennant, Esquire, of Krooth & Altman, Washington, D.C., formerly Counsel, Urban Renewal Section, Office of the General Counsel, Federal Housing Administration, for his helpful suggestions.

[1] Ch. 13, § 3, 52 Stat. 16 (1938), *as amended*, 12 U.S.C. § 1713 (1964, Supp. II, 1965-66).

[2] Ch. 319, § 11, 56 Stat. 303 (1942), *as amended*, 12 U.S.C. § 1743 (1964, Supp. II, 1965-66).

grams for, and performance in, assisting multifamily housing production must be measured against these needs.

I

GENERAL BASIS FOR FHA ASSISTANCE

All FHA multifamily housing programs are based on the insurance of long term (usually forty years), high ratio (90 per cent to 100 per cent) mortgage loans at relatively low interest rates. In the case of new construction, the loan ratio, which varies between programs as well as types of mortgagors, is a percentage of project value or of project replacement cost. In the case of repair and rehabilitation, the loan ratio is based on the sum of the estimated cost of repair and rehabilitation and the Federal Housing Commissioner's estimate of the value of the property before such repair and rehabilitation, with a limitation that, where any such case involves refinancing existing indebtedness, the FHA-insured mortgage may not exceed the estimated cost of repair and rehabilitation plus the amount (as determined by FHA) required to refinance the existing indebtedness secured by the property to be repaired or rehabilitated.

Under existing law, the maximum interest rates are as follows: (1) sections 207[3] and 213[4] management type—5-¼ per cent; (2) section 234[5] condominiums—5-¼ per cent on the blanket mortgage, but six per cent on the release out individual mortgages; (3) sections 220[6] and 221[7] market rate cases—six per cent; (4) section 231[8]— 5-½ per cent; and (5) section 221(d)(3)[9] below market interest rate cases—six per cent during construction and reduced at final endorsement (*i.e.*, after completion of construction) to three per cent.

In the case of section 207, the loan ratio is based on the FHA estimate of the value of the property when the proposed improvements are completed. In all other cases involving new construction, the loan ratios are based on the FHA estimate of the replacement cost of the project.

The value or the cost of the project may include the FHA's estimate of the fair market value of the land (prior to the construction of the improvements to be built as a part of the project) when owned in fee by the mortgagor, the proposed physical improvements, utilities within the boundaries of the property, architect's fees, taxes and interest (and, in leasehold cases, ground rent) during construction, and "other miscellaneous charges incident to construction and approved by the Commissioner." These latter charges include insurance during construction, premium on the contract bond, quantity survey, FHA fees (*i.e.*, examination and inspection fees and mortgage insurance premiums during construction), financing expense not exceeding two per

---

[3] 12 U.S.C. § 713 (1964, Supp. II, 1965-66).
[4] 12 U.S.C. § 1715e (1964, Supp. II, 1965-66).
[5] 12 U.S.C. § 1715y (1964, Supp. II, 1965-66).
[6] 12 U.S.C. § 1715k (1964, Supp. II, 1965-66).
[7] 12 U.S.C. § 1715l (1964, Supp. II, 1965-66).
[8] 12 U.S.C. § 1715v (1964, Supp. II, 965-66).
[9] 12 U.S.C. § 1715l(d)(3) (Supp. II, 1965-66).

cent of the face amount of the mortgage, title and recording expense, legal and organization expense, and builder's profit. The builder's profit allowance and general overhead allowance is hereinafter discussed in greater detail.

In the case of cooperatives and condominiums under sections 213 and 234, there is also included an allowance for sales and marketing expense. In the case of nonprofit mortgagors (including cooperatives) under section 221(d)(3) below market interest rate projects, there is also included in the estimate of project replacement cost the FNMA commitment fee of one per cent of the face amount of the mortgage. In all multifamily housing cases, FHA requires the mortgagor to escrow for working capital an amount equal to two per cent of the face amount of the mortgage. This can be in the form of cash or an unconditional irrevocable commercial letter of credit. However, for nonprofit mortgagors (including cooperatives) under section 221(d)(3) below market interest rate cases, there is also included in the estimate of project replacement cost this two per cent working capital item—although, in FHA jargon, it is called an allowance to make the project operational (AMPO).

II

LIMITATIONS ON MAXIMUM AMOUNT OF LOAN

There are several limitations on the maximum amount of the insured mortgage loan. They are (1) the ratio of loan to estimated value or replacement cost, (2) dollar limitations per dwelling unit and per type of mortgagor, and (3) debt service (*i.e.*, the maximum mortgage supported by net income, determined by dividing ninety per cent to ninety-five per cent of net income by the sum of (i) mortgage interest rate, (ii) mortgage insurance premium and (iii) initial curtail factor). The loan to value ratios and dollar limitations vary depending on the section of the act and the type of mortgagor involved.

A. Loan Ratios

The loan ratios for the various programs are as follows:

(a) Section 207—ninety per cent of the value of the project.

(b) Section 213—ninety-seven per cent of estimated replacement cost in the case of management type cooperatives; ninety per cent estimated replacement cost in the case of an investor-sponsor (*i.e.*, a mortgagor approved by FHA who, as a condition of obtaining mortgage loan insurance, certifies that upon completion of the project he intends to sell the same, at certified project cost, to a management type cooperative, such purchasing cooperative getting a ninety-seven per cent of project replacement cost loan).

(c) Section 221—ninety per cent of estimated replacement cost in the case of limited distribution mortgagors; 100 per cent of estimated replacement cost in the case of cooperatives (including investor-sponsor cases), nonprofit mortgagors (including builder-sellers who, prior to submitting an application for mortgage insurance, have entered into an agreement with a nonprofit mortgagor eligible for a section 221(d)(3) insured mortgage loan to sell the project at completion at certified project cost), or a public body not receiving financial assistance from the United States exclusively pursuant to the Housing Act of 1937. It is to be noted that in the case of investor-sponsor and builder-seller mortgagors obtaining 100 per cent loans under section 221(d)(3), not less than ten per cent of such loan is escrowed or retained until the project is actually transferred to the purchasing cooperative or nonprofit mortgagor, at which time it is paid over to the investor-sponsor or builder-seller. If the project is not so transferred, such retention is applied to reduce the mortgage, and the investor-sponsor or builder-seller mortgagor is required to operate as a limited distribution mortgagor.

(d) Section 234—ninety per cent of estimated replacement cost on the blanket mortgage.

(e) Section 231—100 per cent of estimated replacement cost for nonprofit mortgagors; ninety per cent of estimated replacement cost for "profit motivated" mortgagors.

B. Dollar Limitations Per Dwelling Unit

Different dollar limitations are established for non-elevator and elevator type structures, and for various sections of the act, as shown below.

	Sections 207, 213 and 220		Sections 221(d)(3), 221(d)(4) and 231	
	Non-Elevator	*Elevator*	*Non-Elevator*	*Elevator*
0-BR	$ 9,000	$10,500	$ 8,000	$ 9,500
1-BR	12,500	15,000	11,250	13,500
2-BR	15,000	18,000	13,500	16,000
3 or more BR	18,000	22,500	17,000	20,000

The Commissioner may, by regulation, increase any of the above dollar limitations by not to exceed forty-five per cent in any geographical area where he finds that cost levels so require. Also, the dollar limitations shown for section 221(d)(3) are applicable to the market rate program only. For the section 221(d)(3) below market interest rate programs, special dollar limitations (as well as family income limitations for purpose of admission) are fixed by FHA on a community-by-community basis.

In connection with the dollar limitations established for section 231 elderly housing, there is a disadvantage, compared to section 207 or section 220, of from $1,000 to $2,500 per unit. This disadvantage to section 231 elderly housing is not based on facts as to cost. In fact, elderly housing costs more than the typical multifamily rental housing projects under sections 207 and 220 primarily because:

1. State licensing requirements require satisfaction of fire control standards far

in excess of those applicable to such other multifamily rental housing projects. These take the form, for example, of smoke and heat sensing devices in both private and public areas; extra lighting; two means of egress from every apartment; fire retardant and resistant materials requirements;

2. Community facilities must be more extensive than in other multifamily rental housing projects. Ill-defined criteria pertaining to "nondwelling" qualifications of common areas may result in excessive dependence on "unit count" limitations. This condition causes either unnecessary disputes with local FHA insuring offices or apartment and public area design ill-suited to the elderly housing market. For example, elevators, hallways, laundry rooms, elevator lobbies, required exit stairs, smoke towers, janitor closets, maintenance shops, and general storage areas would be of the approximate same design and cost with each program. Under section 231, however, there are numerous requirements for additional common areas in keeping with section E401-3.1 of the FHA *Minimum Property Standards for Housing for the Elderly,* which states:[10] "Lounges and other rooms for social and recreational facilities are required and shall be provided to the extent needed to enhance living in the project." Other examples of these common areas required by housing for the elderly are linen rooms, maids' storage and day rooms, employees' rest rooms and women's cot rooms. FHA should make it clear that in section 231 cases all common areas (*i.e.,* areas outside of dwelling units), except those which in a typical section 207 or section 220 project would normally be classified as required for dwelling purposes, are to be classified as nondwelling facilities.

C. Dollar Limitations on Mortgage Amount

These limitations are based on the type of mortgagor—public mortgagors and any other eligible mortgagors. In general, public mortgagors are defined as federal or state instrumentalities, municipal corporate instrumentalities of one or more states, or limited dividend or housing corporations (in section 213 cases, only "nonprofit" as distinguished from "limited dividend" corporations) restricted by federal or state laws or by regulations of state banking or insurance departments as to rents, charges, capital structure, rate of return or methods of operation. The applicable dollar limitations are as shown below:

Section	Public Mortgagor	Other Eligible Mortgagor
207	$50,000,000	$20,000,000
213	25,000,000	20,000,000
220	50,000,000	30,000,000
221	12,500,000	12,500,000
231	50,000,000	12,500,000
234	25,000,000	20,000,000

[10] U.S. FEDERAL HOUSING ADMINISTRATION, DEP'T OF HOUSING AND URBAN DEVELOPMENT, MINIMUM PROPERTY STANDARDS FOR HOUSING FOR THE ELDERLY § E401-3.1 (1967).

III

LIMITATIONS ON COMMERCIAL AND COMMUNITY FACILITIES

The limitations on the type and extent of commercial and community facilities which may be included in multifamily housing projects vary considerably, depending on the section of the act involved. These limitations are as follows:

(a) Sections 207, 213, 231 and 234—Such commercial and community facilities ("special" instead of "community" in the case of section 231) as the Commissioner deems adequate to serve the occupants.

(b) Sections 221(d)(3) and 221(d)(4)—Such commercial and community facilities as the Commissioner deems adequate to serve the occupants, except that in the case of any such property or project located in an urban renewal area, the provisions of section 220 apply to the nondwelling facilities which may be included in the mortgage if the mortgagor waives the right to receive dividends on its equity in the portion thereof devoted to community and shopping facilities.

(c) Section 220—Such nondwelling facilities as the Commissioner deems desirable and consistent with the urban renewal plan. However, the project must be predominantly residential, and any nondwelling facilities included in the mortgage must be found by the Commissioner to contribute to the economic feasibility of the project. Also, the Commissioner is required to give due consideration to the possible effect of the project on other enterprises in the community.

(d) General Comment—The restriction of commercial and community facilities strictly to those deemed necessary to serve the occupants militates against sound urban planning. It would appear that, if FHA is to advance rather than retard sound urban planning, the standards as to the inclusion of nondwelling facilities should approxi-- mate the present standards for section 220.

IV

ALLOWANCES FOR BUILDER'S PROFIT AND GENERAL OVERHEAD

A. General

There are two types of builder's profit allowance: the regular allowance, and the ten per cent allowance. The regular allowance is whatever the local FHA insuring office finds that contractors in the area would require as a construction fee to erect a comparable project. In general, this regular allowance will vary from about four per cent to seven per cent of estimated field construction cost. The ten per cent allowance has, in the main, been established by the Congress for certain programs at ten per cent of all project costs other than land.

B. Regular Profit Allowance

The regular profit allowance is applied in the following: (a) all section 207 projects; (b) section 213 projects in non-urban renewal areas; (c) section 221(d)(3), all projects (including builder-seller mortgagors) except as noted in subpart C below, whether market interest rate or below market interest rate; (d) section 231, nonprofit mortgagors; and (e) all section 234 condominiums in non-urban renewal areas.

C. Ten Per Cent Profit Allowance

The profit allowance at ten per cent of all estimated projected costs other than land is applied in the following: (a) section 213 projects in urban renewal areas; (b) all section 220 projects; (c) section 221(d)(3) limited distribution mortgagors (excluding builder-sellers) whether market interest rate or below market interest rate; (d) section 221(d)(3) cooperatives (including investor-sponsors) located in urban renewal areas; (e) section 221(d)(4); and (f) section 231 profit-motivated mortgagors.

The FHA has recently advised that its policy of including the ten per cent profit allowance for certain types of cases—see (a) and (d) above—"is presently being reviewed." This may mean that FHA might discontinue this policy, and make the regular profit allowance applicable in these cases.

A further word of caution needs to be asserted here in connection with the ten per cent profit allowance. While the particular section of the act, or FHA policy, may say, without qualification, that such ten per cent allowance is to be included in the estimate of project replacement cost for processing, the mortgagor, at project completion, is confronted with an inconsistency in section 227 of the Act[11] relating to cost certification. The FHA insurance commitment is based upon an estimate of replacement cost. After project completion, however, the mortgagor must certify to FHA the actual cost of the project. If the approved percentage of actual certified cost equaled or exceeded the mortgage loan, no change need be made in the loan. However, if the mortgage loan exceeds the approved percentage of actual cost, the mortgage loan is reduced by the amount of such excess.

Under section 227, however, the ten per cent profit allowance may be included in certified cost in those cases (called "identity of interest" cases) "where the mortgagor is also the builder as defined by the Commissioner." It is, therefore, of critical importance in retaining the ten per cent profit allowance to be sure at initial loan closing that there is an identity of interest between the mortgagor and the general contractor. FHA says such an identity of interest will be construed to exist under any of the following conditions:[12]

> When there is any financial interest of the mortgagor in the general contractor; when one or more of the officers, directors or stockholders of the mortgagor is also an officer, director or stockholder of the general contractor; when any officer, director or stockholder of the mortgagor has any financial interest whatsoever in the general contractor; when the general contractor advances any funds to the mortgagor; when

---

[11] 12 U.S.C. § 1715r (1964, Supp. II, 1965-66).
[12] U.S. FEDERAL HOUSING ADMINISTRATION, A HANDBOOK FOR FHA MULTIFAMILY PROJECTS 33 (1965).

the general contractor provides and pays on behalf of the mortgagor the cost of any architectural services or engineering services other than those of a surveyor, general superintendent, or engineer employed by a general contractor in connection with his or its obligations under the construction contract; when the general contractor takes stock or any interest in the mortgagor corporation as part of the consideration to be paid them; when there exist or come into being any side deals, agreements, contracts, or undertakings entered into or contemplated, thereby altering, amending, or cancelling any of the required closing documents except as approved by the Commissioner.

D. Incentive Provisions

In cases involving nonprofit corporations, the construction contract in all cases (except as otherwise approved by the Commissioner) must be a cost-plus-fixed-fee contract with a guaranteed maximum upset price. In such cases, however, there may be included in such construction contract a "savings incentive provision" whereby the contractor's fee may be increased by fifty per cent of the savings effected below the guaranteed price up to the point where the fee equals ten per cent of all costs other than land. The inclusion of such an incentive provision is also allowed in cooperative and condominium cases where a cost-plus construction contract is used.

E. Builder's General Overhead

In addition to the builder's profit allowance, the FHA includes an allowance for general overhead (as distinguished from job overhead, such as superintendents, field engineer to provide lines and grades for locating structures and utilities on the site, watchmen, temporary offices, telephone, supplies, temporary sheds, toilet, heat, water and power during construction, and so on). General overhead includes such items as office rent, fuel, lights, telephone and telegraph, stationery, office supplies, fire and liability insurance for the office, salaries of office employees, social security taxes, public liability insurance, workmen's compensation insurance, and unemployment compensation taxes for office personnel. Salaries of officers or executives of the general contractor may be included if, during the period for which the salary of such officer or executive is allowed, he performs a type or types of duties which would normally be performed by a nonexecutive employee and his salary is in line with what would be paid to such nonexecutive employee for the performance of the same services. The following scale percentage (based on estimated field construction cost) is used by FHA in determining the builder's general overhead allowance: (i) amounts up to $1,000,000—three per cent; (ii) additional on amounts in excess of $1,000,000 but not exceeding $2,000,000—two per cent; (iii) additional on amounts in excess of $2,000,000 but not exceeding $3,000,000—one per cent; and (iv) additional allowance on amounts in excess of $3,000,000—one-half per cent.

V

OTHER LIMITATIONS

There are other limitations which apply to some of the multifamily housing programs. Section 220 is available only in respect of mortgage loans covering properties located in urban renewal areas. Section 221(d)(3) is available only in communities which have in effect a "workable program" for the elimination of slums and blighted areas[18] approved by the Secretary of Housing and Urban Development. Rent supplements are available only in communities where rent supplements are a part of the "workable program," or which submit evidence of official local approval for participation in the rent supplement program. Such official local approval is by resolution of the local governing body. If a workable program is in effect and does not contain express provision for participation in the rent supplement program, the community must submit a letter from the mayor stating that the workable program of the community contemplates federally-assisted housing of low income families, including housing under such programs as the rent supplement program. If a community once had a workable program under which it received federal assistance for urban renewal or public housing, rent supplements will not be available unless such workable program is reactivated and recertified by the Secretary.

VI

INDIVIDUALS AS MORTGAGORS

Individuals may be mortgagors under FHA-insured mortgage loans without assuming personal liability on the note or mortgage. This is accomplished by including in the note and mortgage exculpatory language which precludes the mortgagee from exercising any right (other than the right to foreclose) to institute any action against the mortgagor for the payment of any sum of money due under the note or mortgage, and also precludes the mortgagee from seeking any deficiency judgment. Exculpatory provisions are also included in the Regulatory Agreement.

VII

OPERATING DEFICIT ESCROWS

In any case where FHA estimates that the rental housing market is such that a substantial period of time will be required before a project can be rented up to a "break-even" point, FHA may require, as a condition of insurance, that at final loan closing the sponsors (as distinguished from the mortgagor entity) shall place in escrow a stated sum to cover any operating deficits which may be incurred during a stated period, generally one or two years. With such a condition, the mortgagee (in order to assure that the loan could be finally closed) would ordinarily require

---

[18] Housing Act of 1949, § 101(a), 42 U.S.C. § 1451(a) (1964).

these funds to be escrowed in cash at initial loan closing. In order to avoid depositing such amount of cash at commencement of construction and leaving it idle for the two or three year construction period, the sponsors may enter into a contract with FHA that they will place such cash in escrow for such purpose at final loan closing, and furnish a bond from an acceptable surety guaranteeing performance of such contract.

VIII

CHANGE ORDERS

It is an established fact that in any sizable construction job there will, during the course of construction, be necessary changes ordered in the work. Such necessary changes arise for a variety of reasons, including errors or omissions in the contract drawings and specifications, unanticipated subsoil conditions, and changes in market acceptability of certain items of equipment. In cases involving cooperatives or non-profit corporations which, as a practical matter, are dependent on the FHA-insured mortgage loan and have no other funds, the cost of such necessary changes can be financed only if there happen to be savings in nonconstruction cost items, or by putting through other "deduct" change orders to offset such increased cost. This seems a very inefficient and hazardous method for dealing with this type of situation. It has been suggested that, in these types of cases, there should be included in the mortgage loan a contingency item of two per cent or three per cent which, subject to strict FHA control, could be used to financed any increased costs resulting from changes during construction deemed necessary by FHA. Thus far FHA has refused to take any such action.

IX

FNMA SPECIAL ASSISTANCE

The Federal National Mortgage Association possesses what are known as "special assistance" functions in connection with some of the FHA multifamily housing programs—principally section 213, section 220, section 221(d)(3) below market interest rate, rent supplements, and section 221(d)(3) and (d)(4) where the housing is for displaced families.

The homebuilding industry operates with two types of mortgage money—interim, or short-term, construction loans and long-term, permanent financing. One type of lender desires to put his money out on short term, one to three year construction loans. He cannot keep it there for forty years, so he does not make the construction loan unless he has a "permanent take out"—that is, when the initial construction loan which he makes is fully disbursed and insured by FHA, another lender has a firm commitment to purchase that loan at a price. Also, in the case of section 221(d)(3) below market interest loans, the current six per cent interest rate during construction reduces to three per cent at final loan closing and no private source would be available to provide the permanent take out for such cases.

Under its special assistance functions, FNMA can provide the permanent take out for these loans by making a commitment to the construction lender to purchase the loan from it when construction is complete and the construction loan has been fully disbursed and insured. For such services FNMA charges a commitment fee of one per cent of the face amount of the mortgage and, if the loan is ultimately delivered to FNMA, a purchase and marketing fee of one-half per cent of the face amount of the mortgage is also charged. The FNMA contract does not require the interim lender to deliver the loan to FNMA; thus, if during the construction period the mortgage market changes, the interim lender may be able to arrange for a take out from conventional sources. Also, if the loan covered by such commitment is not delivered to FNMA, three-fourths of the one per cent FNMA commitment fee is refunded.

In the case of section 221(d)(3) below market interest rate cases, FNMA charges the one per cent commitment fee, but does not charge the one-half per cent purchase and marketing fee. FNMA will make commitments to purchase section 221(d)(3) market rate projects involving rent supplements. However, in these cases it will charge its regular fees of 1-½ per cent: one per cent commitment fee and one-half per cent purchase and marketing fee. All FHA-insured mortgages purchased by FNMA under its special assistance functions are purchased at par.

It is to be noted that in January 1967, FNMA suddenly initiated discounts of from two per cent to four per cent on its mortgage purchases under some of its special assistance programs. These discounts, of course, would be in addition to the regular FNMA fees of 1-½ per cent. This FNMA action seemed a violation of the mandate of the Congress expressed in the Conference Report on the 1966 housing act which said:[14] "While loans are purchased by FNMA at discounts under its regular secondary market, the conferees are strongly opposed to such discounts in the use of FNMA special assistance funds." After public criticism of this action by Congressman Patman, Chairman of the House Committee on Banking and Currency, and Congressman Barrett, Chairman of the Housing Subcommittee, FNMA rescinded this action and resumed par purchases for special assistance mortgages.

Also, it has recently come to light that the administration, during the fiscal year 1967, has been impounding many of the authorizations previously made available by the Congress for various FNMA special assistance programs. For example, of the $450 million projected for section 221(d)(3) below market interest rate mortgages, the administration impounded all but $32.5 million. For section 213 cooperative housing, the administration impounded the entire $148 million uncommitted balance in the revolving fund. These actions were taken without any prior notice; thus

---

[14] H.R. REP. No. 1868, 89th Cong., 2d Sess. 3 (1966).

developers who continued to act in reliance upon the continued availability of these authorizations have been disadvantaged.

Under the Housing Act of 1966, FNMA was authorized to participate in the making of insured advances on the mortgage during construction up to ninety-five per cent of such advances. In other words, FNMA could agree to supply the interim lender with up to ninety-five per cent of funds required to make the construction loan. This authorization applies to any case where FNMA makes a commitment to purchase a mortgage insured under section 213, section 220 or under section 221(d)(3) and executed by a cooperative (including an investor-sponsor), a limited dividend corporation, a private nonprofit corporation or association, or a builder-seller mortgagor. To date, the policy of the present administration has been not to allow FNMA to exercise this power.

X

SECTION 221(D)(3) BELOW MARKET INTEREST RATE

A. In General

Some additional comments are in order with respect to the section 221(d)(3) below market interest rate program. Notwithstanding the administration's current preoccupation with the rent supplement program, the below market interest rate program is regarded by many as the most important recent addition to the array of FHA multifamily housing programs. It is a "going" program today, most of the defects having been already overcome during its six year existence. It has strong acceptance and support in Congress. Experience has clearly demonstrated that it has substantially enlarged the area of housing needs of low and moderate income families which can be served by private rather than public enterprise. Developed to its full potential, the section 221(d)(3) below market interest rate program can be the real savior to our cities.

In my view, if we are to have volume production under this program—and, certainly, this is a must—we are going to get it from the private, "for profit" developer source, rather than the nonprofit source. I do not mean that the nonprofit sources may not be appropriate for the ownership-management end; but, in general, as developers they are not so efficient as the typical private developer. The builder-seller mortgagor, hereinafter described in more detail, can be a great help here.

Further, it seems to me that private limited distribution mortgagors have much to gain in this program. They are enabled to reach a market of vast proportions which, otherwise, they could not reach. The prospect of long rent-up periods and the cash drain of operating deficits is remote. The limited annual return of six per cent on the result obtained by multiplying the face amount of the mortgage by 11.11 per cent is not unattractive if the cash outlay is relatively small. Tax advantages can be achieved in both construction and management periods. FHA needs to be out with a "hard sell" on the advantages of this program to the private limited distribution mortgagor.

B. Waiver of FHA Mortgage Insurance Premium

To further assist in achieving monthly rents or carrying charges which families of low or moderate income can afford to pay, the FHA has waived the requirement that the borrower pay the annual mortgage insurance premium, which amounts to one-half per cent each year on the outstanding unpaid balance of the mortgage.

C. Builder-Seller Mortgagors

Nonprofit mortgagors frequently have motive, but neither money nor requisite skills. Someone has to help them through the intricacies of preparing and processing an FHA application. Someone has to find the funds to pay the costs and fees to get them up to the initial FHA loan closing. While it is possible for a builder to do this by loans or advances payable from the mortgage loan, if and when obtained, there always exists a problem of whether such a relationship creates an improper identity of interest which would make the nonprofit corporation ineligible to obtain an FHA insured loan.

Out of this problem came the "builder-seller" mortgagor. The nonprofit corporation is eligible for a 100 per cent loan. Thus, a builder who, as a condition of securing an FHA commitment, signs a contract to sell the project on completion to a nonprofit corporation approved by the FHA, can get a commitment for a 100 per cent loan. If he does sell the project on completion to the nonprofit corporation, the full 100 per cent loan is disbursed, and the nonprofit corporation merely assumes the loan and takes the completed project. If, for some reason, the builder-seller fails to transfer the project to the nonprofit corporation, he is held to a maximum of a ninety per cent loan and restricted as a limited distribution mortgagor.

This is an over-simplification in respect to this type of mortgagor, but it is enough to indicate that there is a considerable amount of flexibility here which can permit very sensible and proper relationships to be worked out to the mutual benefit of nonprofit corporations and builders or developers, and, more important, to the mutual benefit of the low income people whom the FHA section 221(d)(3) below market interest rate program is intended to help.

D. Mortgage Limits and Income Limits

In addition to the dollar limitations per dwelling unit fixed by the act and hereinbefore described, FHA administratively establishes dollar limitations per unit for zero, one, two, and three or more bedroom units. These limitations are fixed, from time to time, on a community-by-community basis. Typical current limitations are as follows:

City	0-BR	1-BR	2-BR	3-BR
Des Moines	$9,300	$13,250	$15,900	$19,850
New York City	9,950	14,200	17,050	21,300
Atlanta	8,000	11,250	13,500	17,000
Washington, D.C.	9,850	14,050	16,850	21,100

Similarly, family income limitations are fixed by FHA, from time to time, on a community-by-community basis. Typical current limitations are as follows:

City	1 person	2 persons	3-4 persons	5-6 persons	7 or more persons
Des Moines	$5,300	$6,500	$7,650	$8,800	$ 9,950
New York City	5,750	6,950	8,200	9,450	10,650
Atlanta	4,350	5,250	6,200	7,150	8,050
Washington, D.C.	5,700	6,950	8,150	9,350	10,600

For purposes of determining eligibility, gross family income from all sources is considered.

E. Provisions for Inclusion in Tenant Lease

Under the regulatory agreement, tenant leases must contain clauses wherein the tenant (a) certifies the accuracy of the statements made in the application and income survey, (b) agrees that the family income, family composition, and other eligibility requirements shall be deemed substantial and material obligations of his tenancy, (c) agrees that if family income limitations for continuing occupancy, which may be established from time to time by the Commissioner, are exceeded the lease may be terminated, and (d) agrees that at such time as the landlord or Commissioner may direct he will furnish certification of the then-current family income.

F. Spot Checks

Not later than three months after initial occupancy, the local FHA insuring office must make a spot check to assure that initial occupancy requirements are being met. All violations must be reported to FHA Washington headquarters where action will be taken on an individual case basis. Any tenant who was ineligible at the time of initial occupancy must be evicted as soon as legally possible. The usual remedy imposed by Washington thus far is to require the sponsor to deposit, in a special account, the difference between the economic rent and the section 221(d)(3) rent for each month any such unit is occupied by an ineligible tenant. Disbursements from such special account can be made only with the prior written approval of FHA.

G. Recertification of Tenant Income

Two years after initial FHA permission to occupy, and each two years thereafter, tenant incomes must be recertified. On recertification, eviction or refusal to renew leases will not be required where (a) family income exceeds the limitations by no more than five per cent, or (b) the tenant agrees to pay an adjusted market rent.

Adjusted market rent is the rent that would be required if the interest rate on the mortgage loan were at a market rate and FHA was charging the one-half per cent mortgage insurance premium. It is computed by adding to the below market rents the lesser of the following: (i) twenty-eight per cent where the below market interest rate is three per cent, twenty-seven per cent where the below market interest rate is 3-⅛ per cent, twenty-four per cent where the below market interest rate is 3-⅜ per cent, nineteen per cent where the below market interest rate is 3-⅞ per cent; or (ii) twenty-five per cent of the amount of excess family income over the maximum family income limitation. (If twenty-five per cent of the amount of such excess family income is less than $60, no increase in rent payment is required.)

H. Single Person Occupants

The 1966 housing act provides that up to ten per cent of the dwellings in a project may be occupied by low and moderate income single persons who are less than 62 years of age. Otherwise, occupancy is limited to "families" and single persons who are 62 or older.

XI

THE RENT SUPPLEMENT PROGRAM

A. In General

While the administration did not propose it quite that way, when Congress finished working its will upon the rent supplement program it turned out to be a system whereby private housing enterprise would be enabled to provide some housing for families and individuals who otherwise would, in most cases, have to look to low rent public housing in order to secure decent, safe, and sanitary housing.

In its simplest terms, the rent supplement program is one whereby the federal government will pay over each month for the benefit of eligible families or individuals a sum equal to the difference between twenty-five per cent of one-twelfth of the annual gross income of such family or individual and the FHA-approved monthly shelter rent for the dwelling unit occupied by such family or individual. The rent supplement is to make up the difference between the amount which a low income family or individual can afford to pay for housing, and the actual economic rent to be charged in a privately owned and operated multifamily housing project financed with the assistance of a mortgage loan insured under the FHA section 221(d)(3) market interest rate program. Historically, the generally accepted rule of thumb adopted by housing agencies has been that a family can afford to pay twenty per cent to twenty-five per cent of annual income for housing expense.

B. FNMA Fees and Discounts

As previously indicated, for the rent supplement program FNMA charges its regular 1-½ per cent fees. In addition, in the tight money market, the fees required by the interim lender run four per cent or five per cent. In the FHA estimate of replacement cost only two per cent is allowed for financing charges. Nonprofit mortgagors will have to supply cash for all financing fees or discounts in excess of two per cent.

C. Maximum Rents

FHA has established a schedule of maximum gross monthly rents and has indicated that, in high cost areas, the maximum rentals may be increased up to twenty-five per cent. The range of maximum rentals would be as follows:

Unit Size	Monthly Rent Range
0-BR	$ 85-$106
1-BR	105- 130
2-BR	120- 150
3-BR	140- 175

Also, the FHA has clearly stated that these are maximum rents. Accordingly, in areas where suitable housing can be produced for lower rentals, this will be required. This means that the rents approved by the FHA will be the lower of (i) the rents set out in the maximum rent schedule or (ii) the rents needed to meet debt service, operating expenses and the maximum allowable return to a limited distribution mortgagor of six per cent per annum on the result obtained by multiplying the face amount of the mortgage by 11.11 per cent, or, in the case of nonprofit mortgagors, a residual income of five per cent, which will be used as a special contingency reserve. Rents are gross rents and must include all utilities except telephone.

In the case of welfare tenants, the amount of rent paid by the tenant shall be not less than the higher of the following amounts: (i) the rental allowance provided by the welfare agency, or (ii) twenty-five per cent of total household income, including welfare assistance payments.

D. Eligible Tenants

Those eligible to be accepted as tenants are any families or individuals who have incomes which would make them eligible for low rent public housing, as such incomes are established by the Federal Housing Commissioner, and who, in addition, meet any one of the following five qualifications: (a) he has been displaced by governmental action, (b) either he or his spouse is 62 years of age or older, (c) either he or his spouse is physically handicapped, (d) he now lives in substandard housing, or (e) he occupies, or did occupy, housing extensively damaged, or destroyed, by a natural disaster in an area determined by the Small Business Administration, since April 1, 1965, to be a disaster area.

In determining tenant eligibility, gross income from all sources, before taxes or withholding, of all members of the household must be counted. This includes the income of children or other dependents who will live in the unit. No deductions from gross income are allowed for dependents. In addition to income limitations, there are asset limitations—no more than $2,000, except in the case of elderly persons, in which event assets may not exceed $5,000.

E. Amount of Rent Supplement

The basic amount of the rent supplement is the difference between one-twelfth of twenty-five per cent of the gross income and the monthly rent. However, in no case may the amount of the rent supplement exceed seventy per cent of the monthly rent, and it must also be *not less* than ten per cent of the monthly rent.

While no deductions from gross income are permitted in determining tenant eligibility, the following deductions from gross income are permitted in determining the amount of the rent supplement to which the tenant is entitled: (a) up to $300 of income earned by each member of the family under 18 years of age, (b) continuing costs (as determined by FHA) attributable to a permanent disability or a chronic illness not compensated by insurance or otherwise, and (c) expenses incurred for the case of children under thirteen years of age if necessary to the employment of a wage earner in the household.

F. Income Certification and Recertification

Each family or individual who is to occupy a rent supplement dwelling unit must fill out FHA Form 2501, the income and asset certification. The housing manager and his staff will have to help each such tenant to do this. On each anniversary of the date of such first income certification, each tenant, except elderly tenants, must recertify income; and the rent supplement payment will be adjusted on the basis of each such recertification.

The tenant, in his lease, must agree to report immediately any increase in income which will result in a monthly income of four or more times the monthly rental. In such case the rent supplement will be cut off. Otherwise, adjustment in the rent supplement will be made only after each annual recertification. Where a tenant's income decreases due to illness, loss of job or other hardship beyond his control, the FHA may grant a temporary increase in the rent supplement payments for such tenant.

G. The Rent Supplement Contract

The rent supplement contract (FHA Form 2503) will be based on the estimate of the amount of rent supplements required for the units in the project to be supplemented. At the end of the rent-up period, however, FHA will adjust the original estimate to reflect the actual rent supplement requirements plus a contingency allowance of ten per cent. In general, it is intended that future adjustments would be within this ten per cent allowance factor.

Obviously, however, things can occur which could go beyond this ten per cent allowance factor. One would be increases in taxes and other operating expenses in the future. If FHA does not have authorization to increase rent supplements along with increased rents, this could cause serious trouble.

In a mixture of economically and culturally differentiated families, there is a "tipping point"—that is, a point at which, when some given percentage of units are occupied by less economically and culturally privileged families, the achievement of the desired occupancy becomes impossible. This tipping point will vary with the nature of the surrounding community, with the competitive desirability of the dwellings and their rents, and similar matters. If there is any guiding principle which can be suggested it would be that the greater the social and economic distance between the rent supplemented tenants and the non-rent supplemented tenants, the lower the tipping point will be.

Bearing this in mind, suppose that a project starts with fifty per cent of the units supplemented and fifty per cent non-supplemented. After a year or two, suppose the fifty per cent non-supplemented, or a large majority of them, move out and the vacancies cannot be filled at economic rents. Either FHA finds some more rent supplement money or the project defaults. To cover these types of contingencies, FHA undoubtedly will reserve some portion of its rent supplement authorization.

H. Type of Project

The FHA requirements are that all rent supplement projects shall be of modest design and that "swimming pools, two bathrooms per unit, air conditioning, and similar items will *not* be permitted." FHA also says that "projects should . . . not have features that will contribute to premature obsolescence."[15] These requirements are certainly contradictory.

If there are geniuses among the developers—and there are—who can produce projects, within the maximum rents allowed, which have swimming pools, air conditioning, two bathrooms for units to house six or eight persons, why should anyone forbid it, especially in the light of the admonition against features which contribute to premature obsolescence. In this connection, it would also be well to keep in mind that this rule means that such amenities will not be available for non-rent supplement tenants, and that this could well make the rental of those units difficult

---

[15] U.S. FEDERAL HOUSING ADMINISTRATION, DEP'T OF HOUSING AND URBAN DEVELOPMENT, RENT SUPPLEMENT PROGRAM, PUBLIC INFORMATION GUIDE AND INSTRUCTION HANDBOOK 2 (1966). (Emphasis added.)

or impossible. It will also make most difficult the accomplishment of the objective of achieving an economic mix of families in rent supplement projects.

I. Operating Expenses

The FHA Handbook states:[16]

An allowance will be made in the operating cost for expenses incurred by management in certifying and recertifying of tenants for rent supplement eligibility, and for other administrative requirements imposed by the rent supplement program; and typical costs for providing managerial services in connection with housing for low income tenants.

The usual sources of data may not be applicable . . . . Public housing experience in the area should be examined . . . .

For all public housing projects, the national management costs—which they call administration expense—is $7.10 per dwelling per month. Administration expense includes salaries, supervisory and clerical personnel, legal expense, travel, purchase of publications, membership dues and fees, telephone and telegraph expense, and sundry office expense, exclusive of employee benefits. Although the national average is $7.10, the range is from $5.14 to $8.59.

There are other available public housing data which indicate the nature of the problems to be met in rent supplement housing. Of the public housing tenant population, thirty-six per cent of the families with children are one-parent, broken families; thirty per cent are elderly; fifty-three per cent are nonwhite; fifty per cent are receiving assistance benefits; eighty-two per cent of the elderly and twenty-five per cent of the non-elderly have no gainfully employed worker in the family.

The difference between the income limits established for the section 221(d)(3) below market rate program and the rent supplement program is significant. For Washington, D.C., two-person families in rent supplements are at $3,500 compared to about $7,000 for section 221(d)(3) below market; and seven or more-person families at $4,500 in rent supplements compared with $10,600 for section 221(d)(3) below market. Roughly, the income limits for section 221(d)(3) below market rate are double those for rent supplements.

J. Occupancy Interviews

Drawing further on public housing experience, as reflected in recent remarks of Abner Silverman, Assistant Commissioner for Management of the former Public Housing Administration, attention should be directed to some general but quite pertinent information on occupancy interviews and classification of tenant types.

The sponsor had best schedule appointments for interviews. If it is left up to the applicant to drop in at any time convenient for him or her, there will not only be an uneconomic bunching up of applicants, but also long waiting periods in which chil-

---

[16] *Id.* at 9.

dren grow restless, parents' tempers fray, and anything but the proper attitude for a friendly, communicative interview will be created.

Even on a scheduled basis, the sponsor should be ready to cope with children in the application office. Low income mothers are not able to leave the children home with the maid, and parking them with neighbors may not be feasible. Since mothers are the usual applicant spokesmen for the families, the children perforce will have to come along, and they do not stay darling indefinitely.

Should the sponsor wish to interview both father and mother together, some consideration should be given to night office hours. For some wage earners, the interview may involve the loss of a day's pay; it does not seem necessary to put this burden on a low income family merely because of conventional concepts about office hours.

K. Rough Classification of Tenant Types

1. *The Mobile*

These consist of parents and children both of whom are capable of social advancement and improved income. They are characterized, usually, by a stable marriage, by the presence of a skilled or semi-skilled dependable wage earner, personal vigor and drive, eagerness to improve the lot of their children, and great self-respect. They need some help, but they are capable of being influenced by their neighbors. They will seek to emulate and aspire to the same level of achievement—provided only that the social distance between them and their neighbors is not so great that it precludes realistic aspirations.

The type of help they need is knowledge about programs that can assist them in improving their skills, and encouragement to participate in those programs and in other resident or neighborhood activities. The programs may range from vocational training, extension services, household management clinics, adult illiteracy, health service, youth employment—to any one of the many programs that go on in almost every community. Sympathetic, competent management will not only tell them about such programs, but it will also bring them to the project site, and get these tenants interested.

2. *The Partially Mobile*

These consist of a parent or parents who may be non-mobile but whose children are capable of advance. This group is very difficult to help; its need for services runs not only through the entire range of health, educational, welfare, and recreational activities now established, but through some as yet unformulated, or which are now being tested in local community action programs funded by the Office of Economic Opportunity.

Among the more obvious services are day care centers for the children of working mothers, intensive family counselling, intensive household and money management instruction, special tutoring programs for children, vocational rehabilitation services, mental and physical health clinical services, work experience programs, employment services, legal aid and advice—the "works."

These services must be brought into the neighborhood because, by and large, the members of this group are block-bound. They will not travel out of a familiar neighborhood to get to the services. They are also proud and shy and unwilling to expose their inadequacies to strangers. But if the programs are brought close to home, if the other participants are familiar figures, there is a chance these programs will succeed.

3. The Non-Mobile

These consist primarily of the elderly and the physically or mentally handicapped. These are the poor who will not enjoy any significant increase in income resulting from their effort, and for whom the prognosis must be that they will need constant and probably progressively increasing support and service as their capacities fail.

These latter considerations serve to point up a fact which is critical in the success of the rent supplement program. The housing of low income families is not merely a physical activity. It is part and parcel of the larger concept of the elimination of poverty. Management must therefore be a social as well as a physical process. A sponsor who accepts public aid to carry out a public purpose must accept the whole public purpose, not just the parts which are easiest to fulfill. Any sponsor who is unable or unwilling to accept and carry out these social management responsibilities should stay out of the rent supplement program.

XII

BASIC PURPOSE OF FHA

It seems clear that the basic purpose of FHA is to enlarge the area of total housing need which can be served effectively by private, rather than public enterprise. If FHA is to take only such risks as are accepted by the typical conventional mortgage lender, then FHA cannot serve that basic purpose. Further, FHA's contribution toward enlarging the area of total housing need which can be served effectively by private enterprise must certainly be something more than merely enabling conventional mortgage lenders to make mortgage loans with longer terms and higher ratios. If FHA is to serve its basic purpose, it must accept a higher risk of default. To the extent that it fails to do so, it increases the pressure for extending the area of total housing need to be served by public endeavor. The need for FHA to accept a higher risk of default should be understood and accepted by the administration and the Congress.

The chart included herein as table 1 shows that, out of total FHA insurance written covering 1,160,772 dwelling units in multifamily housing, only 114,844, or about ten per cent have gone into default. This is a relatively low default ratio.

TABLE 1

FHA INSURED MULTIFAMILY HOUSING UNITS[1]	Total No. of Units	SECTION OF NATIONAL HOUSING ACT, AS AMENDED								
		207	608[2]	213	220	221 Market Rate	221 BMIR[3]	231[5]	234	Misc.[4]
Total Insurance Written..........	1,160,772	226,399	469,559	107,300	49,304	13,928	39,374	36,093	807	217,978
Default[6].................	114,844	21,510	63,826	5,366	3,667	3,274	954	4,190	0	12,057
Sold.......................	54,492	8,083	37,247	601	0	802	0	539	0	7,220
On Hand..................	60,352	13,427	26,579	4,755	3,667	2,472	954	3,651	0	4,837
IN DEFAULT										
Percent of Total..........	9.89	1.85	5.50	0.46	0.031	0.28	0.08	0.36	0	1.04
Percent of Section Total....		9.50	13.59	5.00	7.44	23.51	2.42	11.61	0	5.53

[1] All figures as of December 31, 1965.   Source: Department of Housing and Urban Development
[2] Also includes Sec. 608-610
[3] Below Market Interest Rate
[4] Military housing under Title 8 and Sections 908 and 810. Section 207 trailer park spaces, etc.
[5] Of the 36,093 unit total, 27,396 units (75.90% of the total) were owned by nonprofit mortgagors and 8,697 units (24.1% of the total) were owned by profit motivated mortgagors. Of the 4,190 units in default, 2,299 units (0.64% of the total and 8.39% of the nonprofit units) were in nonprofit mortgagors and 1,891 units (5.24% of the total and 21.74% of the profit motivated units) were in profit motivated mortgagors.
[6] Includes units in properties acquired by FHA, units covered by mortgage notes assigned to FHA, and units covered by defaulted mortgages but not acquired by, or assigned to, FHA.

In the case of section 608 which produced the largest volume of multifamily housing, 63,826, or about thirteen and a half per cent, of the 469,589 total units have gone into default. Nevertheless, the section 608 insurance fund remains one of the strongest FHA insurance funds.

It should be understood that "default" and "loss" are not coextensive. After a project financed with an FHA insured mortgage loan goes into default, FHA acquires it through assignment or foreclosure. After such acquisition, FHA manages the project until such time as, in its determination, sufficient occupancy is achieved to warrant sale of the property. The difference between (i) the price FHA receives at such sale and (ii) the outstanding balance of the mortgage at the time of default, plus the cost of any capital improvements in the project made by FHA during its management, is the "loss." The amounts collected by FHA from mortgage insurance premiums have been more than adequate to offset the actual losses sustained.

XIII

FHA Benefit to the Housing Consumer

FHA participation in multifamily housing does result in substantial benefits to the housing consumer. As a rough rule of thumb, a project financed with a typical conventional loan would require average rents fifteen per cent to twenty per cent higher than the average rents required if the project was financed with an FHA section 220 insured mortgage loan. For purposes of illustration, assume that there is a market demand sufficient to permit a project with average rentals at $200 per month with conventional financing. If the same project was financed with the assistance of a mortgage loan insured by FHA under section 220, the same facilities can be offered with average rents of $160 to $170 per month. The other alternative is that $30 to $40 more in average rents under the FHA formula will support an additional $3,500 to $4,500 more per unit in improved or additional amenities. In either event the benefit to the housing consumer is substantial—he can get the same product at considerably lower rents, or he can get a considerably better product at the same or somewhat lower rents.

XIV

The Future—Short Run and Long Run

To a large extent housing demand is made up of new household formations and demolition of existing dwelling units. Since 1964, the gap between new household formations plus demolitions (highways, urban renewal, code enforcement, fire and other disasters, and so on) and housing starts has been increasing. In 1967 vacancies will probably hit the lowest point since 1958. Demolitions are at an annual rate of about 700,000 and will likely increase. New household formations run about 1.2 million a year, and will continue at not less than this rate in 1968 and 1969. This translates into a market demand for about 2 million dwelling units a year just to

TABLE 2

YEAR	Total Private Nonfarm Housing Starts	1-2 Family No.	% of Col. 2	Multifamily 3 or More Units No.	% of Col. 2	FHA ASSISTED TOTAL No.	% of Col. 2	1-4 Family No.	% of Col. 3	Multifamily[b] No.	% of Col. 4	207 No.	% of Col. 7	608 No.	% of Col. 7	213 No.	% Col
(1)	(2)	(3)		(4)		(5)		(6)		(7)							
1966	1,197.2	812.4	68%	384.8	32%	158.4	13%	129.1	16%	29.3	8%	2.9	10%			4.3	18
1965	1,482.7	989.8	67	492.9	33	196.6	13	159.9	16	36.7	7	7.3	20			4.7	13
1964	1,530.4	998.0	65	532.4	35	204.6	13	154.0	15	50.7	25	11.0	22			7.9	16
1963	1,581.7	1046.4	66	535.3	34	221.0	14	166.2	16	54.9	10	27.1	49			7.1	13
1962	1,439.0	1016.9	71	422.1	29	259.5	18	197.3	19	62.2	15	28.3	45			10,0	16
1961	1,284.8	990.0	77	294.8	23	243.6	19	198.8	20	45.0	15	23.5	52			9.8	22
1960	1,230.1	1016.7	83	213.4	17	260.9	21	225.7	22	35.2	16	17.7	50			8.0	23
1959	1,494.6	1267.7	85	226.9	15	332.5	22	307.0	24	25.4	11	12.3	48			4.4	17
ESTIMATES[a]																	
1958	1,314.2	1144.0	87	170.0	13	295.4	22	270.3	24	25.1	15	14.0	56			6.8	27
1957	1,174.8	1055.0	90	120.0	10	168.4	14	150.1	14	18.3	15	3.7	20			9.4	51
1956	1,324.9	1245.0	94	80.0	6	189.1	14	183.4	15	5.8	7	.4	7			3.4	59
1955	1,626.8	1542.0	95	85.0	5	276.7	17	268.7	17	8.0	9	4.2	52			1.5	19
1954	1,531.8	1442.0	94	90.0	6	276.3	18	250.9	17	25.4	28	11.9	47			6.2	24
1953	1,402.1	1307.0	93	95.0	7	252.0	18	216.5	17	35.5	37	7.5	21	.2	1%	8.0	22
1952	1,445.4	1360.0	94	85.0	6	279.9	19	229.1	17	50.8	60	7.3	14	5.9	12	10.1	20
1951	1,419.8	1330.0	94	90.0	6	263.5	19	186.9	14	76.6	85	4.7	6	39.8	52	7.7	10
1950	1,908.1	1748.0	92	160.0	8	486.7	26	328.2	19	158.4	99	2.3	1	143.3	90	.1	—
1949	1,429.8	1270.0	89	160.0	11	363.8	25	252.6	20	111.2	70	.8	1	110.0	99		
1948	1,344.0	1239.0	92	105.0	8	294.1	22	216.4	17	77.6	74			77.6	100		
1947	1,265.1	1195.0	94	70.0	6	229.0	18	178.3	15	50.8	73			50.8	100		
1946	1,015.2	965.0	95	50.0	5	69.0	7	67.1	7	1.9	4			1.9	100		
1945	324.9	310.0	95	15.0	5	41.2	13	38.9	13	2.3	15	.2	9	2.1	91		
1944	225.0	210.0	93	15.0	7	93.3	41	83.6	40	9.7	65			9.7	100		
1943	300.0	270.0	90	30.0	10	146.2	49	126.1	47	20.0	67			20.0	100		
1942	450.0	420.0	93	30.0	7	165.7	37	160.2	38	5.5	18	1.2	22	4.3	78		
1941	925.0	865.0	94	60.0	6	220.4	24	217.1	25	3.3	6	3.3	100				
1940	800.0	745.0	93	55.0	7	180.1	23	176.6	24	3.4	6	3.4	100				

keep up, and does nothing to make up the shortage accumulated in prior years. In 1966, housing production was down to less than 1.2 million dwelling units, and in 1967 could, in the views of some, drop to about 1 million. This means that, in the short run period, we are leaving an annual shortage of 800,000 to 1,000,000 dwellings units a year.

By the year 2000, our urban population will double. In the next thirty-three years we will have to build as many dwelling units as were built in the last 200 years; and it is abundantly clear that of what we must build, for both the short and the long run, a much greater percentage of the total must be in multifamily housing projects.

XV

FHA's PERFORMANCE

It is against this background of need, both short run and long run, and this vast array of FHA powers to assist in the development of multifamily housing that we

TABLE 2 (continued)

SECTION OF THE NATIONAL HOUSING ACT

YEAR	220 No.	220 % of Col. 7	221 (d) (3) Market Rate No.	221 (d) (3) Market Rate % of Col. 7	221(d) (3)BMIR No.	221(d) (3)BMIR % of Col. 7	231 No.	231 % of Col. 7	233 No.	233 % of Col. 7	234 No.	234 % of Col. 7	810 No.	810 % of Col. 7	Misc.[c] No.	Misc.[c] % of Col. 7
66																
65	3.7	13%	3.1	11%	12.7	43%	1.3	4%	.1	—	.8	3%	.3	1%		
64	4.2	11	2.8	8	11.3	31	5.2	14	.5	1%	.3	1	.5	1		
63	7.1	14	2.7	5	15.4	30	5.1	10					1.4	3		
62	2.8	5	1.3	2	7.8	14	8.3	15					.6	1		
61	9.9	16	1.3	2	3.0	5	9.7	16								
60	4.3	10	1.2	3			6.1	14								
59	5.2	15	1.9	5			2.4	7								
	7.2	28	1.5	6												
58																
57	3.1	12	1.3	5												
56	5.3	29														
55	1.1	19													.9	15%
54															2.3	29
53															7.3	29
52															19.8	56
51															27.5	54
50															24.5	32
49															12.7	8
48															.4	—

[a] Data in Col. 2 for 1944-40 and in Col. 3 and 4 for 1958-40 are estimated.
[b] Multifamily unit totals exclude mobile housing spaces under Sec. 207, nursing home beds under Sec. 232, and armed services projects classified as public housing under Sec. 803.
[c] Includes Sec. 611, 803 (military housing) and 908.
Figures shown in thousands of units
Source: Census Reports and Reports of the Department of Housing and Urban Development

should ask: "How effective, currently, is the FHA in the use of these powers?" Unfortunately, the facts show that FHA's current performance leaves much to be desired, and must be greatly improved if we are to meet the increasing future needs.

The chart annexed hereto as table 2 shows, among other things, the extent of FHA assistance in financing the development of multifamily housing over the twenty-seven-year period from 1940 to 1966. In 1966, FHA participation was only eight per cent and in 1965 was only seven per cent. Over the twenty-seven year period, FHA participation ranged from six per cent in 1940 and 1941 (when the only FHA authorization to assist multifamily housing was the original section 207 program enacted in 1938 and on a much less liberal basis than the present section 207 program) to ninety-nine per cent in 1950 at the peak of the section 608 program. The average over the twenty-seven year period was about thirty-one per cent.

The facts show that, when FHA is of a mind to do so, it can be an extremely potent influence in assisting the development and construction of multifamily housing. Over a peak six-year period, FHA was assisting multifamily housing production at an average annual rate of 87,000 units a year, compared to less than 30,000 units in 1966. It would, I think, represent a fair consensus that, today, and in the years ahead, FHA's participation in multifamily housing production ought to be in the area of at least thirty-three per cent of the total and that, when it falls below this range, any real national effort toward marked improvement of our urban areas is in very serious trouble.

RENT SUPPLEMENTS AND THE SUBSIDY DILEMMA

THE EQUITY OF A SELECTIVE SUBSIDY SYSTEM

IRVING H. WELFELD*

The issues are rarely right against wrong in the law, but rather right against right.

For the ultimate issues veiled by time and mystery, in law as in life, the most meaningful answer may be the question.

—Paul Freund[1]

I pray to the God within me that He will give me the strength to ask Him the right questions.

—A Transylvanian Beadle[2]

INTRODUCTION

With existing technology, private enterprise unaided cannot meet the needs of the millions of low-income families living in substandard housing. Without a carrot of high caloric content the building industry is unable—in an era in which development costs are rising faster than the personal income of the poor—to produce an adequate supply of housing for families with incomes below the median.[3] As the Senate Committee on Banking and Currency has noted:[4]

> Since the end of World War II, there has been a remarkable increase in new housing production. The accelerated production pace can be attributed in large part to the energy and resourcefulness of American private enterprise, and it has redounded to the benefit of the Nation.
>
> It has become increasingly clear to the committee, however, that lower income families have not been able to participate fully in the benefits of this great burst of new housing production.
>
> . . . .
>
> There are almost 8 million American families who still live in sub-standard housing. The great majority of these families are below the income level needed to afford decent housing.

---

* A.B. 1959, Brooklyn College; LL.B. 1962, Harvard University. Attorney, Office of General Counsel, Department of Housing and Urban Development. Member of the New York and Massachusetts bars.

The views expressed in this article are those of the author, who in no way purports to speak for the Department of Housing and Urban Development, with which Department he is presently employed.

The author would like to acknowledge the generous assistance of Renee Greenfield, Gordon Hagen, Sylvana Kamm, and Patricia Lyons in the preparation of the paper.

[1] Johnson, *Prof. Freund's 'Avuncular Qualities' Help Students Pit Right Against Right*, Harvard Law Record, March 23, 1967, at 2, 12.

[2] E. WIESEL, NIGHT 16 (1960).

[3] *See generally* J. McMURRAY, WAYS AND MEANS OF PROVIDING HOUSING FOR FAMILIES UNABLE TO AFFORD RENTALS OR MORTGAGE PAYMENTS NECESSARY FOR ADEQUATE HOUSING (1960) (an independent study financed by the National Association of Home Builders); Welfeld, *The Condominium and Median-Income Housing*, 31 FORDHAM L. REV. 457, 477-80 (1963).

[4] S. REP. No. 378, 89th Cong., 1st Sess. 3 (1965).

To fulfill an unredeemed pledge to these eight million families the administration brought forth a new incentive to the homebuilding industry—the rent supplement. Paradoxically, although few disagreed with the premise that a subsidy was necessary, and even fewer disagreed with the fact that we were a goodly distance away from fulfilling the pledge the nation made in 1949 to provide "a decent home and a suitable living environment for every American family,"[5] the proposal immediately became embroiled in controversy.

At the heart of the controversy was what we would call the subsidy dilemma. Can an effective program be devised which is fair vis-à-vis non-recipients of the subsidy? Thus the main issue was neither the income floor nor the income ceiling, neither the rent income ratio nor the payment formula, neither the construction standard nor the workable program proviso, but, rather, the fundamental clash between two values—the need to fulfill the pledge to the poor and the need to be fair to the overwhelming majority of non-recipients.

The first part of this article will trace the history of the proposal from its introduction into Congress[6] through its final passage, initial funding, and first days of life. The second part will show how the substantial changes which occurred in the legislative journey—changes which radically transformed the program—illustrate in rather sharp relief the subsidy dilemma.

I

The Legislative History

A. The Administration Proposal

The initial administration proposal[7] authorized the Administrator of the Housing and Home Finance Agency[8] to undertake a program of rent supplement payments to help make certain private housing available to certain lower income families.

The recipients of the supplements would be landlords who satisfied two criteria:[9] (1) that they were non-governmental; and (2) that they were either nonprofit, limited dividend, or cooperative entities. The type of housing eligible for supplements also had to satisfy two criteria:[10] (1) it had to be new or rehabilitated; and (2) the construction or rehabilitation had to be financed with a mortgage loan insured by the

---

[5] Housing Act of 1949, § 2, 42 U.S.C. § 1441 (1964).

[6] No attempt is being made to trace the rent supplement proposal itself or any of its components to specific persons or groups. "[T]he American political structure puts so heavy a premium on diffusion of decision-making power that it is difficult to determine the relationship between the desires of particular persons and groups and what eventually emerges as effective government policy. After all, the drum beater may be credited, or blamed, for the cloudburst, but whether he is responsible is another matter." Greenberg, *The Myth of the Scientific Elite*, Public Interest, Fall 1965, at 51, 53. *See also* Foard & Fefferman, *Federal Urban Renewal Legislation*, 25 Law & Contemp. Prob. 635, 636 n.4 (1960).

[7] S. 1354, 89th Cong., 1st Sess. §§ 101-05 (1965); H.R. 5840, 89th Cong., 1st Sess. §§ 101-05 (1965) (Special Provisions for Disadvantaged Persons, Title I, Housing and Urban Development Act of 1965).

[8] The immediate predecessor of the Secretary of Housing and Urban Development.

[9] S. 1354, *supra* note 7, § 101(b).

[10] *Id.*

Federal Housing Administration (FHA) under the section 221(d)(3)[11] market interest rate mortgage insurance for low and moderate income families.

The subsidy would be on the behalf of a tenant who satisfied two criteria:[12] (1) he had to have an income below the amount required to obtain standard privately owned housing but above the amount necessary to obtain admission to public housing; and (2) he had to be (a) displaced by governmental action, (b) elderly, (c) physically handicapped, or (d) occupying substandard housing.

The amount of the payment was subject to two limitations:[13] (1) it could not exceed the amount by which the rent of the unit exceeded twenty per cent of the tenant's income (twenty-five per cent in situations in which the tenant was given an option to purchase the unit[14]); and (2) it could not exceed the estimated amount of subsidy payable under the public housing program for a comparable unit.

The location of the unit was governed by local planning and zoning requirements. However, rent supplement housing was not limited to communities which had enacted a workable program for community improvement—a requirement of other federal housing and urban renewal programs.[15]

The size of the program requested was large. Authorization was sought for the appropriation of $50 million in the first year with increases of $50 million in the three following years—to a total of $200 million per annum in the fourth year of the program.[16]

B. Committee Action

1. House Committee

On May 21, 1965, after public hearings,[17] the House committee considering the bill reported out[18] a new bill[19] that contained a number of important modifications.

The bill altered the first of the qualifying tests for tenant eligibility. In order to be eligible, a tenant was now required to be one who, through the expenditure of twenty-five per cent of his income, was unable to obtain standard private housing, whether or not his income was above or below the level necessary to obtain admission to public housing.[20] The provision dealing with the amount of the payment was

---

[11] National Housing Act, 12 U.S.C. § 1715*l*(d)(3) (1964), *as amended*, (Supp. II, 1965-66).

[12] S. 1354, *supra* note 7, § 101(c).

[13] *Id.* § 101(d).

[14] *Id.* § 101(f).

[15] Housing Act of 1949, § 101(c), 42 U.S.C. § 1451(c) (1964), *as amended*, (Supp. II, 1965-66).

[16] S. 1354, *supra* note 7, § 101(a).

[17] *Hearings on the Housing and Urban Development Act of 1965 Before the Subcomm. on Housing of the House Comm. on Banking and Currency*, 89th Cong., 1st Sess., pts. 1 & 2 (1965) [hereinafter cited as *House Hearings*].

[18] H.R. REP. No. 365, 89th Cong., 1st Sess. (1965); HOUSE COMM. ON BANKING AND CURRENCY, 89TH CONG., 1ST SESS., CORRECTION OF MISLEADING AND FALSE STATEMENTS CONCERNING RENT SUPPLEMENT PROGRAM MADE IN MINORITY REPORT ON THE HOUSING AND URBAN DEVELOPMENT ACT OF 1965—H.R. 7984 (Comm. Print 1965).

[19] H.R. 7984, 89th Cong., 1st Sess. (1965).

[20] *Id.* § 101(c).

altered by (1) limiting the payment to the amount by which the rent of the unit exceeded twenty-five per cent (formerly twenty per cent) of the tenant's income and (2) eliminating the requirement that the rent supplement payment not exceed the subsidy payable under the public housing program.[21]

No changes were made with respect to the qualifications of the recipients, the type of housing, the location of the housing, or the size of the program.

2. Senate Committee

On June 28, 1965, after public hearings,[22] the Senate committee considering the bill also reported out[23] a new bill[24] containing a number of important modifications.

The type of housing eligible was broadened by allowing ten per cent of the appropriations to be used as an experiment[25] in housing financed under the section 221 (d)(3) below market interest rate program,[26] the section 231 program of mortgage insurance for the elderly,[27] and the section 202 program of direct loans for the elderly,[28] subject to an additional limitation that the number of units in any such project receiving the benefit of rent supplements was limited to twenty per cent of the total.[29] The Senate bill also altered the first of the qualifying tests for tenant eligibility. In order to be eligible, a tenant must now have an income below the maximum amount that could be established for occupancy in public housing.[30]

The Senate committee also modified the provision dealing with the amount of the payment[31] in exactly the same fashion as had the House committee. No changes were made with respect to the qualifications of the recipients, the location of the housing, or the size of the program.

C. House Floor Action

After debate on the bill,[32] and after a roll call vote in which the rent supplement narrowly survived a motion to recommit,[33] the House bill was passed on June 30, 1965.[34] The major changes were the adoption of the Senate bill's provision limiting tenant eligibility to individuals and families with incomes below the maximum

---

[21] Id. § 101(d).

[22] Hearings on S. 1354 Before the Subcomm. on Housing of the Senate Comm. on Banking and Currency, 89th Cong., 1st Sess. (1965) [hereinafter cited as Senate Hearings].

[23] S. REP. No. 378, 89th Cong., 1st Sess. (1965).

[24] S. 2213, 89th Cong., 1st Sess. (1965).

[25] Id. § 101(d)(3).

[26] National Housing Act, 12 U.S.C. § 1715l(d)(3) (1964), as amended, (Supp. II, 1965-66).

[27] National Housing Act, 12 U.S.C. § 1715v (1964), as amended, (Supp. II, 1965-66).

[28] Housing Act of 1959, 12 U.S.C. § 1701q (1964), as amended, (Supp. II, 1965-66).

[29] S. 2213, supra note 24, § 101(d)(2).

[30] Id. § 101(c)(1).

[31] Id. § 101(e).

[32] 111 CONG. REC. 14,327-51 (daily ed. June 28, 1965); 111 CONG. REC. 14,588-622 (daily ed. June 29, 1965); 111 CONG. REC. 14,669-714 (daily ed. June 30, 1965).

[33] 111 CONG. REC. 14,711-13 (daily ed. June 30, 1965).

[34] Id. at 14,713-14.

amount that could be established for occupancy in public housing[35] and the reduction of the size of the program by twenty-five per cent by limiting the authorization to $30 million upon enactment, with cumulative increases of $35 million for fiscal 1967, $40 million for fiscal 1968, and $45 million for fiscal 1969.[36]

D. Senate Floor Action

The Senate passed its version of the bill on July 15, 1965.[37] A number of amendments had been accepted after lengthy debate.[38]

The major changes were (1) the imposition of a new limitation as to the housing that would qualify, that is, housing whose cost of operation was not in excess of the cost of operation of similar housing,[39] (2) the broadening of the class of qualified tenants to include persons (meeting the income qualifications) whose dwellings were extensively damaged or destroyed in a disaster area,[40] and (3) the reduction of the size of the program by twenty-five per cent (to the same level as the House).[41]

The major differences between the House and Senate bills related to the type of housing and the type of tenant that was eligible. The Senate bill (1) allowed, as an experiment, a limited number of below-market and elderly projects to be used, (2) limited the operating costs, and (3) extended the class of eligible tenants to include disaster victims. The House bill had no comparable provisions.

E. Conference Report

The Conference Committee accepted the Senate's amendments with respect to the broadening of the class of qualified tenants (disaster victims) and the limiting of the operating costs of rent supplement housing.[42]

The experimental program in the Senate bill was also accepted but revised by requiring that fifty per cent of the units that received the benefits of the rent supplement be in 221(d)(3) below-market interest rate projects, and removing the twenty per cent limitation on the number of units in a project that could receive rent supplements (except for properties financed with loans under section 202 of the Housing Act of 1959 on or before the date of enactment of the bill).[43]

The Conference Report was approved by the Senate by a voice vote on July 26[44] and

---

[35] See id. at 14,669-82.
[36] See id.
[37] 111 Cong. Rec. 16,350 (daily ed. July 15, 1965).
[38] 111 Cong. Rec. 16,132, 16,137-42, 16,149-90 (daily ed. July 14, 1965); 111 Cong. Rec. 16,295-304, 16,308-23, 16,325-50 (daily ed. July 15, 1965).
[39] 111 Cong. Rec. 16,171 (daily ed. July 14, 1965).
[40] Id. at 16,161-62.
[41] 111 Cong. Rec. 16,323, 16,325-27 (daily ed. July 15, 1965).
[42] H.R. Rep. No. 679, 89th Cong., 1st Sess. 63 (1965).
[43] Id.
[44] 111 Cong. Rec. 17,630-37 (daily ed. July 26, 1965).

by the House on July 27 by a vote of 251 to 168.[45] The rent supplement program was signed into law on August 10, 1965.[46]

F. The Appropriations Fight

1. *First Round*

On August 26, 1965, the President requested the full $30 million authorization for rent supplements.[47] After hearings,[48] the Supplemental Appropriation Bill, 1966,[49] was reported out by the House Appropriations Committee on October 13, 1965.[50] The bill reduced the first year's authorization from $30 million to $6 million and limited the location of the housing to areas which had workable programs or in which the rent supplement program had been officially approved by the local community.[51] After debate,[52] the entire appropriation for rent supplements was deleted by the House on October 19, 1965, by a vote of 184 to 162.[53]

The Supplemental Appropriation Bill, 1966, was also reported out, after hearings,[54] by the Senate committee on October 19, 1965.[55] The bill[56] reduced the authorization from $30 million to $12 million. No requirement with regard to local approval was contained in the Senate bill. The bill was approved by the Senate[57] after it rejected two motions, one to delete the rent supplement appropriation provision entirely,[58] and a second to reduce the appropriation to $6 million.[59]

The House-Senate Conference denied any funds for rent supplements but appropriated $450,000 for the preparation of plans and criteria for implementing the program.[60]

2. *Second Round*

On February 11, 1966, the President again requested the full $30 million authoriza-

---

[45] 111 CONG. REC. 17,743-51 (daily ed. July 27, 1965).

[46] 12 U.S.C. § 1701s (Supp. II, 1965-66).

[47] H.R. Doc. No. 278, 89th Cong., 1st Sess. (1965).

[48] *Hearings on the Supplemental Appropriation Bill, 1966, Before Subcomms. of the House Comm. on Appropriations*, 89th Cong., 1st Sess., pts. 1-3 (1965).

[49] H.R. 11588, 89th Cong., 1st Sess. (1965).

[50] H.R. REP. No. 1162, 89th Cong., 1st Sess. (1965).

[51] H.R. 11588, *supra* note 49, ch. 4. H.R. REP. No. 1162, *supra* note 50, at 12-13. The question as to whether the proviso was legislation on an appropriations bill was debated. However, the Chair ruled that since the proviso was negative in character it was only a limitation and not legislation. 111 CONG. REC. 26,033-34 (daily ed. Oct. 14, 1965).

[52] 111 CONG. REC. 26,008-45 (daily ed. Oct. 14, 1965).

[53] *Id.* at 26,045-46.

[54] *Hearings on Supplemental Appropriations for 1966 Before Subcomms. of the Senate Comm. on Appropriations*, 89th Cong., 1st Sess. (1965).

[55] S. REP. No. 912, 89th Cong., 1st Sess. (1965).

[56] H.R. 11588 (in the Senate), 89th Cong., 1st Sess. (1965).

[57] 111 CONG. REC. 26,584, 26,587-631, 26,781 (daily ed. Oct. 20, 1965).

[58] *Id.* at 26,604.

[59] *Id.* at 26,607.

[60] H.R. REP. No. 1198, 89th Cong., 1st Sess. 4-5 (1965).

tion for rent supplements.[61] After hearings,[62] the Second Supplemental Appropriations Bill, 1966,[63] was reported out by the House Appropriations Committee on March 25, 1966.[64] The bill reduced the first year's authorization from $30 million to $12 million and again included the workable program or local approval proviso.[65] The House, after debate,[66] approved the bill on March 29, 1966.[67]

After hearings,[68] the Senate committee eliminated the rent supplement appropriation from the bill.[69] The full Senate, however, overruled the Appropriations Committee and accepted the House version of the bill (by a narrow vote of 46-45) on April 27, 1966.[70]

The bill was signed by the President on May 13, 1966.[71]

G. Administrative Sequel

May of 1966 also saw the issuance of the administrative regulations which put flesh on the statutory skeleton.

The main changes contained in the administrative regulations and instructions[72] dealt with the housing and the tenants who were eligible for the rent supplement program and with the amount of the payment. Thus, (1) a limitation on the amount of rent that could be charged for a unit was imposed,[73] (2) the maximum income (in order to qualify) was reduced from the maximum permitted for *occupancy* in a public housing project in the area to the maximum permitted for *admission* of *regular* tenants in a public housing project in the area,[74] (3) a limitation as to the amount of assets which a tenant could have and still qualify was imposed,[75] and

---

[61] H.R. Doc. No. 380, 89th Cong., 2d Sess. (1966).

[62] *Hearings on the Second Supplemental Appropriation Bill, 1966, Before Subcomms. of the House Comm. on Appropriations*, 89th Cong., 2d Sess. (1966).

[63] H.R. 14012, 89th Cong., 2d Sess. (1966).

[64] H.R. REP. No. 1349, 89th Cong., 2d Sess. (1966).

[65] H.R. 14012, *supra* note 63, ch. 4.

[66] 112 CONG. REC. 6708-69 (daily ed. March 29, 1966).

[67] *Id.* at 6768-69.

[68] *Hearings on the Second Supplemental Appropriation Bill, Fiscal Year 1966, Before the Senate Comm. on Appropriations*, 89th Cong., 2d Sess. (1966).

[69] S. REP. No. 1137, 89th Cong., 2d Sess. 8-9 (1966).

[70] 112 CONG. REC. 8651-83 (daily ed. April 27, 1966).

[71] Act of May 13, 1966, Pub. L. No. 89-426, 80 Stat. 141.

[72] It should be noted that the regulations, to the extent they changed the plain meaning of the legislation, were codifying the stormy legislative history. They can in effect be deemed the price the administration had to pay to get the program funded. *See* notes 73-75 *infra*.

[73] U.S. FEDERAL HOUSING ADMINISTRATION, DEP'T OF HOUSING AND URBAN DEVELOPMENT, RENT SUPPLEMENT PROGRAM PUBLIC INFORMATION GUIDE AND INSTRUCTION HANDBOOK 5 (1966).

"As a further means of assuring that the program services low-income families in accordance with the congressional intent, the Secretary will establish in each locality maximum per unit rentals which will cover construction costs and maximum mortgage limits based on project prototypes of modest design and cost." *Hearings, supra* note 62, at 273 (a portion of the administration statement placed in the record).

[74] RENT SUPPLEMENT PROGRAM, *supra* note 73, at 10.

"[F]or initial qualification and eligibility, the income limits will be the same as or below the limits that exist now for public housing . . . ." *Hearings, supra* note 62, at 271 (testimony of Secretary Weaver).

[75] 24 C.F.R. § 5.20 (1967).

MR. EVINS. Mr. Secretary, let us clear upon the record on one thing, a very crucial and im-

(4) a limitation on the amount of the supplement that any tenant could receive was imposed (it could not exceed seventy per cent or be less than ten per cent of the rent for the unit).[76]

Table 1 summarizes the main differences between the original administrative proposal and the Rent Supplement Program as passed by Congress, signed by the President, and administered by the Federal Housing Commissioner.

II

The Subsidy Dilemma

A. The Need for Volume

"One needs only his eyes, his nose, and a willingness to walk through the slums of America's great cities to be aware that we are many leagues away from the goal of tolerable housing for all Americans."[77] The administration, through the use of the rent supplement proposal, attempted to take a giant stride toward the goal. As the Senate committee which held hearings on the proposal stated:[78]

> A number of existing Federal and State housing programs have been of significant value in helping low-income families to obtain standard housing. However, as helpful as these programs have been, they reach only a very small part of the total number of these families. Of the approximately 1.6 million housing starts last year, only a small proportion were units assisted under Federal or State programs designed to help low-income families.
>
> . . . .
>
> Sixteen years ago, Congress and the American people pledged themselves to— "the realization as soon as feasible of the goal of a decent home and a suitable living environment for every American family."
>
> This is our national housing objective. Commendable strides have been made toward achieving that objective, but for too many American families the pledge remains unredeemed. The committee recognizes that to redeem this pledge requires a comprehensive housing program that will provide a substantial volume of housing designed to serve families of low income. The committee has concluded that housing for lower income families can be produced in sufficient supply only through enlisting the experience and resources of private enterprise.

---

portant point. . . . This appropriation got into difficulty last October because some members read from tentative regulations . . . that individuals with assets or income up to $25,000 would be eligible.

That is not the case. That is not the situation and it was not intended by the law. . . .
. . . .
Secretary Weaver. Yes, sir.
Mr. Evins. Your statement is that the asset limitation . . . will be $2,000 except in the case of the elderly, where it will be $5,000. This is correct?
Secretary Weaver. Yes, sir.
Hearings, supra note 62, at 271.
[76] 24 C.F.R. § 5.25 (1967).
[77] R. Vernon, The Myth and Reality of Our Urban Problems 46 (1966).
[78] S. Rep. No. 378, *supra* note 4, at 3.

TABLE I

RENT SUPPLEMENT PROGRAM—SUMMARY OF MAJOR PROVISIONS

Subject	Original Proposal	Operating Program
1. Qualified Owners	Non profit and limited dividend corporations, and cooperatives	Same
2. Eligible Housing	FHA Section 221(d) (3) market interest-rate housing	Limitation placed on operating costs and rents. Program broadened, now includes: A. F.H.A. Section 221 (d) (3) market interest-rate housing B. Experimental Program — 10% of payments authorized by appropriations acts. (1) 5% — F.H.A. Section 221 (d) (3) below market interest rate housing projects approved for mortgage insurance after August 10, 1965. (2) 5% — Housing for the elderly projects (a) Section 202 of the Housing Act of 1959 — Projects approved before and after August 10, 1965. Provided that no more than 20% of the dwelling in a property financed on or before August 10, 1965 may receive supplements. (b) Section 231 of the National Act — Projects whose mortgages have been finally endorsed for mortgage insurance, after August 10, 1965
3. Eligible Tenants	Individuals or families whose incomes are such that they are unable to obtain standard housing at a rental which is equal to or less than 1/5 of their income, and who are 1. occupying substandard housing 2. displaced by governmental action, or 3. elderly or handicapped.	A. Individuals or families who have incomes that do not exceed the the maximum amount that can be established for admission of regular tenants in public housing law, and who are 1. Same 2. " 3 " 4. victims of disaster after April 1, 1965. B. Limitation on assets of tenants
4. Amount of Payment	A. Could not exceed difference between 1/5 of income and rent B. Could not exceed public housing annual contribution	A. Could not exceed difference between 1/4 of income and rent. B. Could not be more than 70% of rent or less than 10%.
5. Location of Unit	Workable program required only in community which had had a program.	Workable program or local approval required in all communities.
6. Financing	Authorization to enter into contracts for up to $200 million in supplement payments during initial four years.	Initial appropriation of $12 million

The conclusions reached by the committee with respect to using the resources of private enterprise rested on something more substantial than a prejudice either in favor of private enterprise or against government bureaucracy.

> SENATOR DOUGLAS. One more question and then I will yield.
> . . . [Y]ou propose your low-rent public housing program and you say it will not meet all of the needs, but it represents our best estimate of what can be done. Now what is it that prevents us from doing more?
> MR. WEAVER. The absorbitive capacity of this program, the availability of sites, the approval of programs at the local level, and these types of problems. These are the things.
> . . . .
> MR. WEAVER. It isn't a matter of bureaucratic hours or a matter of lack of interest. It is a matter of the fact in order to get public housing you have to go through many steps, and even in the city of Chicago, as you know very well, the Chicago Housing Authority would like to do a great deal more, but it has difficulty with sites and this has nothing to do with the efficiency of the Chicago Housing Authority.[79]

Thus, the main reason for rejection of public housing was that it could not serve as a vehicle for a large volume housing program. As the Senate report summed up the issue:[80]

> Valuable as the public housing program is and has been however, it cannot by itself fully meet the housing needs of low-income families. The current waiting list for low rent units has already reached 500,000 families. It is a harsh fact that in recent years the program has been unable to stimulate the construction of more than 30,000 new low rent units a year. There is clearly a pressing need for new programs in addition to this basic tool for low-income housing.

The choice of private enterprise vehicles also revolved around the theme of volume. The 221(d)(3) below-market interest rate program—a program characterized by the administration as successful[81]—was available. Although the interest rate applicable to the program was 3⅞ per cent and as such too high to reach the "rich poor" range which the administration sought to reach, one would have thought that a variant of that program would have been the logical choice.

> SENATOR SPARKMAN. I introduced a bill by request that would have provided for further flexibility in the rate, lowering it down, if necessary, even to zero. That would make available housing units for families much lower in the income levels. Have you seen that bill?
> MR. WEAVER. Yes, sir. I would say this: We have looked at this very carefully and we have found that even if you had a zero rate of interest, which is kind of hard for me, as a practical person, to conceive of getting, you would not be able to go down as low in the income groups as you can with the administration's rent supplementation program.[82]

---

[79] *Senate Hearings, supra* note 22, at 23-24.
[80] S. REP. No. 378, *supra* note 4, at 5.
[81] *Senate Hearings, supra* note 22, at 6.
[82] *Id.* at 17.

This answer went unchallenged. However, it does seem to be but a partial answer since (1) the initial rent supplement proposal did not seek to reach the lowest income groups, and (2) it fails to explain why a program which combined rent supplements and below-market interest was not chosen. It would seem logical and cheaper for the government to take advantage of its credit position and "piggyback" a subsidy on a below-market interest rate rather than to create a program in which a substantial portion of the subsidy is used to reduce a rent based on market rate interest.

The need for volume seemed to have been again the key to the rejection of this approach—albeit indirect:

> SENATOR PROXMIRE. I am concerned also about the temptation that every administration has, when we decide to lease post offices instead of buying them, the impact on the budget in the year you lease is smaller, but over the years it is much bigger, I am convinced.
>
> Isn't it true also with the rent supplement program, the budget will be less in the first year, but over the years it will cost more.
>
> MR. WEAVER. I would say it will not be as great as many people would assume, because the amount of subsidy would decline each year.
>
> On the other hand, I would say that the figures would indicate that the total impact, the total cost on a lower interest rate is less than on a rent supplement.[83]
>
> * * *
>
> MRS. SULLIVAN. . . .
>
> . . . .
>
> As I understand it, the proposal is that the mortgage financing the construction, which would be FHA insured, would carry a market interest rate. In other words, the capital to finance these projects would come from private markets and the only cost to the Government would be the subsidy payments paid over time to eligible tenants in the housing. That is correct, is it not?
>
> MR. WEAVER. Yes, and it reflects, of course, the extremely favorable mortgage market we have now as far as the flow of funds is concerned.
>
> MRS. SULLIVAN. In other words, I have a suspicion that one of the reasons you were able to "sell" your programs to the Budget Bureau was because of the fact that this program would have a minimum initial impact on the Federal annual budget in contrast to section 221(d)(3) below-market interest rate mortgages, for example, where the whole cost of the mortgage is an immediate charge to the budget the minute FNMA buys it. I would like your comments on that.
>
> MR. WEAVER. Two things. Obviously, it did not hurt the program with the Bureau of the Budget, and I think certainly the President has a concern for this and I think the Congress has, too. It has merit.[84]

To illustrate: the administration proposed a program that would finance 500,000 new units in a four year period. The budgetary impact of such a program (on the assumption of a $400 per unit subsidy) would be comparatively small—$50 million—even in the first year of full operation. In contrast, the impact of a below-market

---

[83] *Id.* at 32-33.
[84] *House Hearings, supra* note 17, pt. 1, at 233-34.

interest rate program would have been massive. Since the ultimate source of the funds for (d)(3) was assumed to be the U.S. Treasury, the federal budget would reflect the full amount of the mortgage loan. Thus, in the first year of a (d)(3) oriented program in which 125,000 units are projected with an average mortgage of $10,000, the budget "outlay" would be $1.25 billion, although the actual cost (assuming the interest rate charged to the mortgagor was a full two per cent below the Treasury's borrowing cost) would be $25 million.[85]

The main thrust of the administration's proposal was the necessity for creating a mechanism that would provide a rapid increase in the supply of standard housing within budgetary and cost limitations. In light of this objective, the rent supplement program held another advantage—namely, the payment was keyed to need. Unlike a fixed interest program in which fine tuning is impossible, the amount of the subsidy could be reduced as income rose. The program, thus, had the economic advantage of (a) not wasting a full subsidy on persons who needed only a partial subsidy, and (b) assuming a rise in the income of the tenants, a reduction in the cost of the program, or an expansion of the program with no increase in cost. There was also the sociological advantage of its being unnecessary to evict families whose income had risen above the point of need, thus (a) encouraging housing in which families of different income groups would live together,[86] and (b) eliminating one of the major sore points of public housing—the disincentive to economic advancement produced by a program in which eviction was the mark of economic success.

Such features of the program as the imposition of the income floor and the elimination of the workable program requirement may seem at first glance to be unrelated to the administration's aim to achieve the greatest bang for the budgetary buck, but upon closer examination it becomes clear that they are crucial components. To the extent a person on the bottom of the income scale requires a greater subsidy input per housing unit, the total volume of units must be reduced. To the extent outlying areas are used, lower land costs and lower construction costs (the predominant type of project in such areas being wood-frame construction) would result in rent levels which require a lesser subsidy input per housing unit, thus enabling an increased volume of units.

In conclusion, given a treasury whose resources are finite, the administration's aim was to achieve the largest possible program (using available home-building resources) with the smallest budgetary impact.

[85] At the present time the distinction between the rent supplement program and the below-market interest rate program with regard to budget impact and cost is in the main academic. Section 102 of the Housing and Urban Development Act of 1965 made it possible for the Federal National Mortgage Association (FNMA) to include the (d)(3) mortgages in its portfolio in its arrangements for pooling mortgages and selling participations. The act did this by authorizing appropriations to reimburse FNMA for the amount of the discount the private market would require to purchase a participation which included below-market interest rate mortgages. This eliminated the adverse budgetary impact of (d)(3) mortgages at the cost of the savings the government achieved by using its credit resources to purchase and then to hold the mortgage.
[86] See H.R. Doc. No. 99, 89th Cong., 1st Sess. 8 (1965).

B. The Need for Equity

Whereas, the administration was concerned with fulfilling the nation's housing objectives, Congress was concerned with the fairness of the new program to non-recipients, both poor and rich.

Thus the income floor was an immediate target of attack. As a politicoeconomist stated during the congressional hearing:[87]

> But there is a grave question raised here as to whether when there are vast un-met needs of people with incomes of below $2,000 or $3,000 a year, you then ought to launch a new program to help people who are above the poverty level?

Congress reacted to this argument by striking the economic floor. The program thus avoided the rocks of Scylla by throwing overboard some valuable cargo—housing units.[88] However, having avoided one hazard, the proposal immediately found itself in the whirlpool of Charybdis—the implications of a program which provides better housing for the poor, at a subsidized rent, than is available for a large number of more successful (and possibly harder working) citizens who must pay the full economic rent. A policy of taxing Peter to provide housing for Paul, who would otherwise have to live in squalor, may rest on sweet virtue. A policy of taxing Peter to provide better housing than his own for Paul is a bitter pill.

Can this unappealing prospect be avoided? And if it can, what are the costs? These two questions will be considered in light of the legislative history of the rent supplement proposal.

The administration was aware of the problem and limited the categories of poor that this program would serve. Thus the qualification for tenancy included not only low income but also being in a category that few would begrudge—the handicapped, the elderly, the displaced, and subsequently the disaster victim. The occupant of substandard housing may not qualify as deserving but at least he has served his time in squalor.

Congress added an additional requirement—tangible evidence of the occupant's deservedness. One of the earliest amendments required the occupant to pay an extra five per cent of his income for his new housing. A representative of the American Bankers Association gave the following explanation why this was needed:[89]

[87] *Senate Hearings, supra* note 22, at 18 (Senator Douglas).

[88] The argument was made that by increasing the amount to be paid by tenants from 20% to 25% of income, the lowering of the income ceiling by Congress did not affect volume. *See* 111 Cong. Rec. 16,059 (daily ed. July, 13, 1965) (statement by Senator Douglas). In response it should be noted: (1) that the administration proposal originally contemplated supporting 500,000 units at an annual cost of $200 million. Secretary Weaver, however, in testimony seeking appropriations after the income limit was dropped, estimated that 250,000 units would be supported by an appropriation of $150 million— a one-third decrease in the number of units per dollar of expenditure. *Hearings, supra* note 62, at 267; (2) that lowering of the ceiling defeated the purpose of economic integration which was strongly favored by Senator Douglas. *See* 111 Cong. Rec. 16,060 (daily ed. July 13, 1965); and (3) it is this paper's contention that increasing volume was not the prime motive (or even a motive) for raising the tenant's payment from 20% to 25% of his income. This point is discussed in the text *infra*.

[89] *Senate Hearings, supra* note 22, at 379 (Kurt Flexner, Deputy Manager, American Bankers Association). (Emphasis added.)

What we are saying, Senator, is that since it is generally agreed that a person may spend around 20 percent of his income, gross income, on rent, especially in that group, that income group, that the rent supplements should be based on the criteria of need.

Well, now, if a person has to pay 22 percent of his income on rent, *well, it is a little more than perhaps he should to get his housing,* but it doesn't clearly establish need. But if he had to go as high as 25 percent, it would seem that this is substantially higher than an accepted criteria, so that then supplements would be more logical.

Not only does the occupant thereby show effort but he also guarantees that in order to obtain the good housing he is willing to sacrifice luxuries (or necessities).[90] There will be no shiny new cars outside of rent supplement projects.

Is the conflict real? Must a housing subsidy give the poor better housing than is available to higher income neighbors? Theoretically perhaps not, that is, if there is a surplus of standard housing. However, the premise of the problem and the program is a shortage of standard units.

Can the quality of the housing to be given to the subsidized tenant be limited? Must we build "penthouses for the poor"? Limiting the housing to existing structures has the obvious advantages in this regard in that a "used" house is unlikely to be as good as a new house. Thus it should not be surprising that, although the Housing and Urban Development Act of 1965 contained two new housing subsidy programs, the rent supplement program geared to new construction stirred waves, but the provision granting public housing authorities the power to lease low rent housing in private accommodations scarcely caused a ripple.[91] Nevertheless, although a useful tool in areas in which vacancies in standard housing exists or where rehabilitation of substandard housing is economically feasible, the leasing program does not show any promise of redeeming the pledge to the poor.

Can anything be done to avoid the difficulty if we are forced to rely on new construction? If new construction is a necessary evil, it at least can be restricted to the most basic shelter requirements. The amenities (both structural and environmental) of new housing can be limited.

There are, however, severe economic and urban development constraints in following this course. The building must be of sufficient quality to serve a market for at least the life of the mortgage (forty years). It must, therefore, if it is not to be functionally obsolete many years prior to its attaining physical obsolescence,[92]

---

[90] *See generally* on the rent-income ratio, Rapkin, *Rent-Income Ratio,* in URBAN HOUSING 168 (W. L. C. Wheaton, G. Milgram, & M. E. Meyerson eds. 1966).

[91] 42 U.S.C. § 1421b (Supp. II, 1965-66). This provision, especially in regard to the location of the units, can stir calm waters. *See generally* W. L. MILLER, THE FIFTEENTH WARD AND THE GREAT SOCIETY 99-111 (1966), for the experience of a New England city.

[92] "All rent supplement projects must be of modest design and suitable to the market and the location proposed. Swimming pools, two bathrooms per unit, air conditioning, and similar items will not be permitted. Projects should incorporate good design principles and not have features that will contribute to premature obsolescence." RENT SUPPLEMENT PROGRAM, *supra* note 73, at 2.

include certain facilities which were yesterday's (and possibly today's) luxuries.[93] The dangers of false economy go beyond the structure itself. If the model tenements of the nineteenth and early twentieth centuries are the building blocks of today's slums, the overly modest projects of today may be cornerstones of the slums of to-morrow.

The location of the housing can be channeled so as to limit the environmental amenity. A building of superior quality to house the poor does not offend one's sense of equity if it is placed in an inferior neighborhood.[94] If Peter has to pay for Paul's housing, he need not be forced to live next to Paul. The sentiment was put in its universal form by a novelist—"Generally my fellow townspeople, though they would help the poor, were not particularly fond of them."[95] Or as a Congressman put the issue a bit more bluntly:[96]

> I think the time has come to call a spade a spade. . . .
> When the rent subsidy program was before Congress some of us said the pur-pose of the bill was to force integration of better class neighborhoods. This was denied by the sponsors. . . .
> Let me read from a Federal Housing Administration letter, MF Letter No. 63 to all insuring office directors and multifamily housing representatives under date of September 28, 1965:
> > "Important criteria with regard to approval of a rent supplement project will include full consideration of its contribution to assisting in integrating income groups and furthering the legal requirements and objectives of equal opportunity in housing."
> That is in the regulations, in the instructions to those housing officials who will be spending this $6 million, and they are told the first consideration of the rent subsidy program is integrating economic groups and furthering the objectives of equal opportunity in housing. Under this implementation of the program, private homeownership in America is doomed because a man cannot protect the value of his property nor the desirability of his neighborhood.

Must we, therefore, place the home in a less than suitable environment? If one man's home can be his castle, another man's home may be his prison. As another Congressman viewed the issue:[97]

> We can see no reason why private builders should be forced to obtain local approval for rent supplement projects, which are in essence an "FHA for the poor."
>   . . . .

---

[93] *"Design Factors Plague Rent Supplement Program.* The NAHB Rent Supplement Task Force was told . . . that builders refuse to design down proposed rent supplement projects, and for this reason a number of projects have either been canceled or postponed." NAHB COMPENDIUM BULL., Dec. 1966, at 3.

[94] An architecturally striking public housing development has failed to attract a single white family in spite of strenuous activities by the local housing authority. *See* Dixon, *Goldberg's Variation on Chicago Public Housing*, ARCHITECTURAL FORUM, Nov. 1966, at 25.

[95] E. WIESEL, NIGHT 15 (1960).

[96] 111 CONG. REC. 26,019 (daily ed. Oct. 14, 1965) (remarks of Congressman Martin).

[97] 112 CONG. REC. 8667 (daily ed. April 27, 1966) (statement of Senator Clark).

. . . The local veto rider, if it should become law, will be used to confine rent supplement housing to the areas in which the families entitled to rent supplements already live, thus frustrating the clear intent of the Congress. The problems of our cities will never be resolved if we establish walls or immovable curtains beyond which the poor and elderly cannot go to find decent housing.

CONCLUSION

The fate of the rent supplement program illustrates that the inability to fulfill the nation's pledge to millions of low income families living in substandard housing rests on something more than the failure to enlist private enterprise in the task. Rent supplements were proposed and were necessary because public housing could not produce the necessary volume. However, the introduction of new players did not change the rules of the game. The limitations imposed by Congress assure that private enterprise, even though subsidized, will also fail to produce the necessary volume to achieve the nation's housing goal.[98] Both the thirty-year history of the public housing program and the brief history of the rent supplement program illustrate the paradoxical effect of the subsidy dilemma—the creation of powerful instruments whose use has to be restricted because of their capacity to achieve the very goal for which they were designed.

The most promising solution to the dilemma may be the elimination of the need for a subsidy either by lowering development costs or by raising income levels of the poor. It may not, therefore, be a coincidence that 1966 saw major action on both of these fronts. Legislation was enacted to apply technological advances to housing[99] and a conference was convened whose purpose was the ultimate development of new technologies to enable the upgrading of our physical environment to modern standards at feasible cost levels.[100] The model cities program was also enacted[101] —a program whose premise is that "bricks and mortar" will not renew our cities as

---

[98] The problems and criticisms which have plagued public housing—(1) site selection; (2) segregation of low-income families; (3) increasing non-white occupancy; (4) income limits which are criticized as being too high and too low; (5) inadequacy of the program; (6) detailed federal supervision; (7) poor design; (8) high development costs—are all applicable to the rent supplement program. *See generally* U.S. HOUSING AND HOME FINANCE AGENCY, VIEWS ON PUBLIC HOUSING 153-59 (1960).

[99] Demonstration Cities and Metropolitan Development Act of 1966, § 1010, 42 U.S.C. § 3372 (Supp. II, 1965-66).

[100] *See* U.S. DEP'T OF HOUSING AND URBAN DEVELOPMENT, SCIENCE AND THE CITY (1967) (a report on the Summer Study on Science and Urban Development in June 1966 in Woods Hole, Mass., sponsored by the Department of Housing Urban Development). For the problems even in such a worthwhile endeavor:

"Yesterday Haggerty [President of the AFL-CIO Building and Construction Trades Department], clearly tiffed at a report . . . issued after a HUD-sponsored conference, hit back at charges that the craft unions block progress and resist changes that could mean faster and cheaper construction." White, *Ribicoff Jabs HUD on Slum Advisers*, The Washington Post, April 19, 1967, at A2, col. 3. "*High Court Backs Right to Strike Over Automation, Decides, 5-4, Unions May Enforce Contract Ban on Prefabricated Items, . . . Justices Agree Law Allows Carpenters to Walk Out in Fight to Save Jobs*," N.Y. Times, April 18, 1967, at 1, col. 1. (Headlines.)

[101] Demonstration Cities and Metropolitan Development Act of 1966, tit. 1, 42 U.S.C.A. §§ 1453, 3301-13 (Pamphlet, Feb. 1967).

long as millions of poor and disadvantaged Americans lack the training and opportunity to participate fully in our nation's life.[102]

---

[102] For the problems and possibly the dilemmas one again needs only to read the newspapers.

"His name is Jackson, Ernest Jackson. Ernest is something of a celebrity. He's the one-thousandth graduate of the Kilmer Job Corps Center in New Jersey to be placed. Ernest now earns over $200 a week. Not bad for a fellow who dropped out of school in the 11th grade.

At Kilmer, a lot of young men are being changed from untrained dropouts to skilled craftsmen." Otten, *New Allies for L.B.J.*, The Wall Street Journal, April 19, 1967, at 1, col. 6. *But see* Semple, *U.S. Finds Only 1% On Welfare Lists Are Employable*, N.Y. Times, April 20, 1967, at 1, col. 1.

THE IMPLEMENTATION OF THE RENT SUPPLEMENT PROGRAM—A STAFF VIEW

Walter L. Smith*

When the rent supplement program was signed into law in the fall of 1965,[1] the Federal Housing Administration (FHA) was plunged into a new field. The shift in thrust from a moderate-income group to a low-income group demanded a changed approach. A program designed primarily to serve families at the public housing income level would of necessity have different imperatives than would one intended to replace the below-market interest rate program.

I

Administrative Framework

The attitude of Congress made it evident that, unless the program was placed in operation in a very short time, funding would be extremely unlikely. Since speed of execution was vital, a new approach to the problem of information exchange with the field offices became necessary. To accomplish this purpose, the FHA created a special task force, whose job it would be to put the program into motion rapidly and efficiently. The task force personnel were drawn from all over the country, on the basis of the central office's experience with their aptitude and their work. A sympathetic approach to the problems of a new client group was one requirement, and a thorough grounding in FHA methods and practices was another. An open mind was essential, since this was precisely the field which FHA personnel had always avoided as an undesirable mortgage risk, and which the Public Housing Administration had made peculiarly theirs.

The task force met for the first time early in December 1965 for an intensive two-week training session. The full resources of FHA and the Department of Housing and Urban Development were thrown into an attempt to explain the purposes and intent of the program to the task force members. Administrative, underwriting, and technical problems were discussed, but the main thrust of the training was the explanation of the intent of the program.

By the middle of December, the task force was deemed ready to begin operations. Its members were dispersed across the country to explain to the field officers the meaning and intent of the program, and to demonstrate the methods by which the Department intended to demonstrate to the Congress the desire and need for the program. Each task force member was assigned an area of the country. From that

---

* Executive Director, North Carolina Low Income Housing Development Corporation, Durham, North Carolina.

[1] 12 U.S.C. § 1701s (Supp. II, 1965-66). *See generally* Welfeld, *Rent Supplements and the Subsidy Dilemma*, in this symposium, p. 465-81.

area, he was to bring back expressions of opinion and judgments secured from the field.

In late December the task force again gathered in Washington to review the results of the trip and to study the problems foreseen by the directors and chief underwriters in the field offices. After analyzing the results of this study, the task force returned to the field during January 1966 to obtain from the field offices expressions of interest in the application of the program, and to help the directors secure capable sponsors for specific proposals which could be studied.

The results of the second task force journey demonstrated conclusively that a high level of genuine interest had been aroused by the passage of the rent supplement program. Church groups all across the country saw in the program an opportunity to serve a lower income level than they had ever before been able to reach. The FHA office was flooded with inquiries from sponsors who were interested in building rental units. The task force was then asked to help evaluate the proposals within the framework being considered by the FHA.

Early in the spring, a select group of experts was brought to Washington to review the tentative rules and to judge the chances of success in various parts of the country. This one-week meeting led to the conviction that the program could be placed in operation within the FHA framework and could be meshed with the other work of the field staff.

By early May, a handbook for the operation of the program had been written,[2] a tentative modus operandi had been established, and the Washington headquarters was ready to discuss the program in depth. The directors and chief underwriters of all field offices were brought to Washington for a one-week briefing on the prospective operation of the program. During the course of this meeting, Congress appropriated $12 million in rent supplement funds for the current fiscal year.[3]

The adjournment of this meeting put the program into operation. The FHA was now ready to accept applications for rent supplement projects. In less than eight months, a major new housing program had been thought out and placed into operation. By June 30, 1966, the $12 million dollar appropriation (except for a reserve account) had been spoken for. The first rent supplement contract was signed in September for a rehabilitation project in the Hough section of Cleveland, Ohio.

By late October, the task force was shaken down into an operating section of the multifamily operation of the FHA.

II

Operation of the Rent Supplement Program

In order to rush the rent supplement program from its initial conception to full operation within one year, a number of problems had to be overcome. The in-

---

[2] U.S. Federal Housing Administration, Dep't of Housing and Urban Development, Rent Supplement Program Public Information Guide and Instruction Handbook (1966).

[3] Act of May 13, 1966, Pub. L. No. 89-426, 80 Stat. 141.

herent nature of the program signalled a new approach to the housing problems' of the poor. Private enterprise was to be given a chance to see what it could do, in partnership with the government, in attacking slums and poor quality housing. The social intent of charitable and other nonprofit institutions would be put to the test.

The idea of re-housing the poor through payment by the government of a portion of the rent on privately-built dwelling units required a new look at the problem of economic feasibility. For the first time, an apartment house owner could have a major portion of his rent roll guaranteed. The risk factor in mortgage insurability is entirely changed by this one fact. So long as a supplemented tenant remains in a dwelling unit, his supplement will be paid. The establishment of an upper supplement limit (set at seventy per cent of the gross rent) meant in effect that the FHA would collect a mortgage insurance premium on a mortgage against which it might be making as much as seventy per cent of the payments. Under such circumstances, it was difficult to believe that the FHA could lose. Even so, some of the top technical experts in the agency remained convinced that the program was basically unworkable. Two of the major officials retired rather than face the overthrow of the standards of risk evaluation used for other programs.

The relation of the social concept to the degree of mortgage risk revealed to the agency its deepset distrust of people who could not "pay the freight." It required of agency personnel a re-examination of their own training and judgment. Nothing in the FHA experience had prepared its technical staff for firm judgments on site selection in slum areas. Its previous management experience had been with the middle class; it had few standards of its own to use in facing the new management problems inherent in this program. In previous multifamily projects the agency's work had involved definite criteria based on the mores and living habits of an income group far above that to be served with rent supplements. Even with the section 221(d)(3) below-market interest rate program,[4] the social group served accepted much the same standards and could, for the most part, be handled on the same basis. The selection of FHA as the operating agency caused its members a great amount of honest soul-searching, as the responsible field officers attempted to understand the driving principles of housing poor people.

One positive benefit of the selection of FHA as the operating arm was that its primary interest lay in the economics of making such an idea a working reality. The agency was not frozen into an established pattern of acceptance of local mores, nor was it inclined to make moral judgments on tenant acceptability. Once it was made pellucidly clear that the FHA was not to pass judgment on the theory, but was instead to put the theory into successful practice, the field officers went to work on that task.

A danger seen from the beginning was that the program could very easily lead

---

[4] 12 U.S.C. § 1715*l*(d)(3) (Supp. II, 1965-66).

to the creation of new, modern ghettos. As a first, practical step in forestalling this problem, the FHA limited the size of any one project to 200 units. Although arbitrary, and recognized as such, the informal limitation was effective in that it made clear the intent to avoid ghettoizing the populace. The danger will exist throughout the life of this or any other similar program.

One of the purposes of the program was to achieve a measure of economic integration. Suburban structuring has proceeded to such a point that it is possible for a developer to know before he starts work the exact income level which will be attracted to his subdivision. Conversely, in low-income groups, the concentration of economic failure has reached formidable proportions. Human nature seems to be such that failure reinforces failure. If the rent supplement program could be used to expose low-income families to moderate-income families, with another set of standards, perhaps a beginning could be made toward de-structurizing that portion of society.

The intent of Congress was expressed on this point through a "modest design" requirement.[5] Individual congressmen may have felt that a modest design standard was essential to keep the program within the client group for which it was intended. The practical result of the criterion was to negate, at least in the beginning, any actual attempt at vertical economic integration. One standard squeezed out of Secretary Weaver was that no dwelling unit could contain more than one bathroom. For a three-or-more bedroom apartment, this starts out as an undesirable unit. Air-conditioning was forbidden, although any unit built in certain sections of the United States without it is automatically substandard. The mortgage term that will be used for the majority of the projects will be forty years. If any serious attempt is made during that period to remove poverty as an important factor in American economics, such apartments will become substandard and virtually unrentable. Rather than an attempt to keep costs within bounds, these requirements were moral standards which said in effect that rent supplement units should be second-class units.

For the technical sections, the establishment of cost limits and upper rent limits was a nightmare. Every conceivable method of arriving at a useable set of cost limits was tried and discarded. Upper rent limits were set at $85 per month for an efficiency, $105 per month for a one-bedroom unit, $120 per month for a two-bedroom unit, and $140 per month for a unit containing three or more bedrooms. In high-cost areas, these limits could be exceeded by up to twenty-five per cent. A pragmatic upper limit of $175 per month for a three-or-more bedroom unit, including all utilities except telephone, was thus created. This limit immediately removed the possibility of large-scale new construction in New York City, Chicago, and other major urban centers. New units simply cannot be produced in quantity in such areas at these rent levels.

---

[5] U.S. FEDERAL HOUSING ADMINISTRATION, *supra* note 2, at 2.

Since the congressional delegations from the large metropolitan areas were a major source of support, the FHA was forced into a ruling that the funds allocated for use in conjunction with the below-market interest rate (five per cent of the total appropriations) could be used only in those areas in which no rent supplement project could be built without the three per cent interest rate. Most attempts to use the joint programs for experiments in economic integration were thereby shut off. Since rehabilitation projects are still feasible at a market interest rate in most of the metropolitan areas, the effort in those cities had to be switched from new construction to rehabilitation.

To those who were directly concerned with the implementation of the program, the establishment of these rent levels made it clear that the program was to be used mainly in medium-sized and smaller cities and towns where costs could be expected to be lower. This is, indeed, what has happened.

The emphasis on participation in the program by nonprofit sponsors revised another early concept. Historically, builders and developers managing rental units have tried, understandably, to skim the cream off the market by accepting as tenants only those families which could reasonably be expected to remain economically stable and which should be relatively trouble-free. The imperative of a church group entering this program is entirely different. Such a group is primarily trying to serve those who are purposely kept out of normal projects. Such families generally have less stable incomes, fewer work options and hence longer periods of unemployment, and are trouble-prone. These factors showed up at once as an increase in the anticipated rent supplement requirement per unit. Originally, the projected average supplement was estimated at $600 per year per unit. The eager participation of the nonprofit sector forced this amount to an average of $1,000 per unit per year almost at once. This, of course, meant that fewer units could be produced under a given appropriation than had been projected. It also meant that the program was to be used by at least some of its sponsors for a genuinely low income group. The relationship between a tenant's income and the amount of supplement payment is shown in table 1.

Nothing has yet appeared in the operation of the program that has caused as much difficulty as the projected management problems of these projects. Estimates of the probable cost of managing a rent supplement project vary so widely as to be ridiculous. Judgments about tenant relations as a management problem have actually kept some sponsors out of the program. The FHA's experience has been with the landlord class; in many cases it has seemed to adopt the landlord's attitude toward low-income tenants. It is extraordinarily difficult to convince a property management officer (who is fully aware of his troubles with middle-income tenants) that a rent supplement tenant could under any circumstances be anything but a problem. A guidebook to effective management has been prepared by the FHA and distributed

TABLE I
Tenant Income and Supplement Payments

Gross Rent / Tenant Income	0-Bedroom $85		1-Bedroom $105		2-Bedroom $120		3-or-more Bedroom $140	
	Tenant Rent	Supplement	Tenant Rent	Supplement	Tenant Rent	Supplement	Tenant Rent	Supplement
$1200	25	60						
1300	27	58						
1400	29	56						
1500	31	54	31	74				
1600	33	52	33	72				
1700	35	50	35	70				
1800	38	47	38	67	38	82		
1900	40	45	40	65	40	80		
2000	42	43	42	63	42	78	42	98
2100	44	41	44	61	44	76	44	96
2200	46	39	46	59	46	74	46	94
2300	48	37	48	57	48	72	48	92
2400	50	35	50	55	50	70	50	90
2500	52	33	52	53	52	68	52	88
2600	54	31	54	51	54	66	54	86
2700	56	29	56	49	56	64	56	84
2800	58	27	58	47	58	62	58	82
2900	60	25	60	45	60	60	60	80
3000	63	22	63	42	63	57	63	77
3100	65	20	65	40	65	55	65	75
3200	67	18	67	38	67	53	67	73
3300	69	16	69	36	69	51	69	71
3400	71	14	71	34	71	49	71	69
3500	73	12	73	32	73	47	73	67
3600	75	10	75	30	75	45	75	65
3700	77	8	77	28	77	43	77	63
3800			79	26	79	41	79	61
3900			81	24	81	39	81	59
4000			83	22	83	37	83	57
4100			85	20	85	35	85	55
4200			88	17	88	32	88	52
4300			90	15	90	30	90	50
4400			92	13	92	28	92	48
4500			94	11	94	26	94	46
4600					96	24	96	44
4700					98	22	98	42
4800					100	20	100	40
4900					102	18	102	38
5000					104	16	104	36
5100					106	14	106	34
5200					108	12	108	32
5300							110	30
5400							113	27
5500							115	25
5600							117	23
5700							119	21
5800							121	19
5900							123	17
6000							125	15

to its offices,[6] but it is likely that only experience will teach the sponsors, the owners, and the FHA the proper blend of supportive services and hard-nosed management

[6] U.S. Federal Housing Administration, Dep't of Housing and Urban Development, Rent Supplement Program Project Management Outline (1967).

practices. The efforts of one organization are illustrated in the appendix that follows this article.

CONCLUSION

Within the next few years, enough projects will be finished so that a pattern may be established. Some facets of the program need revision, but in many parts of the country rent supplements seem a promising answer to low-income housing problems. It is beyond doubt the most widely misunderstood housing program ever put into effect. Its greatest usefulness at this moment is in the southeast and southern middle western regions; yet this is the area of most determined congressional opposition to the concept. In North Carolina, for example, a statewide Low Income Housing Development Corporation has been established by the North Carolina Fund.[7] It is using the rent supplement program under nonprofit sponsorship as its major instrument, and is finding that the tool fits the job; yet the North Carolina congressional delegation votes as a bloc to kill the program.

As experience with the rent supplement program grows—and it must grow, since the appropriations already made commit the government to support of the existing program for up to forty years—and misunderstandings about its purposes and methods lessen, it is likely to become the keystone of the effort to re-house the poor.

* * *

APPENDIX

I

MANAGEMENT PLAN FOR RALEIGH INTER-CHURCH HOUSING, INC.

1. *Professional management.* RICH will hire, for day-to-day management of the project, a competent, experienced real estate firm.
2. *Resident manager.* RICH will include in its project at least one rental unit which shall be reserved for a resident manager.
3. *Property maintenance.* RICH will form, within the sponsoring group itself, a property maintenance committee. This committee shall be responsible to the sponsor for the upkeep and appearance of the project.
4. *Tenant selection.* RICH will form, within the sponsoring group itself, a tenant selection committee. This committee shall be responsible for the determination of tenant selection, in accordance with the requirements of the FHA and the policies of the sponsoring group. It shall make, or cause to be made, an investigation of the income, assets, family size and composition, of each prospective tenant. It shall make a determination for the sponsor of the required amount

---

[7] The corporation is now completely independent.

of supplement for each tenant, and shall furnish to the management firm a completed application form for each tenant.

5. *Social support and assistance.* RICH will form, within the sponsoring group, a committee (which shall include representatives from all churches involved) which shall be responsible for making available to the tenants and to the project any and all socially supportive services needed or desired to assist the tenants. The information secured by the tenant selection committee shall be made available to the tenant assistance committee.

6. *Financial management.* RICH will form, within the sponsoring group, a financial committee which shall be responsible to all concerned for the management of residual receipts, replacement reserves, maintenance and decorating reserves; mortgage management; rent supplement funds computations and management; loans and grants.

7. *Tenant advisory committee.* RICH shall form a tenant advisory committee, which shall be responsible for giving the tenants financial and credit advice, job opportunity information, and other information and advice.

8. *Steering committee.* The chairman of each of the above committees shall also serve as a member of a steering committee which shall coordinate implementation of the policies of the board of directors, and which shall recommend policies and policy changes to the board of directors. This committee shall contain representatives of the tenants.

9. *Open occupancy.* No policy determination may be made by RICH or any of its constituent bodies or agents which contravenes the occupancy policies of FHA.

10. *Tenant privacy.* RICH will prohibit its members, constituent bodies, and agents from making public, inside or outside the project, the financial situation or supplement requirements of any tenant.

II

Organization of Raleigh Inter-Church Housing, Inc.

Board of Directors

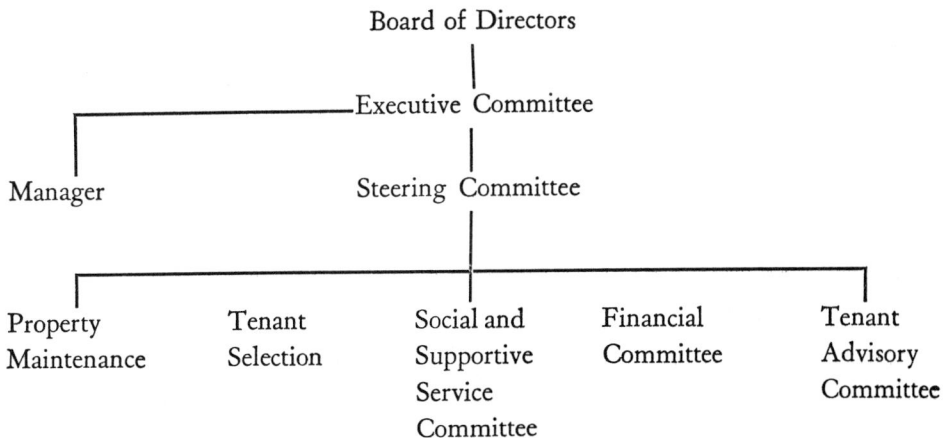

| Property Maintenance | Tenant Selection | Social and Supportive Service Committee | Financial Committee | Tenant Advisory Committee |

PUBLIC HOUSING – A SOCIAL EXPERIMENT SEEKS ACCEPTANCE

WILLIAM H. LEDBETTER, JR.*

INTRODUCTION

The large and expanding melange of projects and propositions designed to improve the living conditions of the less privileged members of the citizenry has become known to twentieth-century Americans as social welfare. Under this comprehensive, somewhat amorphous rubric are catalogued the manifold services of the federal, state, and local governments, the secular charities and foundations, and the church-related organizations.

Social welfare, particularly that part funded by the public sector, has become a topic of concern today because, despite America's heralded affluence, the problems of the poor are still with us. With nearly eighteen per cent of all American families who live in housing units surviving on an income level of less than $3,000 per year,[1] with the advances of the technological age relegating the unskilled and uneducated to frustrating unproductivity, with medical science increasing longevity and sustaining the mentally and physically handicapped, and with the traditional reliance on stoic individualism and family responsibility being sacrificed to mobility and interdependence, the task is formidable; and it apparently has just begun.[2]

At least since the mid-1930s the various programs of housing and home finance assistance that involve the public sector have constituted an essential component of the social welfare effort. All of these government programs have not been aimed directly at alleviating poverty—some were temporary war measures to improve the military machine at home, some are designed to assist middle-class families to flee to the suburbs, some attempt to maintain a high level of activity in the field of real estate investment and finance, and others are calculated to improve the livability and beauty of the cities and the countryside. But the nation has come to realize that, if poverty is to be abolished, an integral part of the assault must be the provision of adequate housing. It is also now realized that, given the shortage of adequate housing (especially in the central parts of the cities) and the apparent inability of private enterprise to supply a sufficient amount of housing for low-income families, the public sector must increase its efforts.

---

* B.A. 1963, Campbell College; LL.B. 1966, University of Richmond; LL.M. 1967, Yale University. Assistant Professor of Law, University of South Carolina. Member of the Virginia bar.
[1] U.S. BUREAU OF THE CENSUS, DEP'T OF COMMERCE, STATISTICAL ABSTRACT OF THE UNITED STATES: 1966, at 336, table 472.
[2] *See generally* on the many facets of social welfare, NEW PERSPECTIVES ON POVERTY (A. Shostak & W. Gomberg eds. 1965); G. STEINER, SOCIAL INSECURITY (1966); *Symposium: Law for the Poor*, 54 CALIF. L. REV. 319 (1966); *Symposium—Antipoverty Programs*, 31 LAW & CONTEMP. PROB. 1 (1966).

With the increased concern with slum clearance and urban renewal, housing will undoubtedly retain its important position, and may in fact become the fulcrum of the entire crusade against poverty.

> The best security for civilization is the dwelling, and upon proper and becoming dwellings depends more than anything else the improvement of mankind. Such dwellings are the nursery of all domestic virtues, and without a becoming home the exercise of those virtues is impossible.[3]

A detailed study of all of the programs of housing and home finance assistance would be too unwieldy.[4] It is the purpose of this article to consider only that segment of housing referred to as "public housing." The word *only* is hardly appropriate, other than to emphasize the relative degree of constriction, because public housing involves several programs under the auspices of the Housing Assistance Agency (formerly the Public Housing Administration) and hundreds of local housing authorities. Some of the programs are remnants of the oldest and most controversial of the government efforts in the field of housing, and are progenitors of many of the more recent endeavors. Others are of more recent vintage, and are attempts to supplement or supplant portions of the older ones.

In analyzing this social experiment which, after twenty-nine years, is still seeking acceptance, this article first describes the origin and history of public housing and then offers a brief summary of how the program works. Next, the most common criticisms are surveyed and evaluated, after which new approaches to public housing are studied in an effort to see whether the program can rise to acceptance from the present nadir of its fortunes.

I

ORIGINS AND HISTORY OF PUBLIC HOUSING

The federal government did not enter the field of housing assistance until the First World War, except to provide housing for military personnel and certain government employees, and to appropriate small sums for the study of slum problems (as Congress did in 1892 with an authorization of $20,000).

In 1917, the government enacted a two-part program which resulted in the construction of 5,000 single-family units plus apartments and other dwelling space during the war.[5] Under the Shipping Act[6] the Shipping Board Emergency Fleet Corporation was organized to lend money to limited-dividend corporations that would build houses

---

[3] R. FISHER, TWENTY YEARS OF PUBLIC HOUSING 62 (1959), quoting Benjamin Disraeli.

[4] *See generally* U.S. DEP'T OF HOUSING AND URBAN DEVELOPMENT, PROGRAMS OF THE DEPARTMENT OF HOUSING AND URBAN DEVELOPMENT (1966), for a summary of the programs administered by that Department.

[5] U.S. DEP'T OF HOUSING AND URBAN DEVELOPMENT, WHAT THE DEPARTMENT OF HOUSING AND URBAN DEVELOPMENT IS AND HOW IT IS ORGANIZED 8 (1966).

[6] Ch. 19, 40 Stat. 438 (1918).

and other quarters for defense workers. The second part of the war effort was the United States Housing Corporation[7] which built housing facilities itself and realized a $26 million net loss.[8] Both operations terminated at the end of the war.

The second federal effort began in 1932 when Congress, goaded by the depression, authorized loans by the Reconstruction Finance Corporation (RFC).[9] The RFC issued loans to limited-dividend corporations until 1933.

The National Industrial Recovery Act, one of President Roosevelt's initial attacks on the depression, created the Public Works Administration (PWA), which included a housing division.[10] This agency also made loans to private limited-dividend corporations. Because of the small number of acceptable applications for these funds, and because the limited-dividend corporations could not build cheaply enough to provide low-rent units for the persons whom the program was designed to benefit, PWA began constructing housing projects itself. This move was also designed to assist the President's effort to provide more employment opportunities for the millions of idle workers. In 1935, a federal district court ruled that the federal government could not use eminent domain to acquire property for low-rent housing and slum clearance.[11] But when, in the following year a state court held that a local government could condemn for housing projects,[12] PWA began encouraging local participation in the housing effort by making available loans up to seventy per cent and grants up to thirty per cent for certain public entities.[13]

On March 13, 1935, Senator Wagner of New York introduced a bill in Congress to establish a permanent low-rent public housing administration within the federal bureaucracy. This bill was reported out of the Committee on Education and Labor on August 2, 1937, and debated until August 6, when it was accepted by the Senate.[14] The New York Senator argued that the bill would stimulate business activity, would increase employment,[15] and would assist the local governments to eliminate slums and unsanitary tenements.

In the House of Representatives, the bill reached the floor from the Committee on Banking and Currency and ran into lengthy debates over the merits of the program,

---

[7] Act of May 16, 1918, ch. 74, 40 Stat. 550.

[8] R. FISHER, *supra* note 3, at 78.

[9] Emergency Relief and Construction Act of 1932, ch. 520, 47 Stat. 709.

[10] Ch. 90, tit. II, 48 Stat. 200 (1933).

[11] United States v. Certain Lands in the City of Louisville, 9 F. Supp. 137 (W.D. Ky. 1935), *aff'd*, 78 F.2d 684 (6th Cir. 1935), *petition for cert. dismissed*, 294 U.S. 735 (1936).

[12] New York City Housing Authority v. Muller, 270 N.Y. 333, 1 N.E.2d 153 (1936).

[13] R. FISHER, *supra* note 3, at 86-89.

[14] 81 CONG. REC. 7967-92, 8368-73 (1937). Senator Wagner's efforts have been oversimplified for the purposes of brevity. Actually, the Senator's first bill was not the same bill that passed both houses in 1937, because a few changes were made as the proposal wound its way through committees and the Congress in 1935, 1936, and 1937. *See generally* M. STRAUS & T. WEGG, HOUSING COMES OF AGE 178-89 (1938), for a more complete history of this era of public housing.

[15] The argument that public housing would increase employment and stimulate business activity was probably specious in view of the fact that the PWA program had proven unsuccessful in providing the quick relief that was anticipated. *See* R. FISHER, *supra* note 3, at 85-87.

the ultimate costs, and an unsuccessful attempt to place the administration officials within the civil service.[16] Congressman Stegall of Alabama managed the legislation in the House and followed the same arguments used by Mr. Wagner. He idealistically proclaimed that the bill would abolish "the spawning places of crime and immorality"; but opponents said that the bill was "atrocious," "rank collectivism," and "government intrusion on a purely local problem."[17] On August 18, the bill passed the House by 274 to 86.[18]

After a Senate-House conference, the bill was resubmitted, and was passed on the final day of the Seventy-fifth Congress.[19] On September 1, 1937, the United States Housing Act became law,[20] representing the government's first major excursion into the field of public housing. The bill established the United States Housing Authority (USHA) within the Department of Interior, capitalized the agency with $1 million, and authorized it to issue its bonds not to exceed $500 million.

The USHA was transferred to the Federal Works Agency in 1939.[21] In 1942 the program was shifted to the National Housing Agency along with the Federal Housing Administration (FHA); and the new organization took jurisdiction over all nonfarm housing programs of the federal government.[22] At that time the public housing segment of the new agency acquired a new name, the Public Housing Administration (PHA). The National Housing Agency was succeeded by the Housing and Home Finance Agency in 1949[23] and PHA became a part of the new and expanded agency.

The final reorganization occurred in 1965 with the passage of the Housing and Urban Development Act of 1965.[24] The act established the Department of Housing and Urban Development. The two key agencies of the new department, PHA and FHA, were brought under direct control of the secretary, Dr. Robert Weaver, in contrast to their semi-autonomous position under the Housing and Home Finance Agency which Weaver had called "an administrative monstrosity."[25]

II

THE PROGRAM AND HOW IT WORKS[26]

The federal agency which now administers the public housing program is called the Housing Assistance Administration (HAA). HAA neither constructs nor

---

[16] 81 CONG. REC. 9234-94 (1937).

[17] N.Y. Times, Aug. 22, 1937, at 1, col. 8.

[18] See N.Y. Times, Aug. 19, 1937, at 1, col. 5.

[19] See N.Y. Times, supra note 17.

[20] Ch. 896, 50 Stat. 888 (1937).

[21] Reorganization Plan No. 1, 53 Stat. 1423 (1939).

[22] Exec. Order No. 9070, 7 Fed. Reg. 1529 (1942).

[23] Reorganization Plan No. 3, 61 Stat. 954 (1947).

[24] Pub. L. No. 89-117, 79 Stat. 451 (codified in scattered sections of 12, 15, 20, 38, 40, 42, 49 U.S.C.).

[25] N.Y. Times, Jan. 14, 1966, at 1, col. 1, at 32, col. 5. The other agencies within the Department are the Community Facilities Administration, the Urban Renewal Administration, and the Federal National Mortgage Association (which retains its independent status).

[26] Diagram showing the initial construction and operation processes are contained in appendix A.

operates housing projects itself, but assists the localities in their efforts to provide adequate housing for low-income families.

In order to avail itself of the largesse and advisory assistance of the federal government, the local governing body (*e.g.,* the city council or the board of aldermen) must adopt an ordinance creating a local housing authority. This is done pursuant to state enabling legislation.[27]

Upon establishing a housing authority, the local government appoints a board of commissioners which represents various interest groups in the community. The board formulates plans and policies for the authority, and appoints an executive director to conduct the day-to-day administration of the program.

When the local authority devises a plan for a housing project, it submits the plan to HAA. The federal agency then issues a "program reservation" which is an informal statement that upon completion of certain prerequisites HAA will assist in the development of the requested units.[28] Among the prerequisites are: approval of the project by a resolution of the local governing body, a showing of need for the particular project, a demonstration that there is a feasible plan for the relocation of families to be displaced by the project, and HAA approval of the site and basic structural concept.

The first formal accord between HAA and the local authority is the preliminary loan contract, executed to provide funds with which the local authority hires an architect and finances surveys and appraisals. A development program is produced by the authority, giving a detailed account of the plans and schedule of the project. During this stage, HAA can lend up to ninety per cent of the cost of the project.[29] If the loans are not needed immediately upon receipt, the local authority invests the funds in short-term securities. The development program report is a prerequisite to the annual contributions contract.

The annual contributions contract[30] is the agreement by which HAA promises to pay annual grants, for up to forty years, to cover capital costs of the project. The operational and maintenance expenses of the project are met by the rental income from tenants, and if there is any surplus—which there often is—it must be used to reduce the annual contribution of the next year.

After the contributions contract is executed, and all objections which HAA may have had are satisfied, the project "goes out for bids." Contractors submit bids in sealed envelopes which are opened at a public hearing and the bid prices announced. Selection of a contractor (which requires HAA approval) is announced several weeks after the hearing; the contract is awarded to the lowest responsible bidder. After the

---

[27] Every state except Utah and Wyoming has an enabling statute.

[28] U.S. PUBLIC HOUSING ADMINISTRATION, DEP'T OF HOUSING AND URBAN DEVELOPMENT, PUBLIC HOUSING FACT SHEET 2 (undated) [hereinafter cited as PUBLIC HOUSING FACT SHEET].

[29] § 9, 42 U.S.C. § 1409 (1964).

[30] § 10, 42 U.S.C. § 1410 (1964, Supp. II, 1965-66).

contractor posts a bond with surety, the local authority issues an "order to proceed," and construction is started. The local authority deals only with the prime contractor—the bidder—who in turn purchases his own materials and supplies and hires subcontractors. The contractor is responsible for clearing the site, grading,[31] construction, and installation of facilities.[32] He must submit monthly reports which are transmitted to HAA for inspection, and any changes must await approval by HAA of a "change order."

During the early stages of the construction, the local authority will issue short-term notes to retire all of the federal loans, with interest. The notes are tax-exempt, low-interest securities, guaranteed by the annual contributions contract. Such notes usually mature within three to six months of issuance, and are paid off by reissues, each issue secured by the contributions contract. In effect, the local authority is "[translating] federal aid into going low-rent projects and *Aaa* credit rating."[33]

When the project is about eighty per cent completed, the authority issues its permanent bonds, usually forty-year securities bearing tax-exempt interest at three per cent to 4.5 per cent. Despite the relatively low yields, these bonds are attractive investments, especially to the institutional investors, because they are backed by the federal commitment.

The local authority sets the rental and income limits (with HAA approval), handles tenant selection (pursuant to HAA guidelines), and then enters the project management phase. A manager is employed, who will be compensated from funds derived from the monthly rentals.

III

THE DISILLUSIONMENT

Almost three decades after the public housing program was inaugurated, few people are willing to support the effort as it now stands. Even those who originally championed the program have since defected and now voice strong criticism.

In 1937 those who opposed the program most vigorously could be divided into two groups: (1) the interest groups—builders, suppliers, mortgage lenders, and real estate associations—who feared that government intervention would disrupt the industry;[34] and (2) conservatives, who opposed the cost and contended that government-subsidized housing would be socialistic, unfair competition with private enterprise, and an

---

[31] However, if the housing authority is working with a local urban development agency, the development agency may have already purchased, cleared, and graded the land.

[32] The contractor is not responsible for supplying cabinets, window shades, appliances, and so forth. These items are purchased through government contracts by the local authority.

[33] R. FISHER, *supra* note 3, at 113.

[34] *Id.* at 21; Mulvihill, *Problems in the Management of Public Housing*, 35 TEMP. L.Q. 163, 165 (1962).

unwarranted subsidy to families who "have no more right to a free new home than to a free new car."[35]

But today, the critics are far greater in number, and represent more than interest groups and conservatives. The new criticism represents the disillusionment of liberals who probably expected too much from the program. As one student of the slums in New York City has said:[36]

> Once upon a time we thought that if we could only get our problem families out of those dreadful slums, then papa would stop taking dope, mama would stop chasing around, and Junior would stop carrying a knife. Well, we've got them in a nice new apartment with modern kitchen and a recreation center. And they're the same bunch of bastards they always were.

Mrs. Catherine Bauer, who helped draft the 1937 act, is an example of ardent supporter turned critic. In a 1957 article,[37] Mrs. Bauer explained that public housing is not like most social experiments in a democratic society. Usually, she said, such experiments begin as an abstract idea, frequently in the atmosphere of theoretical debate, and then either die off or are modified and adapted to actual conditions and become an integral part of the ordinary scheme of things. "Public housing, after more than two decades, still drags along in a kind of limbo, continuously controversial, not dead but never more than half alive."[38]

Lawrence Friedman has attempted to explain why the efforts of twenty-nine years have wrought such controversial products.[39] The program began, he contends, as an effort to assist the submerged middle class, those respectable, honest workers who were unfortunately caught in the depression and needed only a stepping stone to regain their rightful income level. Enacted with this attitude, there was little opposition; most of the early projects were low-rise rowhouses, blending fairly well with their surroundings, and often suburban in location and design. But with the end of the Second World War and the need to prime the pumps to sustain the prosperity of the war years, the government focused its attention on assistance for veterans and the middle class (through tax breaks, insurance, and other subsidies). The fabled flight to the suburbs began in earnest. With this dramatic shift in emphasis, public housing languished: the projects were boxed in the central parts of the cities because the suburbs were reserved for the subdivisions, the projects inherited the "certainly, indisputably and irreversibly poor," and thus the program lost its appeal. Urban land was difficult to find and very expensive when available; thus the vast, high-rise edifices were required. And since the occupants were not respectable, submerged, middle-

---

[35] EDITORS OF FORTUNE MAGAZINE, THE EXPLODING METROPOLIS 105-06 (1957) [hereinafter cited as FORTUNE EDITORS].

[36] Id. at 106.

[37] Bauer, *The Dreary Deadlock of Public Housing*, ARCHITECTURAL FORUM, May 1957, at 140.

[38] Id.

[39] Friedman, *Public Housing and the Poor: An Overview*, 54 CALIF. L. REV. 642 (1966).

class families, the projects could be built without thought of aesthetics or amenities and ineptly run, without much chance of outcry.[40]

Whatever the historical reasons, there is no denying that today the public housing program is subject to many quite plausible criticisms. The most prevalent of these are examined more closely below.

IV

THE CRITICISMS: ANALYSES AND EVALUATIONS

A. Design

The object of most controversy in the program is probably the physical appearance of the public housing structures. Architects and city planners recoil at the sight of the projects, money-conscious politicians refer to them as "barracks" when opposing expansion of the program, the occupants themselves are apparently not pleased with the surroundings, and the liberals who fight for better housing tend to employ the art of evasion to escape reference to design when praising the products of the program.

1. *Role of the Architect*

Project planning and design are responsibilities of the local housing authority. Once an authority decides to construct a project, it retains the architect, cooperates with him, and compensates him for his services. The federal government, however, is not a distant benefactor. Throughout the process, the low-rent housing manual of HAA—a dictionary-thick set of regulations and standards—must be consulted for minimum standards, maximum allowances, cost limitations, room size, required facilities, and so on. And when an issue is unclear or the architect wishes an administrative variance, consultation and negotiation with the HAA regional office are necessary.

An architect who has designed several New England public housing projects describes the process as follows.[41] First, the architect is retained by the local authority for a feasibility study. He is told the number of units that are desired and the site of the proposed project. After the study, any revisions in the authority's original plan are made, and the revised plan is sent to HAA regional headquarters for approval. If approved without further changes, the architect next draws up a very detailed preliminary work (the federal manual requires greater specificity than a designer would ordinarily use for a private project). This drawing, in turn, is screened by the regional office which may reject it, approve it, or approve it with modifications. If the architect has attempted to employ ingenuity and thus has deviated from the traditional patterns, the regional staff of accountants and draftsmen may balk; if, however, the regional

---

[40] This analysis by Professor Friedman needs further investigation. Several persons with whom I have spoken suggest a similar historical factor in the public housing program, but this theory does not seem to be substantiated in the literature.

[41] Interview with Carl Granbery, architect, Nov. 1, 1966.

office is attuned to the current emphasis on aesthetics, a conference may be called at which the architect and the local authority officials will be expected to support the sketches with a persuasive argument and a good-faith showing of confidence in the plan, after which approval will be given. The architect then produces a "working drawing" to be used by the contractor during construction. During the construction process, the architect acts as the housing authority's "agent" in seeing that the contractor abides by the plans. Any deviation requires approval of the architect, the housing authority, and HAA, and involves complicated "change order" procedures that can take as long as a working day to prepare and transmit.

2. *Design Framework*

In designing a public housing project, an architect is confronted with the same problems that face any architect designing a large urban development; but the problems are exacerbated by the miles of red tape and the already-formulated federal standards.

There are three considerations in design of a project:[42]

(1) Design of the units. This step concerns the arrangement of the rooms within the unit, the shapes and sizes of the rooms, placement of doors and windows, and location of interior facilities. In the jargon of the architect, most of the facts in this consideration are "given" in public housing projects. The architect has little room to maneuver with new formulae and innovation because of the HAA regulations.

(2) Design of the building. This involves the lay-out of the various units within the structure, the location of stairways, elevators and corridors, and the design of the exterior. Again, this is largely a "given" in public housing, because HAA wants to cut sizes and costs as much as possible on each structure—a result of Congress's annual demands for production of more units per amounts appropriated. This attitude requires a certain size limitation and a certain density within the structures, factors that combine with cost limitation to give the architect little freedom.

(3) Siting. This aspect of architecture is concerned with the arrangement of the buildings on the project site, the landscaping, and the relationship of the project to "the outside world." The architect here has some degree of latitude and can often apply his imagination to contribute to the appearance of the project. But even so, his freedom is not unbounded. Playgrounds must be provided, parking facilities sufficient to accommodate about one vehicle per unit are necessary, and only the minimum amount of trees, shrubs and ornaments can be financed.

---

[42] Interview with Bruce Adams, Associate Professor, School of Architecture, Yale University, Nov. 1, 1966.

3. High Rise and High Density

Some critics presume that the root of the evil in public housing design is the high density. But as all contemporary city planners and architects would confirm, the principle of high-rise, high-density living is finding acceptance. The concept has swept Europe and England, particularly in those areas where land is scarce; and any Sunday edition of the New York Times illustrates the growing attraction which the concept is receiving in large urban areas of this country.[43]

This modern concept cannot, however, be applied to low-cost housing without becoming distorted. It is suitable for middle- and upper-income families for several reasons: (1) the term "high density," as used in this article, refers to number of families per structure, and in the upper income brackets the families can take advantage of their mobility to frequently break the monotony of the acres of concrete; (2) since the rents are higher, the projects can be aesthetically appealing and the facilities can be comparatively luxurious; and (3) there is no stigma attached to the developments.[44]

Thus it is not the concept of high density and high rise that makes the projects "drab, ugly blocks of cement standing like soldiers,"[45] but rather a combination of these factors with the low-cost feature and the stigma attached to living in the projects.

4. Proposed Design Reforms

Many proposals for change have been offered by designers and planners in recent years; they range from suggestions of minor variances to radical departures from the present program.

Albert Mayer, a New York City architect, lamented, "How can you expect a positive or creative individual or social response to such a grim, unimaginative third-ratedness," and then proposed four alterations in the design concept.[46] He suggested that more open space be provided in the projects to provide sunlight and simple beauty; that more lighting facilities be made available so that the projects can be safer and more suitable for nighttime recreational opportunities; that the acres of asphalt be swept away with a revision in the concepts of parking, even if it requires putting the vehicles away from the immediate vicinity or going underground; and that there be a mingling of high-rise towers with lower structures in the same project to provide diversity and more sunlight but at the same time utilizing the land space. As for the interior of the units, Mr. Mayer concluded that the present condition was

---

[43] *See generally* R. KATZ, INTENSITY OF DEVELOPMENT AND LIVEABILITY OF MULTI-FAMILY HOUSING PROJECTS (U.S. Federal Housing Administration, Technical Study TS 7.14, 1963); R. JENSEN, HIGH DENSITY LIVING (1966).

[44] Interview with Bruce Adams, *supra* note 42.

[45] Friedman, *supra* note 39, at 652.

[46] *Public Housing Design*, 20 J. HOUSING 133 (1963), quoting Albert Mayer.

satisfactory but warned that cost limitations should not be so low and inflexible as to prohibit serviceable bathroom and kitchen facilities.

Mrs. Bauer's 1957 attack described the program as the "bare bones of . . . New Deal theory" not yet "covered with the solid flesh of present-day reality."[47] She criticized the interior design as deficient in space and in privacy; she said that the projects were too large, with high densities and few amenities, thus fostering the "island concept" which reinforced a "charity stigma." While most Americans prefer one-story dwellings, she observed, public housing continues to be high-rise. Her proposals for change recognized the need for more public housing, but focused on the possibility of abolishing the public landlord concept and allowing private enterprise to build the projects, with rents subsidized by the government. A group of prominent architects, sociologists, planners and financiers echoed Mrs. Bauer's criticisms and made suggestions of their own in the next issue of *Architectural Forum*.[48]

James Rouse, a mortgage banker, advocated a halt to the high-rise projects and concentration on the small, scattered structures. A New York social worker, Ellen Lurie, proposed an end to the public landlord and approved Mrs. Bauer's suggestion that private sponsors should build apartment houses with the tenant's rents subsidized by the government. She warned that the private projects would be no better, however, unless consideration is given to livability. To make her point, she queried: How can a mother manage five kids from a twelfth-floor window? William Wheaton, professor of city planning at the University of Pennsylvania, suggested that the projects be eliminated and replaced with rowhouses, garden apartments, and scattered units, so as to blend with the community.

Charles Abrams, noted author and student of urban problems, emphasized the need for ownership. The poor look to ownership of property as security and prestige just as do other Americans, he pointed out. He recommended tenant co-operatives, and loans to low-income families so that they could buy modest houses in the suburbs at 0-3 per cent interest. In a more poignant vein, Henry Churchill, architect, proclaimed that the word "project" should be declared unconstitutional and stricken from the dictionary. He favored abolition of all local housing authorities and transferral of their responsibilities to the municipal agencies concerned with physical change in the community. He, too, advocated private construction of apartments with government subsidy.

Some observers have suggested that the best way to improve the design of the cities is to concentrate on construction for middle-class homes, and allow the currently unpopular "filter down" theory to operate for the benefit of the low-income families.[49] Mrs. Bauer, on the other hand, has contended that this theory can-

---

[47] Bauer, *supra* note 37.

[48] *The Dreary Deadlock of Public Housing—How to Break It*, ARCHITECTURAL FORUM, June 1957, at 139.

[49] Interview with Bruce Adams, *supra* note 42. Adams referred to this theory as an alternative expounded by many persons, but did not propose it himself.

not help "within a thousand years" because of the constant increase in urban growth, the continuing low-income status of many persons, racial discrimination, and the fact that much slum housing is so intolerable that it should be torn down immediately.[50] Secretary Weaver has explained that "by the time high-priced housing has depreciated enough to be within the financial reach of the poor, it is pretty bad housing, either in terms of its physical condition or its overcrowded pattern of occupancy."[51]

B. Isolation and Segregation

A frequent indictment is that public housing sets low-income families apart from the rest of the community instead of helping these people break through the barriers which the slums have built between them and the middle-class subculture. And since most often the low-income bracket is composed largely of nonwhites, vehement protests from civil rights advocates assert that the traditional large-project approach to public housing segregates the nonwhites from the white community at a time when national policy is quite the contrary.

Although the problems of social isolation of the poor and racial segregation are too often inextricably intertwined, for purposes of this article the two are considered separately.

1. *Isolation*

One of the causes of disillusionment with the program is the way in which it tends to herd low-income families into institutionalized settings, separating them from the rest of society. It was once thought that decent housing would automatically transform the slum-dwellers into ideal citizens and social integration would take care of itself. But the vast, high-rise projects with their cold and impersonal appearances "constitute a continuing, humiliating reminder that occupants are wards of the state."[52] The reminder is not only obvious to the occupants—any observant passer-by can recognize the projects for what they are.

An example of this enclave-like project is Pruitt-Igoe of St. Louis. Built in 1954 at a cost of $36.8 million, this monstrosity houses 10,000 persons in several eleven-story buildings. Even the much-needed $7 million rejuvenation of the project, now in progress, will further the isolation with eleven picnic areas, thirteen playgrounds, a beer garden, a theatre, and a community center.[53]

This situation is repeated time and again in city after city, especially where land is scarce and the housing shortage is acute. Even in New Haven, a city which has been praised for its redevelopment efforts, the main low-rent project is a drab looking area of town where even the street patterns contribute to the detachment.

---

[50] Bauer, *supra* note 37.
[51] R. WEAVER, DILEMMAS OF URBAN AMERICA 102 (1965).
[52] FORTUNE EDITORS 107.
[53] Wall Street Journal, Sept. 26, 1966, at 18, col. 4.

The recent Logue Report on New York City's urban problems attacked the isolation in the city's projects. It charged that the large-scale projects "have concentrated low-income families in isolated areas and failed to blend with or complement existing neighborhoods."[54]

Largely because of the criticisms of the institutionalized setting which the project presents, HAA no longer favors the large-scale project; one official calls it "a thing of the past."[55] Although this may be wishful thinking, particularly since many cities continue to erect the structures, emphasis seems to be shifting to new approaches, when possible; the most promising of these new approaches are discussed later in this article.

One proposal which is not presently being tested, except in projects for the elderly, is for dispersal of new low-rent housing projects in smaller apartments throughout the community. This would eliminate the detachment and institutionalized atmosphere of the projects, and would also improve design; but there are several very difficult problems.

First, the cost per unit rises appreciably with a diminution of units per project, so that such a plan, if submitted to HAA, would probably be rejected as too expensive. It has been argued in rebuttal that funds already appropriated but not expended by the local authorities could be used in accord with such an approach. Another argument goes further and asserts that Congress should loosen its grip on the public purse strings and allocate as much as ten per cent of the total national income to housing.[56]

Second, myriad small projects cannot house as many families as a couple of well-located large projects. This is a logical criticism, particularly as to those areas which are destroying by slum clearance and urban renewal whatever low-income housing does exist. On the other hand, it could be said that perhaps the emphasis should shift from an effort at wholesale rehousing to concentration on fewer families—providing new housing for a few persons at a time but providing the services and facilities in such a manner that they can have the opportunity to break the social barrier.

A third objection is that land is simply unavailable, except at very high prices, in those neighborhoods into which the proponents of this approach wish to send the low-income families. Where land is available in large parcels sufficient to accommodate three- or four-unit projects, the expense, the zoning and building code regulations, and the vigorous opposition from the residents of the invaded neighborhood would pose grave problems. Although there are those who would overlook the

---

[54] INSTITUTE OF PUBLIC ADMINISTRATION, REPORT OF STUDY GROUP 12 (E. Logue, Chairman, Sept. 1966).

[55] McGuire, *Rehabilitation for Public Housing*, 22 J. HOUSING 595, 596 (1965).

[56] *See* Lynd, *Urban Renewal—For Whom?*, in NEW PERSPECTIVES ON POVERTY 104 (A. Shostak & W. Gomberg eds. 1965). This view was reiterated in an interview, Nov. 8, 1966.

cost factor, a different view would be taken by the taxpayer—who would ask why he is supplying suburban living for the poor when he can hardly afford it himself. The opposition forthcoming from the neighbors would be to a great extent justified: land values would go down, there is strong evidence that the project property would not be kept presentable, and the single-family zoning pattern would be cracked. In fact, it is questionable whether such a move would be of social value to the tenants, unless only those well-adjusted, responsible families were chosen, thereby leaving the projects to the "rock-bottom poor."[57]

2. The Race Problem

When discussing the race issue in public housing, there are two factors to consider: tenant selection and site selection. The manner in which local authorities select applicants for particular projects obviously has a direct bearing on the racial composition of the projects. The way in which local authorities select sites for projects also has a bearing on racial composition. If the units are built in an all-white neighborhood, the project will probably be all white. If the project is located in a nonwhite area—as most of them are—the project will probably be exclusively or predominantly nonwhite.

When the Housing Act was enacted, little attention was given to racial composition of the projects. The separate-but-equal philosophy prevailed, and enjoyed judicial sanction. As late as 1949, an effort to ban discrimination in housing projects was defeated in the Senate, 49-31.[58] Even after the United States Supreme Court removed official imprimatur from the old separate-but-equal doctrine in 1954,[59] the Public Housing Administration did little to apply the mandate to the field of public housing. Agitation was avoided in an effort to retain the support of southern congressmen whose votes were needed to prevent the program from being swept away by the tide of disenchantment that prevailed in the 1950s.[60]

In 1962, Executive Order No. 11,063[61] ordered an end to racial discrimination in tenant selection; a provision to this effect was to be included in all annual contributions contracts after November 20, 1962.

Title VI of the Civil Rights Act of 1964[62] and the PHA regulations adopted pursuant thereto make it clear that all funds disbursed by PHA must have non-discrimination features attached, regardless of the date of the contract. Some writers say that these provisions were aimed as much at site selection as at tenant selection.[63]

---

[57] Friedman, *supra* note 39, at 667.

[58] *See* R. FISHER, *supra* note 3, at 260.

[59] Brown v. Board of Education, 347 U.S. 483 (1954).

[60] *See generally* Comment, *The Public Housing Administration and Discrimination in Federally Assisted Low-Rent Housing*, 64 MICH. L. REV. 871 (1966), for a historical study of discrimination in public housing.

[61] 3 C.F.R. 261 (Supp. 1962), 42 U.S.C. § 1982 (1964).

[62] 42 U.S.C. §§ 2000d to 2000d-4 (1964).

[63] *E.g.*, Comment, *supra* note 60.

At present, the federal agency approves of a local authority's policies if based on "free choice." This policy permits tenants to go to any project they wish so long as there is a vacancy. On paper the plan is free from the onus of discrimination, since nonwhites can go to "white" projects and vice versa. Some local authorities, however, have adopted more positive measures of integration due to local pressures.

The New York City Housing Authority has gone through several gyrations trying to meet the demands of civil rights advocates and at the same time to maintain a realistic approach to the housing problem. Before 1960, the city authority followed the free choice policy, but many leaders in Manhattan complained that this produced racial imbalance in the projects since whites were always selecting all-white projects, leaving the nonwhites in predominantly nonwhite projects. Thus, in August of 1960 the authority adopted a plan whereby all vacancies in the projects which were largely composed of whites would be held for nonwhites, in an effort to produce racial balance. After four years, however, this measure met ironically with disapproval of Harlem leaders, who claimed that the vacancies in Harlem projects were being held for outsiders (whites) when they should be filled as quickly as possible by Harlem slumdwellers. With 85,000 applicants per year and only 6,000 available units, the denunciations of the "holding" policy were valid. So, in January of 1964 the authority announced that its "holding" policy had been abandoned and it would fill vacancies on a first-come-first-served basis.[64]

Jersey City, meanwhile, was adopting a plan whereby all vacancies in predominantly Negro projects would be filled two-for-one by white applicants and vice versa, and that anyone who refused to accept an assignment would be pushed to the bottom of the project preference list.[65]

There are those who think that any concentrated effort intentionally to integrate housing projects is an abuse of freedom of association, and that the only fair method of tenant selection is that of free choice. One writer has contended that the primary objective of the program should be slum clearance and decent housing, not racial integration, and that forced integration is "social compulsion manipulated according to plans of self-appointed social engineers."[66]

The site selection issue is even more difficult than the tenant selection problem. Since one purpose of the program is to eliminate slums, most projects are built in or near the blighted areas of the central part of the city, which are usually heavily nonwhite areas. Obviously such projects will not have a balanced racial composition unless the local authority brings in persons from other neighborhoods under a compulsory placement plan such as that which lost favor with all sides in New York City.

---

[64] N.Y. Times, Jan. 27, 1964, at 16, col. 7.

[65] N.Y. Times, June 19, 1964, at 12, col. 1.

[66] Avins, *Anti-Discrimination Legislation as an Infringement on Freedom of Choice*, 6 N.Y.L.F. 13, 37 (1960).

The scattered-site approach could solve many of the racial problems in public housing; but all of the difficulties of that approach would still be present, accentuated by the race issue.

C. Problems of Management

A public housing project cannot be managed like a private middle-class apartment house. Discipline must be maintained to preserve the reputation of the program and to prevent the tenants from living in terror. The central problem seems to be: How can a project be effectively managed with the regulations, policing techniques, and necessary disciplinary demands, but yet provide an atmosphere of minimum interference, self-improvement, and responsibility.

To abolish the large projects would certainly eliminate some of the managerial problems, but since the existing structures are expected to last for a long time, and new ones are springing up every year despite the disdain for them, there must be some consideration of solutions to the problems of management in the projects.

1. Income and Rent Limits

One of the chief complaints, usually categorized as a management problem— although it could be a topic of discussion in itself—is the income limit rule, which sets a limit as to how much a tenant can earn before he must leave the project. To be eligible for admission to a project, an applicant must be within the statutory definition of "low-income family."[67] Formerly, this was set as one whose income did not exceed five times the annual rental of the unit. Since 1959 this statutory definition has been abolished and the local authorities set their own income limits for admittance, with HAA approval. The local authorities are still following the old statutory standard, with some flexibility. The rentals, on the other hand, are governed by section 14(7) of the Act,[68] which provides that there must be a gap of at least twenty per cent between the upper rental level for admission into a public housing project and the lowest rents at which private enterprise is supplying a substantial amount of adequate housing in the area. Thus, an applicant whose income is $300 per month would pay a monthly rental of about $60 (1/5 of 300). If there is at least a twenty per cent gap between this amount ($60) and the lowest rents at which private enterprise is providing a substantial amount of adequate housing, the applicant is eligible for public housing. Once admitted, his rental will increase with any increase in income. Once the tenant's income has increased beyond the approved maximum income limits for continued occupancy (*i.e.*, once the tenant's income is so high that his monthly rentals are more than four-fifths the amount of rent at which private enterprise is providing housing), the tenant must be evicted.

This rule has been roundly criticized. Charles Abrams, for example, says,[69]

---

[67] § 2(2), 42 U.S.C. § 1402(2) (Supp. II, 1965-66).

[68] 42 U.S.C. § 1414(7) (1964).

[69] C. ABRAMS, THE CITY IS THE FRONTIER 37 (1965).

Income limitations in public housing have brought no end of troubles. Some tenants have concealed their incomes, some have refused to work overtime, and some have even turned down better-paying jobs. A child reaching working age may disqualify the family for continued occupancy unless he moves out. Where the American family normally boasts of financial improvement, a public housing tenant may find it the prelude to an eviction notice. The more successful occupants who could give leadership to the community are usually those forced to go. . . . Departure of the better wage earners, white and Negro, also tends to stamp the project as the haven of the poor.

Since there exists a twenty per cent gap between what the tenant will be paying in rent and what he would have to pay for an adequate dwelling on the open market, an evicted tenant is often tossed back into the slums or at least into substandard housing.

As amended in 1961, the Housing Act provides that local authorities must require a tenant whose income has increased beyond the approved maximum income limit to leave the project "*unless* the public housing agency [the local authority] determines that, due to special circumstances, the family is unable to find decent, safe and sanitary housing within its financial reach although making every reasonable effort to do so."[70] It would seem that this amendment could be used by the local authorities in a flexible manner to permit a tenant to stay when his income has increased above the prescribed limit but has not risen so high as to elevate him above the twenty per cent gap into an income bracket that would allow him to obtain adequate housing with a reasonable percentage of his earnings.

There are several reasons why these persons should be allowed to remain in the project. Although they may not be the pillars of the community, the very fact that their incomes have risen above limit illustrates that they are to some degree at least conscientiously attempting to improve themselves. Thus, they can provide some measure of socioeconomic integration; and perhaps their ambitions and desires to break the cycle of dependency can influence some of the unmotivated crowd which inevitably will be a part of the project population. Another reason for allowing them to remain is that such a policy would provide a degree of permanency or stabilization for the poor; such an attitude is needed in the projects to give the tenants a desire to improve the appearance of the place and to participate in the social life, such as it is, of the community. A third reason is purely economic. Since the annual rental income carries the operational and maintenance expenses of the project, the local authority should want to retain these families paying higher rents. The higher rent payments help to make up for the very low rents which some families pay and thus aid many marginal projects to remain solvent. Finally, since those persons whose incomes will usually rise above the limit are white, a rigid

---

[70] § 10(g)(3), 42 U.S.C. § 1410(g)(3) (1964). (Emphasis added.)

income limit policy could tip the delicate scales and thus cause the project to become a subsidized ghetto for the lowest-income nonwhites in the community.[71]

There is some evidence that many, if not most, local housing authorities are now more flexible in their application of the income limit rule. There are several ways of accomplishing this flexibility. The local authority can interpret liberally the new provision in section 10(g)(3) and allow the family to remain in the project unless it can find adequate housing within its financial means in the private market. Or the local authority can juggle the figures in determining the tenant's "income." Since the determinative income is not gross income, the authority can play with several types of deductions and exemptions. Also, the manner in which the local authority considers assets other than income differs from place to place.[72] For example, a southern authority allows "administrative exemptions" for child care in cases of members of the Armed Forces and for a portion of the income of a minor. In that city, a family of four who is admitted to the project with a net income of $3400 may continue occupancy at least until its net income is $4200.[73] There is evidence that managers "go along" with high paid tenants in other cities, even for a year or two; a Chicago manager has said that these are "good" tenants whom he does not want to lose.[74]

Many critics have been arguing for some time that one way to cure the harshness of the income limit would be to allow the local authority to sell the unit to a tenant when his rent payment becomes so high as to be sufficient to cover debt service on the unit.[75] Charles Abrams has suggested that HAA consider tenant co-operatives.[76]

The Housing and Urban Development Act of 1965 amended the Housing Act to incorporate some of these proposals to a certain extent. Section 15(9) of the Act now provides that a local authority may permit a tenant to acquire a dwelling unit within a project as long as it is "suitable by reason of its detached or semidetached construction for sale and for occupancy by such purchaser or a member or members of his family."[77] Although the new provision would seem of no value to those families living in the high-rise projects, since by no stretch of the imagination could those units be described as "detached" or "semidetached," the enactment could benefit occupants of triplexes and quadriplexes and those persons in the projects for the elderly.

[71] C. Abrams, supra note 69; Friedman, supra note 39, at 659.

[72] Mulvihill, supra note 34, at 182.

[73] Letter from the office of Frederic Fay, Executive Director, Richmond Housing and Redevelopment Authority, Richmond, Virginia, to the author, Oct. 1966.

[74] Friedman, supra note 39, at 664.

[75] E.g., The Dreary Deadlock of Public Housing—How to Break It, Architectural Forum, June 1957, at 139.

[76] Discussed at p. 500 supra.

[77] 42 U.S.C. 1415(9) (Supp. II, 1965-66). S. 2343, 90th Cong., 1st Sess. § 1 (1967), now pending in the Senate Committee on Banking and Currency, was introduced on August 24, 1967, by Senator Tydings and Senator Mondale to amend section 15(9) of the Act. This bill would permit a tenant to acquire a dwelling unit in any project, and to make monthly payments to the agency sufficient to amortize a sales price, equal to the greater of the unamortized debt or the appraised value of the unit at time of purchase, in not more than forty years.

2. *Tenant Discipline*

Some observers think that it was the postwar emphasis on government programs for the middle-class that left the housing projects to the permanently poor.[78] Whether or not these programs are the proximate cause, it is evident today that a chief characteristic of too many projects is the number of chronically unemployed, the alcoholics and addicts, the unmarried women with children, and the police cases. This less-than-desirable set of circumstances presents the housing officials with serious management problems. It is reported, further, that the move-out rate for public housing tenants is one out of four per year, with a large number of these families apparently leaving because of the inability of the housing authority to deal with the problem of misfit families.[79]

The family with no male head is particularly troublesome. In the case of a woman with several children by different fathers, officials realize that the welfare and reputation of the project must be given as much, or more, consideration than the indigence of the family in question. One housing official recalled for this writer a recent case in which municipal social workers were attempting to gain admittance to a housing project for such a family. The official felt that, despite the unfortunate financial condition of the family, it would be detrimental to the project to allow this family into the project. New Bern, North Carolina, has adopted a rule calling for eviction of any tenant to whom an illegitimate child is born during occupancy,[80] and officials in Chicago and Cincinnati, among others, have formulated similar policies.[81]

3. *Building Maintenance*

Vandalism and filth pose other problems for those in charge of management. It is said that vandalism in New York City costs, in some years, as much as $40,000 per project.[82] Chicago reports that in some years one fourth of all federal assistance to the local authority is used to cover the costs of vandalism, waste, mismanagement and union featherbedding.[83] In the Pruitt-Igoe project in St. Louis[84] much of the $7 million now being spent on renovation will be used to improve the lighting in the stairs and corridors to lessen crime, modernize the elevators to decrease the number of muggings and sexual assaults, install break-proof ornaments and fixtures to protect them against vandalism, and enclose light bulbs to prevent the constant intentional breakage. At present, the St. Louis authority spends $91,000 per year for guard service to supplement local police efforts at the project.[85]

[78] *E.g.*, Friedman, *supra* note 39.

[79] Mulvihill, *supra* note 34, at 174-75.

[80] Friedman, *supra* note 39, at 658.

[81] Wall Street Journal, April 10, 1958, at 1, col. 8, at 19, col. 2.

[82] Mulvihill, *supra* note 34, at 179.

[83] Wall Street Journal, *supra* note 81.

[84] Discussed at p. 501 *supra*.

[85] Wall Street Journal, Sept. 26, 1966, at 18, col. 4.

A costly maintenance problem is featherbedding. In Chicago, for example, it has been reported that union pressures require that electricians install light bulbs, and carpenters replace screws in brackets. The removal of a hot water heater requires a pipefitter to disconnect the hot water pipe and a plumber to disconnect the cold water pipe. In one Chicago project a survey showed that thirteen janitors working eight hours a day were doing work that should require only five janitors working four hours a day.[86]

In a large operation, such as that conducted by the New York City Housing Authority where $48 million has been spent on painting contracts in the last ten years, corruption can be costly. A recent scandal in Manhattan involved a union official and several housing officials, among others, and led to indictments for rigged bidding and bribery.[87]

D. Costs

Public housing is expensive. Outlays have thus far exceeded a billion dollars, most of which has been paid for by the nation's taxpayers.[88]

The loan contracts that obligate the federal government to lend money to local authorities in the process of construction do not impose upon taxpayers. The loans are repaid by the local authorities, with interest, when they issue their first short-term notes.

The annual contributions contracts, however, obligate the federal government, over a period of up to forty years, in a way that does affect the taxpayer's pocketbook. This contract is an agreement by which HAA promises to pay annual grants to the local housing authority to cover the capital costs of the project. The Housing Act provides, "The faith of the United States is solemnly pledged to the payment of all annual contributions contracted for . . . and there is hereby authorized to be appropriated in each fiscal year . . . the amounts necessary to provide for such payments."[89]

Once Congress authorizes HAA to sign annual contributions contracts for a given number of units, it is, in effect, binding future Congresses to appropriate enough money to meet the capital expenses of the units. Instead of each project costing the government one large lump sum upon construction, the authority receives relatively smaller annual grants toward capital costs over a period of years, with no visible increase in the public debt at that point.[90]

These contributions contracts are also used as security for the notes and bonds

---

[86] Wall Street Journal, *supra* note 81.

[87] N.Y. Times, Oct. 19, 1966, at 1, col. 8.

[88] In 1957, it was estimated that costs had exceeded $626 million to that point. R. FISHER, *supra* note 3, at 126. The figure in the text is obtained by adding the authorizations from 1957 to 1966 to that amount.

[89] § 10(e), 42 U.S.C. §1410(e) (Supp. II, 1965-66).

[90] R. FISHER, *supra* note 3, at 127.

which the local authorities issue. If a local authority should default, the federal government would meet the principal and interest payments on these obligations, paying the bondholders directly. But this arrangement imposes little additional expense to the federal government; it only pledges to bondholders a sum which has already been pledged to the local authority.

The first authorization under the 1937 act was for annual contributions contracts aggregating $5 million for the first year and $7.5 million for each of the next two years.[91] Through the years Congress has repeatedly raised the authorizations.[92] By 1965, in contrast to the 1937 legislation, the authorization was for an increase to $47 million per year over a four-year period.[93]

Costs to the local government are slight. Although the local governing body must agree to exempt the projects from taxation if federal subsidies are to be forthcoming, the local authority may be required by the local government to make payments in lieu of taxes equal to ten per cent of the annual rental income of the project.[94] This usually provides more income for the local government since the projects are often built on sites where slum tenements formerly stood or on vacant land. On the other hand, there may be a hidden cost involved, since the space occupied by the project could some day have been used by an industrial complex.

Another hidden cost to local government may exist in the competition that local authority bonds provide for municipal bonds. Both are long-term, low-interest, tax-exempt obligations. It would seem, however, that authority bond issues would hardly hinder municipal bond sales since there is, at least for the present time, a sufficient market for both.

Many think that public housing is inordinately expensive. It has been said that the capital costs in big projects, which must be met with the annual contributions from the federal government, run as high as $13,000 to $20,000 per unit.[95] For this price the government could buy houses in the suburbs for the poor and turn the family free from the many annoyances of the projects. Charles Abrams has proposed something similar.[96] Whether this approach is advisable is debatable. It would be in direct competition with the private homebuilders and realty companies, a situation which the government has consistently sought to avoid. The many problems associated with scattered-site housing could be reiterated to rebut the argument for suburban houses. And consideration should also be given to the tenants; they may not be able to afford such a program, since they would be left with the expenses of

[91] United States Housing Act of 1937, ch. 896, § 10(e), 50 Stat. 892.

[92] See generally HOUSE COMM. ON BANKING AND CURRENCY, 89TH CONG., 1ST SESS., BASIC LAWS AND AUTHORITIES ON HOUSING AND URBAN DEVELOPMENT 169 n.24 (Comm. Print 1965), for a chronological listing of congressional authorizations.

[93] § 10(e), 42 U.S.C. § 1410(e) (Supp. II, 1965-66).

[94] § 10(h), 42 U.S.C. § 1410(h) (Supp. II, 1965-66).

[95] FORTUNE EDITORS 108.

[96] The Dreary Deadlock of Public Housing—How to Break It, ARCHITECTURAL FORUM, May 1957, at 139.

maintenance, insurance, ad valorem taxes, and the other problems that accompany home ownership.

V

THE NEW STRATEGIES

An effort has been made to take note of the more common criticisms of public housing and to evaluate the suggestions and counter-arguments associated with these criticisms. In the past few years the federal government has been attempting to answer some of these objections by statutory revisions, and by deviating from the old traditionalism with several new programs.

A. "Section 23 Leasing"

Leased-housing programs for low-income families had been tested prior to 1965 in several cities, including Boston, New Haven, Ann Arbor, and Washington. They had been effective and workable. Thus, in 1965, Congress enlarged the leased-housing program by enacting legislation designed to aid the housing authorities in providing quarters for low-income families in private accommodations. This enactment was a part of the Housing and Urban Development Act and it added section 23 to the Housing Act.[97] Of the units authorized by Congress for 1965-69, 40,000 of these units may be obtained through this leasing procedure.[98]

Before initiating a section 23 program, a local authority must obtain local government approval. Then, the authority makes application to HAA, showing, among other things, that the leasing of existing units will not put a strain on the total housing supply in the community.[99] Once approved, the local authority can lease standard housing and sublease to persons eligible for public housing; or the authority can enter into agreements with owners of substandard dwellings whereby the owners will upgrade the units to code standards before the authority will accept them. The latter practice is more common; and it has the value of involving public housing in the total neighborhood improvement effort.

When improvement of the dwelling is required, commitment is made prior to the renovation so that the owner can obtain financing to do the work. Once the work is completed, and if it meets HAA standards, the local authority can either lease the unit from the owner and sublease to a tenant, or it can enter into a working contract with the owner and allow the owner to lease directly to the tenant. The property owner may select the tenants, or he may choose to give the responsibility to the local authority. In either case, the local authority retains the sole right to evict

---

[97] 42 U.S.C. § 1421b (Supp. II, 1965-66).

[98] PUBLIC HOUSING FACT SHEET 4.

[99] U.S. DEP'T OF HOUSING AND URBAN DEVELOPMENT, THE LEASING PROGRAM FOR LOW-INCOME FAMILIES 2 (1966) [hereinafter cited as LEASING PROGRAM].

the tenant (but it agrees to consider any complaints which the owner may have during the course of the lease). If the owner is to select the tenants, he must agree to approve them without regard to race, creed, color, or national origin.[100] The lease must be for not less than twelve nor more than sixty months in duration.[101]

The rental provisions of the Housing Act are also applicable under this program. The tenant's rent is approximately one-fifth of his income; and the difference between this figure and the actual cost of the rent and utilities (except water) is paid by the local authority with the annual contributions from the federal government. The federal contribution cannot exceed the amount that would be available for a newly-constructed project to accommodate comparable numbers, sizes, and kinds of families.[102] An additional federal contribution of up to $120 per annum can be provided to assist the tenants if they are elderly, disabled or, in some instances, displaced.[103]

This program is not intended as an eventual substitute for new construction; HAA states that the section 23 program "can be useful in a community as a short-term supplement to the basic supply of housing owned by the local housing authority."[104] This program is available mainly for two-parent families eligible for public housing but who show a preference for nonproject residence and demonstrate a potential for adjusting to the neighborhood in which they will live.[105] The program also seems to be directed to the large families who can seldom find accommodation in the projects because statutory cost ceilings limit unit size. In Washington, for example, only thirteen five-bedroom units were available for applicants in 1964, although there were 478 families on the waiting list for that size unit.[106]

The new leasing program has three advantages, other than the obvious one of eliminating the management problems found in the big projects:

(1) There is less restraint on a tenant's increasing his income, because if he should rise above the public housing limit he can renew the lease with the property owner on his own accord and thereby remain in the house.

(2) The program encourages homeowners to upgrade their deteriorating residential properties to lease; this improves neighborhoods that are about to slip into "slum" status.

(3) The problems of isolation and racial balance are diminished, although there would still be difficulties in those neigbhorhoods that would rebel against a nonwhite family.

---

[100] Id. at 7.
[101] § 23(d), 42 U.S.C. § 1421b(d) (Supp. II, 1965-66).
[102] § 23(e), 42 U.S.C. § 1421b(e) (Supp. II, 1965-66).
[103] LEASING PROGRAM 3-4.
[104] Id. at 4.
[105] Marindin, Combined Rent Supplement, Rehab Demonstrations, 23 J. HOUSING 255, 256 (1966).
[106] Id.

In those states that require local referendum before a housing project can be started, there is a possibility that such requirement would not apply to section 23 leasing. Of course the language of the statute or constitutional provision would be important; but the California attorney general has ruled that the leasing program "does not constitute the acquisition or establishment of a low-rent housing project" but rather contemplates "individual units located among various separate and un-related buildings" and thus no local referendum is necessary.[107] This would be of practical importance in those localities which have rejected public housing projects.

HAA has announced that the Office of Economic Opportunity (OEO) will take part in the effort under the section 23 program. Community Action Agencies are to assist the local housing authorities and the tenants by finding owners willing to lease units, by training and counseling families moving into leased units, by assisting the families in their moving with provision for babysitters, and so forth, by compiling market survey and other data to aid the authority in meeting HAA requirements for the program, and by assisting the tenants who are leaving leased housing to take best advantage of available housing opportunities in the private market.[108]

B. Rehabilitation

When Congress in 1965 authorized 240,000 additional units of low-rent housing over the next four years, it permitted 60,000 of these units to be obtained through acquisition and rehabilitation of existing housing.[109] In fact, rehabilitation of existing housing may become the principal tool of the urban renewal program.

Rehabilitation represents a shift in emphasis for public housing—it brings public housing more than ever before into the total urban renewal effort. The local authority will be attempting to save neighborhoods, working closely with local and federal government and with private organizations and developers.

Rehabilitation of existing housing has many advantages. It adds to the inventory of standard housing without the need for as many large projects.[110] It is more

---

[107] Opinion No. 65-246, 47 Op. Att'y Gen. Calif. 17 (1966). The California constitutional provision referred to is article 34. On September 2, 1965, Joseph Burstein, General Counsel of HAA, handed down a similar opinion with reference to California.

[108] U.S. Office of Economic Opportunity, Community Action Memorandum No. 41 (June 29, 1966; U.S. Public Housing Administration, Dep't of Housing and Urban Development, Circular to Local Authorities (June 29, 1966).

[109] Public Housing Fact Sheet 4. This program is not to be confused with the new section 221(h) program which provides mortgage insurance to finance purchase and rehabilitation by nonprofit organizations of housing for resale to low-income families. 12 U.S.C. § 1715l(h) (Supp. II, 1965-66). This program is administered by the Federal Housing Administration, and is similar to the 221(d)(3) and rent supplement programs discussed briefly at pp. 519-20 infra.

[110] This statement refers to additions to standard housing inventory, not to the overall inventory of housing. There is a shortage of housing in this country, but an even more serious shortage of adequate low-cost housing for the lower-income families. See generally W. Grigsby, Housing Markets and Public Policy (1963). This shortage in low-cost housing is thought to be a primary reason for the poor tenant's troubles—namely, he is subject to onerous leasing terms, high rent, minimum facilities, and so on, because it is a "landlord's market." See generally Schoshinski, Remedies of the Indigent Tenant: Proposals for Change, 54 Geo. L.J. 519 (1966). Therefore, while rehabilitation adds to the

economical than construction of new units. It can be more quickly acquired and put to use. It provides the social integration which many critics consider essential by supplying less identifiable types of housing. It permits greater choice by the low-income family, thereby providing a degree of independence and responsibility. And it serves to improve the entire fabric of those neighborhoods suffering from blight and high vacancy rates.[111]

Of course, it has its deficiencies: it is no substitute for an increased inventory of new construction for low-income families since the program cannot provide enough housing for those who need it; it does not permit close coordination of social services for the poor such as in the housing projects; and it does not provide as much opportunity for innovation with new and modern designs and materials (although there is little evidence that the projects were ever testing grounds for new designs and materials). And since the program will have to be for the benefit of the more responsible families (since they will be going into already-established neighborhoods often with moderate- and middle-income predominance), this may leave the housing projects to the problem families, the misfits, and the chronic unemployed, which would be an unhealthy and uneconomical situation for the projects.

There are three basic methods which the housing authorities can use in rehabilitating existing units. First, the authority can select and acquire properties on its own initiative and contract the rehabilitation to private builders through competitive bidding. Second, it can buy properties and rehabilitate them itself with its own staff and some additional personnel. If competent supervision and an adequate staff are available, this obviates the many delays and expenses incident to the administration of contracts. On-the-spot decisions can be made more easily without loss of time and money. But in using this method, the local authority must hire more workers and assume the responsibilities of purchasing and storing the materials, insuring the property and the construction process, and the handling of detailed cost control accounting.

A third method enables a local authority to select properties which have already been renovated by private builders. This contemplates a contract for purchase and sale of the property; it eliminates the problems and delays encountered when the local authority contracts the work, and eliminates the reponsibilities when the authority does the work itself. Properties offered under this arrangement are, of course, inspected, and must follow HAA rules. A price is negotiated which will include a profit for the builder. Before the rehabilitation is begun, an agreement is executed, enabling the seller to get financing for the rehabilitation. Usually the properties involved are housing units in a designated development area and include several different dwelling units. (This is the turnkey method, which is presently

---

amount of standard housing available, it does not necessarily improve the total inventory of housing so that the landlord's market can be modified.

[111] McGuire, *supra* note 55, at 595.

the object of experimentation in the field of rehabilitation as well as in new construction.[112])

There are several general standards which apply to the program. The house must be decent and safe, and the neighborhood must be residential, properly zoned, without nuisances and land uses, and with an adequate supply of schools, playgrounds, churches, shops, and so on. The room cost limitations of section 15(5) of the Housing Act apply, but exclude the cost of the land and the nondwelling units on the property.[113] The total cost of the acquisition and rehabilitation cannot exceed ninety per cent of the amount that would be allowed for new construction.[114] It has been estimated that rehabilitation can be done for eighty to eighty-five per cent of the cost of new construction.[115]

Philadelphia has been the pacesetter in this new program. Before it exhausted its authorization of 1,380 units, it had already asked Washington for money to acquire another 5,000.[116] The Philadelphia authority has experimented with all three methods of rehabilitation described above, and now prefers the turnkey method, by which it has produced 300 units.[117] It designates certain areas within the city in which to focus its efforts; certain blocks are called "in" blocks in which any house properly rehabilitated will be purchased, and certain blocks are "out" blocks in which the authority will buy enough houses to make an impact on the character of the street.[118]

C. Housing for the Elderly

The problems of the elderly have gained increasing attention during the 1960s, as the nation begins to realize how large a proportion of American society is comprised of the aged and how unique and demanding their difficulties can be. More than twenty-two million persons in this country are aged; and, more significantly, more than half of the elderly families have incomes of less than $3000, about one-third have incomes of less than $2000, and nearly half of the elderly single persons have incomes of less than $1000. More than 3.5 million of these people live in substandard housing, which poses particular problems for aged persons because of their special needs and difficulties.[119]

[112] The turnkey technique is examined in its larger context at pp. 517-18 *infra*.

[113] 42 U.S.C. § 1415(5) (Supp. II, 1965-66).

[114] The information on rehabilitation is obtained from a PHA circular of November 12, 1965, transmitted to local authorities and regional offices setting forth procedures and standards to implement the program.

[115] Interview with Carl Anderson, Assistant Director, New Haven Housing Authority, Oct. 24, 1966.

[116] *Public Housing Gets a Facelifting*, AM. BUILDER, June 1966, at 70, 71.

[117] Letter from Christy Emerson, Director of Development, Philadelphia Housing Authority, to the author, Oct. 31, 1966.

[118] *Public Housing Gets a Facelifting*, AM. BUILDER, June 1966, at 70, 72-73.

[119] U.S. PUBLIC HOUSING ADMINISTRATION DEP'T OF HOUSING AND URBAN DEVELOPMENT, PUBLIC HOUSING PROGRAM FOR SENIOR CITIZENS 1 (undated) [hereafter cited as SENIOR CITIZENS HOUSING].

Congress has written special provisions into the Housing Act for the elderly. In 1961, the Act was amended to provide that the government

> may, in addition to the payments guaranteed under the [annual contributions] contract, pay not to exceed $120 per annum per dwelling unit occupied by an elderly family . . . where such amount . . . was necessary to enable the public housing agency [the local authority] to lease the dwelling unit [to an elderly person or family] . . . at a rental it could afford and to operate the project on a solvent basis.[120]

The Act also allows a larger cost allowance for constructing and equipping low-rent projects which are specifically for the elderly. While $2400 per room is the basis upon which annual contributions are computed in most cases, accommodations designed for the elderly have a $3500 per-room basis.[121]

These two provisions enable the local authorities to spend more money on projects for the elderly, and they assure the authorities of federal assistance when these families cannot pay rent sufficient to defray expenses. It also seems evident that Congress and HAA are not particularly concerned with high densities and corner-cutting, as in the traditional low-rent projects.

With these federal incentives and the current disapproval of the traditional low-rent projects, the local authorities have enthusiastically embraced the program. In New Haven, the last six construction projects have been for elderly persons.[122] Four of every five units recently constructed in Chicago were reserved for the elderly,[123] and a California county which had defeated public housing by referendum reversed its judgment and accepted housing for the elderly.[124] In all, 250 localities now have projects occupied exclusively by elderly persons, and 1500 have projects with units for the elderly in them. Almost 100,000 units have been completed since the new emphasis began.[125]

There are several factors which encourage the local authorities to build these specially-designed projects and units for the elderly. First, there is much less objection to racial integration in the elderly housing projects, and thus the local authority and the federal government can meet their "obligations" in the race relations field without arousing too much resentment. A second factor is that with the increasingly vociferous objections to the large projects, the local authority can meet the demands for scattered housing by building for the elderly. Neighborhoods which will not tolerate a huge low-rent project packed with Negroes on Aid for Dependent Children may go along with a high-rise for sweet but impoverished old folks. These elderly families are most often "white, orderly, and middle-class in behavior," and more

---

[120] § 10(a), 42 U.S.C. § 1410(a) (Supp. II, 1965-66).

[121] § 15(5), 42 U.S.C. § 1415(5) (Supp. II, 1965-66).

[122] Interview with Carl Anderson, *supra* note 115.

[123] Friedman, *supra* note 39, at 653.

[124] *Id.*

[125] SENIOR CITIZENS HOUSING 3. *See also Public Housing for the Elderly*, 20 J. HOUSING 77 (1963).

than likely will be "grateful, docile and unseen." They are never vandals, and "they do not whore and carouse."[126]

Finally, although the traditional low-rent projects hamstring the architects and contractors with miles of red tape and the many regulations and standards, the projects for the elderly provide more money and less stringent density requirements. Also, HAA is apparently more willing to allow greater experimentation with design than it is with low-rent projects. The results of this flexibility and relaxation of high-density requirements are apparent in the products of the elderly-housing program to date.[127]

In building these projects for the elderly, special consideration is given to wide doors, ramps for wheel chairs, safety features, and the like.[128]

D. A New Approach to Construction—The Turnkey Technique

The Housing Assistance Agency has recently developed a technique for public housing which permits a local housing authority to purchase a "packaged deal" from a builder or developer. Simply stated, under the turnkey method (called Turnkey) the local housing authority invites a landholding private developer to build a project, fixes a price, and buys the finished product. The technique may prove to be less expensive to the authorities (and, consequently, to the taxpayers).

Under Turnkey a developer or builder who has a site, or an option to buy one, approaches the local authority with a proposal to build. If the plan is acceptable, the applicant is invited to submit plans and specifications. After the local government has approved the project, the proposal is submitted to HAA. If approved, a letter of intent is entered into between the local authority and the developer which sets forth the detailed plans and a cost estimate. The price of the project will be (1) the price given in the letter of intent, or (2) the midpoint of two independent appraisals, whichever is less. If the midpoint of the appraisals is less than ninety-five per cent of the price asked by the developer, neither the developer nor the authority is bound to proceed further, and the authority pays the developer for his drawings and, if the developer desires, purchases the site from him. If the parties agree on the price, the developer retains a registered architect to draw up detailed "working" plans and specifications. The developer must agree to refrain from discrimination in hiring, and must submit his wage rates to the Department of Labor. When these documents have been approved by HAA, the federal agency enters into a federal assistance contract (for annual contributions) with the local authority just as it does for the usual project.

The next step is the contract of sale, which contains provisions as to quality, materials to be used, completion date, cost, and a one-year clause for remedying

---

[126] Friedman, *supra* note 39, at 654.
[127] Interview with Bruce Adams, *supra* note 42; interview with Carl Granbery, *supra* note 41.
[128] SENIOR CITIZENS HOUSING 2.

defects which the developer must guarantee with surety in the amount of 2½ per cent of the purchase price. The federal government backs the promises of the local authority, just as it backs the bond issues in the low-rent projects constructed in the usual manner.

With the contract of sale and an opinion letter from the general counsel of HAA, the developer can get credit from a private lending institution. The lender relies on these documents and the developer's credit standing in making the loan. It can be assured of having the mortgage taken off its hands by an arrangement for "take-out financing," similar to the FHA programs which involve prior commitments by the Federal National Mortgage Association to purchase the mortgage.[129]

Contractor News, a trade magazine, has stated that the turnkey method will put the general contractor "back in command of his own team on government jobs."[130] Joseph Muscarelle, a contractor who has done some turnkey jobs in Newfoundland, contends that many reputable contractors who do not bid on public housing projects because of the disadvantages will now be attracted to the projects.[131] Another builder says that elimination of the local authority's "clerk-of-the-works" will save untold delays. "These guys," he said, "block projects for days arguing about silly job changes; it's a rare bird who knows what he's talking about—they have little training."[132] (Only those change orders which increase or decrease the contract price by a substantial amount must be approved by HAA under Turnkey, in contrast to the tedious requirements of ordinary construction process.[133])

The first new-construction job built with Turnkey is a 343-unit high-rise apartment in Washington, D.C. The method is being used in several rehabilitation projects, notably in Philadelphia. Some local authorities are dragging out old plans and giving them to developers to "cost out," in an effort to see whether turnkey production can be less expensive.[134]

Because of the novelty of the method, there is little information available. There is no way to analyze the advantages as yet, because few authorities have tried it. The obvious values include more freedom for the contractor and less red tape for the local authority and the contractor. Both the federal agency and the building industry are approaching the new procedure with cautious optimism.

---

[129] The information in the three preceding paragraphs is obtained from U.S. Public Housing Administration, Dep't of Housing and Urban Development, Buying from Developers (1966) [hereinafter cited as Buying from Developers]; *An Enlightened Approach to Construction*, Contractor News, July 1966; and *Public Housing Gets a Facelifting*, Am. Builder, June 1966, at 70, 72-73.

[130] *An Enlightened Approach to Construction*, Contractor News, July 1966.

[131] *Id.*

[132] *Id.*

[133] Buying from Developers 6.

[134] Letter from Christy Emerson, *supra* note 117. The Philadelphia Authority has a firm proposal for new construction from an Indiana firm, and has given another set of old plans to a developer so that he can "cost them out" for comparative cost analysis.

VI

Related Housing Programs

To put public housing in proper perspective, it is necessary to refer briefly to several of the more important programs which are related to, or connected with, the public housing program. Thus, it can be made clear that public housing is not alone in this assault on inadequate shelter and that, despite the deficiencies and perplexities of the public housing program, none of these allied efforts was intended as, nor can it become, a substitute for public housing.[135]

A. Rehabilitation Loans and Grants to Individuals

The Housing Act of 1964 expanded earlier provisions for rehabilitation loan assistance by providing "Section 312 Rehabilitation Loans."[136] This section authorizes government loans to owners or tenants of property in urban renewal or code enforcement areas to enable them to bring the property up to local code requirements or to carry out the objectives of the urban renewal plan for the area. Interest rates are only three per cent, and loans up to $10,000 can be repaid within twenty years, or within a period equal to three-fourths of the remaining life of the property, whichever is less. These funds are available only to persons who cannot get credit from other sources at comparable terms and conditions.

The Housing and Urban Development Act of 1965 added section 115 to the Slum Clearance and Urban Renewal division of the Housing Act of 1949, making federal grants available to qualified low-income owner-occupants of housing in urban renewal or code enforcement areas for the repair and improvement of property.[137] The maximum grant that can be made is $1500. An applicant whose income is less than $3,000 per year can receive more favorable terms than higher-income families.

B. The "221(d)(3)" Program

Among the several housing programs within FHA, the section 221(d)(3) program[138] is one of the most publicized. By this provision certain types of developers (nonprofit corporations, limited-dividend corporations, cooperatives, and certain public bodies) can obtain mortgage insurance from FHA which allows them to obtain low-interest loans from private lending institutions in order to build multi-unit rental projects.

The purpose of the program is to provide housing for those families, particularly displaced and elderly families, whose incomes make them ineligible for public

---

[135] *See generally* for compilations of federal housing laws, House Comm. on Banking and Currency, *supra* note 92; Urban America, Inc., Summary of Federal Housing Programs for Low and Moderate Income Families (1967).

[136] 42 U.S.C. § 1425b (1964).

[137] 42 U.S.C. § 1466 (Supp. II, 1965-66).

[138] 12 U.S.C. § 1715*l*(d)(3) (Supp. II, 1965-66).

housing but who cannot afford adequate housing on the open market with a reasonable amount of their income. These are the families in the "twenty per cent gap"
between the highest rentals in public housing projects and the lowest rentals in the
open market.

The 221(d)(3) housing program can be combined with public housing. For
example, a nonprofit organization or a church group could build a 221(d)(3) project
and sell an undivided interest in the property to the local housing authority. The
authority could make a prior commitment to purchase such an interest, so as to
assure adequate financing from a private institution. This arrangement allows low-
and moderate-income families to live together, and the apartment is not identified as
a public housing project. When the low-income tenants exceed the income limits,
they would not have to move out, but would simply be stricken from the public
housing rolls and would pay their rent without subsidy. A variation of this arrangement would be a plan whereby the local authority does not own an interest in the
apartment, but agrees to lease a certain number of units under the new section 23
leasing program. In either case, if it became necessary, the local authority could
buy the project from the sponsor.[139]

C. Rent Supplements

One of the more recent items of legislation in the field of housing is the rent
supplement provision of the Housing and Urban Development Act of 1965.[140] As
originally planned by the Johnson Administration, this program was intended to be a
companion to the 221(d)(3) program in providing housing for the moderate-income
families. As passed by the Congress, the program is aimed at assisting public housing
in providing for the low-income group.

Under this program, FHA will enter into contracts with limited-dividend corporations, nonprofit corporations and cooperative housing corporations, who will obtain
financing from approved mortgagees, generally following the pattern of 221(d)(3)
arrangements. To be eligible for these projects, a family must, as a general rule, be
eligible for public housing, and must also be either elderly, physically handicapped,
affected by a natural disaster, living in substandard housing, or displaced by government action. The tenant will pay the owner of the project the amount that he can
afford, which will be at least twenty-five per cent of his income, and FHA will pay
the difference between this amount and the fair rental value of the unit.[141]

---

[139] These arrangements, and others, were discussed in an address by Marie McGuire, Acting Deputy
Assistant Secretary, Department of Housing and Urban Development, National Conference of Catholic
Charities, New Orleans, Louisiana, Oct. 11, 1966.

[140] § 101, 12 U.S.C. § 1701s (Supp. II, 1965-66).

[141] See generally Kates, Current Legislation, 7 B.C. IND. & COM. L. REV. 314 (1966); Welfeld, Rent
Supplements and the Subsidy Dilemma, in this symposium, p. 465; Smith, The Implementation of the
Rent Supplement Program—A Staff View, id., p. 482. Kates discusses § 103 of the 1965 Act in his
article on rent supplements. But § 103 amended the 1937 Act, adding the § 23 leasing program which is
not considered a part of the rent supplement program.

VII

CONCLUSION

Housing problems can be allayed in the higher economic strata by private enterprise, or at least by private enterprise assisted by a few tax incentives and government-sponsored mortgage insurance. But the inadequate supply of decent housing is an acute problem to the lower income segment.[142] It is evident that the building industry cannot cope with the problems of this group without assistance.[143] Building for those who cannot pay is patently imprudent in our capitalist society, and building so cheaply that these persons could afford to pay would only be erecting tomorrow's slums. Therefore, some sort of government-subsidized effort seems necessary to provide decent housing for the low-income group.

As we have seen, there are many difficulties in the program which the government has launched, some of which have been spotted and subjected to valid criticisms. How can we attack these problems and render the program more effective?

A starting point for such a problem-solving attempt should be to define the goals of the program. It is imperative that the primary purpose of the endeavor be recognized and clearly understood. It "is not the relief of unemployment in the building trades, nor the demolition of substandard housing, nor the stabilization of real estate values, nor the reduction of crime—the purpose is simply the provision of housing."[144] This may be an overstatement of the case, but it must be emphasized that the provision of housing for low-income families is the central theme, and side issues should not cause us to deviate unawares from this purpose.

Despite the foibles and the many objections, there is no realistic alternative to "the project" in the large urban areas where there is an immediate necessity to bulldoze the slums and provide decent housing for thousands of low-income families. Land is too scarce and too expensive to talk of scattered projects in the big metropolitan areas where square footage of soil is as valuable as gold.[145] Thus, attention

---

[142] See appendix B.

[143] The building industry produces about 1.6 million units annually, whereas it is estimated that it should be producing 2 million, or even 2.5 million per year. C. ABRAMS, THE CITY IS THE FRONTIER 277 (1965).

[144] M. STRAUS & T. TWEGG, HOUSING COMES OF AGE 26 (1938).

[145] A letter from Oscar Kanny, Director of the New York City Housing Authority, Public Information Division, to the author, Nov. 10, 1966, supports this writer's thesis that the large projects cannot be abandoned in the larger metropolitan areas. Mr. Kanny writes:
"Because of the severe budget limitations imposed by the lending agencies, it is almost essential that we provide as high a density as the zoning regulations permit in order to keep to a minimum the unit cost per apartment. This condition almost always dictates highrise buildings. Also, because of the zoning regulations regarding spacing of buildings, generally a number of low buildings would create practical difficulties of design . . . . Furthermore . . . a certain percentage of parking is required in every project, and the less the number of buildings, the greater the amount of ground area available to accommodate parking. In addition, we provide a considerable amount of play and recreation space for each project, thus requiring as much open area as practical."
The supply of housing needed for low-income families in New York City is best understood by citing

must be focused on marked improvement in the design, appearance, management, and composition of the projects.

A. Design and Appearance

The problems with design and appearance can best be remedied by increasing the cost allowance to a more appropriate figure, and by reducing the density requirements to a respectable limit. Although cost limits have been raised over the years, they have constantly lagged behind the increasing costs of construction. The cost limits set by Congress are in direct conflict with the programs of urban beautification and redevelopment into which so many millions of dollars are being pumped. This is not to propose that low-rent projects be decorated with lavish ornaments and luxuries but only that they be designed and built with the view that they are going to last at least half a century; they should not be allowed to clutter the urban skylines and provide drab warehouses for the poor for so many years. Densities cannot be reduced to such levels that government funds would be wasted on spaciousness, but the family-to-structure and family-to-acre ratios should be such that an architect can design a creditable edifice and families can live in some degree of privacy and comfort.

B. Management

This problem cannot be resolved by reducing public order to chaos; but the tenants can be given as many privileges as possible to enable them to learn the merits of independence and responsibility. A few suggestions are set out below.

Despite the unfortunate consequences of such a policy, the problem families must be denied admittance into the projects if the projects are to become suitable places in which conscientious families can try to break the barriers which the slums and poverty have placed between them and the rest of society. The alcoholics, the drug addicts, families with proven propensities for trouble and delinquency, and unwed mothers who show no signs of reform, must be barred. Ivory-tower critics seldom mention this as a possible remedy to many of the public housing difficulties because, at first glance, it seems a bit cruel. But there is no alternative if we sincerely want a housing program which can answer the social, as well as economic, needs of these low-income persons. It is clear that a vast majority of the taxpayers, the housing authority officials, and particularly the occupants of the projects, want such a policy.

The occupants of a project should be allowed more voice in the affairs of community life. They should, for example, be allowed to elect an "advisory board" to assist the project supervisors in matters of public concern and to represent tenants in discussions with the "public landlord." Such a body should not be given power

---

Mr. Kanny's figures. In the city, there are 149 projects with 142,817 units, and seven co-ops with 6,173 units. At present, more than 12,000 additional units are either under construction or on the drawing boards.

to control administration of the project or to make decisions which would bind taxpayers to the will of the tenants, but the panel could provide the tenants a sense of participation in community affairs, a feeling of responsibility in decision-making.

The uncommendable attitudes of many project managers toward privacy must be reversed. Intrusion upon the privacy of tenants should be unconditionally halted except in clearly justified investigations and examinations of records for the sake of the primary purposes of the program.

Formal leases should take the place of the month-to-month situation which now exists. Such leases would have to be subject to right of expulsion for certain violations of regulations (as even commercial leases are) and would probably have to be subject to the right of the authority to evict when the tenant's income rises above the stated income limit, unless our philosophy on this point were changed. But even with these conditions in the leases, such papers would be symbols of a tenant-landlord relationship such as exists elsewhere in society, brushing aside the attitude that public housing tenants are just temporary wards of an institution.

The right of judicial review of all grievances may be too cumbersome, and not even in the best interest of tenants in many cases, but some sort of administrative procedure should be devised, particularly for rulings which affect the tenant's continued occupancy once he is in the project.

There should be more experimentation with ways to mitigate the harshness of the present income-limit rule. Certainly tenants should be allowed, once in the projects, to continue occupancy when eviction would only return them to the slums. Of course, rent payments should rise, until the payments were equal to the fair rental value of the units. The idea proposed that would allow a tenant to purchase his unit once his rent is sufficient to pay operational expenses and cover debt service should be explored, particularly in those projects that are becoming havens for the lowest income nonwhites of the community. Congress has allowed this approach as to detached or semidetached units, but there are concepts within the relatively new law of condominium which may permit it even in high-rise projects. To permit these families to remain in the project would add a feeling of attachment and permanancy which is direly needed. The tenant would acquire an attitude of "home," which in turn would go far toward improving the appearance of the housing projects. Perhaps such a plan would be too attractive, and valuable unit space would become even more unavailable for the poorer families who need it most. If and when such conditions occurred, the plan would have to be scrapped, and those persons with higher incomes encouraged or forced to leave the projects in deference to the slumdwellers on the waiting lists.[146]

---

[146] C. ABRAMS, *supra* note 143, at 37, 266, discusses these problems of the income-limit rule, but he does not suggest what would happen if *too* many of these higher-income tenants decide to stay on, pay the rent, and thus lengthen the waiting lists. Staughton Lynd, professor of history at Yale University and author of an article on urban renewal (note 56 *supra*), said in an interview Nov. 8, 1966, that his

Authorities should tackle the problems of isolation. Provision for social services and participation in community affairs should be further fostered. More physical amenities are needed, preferably to be shared with those outside the projects. Such things as inexpensive clubhouses and playgrounds would require higher cost allowances; but the costs would not be unjustified since such efforts may hasten the day when these families can be independent citizens.

There is no question but that tenant selection practices should be devoid of racial discrimination. As for the tougher problem of site selection, there is little hope that this situation can be quickly and completely resolved. If the purpose of this program is to provide housing for low-income families, it is logical that the projects will be built in those blighted areas where slums are being torn down under urban renewal programs, and where the lack of adequate housing is lining the landlords' pockets. Since a large number of these areas are predominantly nonwhite, it is inevitable that projects built in these sections of town will be predominantly nonwhite. A policy of compelling whites to enter the nonwhite projects raises several questions. Is compulsory placement socially desirable? Is this influx of whites beneficial to the many nonwhites who wish to enter the project in their own neighborhood but find many of the units occupied by these persons brought in from other areas?

Of course, in integrated neighborhoods, there should be no problems. And if a nonwhite slum and a white slum are located in such a way that a project can be built between them, a proper approach would be to build a single project between them to serve the needs of both areas. Aside from these easier situations, however, the site-selection dilemma remains complex and possibly insoluble.

Outside of the more densely-populated urban areas, where land is available and less expensive and there is not an over-abundance of low-income families needing housing assistance, several smaller projects, scattered throughout the community, would seem more suitable than the massive high-rises required in the big cities. There is evidence that this theory is being accepted; and it should continue, because scattered housing is probably the best solution to the many problems of the large projects.

The several new strategies—section 23 leasing, rehabilitation, housing for the elderly, Turnkey—should continue. The leasing program and the rehabilitation effort offer excellent supplements to the traditional project approach, and will involve the public housing program in the larger effort to save neighborhoods and beautify cities. If the turnkey technique proves effective as a method of saving time, red tape, and money, the experimentation will have been a giant step from the traditionalist attitude of most government administrative agencies. In all of these programs, in fact, this writer finds hope not so much in their content, as worthy as this content may

---

experiences with low-income families in Manhattan had disclosed that a primary reason for the reluctance to enter housing projects was the feeling of detachment, "temporariness" and an inability to feel as if the unit were "home." Professor Lynd agreed with the many critics who believe that a relaxation of the income-limit rule would help remedy this attitude.

be, but in the fact that they appear to represent a new trend in public housing: a shrugging off of bureaucratic lassitude and a new effort to find solutions with experimentation and change.

Finally, public housing should be more than a receptacle for displaced families from urban renewal areas. In many communities public housing is being relegated to the role of receiver of the displaced families when the slums are bulldozed and the land is sold for commercial purposes or for construction of more respectable moderate- or middle-income housing. Families forced into public housing under such conditions cannot be expected to fall in love with the project. And public housing cannot get on with the business of eroding the housing shortage for low-income families when all of its efforts are expended in just keeping up with the displacees.[147]

Public housing cannot be replaced by any of the new programs thus far developed.[148] It can be supplemented with many endeavors, private and public, and it can improve with persistent determination to face the problems and solve them. Some questions have been raised, and suggestions offered. Lest anyone think that the many problems of public housing can be resolved swiftly and decisively, a statement by Dr. Weaver seems particularly apropos:[149]

> Because of the heterogeneity of the country, its governmental structure, our traditions relative to land and home ownership, and the paradoxes in race and housing, definitive formulations of policy are difficult. . . . [W]e must avoid doctrinaire approaches. There are no simple answers. Indeed, there are few single answers or pat solutions which will be effective.

* * *

[147] Because of the involuntary and compulsory aspects of urban renewal displacement, many former slum dwellers refuse to go into public housing projects. In Philadelphia 80% of the dislocated families qualified for public housing but less than 15% moved in; in a large Los Angeles program less than 1% were willing to occupy public housing; in New York's West Side area, only 16% of the 68% eligible for public housing accepted it; and in one Detroit area only 3% wanted to go into public housing projects. Nationwide, it is estimated that only 13-22% of displaced families move into public housing. C. ABRAMS, *supra* note 143, at 35, 267. Professor Lynd, in an interview Nov. 8, 1966, reported that his experience with Manhattan families suggested that these families should be allowed to participate more in urban renewal programs to eliminate some of the compulsion. He also suggested that for those families who did not want public housing, provision should be made for temporary quarters while redevelopment occurs and then allow them to re-enter the neighborhood in new or improved housing units, instead of the mass dislocation approach now being used. His criticisms of urban renewal are further defined in his article, note 56 *supra*.

[148] Some persons who object to the projects in public housing see the solution only in programs such as 221(d)(3) and rent supplement. But given the present state of things, it would be very unwise to shift the emphasis of the low-cost housing effort to programs such as this. The several persons with whom this writer discussed public housing were convinced that 221(d)(3) housing is cheap and poorly constructed, with less quality than the public housing program construction. Since rent supplement housing will follow the pattern of section 221(d)(3), there is no reason to believe that this program will be any different. In New York City, where real estate investment is supposed to be the keenest, 221(d)(3) housing is scarce, and "slum areas which require clearance present a financial obstacle that effectively rules out 221(d)(3) housing." Letter from Oscar Kanny, *supra* note 145. Mr. Kanny concludes, therefore, that the similar program of rent supplements has little potential. This is not to say, of course, that public housing cannot join with 221(d)(3) efforts in many areas.

[149] R. WEAVER, DILEMMAS OF URBAN AMERICA 116 (1965).

APPENDIX A

PUBLIC HOUSING TRANSACTIONS

Initial Construction

Contractor

Contract Award

Construction of Buildings

Local Housing Authority (funds lent by Federal Govt.)

Purchased

Condemnation awards to slum landlords

Slum Houses

Operation

Expenditures

Employees and Materials

Local Govt.

Holders of Public Housing Bonds

Operating Expenses

Payment in lieu of taxes = 1/10 of 1/5 of incomes of PH occupants

Interest & Amortization

Local Housing Authority

Rent = 1/5 of income

Annual contributions = debt service

Corporate & Personal Income Taxes, Excise Taxes, etc.

Households and institutions paying income and other Federal taxes

Receipts

Public Housing Occupants

Public Housing Administration

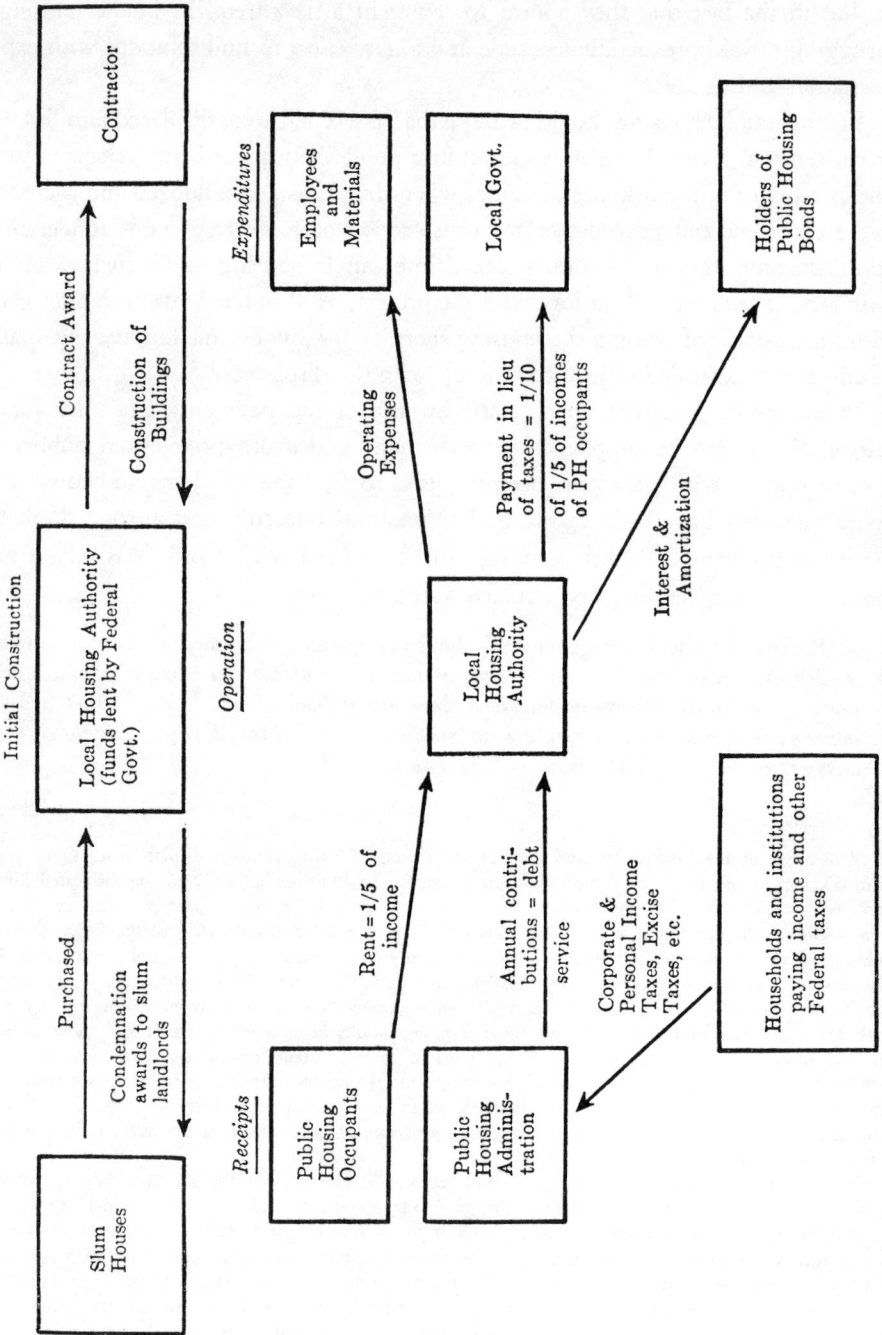

Source: This diagram was originally published in Nourse, *Redistribution of Income from Public Housing,* 19 NAT'L TAX J. 27, 37 (1966), and is reprinted here with permission of the *National Tax Journal.*

APPENDIX B

INCOME GROUPS AND HOUSING

Top Income

Most of the new housing produced by private enterprise for rent and for sale, with or without FHA insurance, is built for this income group.

Tax breaks (such as deductions for interest on mortgage loans), VA programs, and FHA insurance are available for families within these groups, particularly the top income bracket.

An insufficient supply of housing is produced by private enterprise for this group, but the supply is augmented by livable second-hand houses.

This is the "20% gap," and very little-housing is produced for this group.

221(d)(3), rehabilitation loans and grants, and a few other programs are aimed at this group.

Except for a few shacks in the rural areas and in communities without adequate zoning codes, no new housing is supplied by private enterprise for this group.

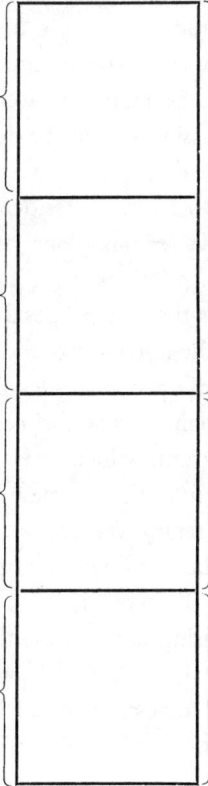

Subsidized public housing is essential to meet the needs of this income group.

Zero Income

Source: This chart is based on a similar sketch in N. STRAUS, THE SEVEN MYTHS OF HOUSING 175 (1944). It is presented only to illustrate the strata of income groups in this country and the availability of adequate housing to members of each group, and not as a demographically or mathematically precise division.

NEW TECHNIQUES IN PUBLIC HOUSING

INTRODUCTION

By a Memorandum of August 17, 1967, to Secretary Robert C. Weaver, President Johnson announced with dramatic suddenness his approval of "a pilot program, under existing authority, to stimulate private enterprise to build and manage low-income housing"; and he directed Secretary Weaver "to institute . . . a project of the type recommended by the Commission so that the desirability of a large scale program along these lines can be determined as soon as possible."[1]

The "Commission" referred to by the President was his Committee on Urban Housing, chaired by Edgar F. Kaiser, and representing a cross-section of industry, banking, and labor. Its recommendations are contained in a Memorandum dated August 16, 1967,[2] which mentions that the proposal had been submitted by Secretary Weaver to the President, who then requested the Kaiser Committee to review it. The Committee concluded that the proposal "deserves prompt attention."

The same Memorandum explained that the new program is a variation of the "Turnkey" public housing program, which was already underway. Under that program private developers build housing for sale to local public housing authorities;[3] the new feature proposed by Secretary Weaver was the application of the Turnkey principle to management of public housing projects by private firms.[4]

This article will first discuss Turnkey I, the production of housing by private developers for sale to public housing authorities; then it will treat Turnkey II and the even more recent Turnkey III.[5] Next, the article will consider the utilization of privately owned, existing, or to-be-constructed housing for low-income families financed under section 23[6] or section 10(c)[7] of the United States Housing Act. Un-

---

* LL.M. 1941, National University School of Law. Associate General Counsel (Legal Services), Department of Housing and Urban Development; General Counsel, U.S. Public Housing Administration, and thereafter for the Housing Assistance Administration, 1961-67. The views expressed herein are personal to the writer and do not necessarily reflect the views of any government agency.

Mr. Burstein has received the Distinguished Service Award from the Department of Housing and Urban Development for his work in developing the Turnkey process in public housing construction.

[1] Memorandum from President Johnson for Secretary Weaver, Aug. 17, 1967, in 3 WEEKLY COMPILATION OF PRESIDENTIAL DOCUMENTS 1166 (1967).

[2] Memorandum from Edgar F. Kaiser for President Johnson, Aug. 16, 1967, in 3 WEEKLY COMPILATION OF PRESIDENTIAL DOCUMENTS 1166 (1967) [hereinafter cited as *Kaiser Memorandum*].

[3] The original program of sale to local public housing authorities is designated in this article, and has been referred to elsewhere, as Turnkey I.

[4] This later-conceived program is often termed Turnkey II. The management of the public housing can be by nonprofit groups, profit-motivated enterprises, or organizations of the occupants.

[5] Turnkey III is a designation for a program which contemplates ultimate ownership by the occupants of the public housing, this ownership being attained through lease-purchase and self-maintenance arrangements. The program was developed subsequent to the *Kaiser Memorandum, supra* note 2; but it was anticipated in Secretary Weaver's proposal and in the Memorandum.

[6] 42 U.S.C. § 1421b (Supp. II, 1965-66).

[7] 42 U.S.C. § 1410(c) (Supp. II, 1965-66).

der these provisions, various arrangements are possible to achieve low-income and middle-income housing combinations—including home-ownership—in a completely "private" or "nongovernment" setting. Finally, there will be discussed new approaches to federal-local governmental cooperation in carrying out such federally assisted projects.

For simplicity, the article will not deal with Turnkey rehabilitation; but the reader will recognize its applicability to property which is rehabilitated for ultimate sale to the housing authority. Indeed, Turnkey, in an informal way, started with the "Used House" program in Philadelphia, financed by the Public Housing Administration. Under this program, 1,000 scattered row-houses have already been completed; and an additional 5,000 units (3,300 to be rehabilitated and 1,700 to be replaced over a three-year period) were contracted for in the spring of 1967.[8]

For all of the programs discussed here, the basic federal vehicle is the United States Housing Act,[9] which is currently administered in the Department of Housing and Urban Development (HUD) by the Housing Assistance Administration (HAA). The local instrumentality is the public housing authority, which exists under the housing authorities laws of the various states. These laws are in force in every state except Utah and Wyoming and also apply on eighty Indian reservations (including reservations in those two states) and in Puerto Rico, the Virgin Islands, and Guam. Federal public housing legislation includes almost any public body engaged in slum clearance or low-income housing;[10] but the necessity of marketing local tax exempt obligations excludes other than local housing authorities from the program, except for the leasing programs,[11] which do not require the issuance of such obligations.

I

TURNKEY I

The term Turnkey, although long in common usage in other areas,[12] entered the public housing field on January 20, 1966, when Secretary Weaver, two days after his appointment, announced an experimental program of Turnkey public housing.[13] Under this program the local housing authority (LHA) would contract for a com-

---

[8] Amendatory Agreement No. 19, June 27, 1967, to Annual Contributions Contract between the U.S. Government and the Philadelphia Housing Authority, April 1, 1959.

[9] 42 U.S.C. §§ 1401-30 (1964, Supp. II, 1965-66).

[10] 42 U.S.C. § 1402(11) (1964) defines the term "public housing agency" to mean "any State, county, municipality, or other governmental entity or public body . . . which is authorized to engage in the development or administration of low-rent housing or slum clearance."

[11] These programs are discussed at pp. 540-44 *infra*.

[12] WEBSTER'S THIRD NEW INTERNATIONAL DICTIONARY 2468 (1961) defines "turn-key job" as "a job or contract in which the contractor agrees to complete the work of building and construction to the point of readiness for operation or occupancy." For other definitions, see 42A WORDS AND PHRASES (1952, Supp. 1967). In public housing usage, "Turnkey" has not been hyphenated; and, accordingly, that spelling is adopted in this article.

[13] HUD News Release No. 66-5, Jan. 20, 1966.

pleted development to be produced by the developer on his own land and with payment to be made upon the "turning over the keys" of the development to the LHA.

Although simple in concept, the Turnkey system completely reverses the traditional method of producing public housing—site acquisition by purchase or condemnation, preparation of competitive-bidding type plans and specifications by an architect retained by the LHA, competitive bidding and award, and construction by the low bidder. This "conventional" system followed the pattern of public construction with its built-in safeguards and its concomitant built-in delays and expenses. More important from the standpoint of residential construction, the system excluded the great bulk of private entrepreneurs engaged in private construction[14] and thereby lost the potential benefit of their expertise and efficiency, developed in the residential field through competition for public acceptability. The purpose of Turnkey was to permit more adequate utilization of the means and knowledge of private enterprise in producing the finished public housing.

Fortunately, this method of procuring public housing is authorized by federal and state public housing legislation. Federal law authorizes financing of the "acquisition" as well as the "development" of public housing.[15] Similar wording appears in the state enabling acts.[16]

Fortunately, too, the federal provisions which permit a federal guarantee for the issuance by local housing authorities of obligations which will finance the capital cost and subsidies for public housing also authorize the providing of federal guarantees whereby private developers can obtain interim financing to develop projects for sale to the housing authorities.[17] However, it was necessary to develop special contract provisions in close association with lending institutions and developers, so that there would be no doubt that the provisions in the United States Housing Act, developed and nurtured meticulously over thirty years to assure the sanctity of local housing

---

[14] Although invitations for bids are open to all, only a limited number of contractors generally respond. Usually there are three or more bidders, but rarely more than six or seven. Under this system the great mass of developers and residential builders (and their associated architects, subcontractors, and suppliers), who are accustomed to building on their own sites, have not participated in the construction of public housing.

[15] 42 U.S.C. § 1402(5) (1964) defines the term "development" to mean "any or all undertakings necessary for . . . land acquisition . . . in connection with a low-rent housing project." 42 U.S.C. § 1402(8) (1964) defines "acquisition cost" to mean "the amount prudently required to be expended by a public housing agency in acquiring a low-rent housing . . . project." 42 U.S.C. § 1409 (1964) provides that HUD "may make loans to public housing agencies to assist the development, acquisition . . . of low-rent-housing . . . projects." 42 U.S.C. § 1410(b) (1964) provides that the rates of annual contributions may be based upon "development, acquisition . . . cost."

[16] E.g., MINN. STAT. ANN. § 462.445, subd. 1(4) (1963) (which empowers a housing authority to "provide for the construction . . . of any project"); § 462.421, subd. 12(3) ("The term 'housing project' . . . may be applied to . . . the acquisition of property . . . the construction . . . of the improvements . . . ."); § 462.445, subd. 1(6) (which empowers a housing authority to "acquire real . . . property"); LA. REV. STAT. § 40:382(10) (1950) ("The term 'housing project' . . . may be applied to . . . the acquisition of property . . . the construction . . . of the improvements . . . ."); § 40:474(8) (which empowers a housing authority to "acquire . . . any property in any legal way").

[17] 42 U.S.C. § 1421a (1964, Supp. II, 1965-66).

authority notes and bonds, would similarly assure the federal government's commitment to the developer of Turnkey housing and to his lender.

This commitment is that if the developer complies with the Letter of Intent and the Contract of Sale, in accord with their terms and with the plans and specifications for the project, then the housing authority will carry out its obligations under the Letter of Intent and the Contract of Sale. Furthermore, if the housing authority fails for any reason to carry out its obligations, whether the failure stems from inability or unwillingness, the federal government has, and will exercise, the unilateral right to take possession or title and proceed to perform in place of the housing authority.[18] Thus, even if an injunction should be issued against the housing authority to prevent it from performing, the federal government agrees to fulfill the authority's obligation. Then with possession of, or title to, the project, the federal government could remove the court proceeding to the federal courts and the contract would thereafter be carried out as a federal contract pursuant to the United States Housing Act. When lending institutions and the legal profession become fully aware of the "performance

---

[18] The pertinent clause of the Annual Contributions Contract reads as follows:
"The Local Authority will acquire Project No. — pursuant to a Contract of Sale to be entered into between the seller and the Local Authority. Prior to the execution of such Contract of Sale the Local Authority may issue a Letter of Intent to the seller to enter into such Contract. Such Letter of Intent and such Contract shall bear the written approval of the Government. Failure of the Local Authority to expeditiously continue the undertaking of the Project or to comply with the Letter of Intent or Contract, or if the Letter of Intent or Contract is held to be void, voidable or ultra vires, or if the power or right of the Local Authority to issue the Letter of Intent or enter into the Contract of Sale is drawn into question in any legal proceeding, or if the Local Authority asserts or claims that the Letter of Intent or Contract is not binding upon the Local Authority for any such reason, the occurrence of any such event, if the seller is not in default, shall constitute a Substantial Default for the purpose of Article V hereof and, in such case, the Government will continue the undertaking of the Project and will take delivery of such right, title or interest in the Project as the Local Authority may have and perform such Letter of Intent or Contract of Sale, as the case may be. The provisions of this paragraph are made with, and for the benefit of, the seller and his assignees who will have been specifically approved by the Government prior to such assignment. To enforce the performance of this provision the seller and such assignees, as well as the Local Authority, shall have the right to proceed against the Government by action at law or suit in equity. In order to assist in financing the acquisition cost (herein called Development Cost) of the Project the Government, notwithstanding the provisions of Sec. 410, shall lend to the Local Authority an amount equal to the Maximum Development Cost of the project: Provided, that the Government shall not be obligated to make annual contributions with respect to the Project until the Local Authority has sold an issue of its Bonds to finance such cost."
In connection with the last sentence of this clause, see also 42 U.S.C. § 1409 (1964), which limits loans to 90% only at the point where the annual contribution is actually to be paid. By implication, therefore, this section allows a 100% loan prior to that time.
U.S. HOUSING ASSISTANCE ADMINISTRATION, DEP'T OF HOUSING AND URBAN DEVELOPMENT, LOW-RENT HOUSING MANUAL § 221.1, exhibit 1 (Sept. 1967) [hereinafter cited as LOW-RENT HOUSING MANUAL], contains the following statement with respect to this contract clause:
"The developer will undertake the construction financing in his usual way. However, under the above annual contributions contract provision, he and his lender can rely upon performance of the contract by the Federal Government, if necessary, from the time of the execution of the Letter of Intent through the conveyance of the property. The developer and lender are assured that the transaction will be consummated either with Local Authority or with Government funds. If it is deemed desirable, an arrangement could be made whereby payment by the Local Authority, or by the Government, would be made directly to the lending institution."

take-out" guaranteed by the federal government, they should have no question as to the security of the local housing authority's commitment.

On the other hand, HUD has been careful to make as certain as possible that the lending institution which provides the interim financing is responsible, along with the developer, for the completed result.[19] This, indeed, is a key feature of the Turnkey system. The housing authority does not require any special guarantee, performance bond, or other assurances of the competency of the developer; its safeguard is that it makes no advances to the developer and does not pay until it is provided with the finished result in compliance with the requirements of the Contract of Sale. Any assurances that the lender requires of the developer are completely within its domain; and if the developer cannot find a lending institution which will finance him, then he cannot participate in a Turnkey project.

While some federal requirements for public construction, such as equal opportunity in employment[20] and the requirements of the Davis-Bacon Act,[21] continue to apply, others do not, including requirements as to performance and payment bonds.[22] Similarly, the usual provisions concerning delay, damage, and liquidated damages are not part of the arrangement, for the simple reasons that they are not required by law and that the running of interest and overhead against the developer is a self-policing limitation on delay. The benefits to the developer for completion ahead of schedule provide an additional incentive for promptness.

Under the revised procedures contained in section 221.1 of the HUD *Low-Rent Housing Manual*,[23] the developer is selected from among others on the basis of his site and the feasibility and desirability of his proposal. No formal advertising is required because each site is unique and, as it belongs to the developer, would not be susceptible to competitive bidding.[24]

The selection is made by the local housing authority on the basis of very inexpensive general outline information submitted by interested developers; and the selected developer is given a "Letter Designating Turnkey Developer,"[25] which advises him that his proposal has been approved and requests him to proceed with preparation of the necessary preliminary drawings and specifications and the state-

---

[19] In short, the lending institution out of its own self-interest should make sufficient inspections to assure that the developer is complying with the terms of the Letter of Intent and the Contract of Sale; if the developer does not provide the specified finished product, then the housing authority is not obligated to perform.

[20] Form HUD-53010, Annual Contributions Contract, Part One, § 304; Exec. Order No. 11,246 (Sept. 24, 1965); Low-Rent Housing Manual § 221.1(8b).

[21] 40 U.S.C. §§ 276a to 276a-5 (1964); Form HUD-53011, Annual Contributions Contract, Part Two, § 115(B); Low-Rent Housing Manual § 221.1(8b).

[22] Low-Rent Housing Manual § 221.1 does not require performance or payment bonds for turnkey projects.

[23] Issued in September 1967.

[24] The time-honored "uniqueness" of land, which is the basis for the right to specific performance of contracts for the sale of realty, provides the justification for the housing authority's use of "negotiation," rather than competitive bidding.

[25] Low-Rent Housing Manual § 221.1, exhibit 3. Exhibit 3 is reprinted as an appendix to this article.

ment of selling price required for the Letter of Intent. The developer then proceeds, at some expense, to prepare these documents and to comply with other requirements.[26] The data and material supplied by the developer must be fairly complete because they provide the basis for two independent cost estimates of the proposed development; and on the basis of these estimates the Letter of Intent price is negotiated by the housing authority, with the approval of the Housing Assistance Administration.

A key safeguard in the Turnkey process, both from the standpoint of the developer and of the government, is the cost estimating step. It is essential, therefore, that both the developer and the cost estimator know as nearly as possible the items of cost to be considered. The Turnkey process needs further development in this regard because of the relative absence in this country of a cost estimating profession.[27] Unlike appraising, cost estimating in the United States is generally done very informally and not on a fee basis. Moreover, the estimate usually includes only those elements having to do with direct construction costs. Such items as financing costs, taxes on land and improvements during construction, overhead and profit, entrepreneur and builder's risk must be specifically called to the attention of the cost estimators.

Section 221.1 includes a standard cost estimating contract, and an exhibit to this contract contains a summary of items of cost;[28] but it is not complete and will be supplemented in the future. The amount of such items as overhead, profit, and developer's and builder's risk is not specified. Therefore, the cost estimators are required to state what they consider reasonable for those items in that locality for that type of contract or arrangement. This flexibility was provided deliberately to take account of the variations that occur with the locality and with the risk involved under different circumstances. The requirement that these amounts be stated specifically, justified by the cost estimators, and subject to review by the local housing authority and by the HAA should (a) afford adequate safeguards through exposure and (b) eventually provide a guide to the establishment of standards.

The land is also subject to two independent appraisals, which serve as guides for determining the value attributable to the site. The combined land appraisals and cost estimates, together with the developer's asking price, form the basis upon which the housing authority and the HAA negotiate the Letter of Intent price. That price is of key importance because it will be the final price, subject to modifications based on the conditions set forth in article four of the Letter of Intent.[29]

---

[26] The developer is now involved in Phase II of the procedure for developing a turnkey project. This Phase covers the period from the Development Conference through Execution of Letter of Intent. See Low-Rent Housing Manual § 221.1.

[27] The writer infers that the cost estimating profession is much more formally developed in the United Kingdom where chartered quantity surveyors may be retained to provide a "package" type of cost estimate. See Royal Institution of Chartered Surveyors, The Services of the Chartered Quantity Surveyor (April 1966).

[28] Low-Rent Housing Manual § 221.1, exhibit 6, exhibit A.

[29] Low-Rent Housing Manual § 221.1, exhibit 8. Exhibit 8 is reprinted as an appendix to this article.

After the Letter of Intent price is established, a third Phase of the turnkey procedure is entered.[30] In this phase, the developer's architect produces final working drawings and specifications, and the two cost estimators are each required to provide an independent up-to-date cost estimate based on these final plans.

Article four of the Letter of Intent then comes into play. If the midpoint of the cost, based on the two final cost estimates, is above the Letter of Intent price, the developer must produce the project for the Letter of Intent price. If the midpoint is within five per cent below the Letter of Intent price, the developer must produce the project for the price established by that midpoint. If the midpoint is less than ninety-five per cent of the Letter of Intent price, then either party is free to withdraw from the transaction or to negotiate a price satisfactory to the local housing authority and to the HAA. Article four provides further that, if a negotiated price cannot be agreed upon, the developer, at his option, may sell his land and plans to the housing authority for prices previously established and may be reimbursed for his expenses up to that point. In the event of such reimbursement, cost certification is required. Also, an additional fee is permitted to the architect for revising the plans to make them suitable for competitive bidding.

By this method both the developer and the government benefit. The developer benefits because he knows that, once he has received a Letter of Intent, his risk is minimal; even if a Contract of Sale does not result, he can, at his option, be reimbursed for the bulk of his investment and expenses. Under those circumstances, the housing authority will obtain a site, which it has already approved, and plans, which, after revision, can be used as a basis for advertised bidding.

In any case, the Turnkey procedure tends to telescope the time and expense involved in acquiring the site and developing final plans for the public housing project. Since the period up through the development of final plans probably accounts for the greatest delay in procuring public housing, the saving of time provided at this point by the turnkey procedure is a considerable benefit.

In addition to a saving of ten to fifteen per cent in cost, Turnkey also provides greater speed and volume—unquestionably prime considerations in its adoption by HUD and by the President. By its very nature Turnkey forces a compression of time; the developer's own overhead, interest, and other costs are running during the development period and so he expedites the transaction by pressure on his staff, his architect, and the staffs of the local or federal agencies involved. This pressure, which does not exist in the conventional system of procuring public housing, makes it possible to envisage an interval of only seven to nine months from approval of any application by the housing authority up to the start of construction.[31] The average

---

[30] See LOW-RENT HOUSING MANUAL § 221.1. This Phase extends from the Letter of Intent through execution of the Contract of Sale.

[31] The time span is illustrated in the chart contained in LOW-RENT HOUSING MANUAL § 221.1, exhibit 2, where the thirty steps from approval of a progam reservation up to the start of construction are set forth along with the time periods involved.

is twenty-eight weeks; but standard plans permit a much shorter period, while high-rise complicated construction will probably require a longer period because of the architectural and engineering work involved.

The pressure of time and need resulted in Secretary Weaver's directive of September 7, 1967, which provides the basis for a priority system for projects that can be under construction within nine months. While many public housing projects to be produced conventionally will probably be able to qualify, because they already are in advanced stages, only Turnkey has so far been able to achieve anywhere near this time schedule. The average period has been between three to four years for "conventional" public housing.

Of special interest is the possibility of constructing Turnkey I on urban renewal sites. In view of the considerable amount of unused urban renewal land and the greater emphasis on utilization of urban renewal powers and funds to provide housing for low- and middle-income families, urban renewal sites and the use of urban renewal or urban redevelopment powers to generate sites should receive special attention.

The developer in such cases would be selected on the basis of the desirability and feasibility of his proposal by the local public renewal agency (LPA).[32] He would then be provided with an appropriate contract under which he would be authorized to approach the LHA with the proposal to build a Turnkey development for sale to the LHA. When he satisfies the LHA to the point of execution of a Letter of Intent, he is provided with title to the site on which to build the development. If he fails to satisfy the LHA, his right to proceed is withdrawn, and the site made available to another developer.

The utilization of urban renewal or redevolpment powers should become increasingly important as in-town sites become harder to obtain and more costly. Such powers can be used much more flexibly, selectively, and specifically for land assembly for low- and middle-income housing than has heretofore been the case. Especially important and unusual are the possibilities of utilizing the state statutory powers of acquisition, clearance, and rehabilitation for generation of sites and properties for Turnkey development *apart from federal urban renewal assistance.* These powers are very broad and flexible and, because they need not be circumscribed by federal urban renewal requirements, could separately provide a major source of Turnkey sites. The significance of this possibility should be understood in light of the fact that the great majority of Turnkey developers will be builders who will have to find sites or look to others for land. Such builders will be eager for ready-made sites or properties supplied by the LPA and will complete for their use.

---

[32] In those states where the LPA and the LHA are the same, the developer would be selected by the local agency in its LPA capacity.

II

TURNKEY II

Turnkey II was announced by the President as a pilot program to invite private management firms to operate public housing projects. The genesis was Secretary Weaver's recommendation approved by the Kaiser Committee on August 16 and announced by the President on August 17. The purpose stated by the Kaiser Committee was that the "private management concept could encourage the development of a management industry skilled in handling the special problems of operating low-income housing." Other possibilities cited by the Committee were reductions of cost and of prejudices against public housing and the introduction of competing private professional management techniques to encourage flexibility in the traditional management approach of local public housing authorities.[33]

The first three pilot projects announced by Secretary Weaver at his press conference of August 25, 1967, illustrate the ways in which the principle could be applied. The first of the three is of particular interest because it involves the Lavanburg Foundation project, originally conceived in 1964 for a four-block development in the Bronx in New York City and comprising low- and middle-income housing with commercial, recreational, medical, and community facilities to serve not only the 930-unit project but also the surrounding area. Under this arrangement, the housing authority purchases, on the Turnkey I basis, an undivided interest in the entire project; and thereby it is able to subsidize a portion of the families in the project. The project will be constructed for the Lavanburg Foundation by a private builder and will be managed by a private management firm under a contract with Lavanburg which covers its responsibilities regarding the low-income aspects of the project. The purpose of the entire concept in this instance is to provide a private environment for the public housing tenants in a rental project which is privately-publicly owned on an undivided interest basis. Thus, the low-income families are enabled to stay in the development even though their rents increase above public housing limitations and the middle-income families are enabled to benefit from the public housing subsidy if their income should go down. The undivided interest arrangement, together with flexibility achieved through some use of the leasing program referred to later in this article, makes it possible for the families to be unidentified publicly as to income category and to remain in their units; the transfer between low- and middle-income simply takes place on the books of the managing organization.

The pilot Turnkey II project approved in St. Louis points to the social aspects of the private management function; the Executive Director of the St. Louis Housing Authority announced that, in looking for a private firm to undertake the management of an existing public housing 700-unit project, the Housing Authority "must continue to retain its interest in the social needs of the tenants and put forth its

---

[33] *Kaiser Memorandum, supra* note 2.

efforts to assist private management by involving many public and private organizations in the community with respect to the social needs of tenants." The third pilot project will involve private management of a Turnkey I development in Indianapolis.

The first group of Turnkey II projects show that they do not necessarily involve a Turnkey I development. Projects of the Lavanburg type appear to offer the greatest possibility for early consideration. A number of this type are already in prospect—some on urban renewal sites and comprising fairly large areas. Their common characteristics are combinations of middle- and low-income housing, community, recreational, and commercial facilities. They are usually either totally or predominantly privately-owned and thus provide a natural setting for private management. Such projects can and will include combinations involving rent supplement, 221(d)(3) below-market, public housing leasing, and public housing Turnkey components.

Perhaps the most interesting and significant Turnkey II involvement is in connection with the North Gulfport, Mississippi project, which utilizes Turnkey I, Turnkey II, and Turnkey III.[34] Turnkey II is different in the context of this project because the ultimate purpose is homeownership for the occupants—achieved in part through a "sweat-equity" developed by maintenance of the property by the occupants, rather than by the LHA.

Turnkey II in the setting of this project will involve first an interim "management" organization which, before the development is constructed, will contract with the LHA to assist in the selection of the types of families most suited to a homeownership-type development and to provide the selected families with intensive pre-occupany training in how to live in and maintain their homes, develop financial neighborhood responsibility, and so forth. The interim Turnkey II contractor will also provide post-occupancy training and guidance and will help the occupants organize themselves into a self-management homeownership association. The homeownership association will then become, in effect, the Turnkey II management contractor vis-à-vis the LHA, since it will be the organization responsible collectively for management of the development and will represent the occupants as a group with respect to their financial and property rights.

While it was assumed that professional private real estate management firms would be the source of Turnkey II contractors, it appears that the type of expertise involved in the training of occupants might very well be the subject for exploration by the large industrial enterprises which have contracted to undertake technical training in connection with government-sponsored educational or job-training programs. This approach seems especially promising in the case of homeownership type projects,

---

[34] *See* Home Ownership Pilot Program Through Turnkey Process Announced by Secretary Weaver, HUD Press Release No. 4538, Sept. 18, 1967. Turnkey III, which involves homeownership, is discussed later in this article.

where greater emphasis will be placed on total maintenance of the units and on training in homeownership responsibilities, family budgets, savings, and so forth.

As is apparent, there are no definitive guidelines for the type of Turnkey II management agreements that are possible. The assumption is that they will range from
minimum to maximum involvement of the private management organization in the
social problems of the tenants. Naturally, the staffing and fees will vary accordingly;
and the receptivity to such arrangements will also differ with the groups involved
and with the desires of the particular local housing authority.

The Supreme Court recently considered, but did not decide, the question of the
extent to which the local housing authority is in the position of the conventional
landlord.[35] The problem might vary under the private management contract. The
dozens of suits involving tenants' rights with respect to admission, eviction, and rights
to hearing, and the far-reaching legal issues involved, are beyond the scope of this
article. However, the involvement of private management adds an interesting new
dimension to the growing body of discussion and concern about the relationship
of landlord to tenant, especially where government subsidization is involved.

III

Turnkey III

Turnkey III was first announced by Secretary Weaver in the press release of
September 18, 1967,[36] which provided the background for the Turnkey I, II, and III
project to be developed in North Gulfport, Mississippi. A Turnkey III project is
a project owned by the LHA which provides private ownership opportunities for
the low-income occupants. Initial ownership by the LHA distinguishes Turnkey III
from the homeownership systems which are being separately developed under the
leasing program discussed later in this article.

Under Turnkey III as exemplified by the North Gulfport project, the tenants will
be given lease-purchase contracts when they have earned, out of the self-maintenance
of their units, a "sweat equity" of at least $350. All the tenants will need to have
is sufficient income so that twenty per cent of that income will cover all maintenance,
operating, and administrative expenses, including utilities. As the income of the
tenants increases, they will be required to continue paying twenty per cent of their
income for rent, thus reducing the federal subsidy which is available for the debt
service on the obligations issued by the LHA to pay for the acquisition under the
Turnkey I contract. Tenants who wish to acquire ownership sooner can contribute
more than twenty per cent of their income, and such additional contribution will
be added to their maintenance "sweat equity" to enable them to purchase the unit
more quickly.

---

[35] Thorpe v. Housing Authority, 386 U.S. 670 (1967).
[36] Home Ownership Pilot Program Through Turnkey Process Announced by Secretary Weaver,
supra note 34.

While they are occupying these units as low-income families, the families will be receiving the benefits of the federal subsidy available for public housing—that is, the amount, which, in addition to what they can afford, is required to meet debt service. If the family income should increase to the point where the family is ineligible for public housing, it is required to purchase the house for the balance then remaining unamortized, to which will be applied the amount in its equity account. The family should be able to obtain a loan for the balance from private sources. That unit would then stop receiving federal subsidy and would go on to the tax rolls, thus fulfilling both federal and local requirements that only low-income families can receive federal subsidy and the benefits of local tax exemption.

The over-income family has the choice of not purchasing the house and moving from the project. In that event, it can take the amount remaining in its equity account with it; but it cannot receive the benefit of the reduction of the debt on the house through the combination of its rent payments and the federal subsidy. The new family moving into a vacated house has to earn the minimum maintenance "sweat equity" in order to get a lease-purchase contract; and the second family's rights to purchase of the house are based on the fair value appraisal of that house or the unamortized balance, whichever is higher.

Turnkey III is patterned after the HAA-assisted mutual-help program on Indian reservations which was developed by administrative interpretations in November 1962.[37] Under that program a group of Indian families helps to construct their own houses and thereby earn an equity from fifteen to twenty per cent. The amount representing this equity is not advanced by HUD but is available at the request of the LHA in the event that it determines the occupants do fail to maintain their houses adequately during their lease-purchase occupancy. If the occupants maintain their own houses and do not use this equity, they are able to have full title in about fifteen to seventeen years. If the equity has to be used for maintenance, obtaining title is necessarily deferred.

The essential difference between the Indian reservation program and Turnkey III stems from the fact that the Indian family initially develops a considerable equity, which has the immediate effect of reducing the capital cost, or principal; and the family is fully obligated initially to maintain its own house, upon penalty of reduction of this equity and postponement of acquisition of title. The Turnkey III type project assumes no initial principal reduction through "sweat equity," but a gradual building up of earned equity through self-maintenance and through voluntary payments by the family above the required twenty per cent of its income.

The Indian mutual-help program was developed prior to the amendment of the United States Housing Act of 1937 by the Housing and Urban Development Act of

---

[37] Memorandum on PHA Mutual-Help Housing Program in Conjunction with the Bureau of Indian Affairs, from PHA General Counsel for PHA Commissioner, Nov. 30, 1962, as transmitted by PHA Circular on PHA Mutual-Help Housing for Indians, Dec. 5, 1964, and as issued by the Commissioner to all Regional Directors.

1965[38] which added section 15(9) authorizing sale of detached or semi-detached public housing units.[39] The legislative history of that amendment stated clearly, however, that it was not intended to limit any authority to sell pursuant to other provisions of the Act; and Turnkey III has been developed pursuant to these other provisions.[40]

The major advantages of the Turnkey III, Indian mutual-help, and homeowner-ship programs being developed under the leasing powers[41] are that, with essentially the same subsidy as in conventional rental public housing (or even less, due to the savings resulting from the self-interest of the tenants in their own property and the more rapid amortization of the federal debt covering the capital cost) low-income families are able to aspire to homeownership. Moreover, there is absent the danger inherent in other proposed systems which provide the family with title that they will lose the property if they cannot carry through on their mortgage obligations. While it is true that the family, in the programs discussed in this article, initially has only a lease-purchase contract and not full title, its right to purchase is fully protected if it meets its obligations and maintains its property.[42] Its earned equity is available additionally to enable it to acquire title sooner and belongs to it if it should wish, or be compelled, to leave the project. The great advantage to the family, however, is that, at the worst, it will be able to continue living in the unit as a renter at the minimum rent; and if it should be able to do nothing more than pay for LHA administrative expenses and take care of maintenance and its utilities, the lease-purchaser and occupant will still acquire ownership at the end of the amortization period.

IV

LEASING PRIVATELY OWNED HOUSING

The involvement of the private sector in construction and management and the possibility of ownership for tenants is not limited to Turnkey I, II, and III which involve publicly owned housing. These objectives can also be accomplished by utilizing privately owned existing housing in good condition or to be rehabilitated, or new housing to be constructed, which the housing authority leases or

---

[38] Pub. L. No. 89-117, 79 Stat. 451 (codified in scattered sections of 12, 15, 20, 38, 40, 42, 49 U.S.C.).

[39] 42 U.S.C. § 1415(9) (Supp. II, 1965-66).

[40] The Senate Committee commented,

"The committee commends existing efforts to promote policies and programs providing home-ownership possibilities for low-income tenants, such as the mutual-help housing plan for Indian reservations. The provisions of the bill are intended to provide specific authority for sale of public housing units to its tenants, under appropriate circumstances and conditions and subject to prescribed standards, which might not otherwise be authorized by the other provisions of the U.S. Housing Act. They are intended to supplement and not to inhibit the efforts of the PHA to provide other homeownership incentives and possibilities for low-income families."

SEN. REP. No. 378, 89th Cong., 1st Sess. 41 (1965). See also id. at 43.

[41] Discussed in part IV infra.

[42] In many states it is not unusual for land to be purchased under a lease purchase arrangement or through an installment sale contract with title reserved by the seller. Thus, there is nothing extraordinary about the use of the lease-purchase in connection with Turnkey II.

agrees to lease from the private owner or developer for low-income families eligible under public housing rules. The arrangement may alternatively provide for a lease between the owner and the tenant with the LHA agreeing with the owner to carry out the lease terms, including full payment to the owner of the rent and maintenance of the property if the tenant fails to do so. The necessary subsidy is provided by HUD through the HAA under either section 23 or section 10(c) of the United States Housing Act.[43] As in the case of Turnkey, the local powers are derived from provisions in the state laws which authorize housing authorities to lease or otherwise contract for the provision of housing for low-income families.

The federal provisions are limited to the leasing of *existing* housing.[44] However, the state provisions are not so limited, and housing authorities may contract for the leasing of dwellings to be constructed or rehabilitated. The federal annual contributions contract which assures the necessary federal subsidy restricts the commitment of federal funds until the units are actually constructed in compliance with the requirements of the federal statute which limits the contributions to "existing" structures.[45] Thus, with respect to new construction (or to units to be converted or rehabilitated), there is involved the same Turnkey principle and mechanism as in Turnkey I, that is, the federal assurance that, when the units are brought into

---

[43] § 23, 42 U.S.C. § 1421b(e) (Supp. II, 1965-66) provides:
"The annual contribution under this chapter for a project of a public housing agency for low-rent housing in private accommodations under this section in lieu of any other guaranteed contribution authorized . . . shall not exceed the amount of the fixed annual contribution which would be established under this chapter for a newly constructed project by such public housing agency designed to accommodate the comparable number, sizes, and kinds of families."
Substantially the same formula is contained in the last provision of § 10(c), 42 U.S.C. § 1410(c) (Supp. II, 1965-66):
   "*And provided further,* That the amount of the fixed annual contribution which would be established under this chapter for a newly constructed project by a public housing agency designed to accommodate a number of families of a given size and kind may be established, as a maximum annual contribution in lieu of any other guaranteed contribution authorized under this section, for a project by such public housing agency which would provide housing for the comparable number, sizes, and kinds of families through the acquisition, acquisition and rehabilitation, *or use under lease of existing structures* which are suitable for low-rent housing use and obtainable in the local market."
(Emphasis added.)
[44] 42 U.S.C. § 1421b(a)(3) (Supp. II, 1965-66) provides:
"As used in this section, the term 'low-rent housing in private accommodations' means dwelling units in an existing structure, leased from a private owner, which provide decent, safe, and sanitary dwelling accommodations and related facilities effectively supplementing the accommodations and facilities in low-rent housing assisted under the other provisions of this chapter in a manner calculated to meet the total housing needs of the community in which they are located; and the term 'owner' means any person or entity having the legal right to lease or sublease property containing one or more dwelling units as described in this section."
See also 42 U.S.C. § 1410(c) (Supp. II, 1965-66); § 23(d), 42 U.S.C. § 1421b(d) (Supp. II, 1965-66). Although the federal and state laws refer to leasing, they do not require that the leasing be by the housing authority to the tenant. Instead, an arrangement would be permissible whereunder the housing authority did not serve as lessor but participated by providing a subsidy under the annual contribution contract. Such an arrangement would be consistent with § 23(a)(3) and § 23(d) but might not be subject to certain limitations of state law that apply when the housing authority is itself the lessor.
[45] The contract contains a proviso that "the Local Authority shall not commit any annual contribution hereunder in respect to such dwellings until they have been constructed."

existence (or brought up to the agreed-to condition in the case of rehabilitation), the housing authority will have the funds available to meet its commitment to the developer, and that if the housing authority does not meet its commitment, the federal government will.

This arrangement provides an extremely flexible method of (1) making use of existing housing in good condition to absorb vacancies, (2) inducing the rehabilitation, conversion, or modernization of substandard or unsuitable housing for low-income use, and (3) inducing the construction of new housing. In every one of these categories, if the owner is willing, suitable and very attractive arrangements can be worked out for providing the tenants with lease-purchase contracts which enable the tenants, as their incomes increase, to become owners. As of this writing, the homeownership aspects are well along in being worked out. The problem areas lie in establishing the appropriate price for the rehabilitated or newly constructed unit; the protection of the lease-purchase tenant's equity against the insolvency or bankruptcy of the owner and possible prior liens; and the capital financing required for the rehabilitation, improvement, or construction of the units.

The type of private capital financing is especially important because it must result in sufficiently low monthly debt service to enable low-income families with about twenty per cent of their income, plus the limited public housing subsidy, to live in the units. Since the capital cost is *not* financed by tax exempt housing authority bonds or notes, and since the project is not exempt from local taxes,[46] as is the case of LHA-owned housing under the conventional or Turnkey I system, it is necessary to obtain the longest-term, lowest-interest private financing available. It is certain at this writing that such sufficiently long-term, low-interest financing can be worked out.

The types of dwelling units and the types of ownership are limited only by what is achievable by the private financing arrangements that exist or can be brought into existence. The most simple would be detached, semi-detached, row-house or town-house dwellings, capable of ultimate division under separate mortgage. More complex would be the planned unit development under which the common areas and facilities are owned in common. The system can be applied in condominiums as well as in cooperatives. Also, it can be applied to identified units comprising a portion of the private development as well as on the basis of an undivided share of the whole development. It goes without saying that the arrangements should be as simple as possible. There is a point of diminishing returns between ideal objectives that can be achieved (at least theoretically) by a complicated arrangement and the complications and delays that an intricate arrangement can cause in working out individual property interests.

From the standpoint of the types of developers that might be interested in such an arrangement, the most likely to involve major investment and activity are individual

---

[46] Except for § 10(c) leasing, discussed at pp. 543-44 *infra*.

or corporate investors with sufficient income to be attracted by the accelerated depreciation over a ten-year period, during which the developer would usually wish to retain ownership and be assured of rental income and maintenance by the LHA with the federal back-up.[47] From the standpoint of the public interest, arrangements can channel investments and activity that would otherwise go towards tax shelter areas not so crucially in the public interest as housing for low-income families, especially where such housing additionally can serve the purpose of promoting individual pride and self-reliance induced by the homeownership possibilities.

The public housing authority in these arrangements automatically serves an even lesser "government landlord" role than in Turnkey I, II, and III and a role which can be tailored to the minimum or maximum required to serve the interests of the owner-investor, on the one hand, who wishes to be relieved of responsibility, and the occupant-potential-owners, who need the subsidy and the training and guidance towards self-reliant ownership status.

The essential differences between section 23 leasing and section 10(c) leasing under the United States Housing Act are: (1) section 10(c) requires that all the local conditions relating to LHA-owned housing be met, including the existence of a "workable program," partial tax exemption or remission, and so on, while section 23 requires only that an approving resolution be passed by the governing body, and (2) section 23 provides for a maximum of five years with option to renew, whereas section 10(c) is not so limited. The latter difference does not stand in the way of working out an appropriate arrangement, however, since the option to renew can be made exercisable by the owner upon the meeting of certain conditions, thus assuring him or his lender that the length of the term is in his control.

The benefits of utilizing section 10(c) stem from the fact that it requires that local tax exemption or remission be provided equal to that required for LHA-owned housing. The United States Housing Act requires that LHA-owned housing be tax exempt but provides for payments in lieu of taxes (PILOT) not exceeding ten per cent of shelter rents (rents less utilities). These payments on a national average are about $40 per year. Since the property under the leasing arrangements discussed here is privately owned, it is normally not tax exempt; and therefore, section 10(c) requires tax remission equivalent to the difference between the value of full tax exemption and payments in lieu of taxes. This difference varies locality by locality but can often be as much as $300 per year. Where the difference is substantial, the effect of such tax remission is to permit the leasing program (using a twenty per cent ratio of income to rent) to serve a substantially lower income group (lower by $1500 per annum in the $300 case).

In so far as net loss to the community is concerned, the payments in lieu of taxes

---

[47] Depending on his tax position the developer might wish to build the project for almost immediate sale to a nonprofit corporation. The nonprofit corporation could qualify for a 100 per cent loan while the private developer could not.

will generally equal the tax revenue from the property prior to its improvement. The benefit to the community is that the income group to be served will approach that served by LHA-owned housing, to whom the tax-exemption subsidy applies automatically.

This local tax remission can practicably and easily be accomplished by virtue of the standard "cooperation law" provisions found either within[48] or associated with[49] the state housing authorities laws. They provide exceedingly broad powers to cities, counties, states, and other public bodies to cooperate with the housing authority and the federal government in carrying out housing projects. Among these powers are the powers to make donations and enter into long-term agreements. In localities where there are in existence, or will come into existence, LHA-owned projects which are contributing or will contribute PILOT, the local governing body, in its cooperation agreement with respect to the section 10(c) leasing project, can provide that the LHA withhold from such PILOT payments the difference per number of units covered by the 10(c) program between the taxes on the units and the PILOT that would be paid with respect to them if they were LHA-owned. This is the amount that would be necessary for local tax remission.

V

FEDERAL-LOCAL COOPERATION TO EXPEDITE ACTION

Areas which offer new directions to promote expeditious execution of federal-local programs relating especially to low-income housing may be found in the "cooperation laws" referred to earlier. These laws provide a ready-made system under which the federal government by direct agreement with the governing body involved can carry out the contract if they feel that it is not being carried out by the local housing agency. The most critical area of federal-local effectiveness is the competency and zeal of the local administrative instrument designated by the federal and local statutes. Very often its lack of effectiveness is due to political rather than technical considerations—as where a newly elected city administration inherits a hold-over housing authority board and executive head, which under the state laws can be terminated only for cause.

Under the "cooperation laws" referred to above, it is possible for the city, county, state, or other political entity involved to agree with the federal government to cooperate in carrying out the development if the chosen instrument, such as the LHA, does not do so. For example, in the case of a Turnkey project, the local governing body and the LHA could agree with the federal government that if the project is not under construction within a prescribed period, the federal government could declare a default, take possession or title to the project, and call on the local government to

[48] *E.g.*, WIS. STAT. § 66.403 (1965).
[49] *E.g.*, CALIF. HEALTH & SAFETY CODE §§ 34500 to 34521 (West 1955, Supp. 1965).

exercise its powers given it by the cooperation laws in helping the federal government execute the project. This consent by the local governing body and the LHA, and the fact that the local governing body would be acting under local law to help carry out the project would avoid the constitutional inhibitions that could prevent direct federal action. In view of the broad provisions of the cooperation laws, it is difficult to perceive a situation under which a project could not be successfully and quickly concluded if the local governing body in good faith cooperates in providing the assistance of which it is legally capable under the cooperation law, including land assembly, donation of facilities and services, and so on.

Conclusion

Creative new programs have been devised to implement goals of public housing and to provide homes—and sometimes homeownership—for low income families.[50] Fortunately, the legal profession has used its tools and skills to make these programs a reality, rather than merely a dream. The extent of the lawyers' contribution in this regard serves to corroborate the writer's conclusion several years ago that: "We are approaching a period where the country will again be calling upon the talents of lawyers to lead, if possible, but at least to guide the policy makers in a major effort to implement the vision of the 'Great Society' and to make that vision a reality for every American family."[51]

* * *

APPENDIX

EXCERPTS FROM HAA LOW-RENT HOUSING MANUAL[52]

I

Exhibit 3—Letter Designating Turnkey Developer

Date: . . . .

Gentlemen:

This has reference to your proposal to sell to the undersigned Authority a completed property consisting principally of . . . . dwelling units and related appurtenances upon the site situated at . . . . ·

The Authority generally approves your proposal and requests that you proceed with the preparation of preliminary drawings and specifications and statement of your selling price as required by the Department of Housing and Urban Development (Government) as the basis for an annual contributions contract.

If the drawings, specifications and price are satisfactory they will be submitted to the

---

[50] See generally on the programs up to 1964, Burstein, Housing Our Low-Income Population: Federal and Local Powers and Potentials, 10 N.Y.L.F. 464 (1964).

[51] Id. at 491.

[52] U.S. Dep't of Housing and Urban Development, Housing Assistance Administration, Low-Rent Housing Manual § 221.1 (Sept. 1967).

Government with a request for an annual contributions contract under which the acquisition of the property will be financed. The Authority will promptly execute such contract when it is tendered by the Government.

Promptly upon the execution of such contract between the Government and the Authority, the Authority will issue to you a firm Letter of Intent setting forth the conditions under which you will prepare working drawings and specifications and under which you and the Authority will enter into a Contract of Sale of the property.

The Authority will diligently carry out its obligations under said contract and Letter of Intent.

Yours truly,

. . . .

(Local Authority)

By . . . .

II

EXHIBIT 8—LETTER OF INTENT TO ENTER INTO CONTRACT OF SALE OF
LOW-RENT HOUSING PROJECT TO LOCAL AUTHORITY[1]

(Addressed to Seller   Date: . . . .
by Local Authority)

The undersigned Housing Authority (LHA) has entered into an annual contributions contract with the United States of America (Government) providing for a loan and annual contributions by the Government to assist the LHA to undertake to acquire and to operate a low-rent housing project (designated as Project No. . . . .) in accord with proposals and representations made by you (Seller) to sell to the LHA the completed project consisting of improvements and land; the improvements to consist principally of . . . . dwelling units and related appurtenances completed upon land situated in . . . . and described generally as . . . .

In furtherance of your proposal to complete and sell the project, the parties shall enter into a Contract of Sale of the project by the Seller to the LHA, subject to the following conditions:

1. The Contract of Sale shall be in substantially the form of HUD-53015 which is incorporated herein by reference.

2. Within . . . .[2] days after the date of this letter, the Seller shall present to the LHA complete working drawings and specifications for the completion of the project which (a) will have been prepared by a registered architect or under his supervision and shall be signed or sealed by the architect (and engineer if required) responsible for their preparation;[3] (b) shall set forth in detail all work necessary to the acceptable completion of the project, including the materials, workmanship, finishes, and equipment required for the architectural, structural, mechanical, electrical, and site work shown, described, or implied by the preliminary drawings and other data submitted with the Seller's proposal and approved by the LHA and the Government; and (c) shall comply with all applicable State and local laws, codes, ordinances, and regulations as modified by any waivers which have been obtained from the appropriate jurisdictions and which will meet the Government's requirements for approval of the Contract of Sale.

3. Within . . . .[2] days after the receipt of the working drawings and specifications, the LHA shall notify the Seller whether such documents are approved. Promptly upon approval of such documents by the LHA and the Government, the LHA shall, at its own expense, obtain two independent cost estimates of the proposed improvements, including

insurance, taxes, financing, developer's and builder's fee, and overhead.⁴ If the LHA and/or the Government delays its approval of the working drawings and specifications and execution of the Contract of Sale pursuant hereto for more than ....² days after submission by the Seller of the working drawings and specifications, or any revisions thereof, as required in paragraph 2 above, then the purchase price as determined pursuant to paragraph 4, exclusive of the stipulated value of the site(s), shall be adjusted in accordance with the percentage of any change in the United States Department of Commerce composite construction cost index from ....² days after such submission to the date of such approval and execution of the Contract of Sale.

4. The purchase price of the project to be stipulated in the Contract of Sale shall be (a) the sum of (i) the midpoint between the lower cost estimate and the higher cost estimate, obtained pursuant to paragraph 3, plus (ii) the amount of ....⁵ Dollars ($) representing the value of the site, including the Seller's acquisition and other expense in connection therewith, and (iii) the amount of ....⁶ Dollars ($) representing the Seller's costs of architectural and engineering services, including the drawings and specifications, property line, topographic, and utility surveys and subsurface investigations, or (b) the amount of ....⁷ Dollars ($), whichever is the lesser, except that if the amount determined pursuant to clause (a) is less than 95% of the amount specified in clause (b), and the LHA and the Seller cannot negotiate a purchase price acceptable to the Government, the LHA shall pay to the Seller the amount of ....⁸ Dollars ($) for the site and architectural and engineering services and the Seller shall convey the site and deliver the drawings and specifications and results of the surveys and subsurface investigations to the LHA. Seller represents to the LHA and the Government that the amounts included for Seller's acquisition and other expense in connection with the site and the amount stipulated herein as the costs for architectural and engineering services are accurate to the best of Seller's knowledge and belief and agrees that such amounts shall be reduced by any amount which Seller is unable to certify as having been actually expended in connection with such services and site. The Seller, at the request of the LHA, shall revise the drawings and specifications to the satisfaction of the LHA so as to make them adequate in scope, nature and detail to permit competitive bidding thereon, for which service the LHA shall pay the Seller the amount of ....⁹ Dollars ($).

5. If subsurface investigations or analyses subsequent to the date of this Letter reveal that it is not feasible to complete the improvements on the site for the amount specified in clause (b) of paragraph 4 and the LHA and the Seller cannot negotiate a purchase price acceptable to the Government, the LHA and the Seller shall be relieved of all further obligations hereunder.

6. The approval of this Letter of Intent by the Government signifies that the undertaking by the LHA of the acquisition of the property constitutes a "project" eligible for financial assistance under the Annual Contributions Contract identified hereinabove; that said Annual Contributions Contract has been properly authorized; that funds have been reserved by the Government and will be available to effect payment and performance by the LHA hereunder; and the Government's approval of the terms and conditions hereof. If this Letter, prepared in four signed copies, sets forth your understanding of the transaction, please so indicate by signing all four copies in the space indicated and return to the LHA. Upon approval thereof by the Government, an approved executed counterpart will be returned to you.

ACCEPTED:

. . . .

Seller

. . . .

LHA

By . . . .

APPROVED:

UNITED STATES OF AMERICA
SECRETARY OF HOUSING AND URBAN DEVELOPMENT

By . . . .

---

1. This is a suggested form which should be modified to evidence the agreement of the parties.

2. This period (the same number of days in each blank) to be agreed upon by the parties taking into consideration that construction cost estimates must be obtained before the Contract of Sale may be executed.

3. Omit this clause "a" if architect not required. See LRHM Section 221.1.

4. Estimates should include all costs to be borne by Seller, except costs in connection with the site or for architectural and engineering services which are included in [footnotes] 5 and 6 and will be added to the cost estimates as provided in paragraph 4. If any costs such as taxes are prorated only Seller's share may be included.

5. This amount is determined by negotiation between the LHA and the Seller as approved by the Government taking into consideration the appraisals obtained by the LHA and the cost of the site to the Seller, the accretion or diminution in value, if any, since purchased by the Seller and such additional costs as the Seller represents to the LHA are essential in connection with the acquisition of the site and which have been or will be expended by the Seller on or before the date of the Contract of Sale, such as costs of closing, title examinations, title policies, financing, taxes, zoning, legal expenses, and any other necessary costs as may be agreed to by the LHA and the Seller with the approval of the Government. This total amount shall not exceed an amount which if the LHA is to purchase the drawings, specifications, and site and complete the project would make the project financially infeasible.

6. This amount to be agreed upon by Seller and LHA and approved by the Government shall include only costs incurred for surveys, subsurface soil investigations, and architectural and engineering services up to the completion of working drawings and specifications. This amount should be determined in conjunction with the amount inserted in [footnote] 9 and the total of these amounts should not exceed the value of the services required to produce drawings and specifications adequate to permit competitive bidding thereon.

7. Seller's offered sales price.

8. This amount is the sum of the amounts stipulated in [footnotes] 5 and 6. If the Seller does not wish to sell the site he must absorb the costs of architectural and engineering services and this paragraph must be appropriately modified.

9. See [footnote] 6.

III

Exhibit 9—Contract of Sale

. . . .

ARTICLE IX. *Approval by Government.* The approval of this Agreement by the Government signifies that the undertaking by the Purchaser of the acquisition of the property constitutes a "project" eligible for financial assistance under the Annual Contributions Contract identified in Exhibit "C"; that said Annual Contributions Contract has been properly authorized; that funds have been reserved by the Government and will be available to effect payment and performance by the Purchaser hereunder; and the Government approval of the terms and conditions hereof.

THE NEGRO GHETTOS AND FEDERAL HOUSING POLICY

GEORGE W. GRIER*

The summer racial disturbances which have recently become epidemic have focussed attention upon the United States' most important and perplexing domestic problem—rampant racial ghettoization of its major cities. The Negro ghettos are to a considerable degree a product of American housing policies of the post-World War II era. Ironically, they now stand as one of the greatest obstacles to achievement of the nation's goal of decent housing for all its citizens.

These racial concentrations—which are also concentrations of the most deprived of all Americans in virtually every sense of the term—are of impressive size. Today the Negro populations of at least five major cities are estimated to exceed half a million. Negroes constitute close to two-thirds of all residents of Washington, D.C.; more than one-third of the citizens of Baltimore and New Orleans; over one-fourth of those residing in Philadelphia, Detroit, Cleveland, and St. Louis.[1] In all cases they are compressed into limited areas, while large sections of the same cities remain almost exclusively white. In some places like New York and Los Angeles, where the Negro proportions are somewhat smaller, other severely disadvantaged groups like Puerto Ricans and Mexican-Americans are similarly ghettoized in large numbers.

The recent rate of growth of the urban ghettos can best be described as explosive. During the 1950s alone the Negro population of New York increased by forty-six per cent; of Detroit by sixty per cent; of Los Angeles by ninety-six per cent; of Milwaukee by a staggering 187 per cent.[2] Such rapid increase in a problem-ridden population, together with its compression into areas of the central cities which are most deficient in housing and other facilities and services, helps explain why every one of these cities has recently suffered destructive racial violence.

Today, violence is only the most extreme and obvious symptom of the problems which the slum ghettos are causing the major cities and this nation. Washington, D.C., where ghettoization has proceeded farthest of any, affords some illustrative statistics.[3] In the twelve years between 1954 and 1966, Washington's total population

* Senior Associate, Washington Center for Metropolitan Studies, Washington, D.C. Author, THE CHANGING AGE PROFILE: IMPLICATIONS FOR POLICY PLANNING IN METROPOLITAN WASHINGTON (1964), [with Eunice S. Grier] EQUALITY AND BEYOND: HOUSING SEGREGATION IN THE GREAT SOCIETY (1966), PRIVATELY DEVELOPED INTERRACIAL HOUSING (1960), DISCRIMINATION IN HOUSING: A HANDBOOK OF FACT (1960), NEGROES IN FIVE NEW YORK CITIES (1958).

[1] See generally Grier & Grier, Obstacles to Desegregation in Housing, 6 RACE 3 (1964), for a detailed discussion of recent population shifts and their bearing on racial patterns of residence.

[2] Id. at 4.

[3] These statistics are drawn from the Application for a Federal Grant to Plan for a Model Neighborhood in the District of Columbia, submitted to the U.S. Department of Housing and Urban Development by the government of the District of Columbia, April 1967.

held virtually constant at about 800,000 while its Negro population increased from somewhat over one-third of that total to about two-thirds. During the same period, Washington's public school enrollment increased by almost fifty per cent. Its public assistance caseload rose from 7,500 to 11,400 despite stringent restrictions upon welfare eligibility. The number of authorized policemen was increased from 2300 to 3100; but the crime rate rose even faster, elevating Washington to the unenviable position of one of the most crime-ridden of American cities.

Today, Washington has one of the highest venereal disease rates of any major city, and rates of infant mortality and school retardation exceeding many of the most backward states of the Union. In response to the problems the municipal budget has been forced steadily upward, virtually doubling in the last seven years alone. Yet the city still faces pressing shortages of facilities and services of virtually every type to serve the needs of a population which grows increasingly unable to meet the costs.

One of these shortages is a critical lack of decent housing within the economic means of Washington's low-income families. A recent study by the National Capital Planning Commission[4] estimated that half of the city's household population is unable to afford sound, uncrowded rental housing at the prices which prevail in the private market. Almost no new housing is being constructed for this segment of the population; and private rehabilitation and luxury apartment-house construction in the central district continue to chip away at the existing supply priced within their capacity to pay. Meanwhile, the overall condition of the city's housing stock is believed by expert sources to be deteriorating under the pressure of overcrowding and "slumlord" exploitation. Washington's ghettos thus grow not only blacker but more ill-housed with every passing year.

Quite clearly, the needs and problems of Washington's Negro slums have already surpassed the city's ability to cope with them. Even massive infusions of federal grant funds—now exceeding 100 million dollars a year—have failed to close the growing gap between needs and available resources, not to mention reversing the tide of deterioration.

Is Washington, which first passed the fifty per cent mark in Negro proportion at the 1960 Census, merely the prototype for a number of other major cities—including Baltimore, Cleveland, Detroit, New Orleans, Philadelphia, and St. Louis—which will probably have Negro majorities by 1980 at the latest? Can the social and physical blight of such cities be overcome as long as the ghettos exist? Will the American democratic system itself survive continued political and social upheaval to which the riots of the last several summers may well be only prelude?

One thing at least is becoming clear: solutions will not be simple. The ghettos concentrate human problems and frustrations to a degree which immensely increases

---

[4] PROBLEMS OF HOUSING PEOPLE IN WASHINGTON, D.C. (July 1966) (a special report of the National Capital Planning Commission).

the obstacles to their solution. All the public investment to date in experimental anti-poverty programs, job training, compensatory education, and other approaches has not produced solutions which could be guaranteed to make the racial enclaves within the cities economically and socially viable. Particularly unsettling is the evidence that many of the participants in recent outbreaks of ghetto violence have not been among the most abjectly deprived members of the minority population. A goodly number have been persons who have already climbed a certain way up the long ladder to equality, but who realize how very far and filled with obstacles is the distance remaining.[5]

The pressure of needs upon the resources within the ghettos will continue to grow, for the ghettos themselves will almost certainly keep growing. The reason lies in basic demographic facts. Even if migration of minorities from rural areas to the cities were to cease completely, their rate of natural increase is now sufficient to continue the increase of those groups within the urban centers at a rapid pace. The Negro slum populations are young on the whole, with high concentrations in the teen and early adult years.

On the other hand, the recent exodus of whites from cities to suburbs has been heavily concentrated among families of prime childbearing age. Thus, the whites left in the cities tend increasingly to be past the age where they can increase their numbers. Again to cite an example from the nation's capital city, two-thirds of the white adult population of Washington is now past the age of forty.[6] It does not require clairvoyance to foresee that Washington's Negro population will continue to increase rapidly both in numbers and in proportion to the whole.

Thus, there will be continued consolidation and expansion of the heavily-Negro concentrations until they fill the central cities and extend into the suburbs. At the same time, white resistance to the racial conversion of neighborhoods formerly closed to Negroes can be expected to remain high, especially in the solid, highly-organized ethnic areas which still abound in most northern industrial centers. There will be at least two concomitants: first, the areas of Negro residence will continue to expand less slowly than the need. Second, there will be a continuing high level of racial tension and sporadic open conflict, due both to the bottling-up of Negroes with their needs and frustrations within the ghettos, and to white reactions to the expressions of frustration and the inexorable expansion of ghetto boundaries. The economic viability of central business districts will continue to be threatened as they are surrounded by widening areas of social and economic deprivation and conflict.

These will be the virtually inevitable consequences unless measures of sufficient scope are taken to eliminate the racial ghettos as a feature of the American urban

[5] See generally R. CONOT, RIVERS OF BLOOD, YEARS OF DARKNESS (1967), for an excellent analysis of the origins of the Los Angeles riot.

[6] G. GRIER, THE CHANGING AGE PROFILE: IMPLICATIONS FOR POLICY PLANNING IN METROPOLITAN WASHINGTON (Washington Center for Metropolitan Studies, 1964).

landscape, and to replace them with unsegregated patterns of residence. While this will be no easy task, the alternative of a nation both racially divided and continually at war within itself is not a prospect most Americans will accept with equanimity. It is the contention of this article that solutions are possible, albeit difficult. We seek to demonstrate the following points: (1) The racial ghettos are chiefly creatures of public policy, and in large part of housing policy, which fostered and directed their growth into present patterns. (2) To a major degree, the ghettos are also products of the post-World War II era. For example, in 1940 Washington's Negro population was less than half its present size, and was segregated to a much less rigid degree.[7] (3) What public policy has created within a single generation, it is equally capable of undoing in a similar span of time. To achieve this, however, will require a massive reorientation of available resources.

First, let us review the contributions of public policy to the emergence of the ghettos. Its role can best be understood when viewed against the background of the major population trends which shaped the development of the nation as a whole during the period of the ghettos' most rapid growth.

One of these forces was a high overall rate of population increase: twenty-eight million people were added to the United States population in the 1950s alone. A second was urbanization: about eighty-five per cent of this staggering growth was concentrated in only 212 metropolitan areas, while most rural sections had substantial net out-migrations.[8]

National policy unquestionably helped accelerate the cityward migration by encouraging the development of mechanized agricultural techniques and the consolidation of small family farms into huge agricultural "factories" where mass production methods were most feasible. At the same time, the federal government did little or nothing to encourage the development of smaller towns within largely rural areas. Thus, it became necessary for many of those displaced to move long distances to the major cities in search of employment.

The policy factors mentioned so far were largely neutral in terms of race. However, a disproportionate number of the long-distance migrants, especially in a south-to-north direction, were Negro. One reason was that the low-skilled farm workers displaced by mechanization were heavily Negro. A second was less accidental: the traditional discriminatory practices of the south, and the reluctance of the federal government to interfere in these practices, meant that few job opportunities were available for displaced Negro farm workers in southern commerce and industry. Thus, in both positive and negative fashion, public policies and practices paved the route for the Negro migration to the great metropolitan complexes of the north.

---

[7] E. GRIER, UNDERSTANDING WASHINGTON'S CHANGING POPULATION (Washington Center for Metropolitan Studies, 1961).

[8] U.S. BUREAU OF THE CENSUS, DEP'T OF COMMERCE, U.S. CENSUS OF POPULATION, 1960; see particularly the special reports in Series PC(2) on migration.

It was after the Negro migrants arrived at northern destinations, however, that public policy played its most decisive role in shaping the ghettos. The prime guiding forces were applied in the housing area. Both at the federal and the local levels, virtually every aspect of housing policy interlocked to encourage the concentration of Negro newcomers within the central city slums, and to prevent their escape once they had begun to climb the economic ladder.

Until recent years, federal policy in housing was mainly supportive of racial segregation. At the very least, it did little to interfere with discriminatory practices by local authorities and private entrepreneurs; at the worst (and particularly before 1950), it actively encouraged such practices.[9] Not until President Kennedy's landmark Executive Order of November 1962[10] was the federal government placed clearly on record to the effect that racial discrimination in housing was contrary to the national interest.

That presidential directive, even then, may have been more an expression of individual belief than of national policy. Five years later it still had not been backed up by legislation, and a bill strengthening the Civil Rights Act of 1964[11] had failed of enactment in Congress largely because it added housing to the Act's jurisdiction.

Until the late 1940s the Federal Housing Administration's *Underwriting Manual* had advised appraisers to lower their ratings of properties in neighborhoods occupied by "inharmonious racial or nationality groups . . . often to the point of rejection." To assure continuing racial stability in newly developed neighborhoods, it recommended a model restrictive covenant for inclusion in property deeds. A Supreme Court decision of 1948 rendered racial covenants legally unenforceable; but it was not until early in 1950, well into the post-war suburban boom, that FHA ceased insuring new developments covered by them.[12] Prior to 1950, also, FHA's encouragement of segregated development had not been limited to recommending it. Private developers who proposed to build for interracial occupancy were treated to a variety of delaying and obstructing tactics. Some gave up and accepted the requirement of segregation; but in at least two instances, builders who held firmly to non-discriminatory policies were driven out of business by persistent FHA opposition which prevented them from securing mortgage financing.[13]

In varying ways and to varying degrees, FHA's policies and practices were mirrored by other federal agencies influential in the provision of housing. These included the Public Housing Administration, which encouraged the development of

---

[9] The federal role in enforcing housing discrimination is documented in C. ABRAMS, FORBIDDEN NEIGHBORS (1955).

[10] Exec. Order No. 11,063, 3 C.F.R. 261 (Supp. 1962), 42 U.S.C. § 1982 (1964).

[11] Pub. L. No. 88-352, 78 Stat. 241 (codified in scattered sections of 5, 28, 42 U.S.C.).

[12] Shelley v. Kraemer, 334 U.S. 1 (1948); *see* C. ABRAMS, *supra* note 9.

[13] *See generally* E. GRIER & G. GRIER, PRIVATELY DEVELOPED INTERRACIAL HOUSING ch. 8 (1960), for detailed case histories of two post-World War II developments intended for interracial occupancy which were driven to financial ruin by FHA opposition despite powerful private support.

segregated projects according to a "racial equity" formula by which units were separately constructed for whites and nonwhites in proportions based on a statistical estimate of relative need. If the needs of the two groups subsequently changed, the allocation of units usually did not. They also included the Veterans Administration, which guaranteed home mortgages for returning veterans, but followed FHA's lead in regard to the kinds of new developments on which those benefits were made available.[14]

In the years following 1950, there was a gradual liberalization of the policies of the federal housing and renewal agencies regarding race; but the changes were specific and limited, and in no sense did the federal government possess a consistent policy against housing discrimination until the 1962 Executive Order.

Under the terms of the Order, FHA and other federal agencies providing housing assistance are required to withhold their aid from builders who discriminate. The coverage of the Order does not extend to housing already on the books before its effective date, or to housing without federal assistance. It is presently estimated that the Order covers only fifteen per cent of new housing, and between two and three per cent of the *total* housing stock.[15] Further, the enforcement machinery is basically weak, relying almost exclusively on the compliance machinery of the assisting agencies.

Before the federal prohibition, however, a number of the most populous northern states had adopted laws barring housing discrimination within their jurisdictions— and often having coverage which extended beyond housing receiving governmental aid and into the exclusively private sector. They included such important states as New York, New Jersey, Pennsylvania, Massachusetts, and Michigan.

The number of states possessing such laws has continued to increase, totalling twenty-two as of 1967.[16] In addition, a number of jurisdictions have progressively broadened the coverage of their initial legislation. While the enforcement mechanisms vary in effectiveness, most are quite weak and cumbersome. But there is little question that in most parts of the United States today, a minority family possessing the will, the perseverance, and adequate financial means can buy or rent housing approximating their preference as to price, size, and style in a fairly wide range of locations outside traditional "ghetto" areas.

---

[14] *See generally* E. GRIER & G. GRIER, EQUALITY AND BEYOND: HOUSING SEGREGATION IN THE GREAT SOCIETY (1966), for an analysis of the different roles of various federal agencies in denying equal housing opportunity to nonwhites.

[15] This estimate was supplied by the President's Committee on Equal Housing Opportunity.

[16] *See generally* M. FISHER & F. LEVENSON, FEDERAL, STATE AND LOCAL ACTION AFFECTING RACE AND HOUSING (National Association of Inter-group Relations Officials, 1962), for a comprehensive analysis of action at all governmental levels up to the period just before the 1962 Executive Order. The texts of state and local laws as of the end of 1961 are summarized in U.S. HOUSING AND HOME FINANCE AGENCY, STATE STATUTES AND LOCAL ORDINANCES PROHIBITING DISCRIMINATION IN HOUSING AND URBAN RENEWAL (1961). The most complete and reliable source of up-to-date information on the status of anti-discrimination laws and ordinances throughout the nation is *Trends in Housing*, published by the National Committee Against Discrimination in Housing.

Does this mean that the problem is well on its way to solution? The answer must be in the negative. At this point in history even the broadest "Fair Housing" legislation, however adequately enforced, would be insufficient to reverse or even to stabilize the growth of the ghettos. Would nondiscrimination in the administration of the programs from their inception have prevented the ghettos from expanding to their present magnitude? However paradoxical it may seem, the answer to this question is also "No"—and for the same reason. The major source of difficulty has never been in discriminatory administration of the federal housing programs. The basic legislative provisions governing the provision of most such benefits assure that the bulk of minority members are unable to take advantage of them, however fairly they are administered.

The entire thrust of federal involvement in the housing field has worked against the availability of federal benefits to deprived minorities such as Negroes. One key lies in the following statement of policy quoted from a recent publication of the U.S. Bureau of the Budget: "The Federal Government encourages better housing for the Nation primarily by assuring the availability of private credit on reasonable terms."[17] This emphasis, which derives from the origin of federal housing programs as an economic stimulator in the post-1929 depression, means that the benefits of federal involvement are made available chiefly to those who can pay their own way in the private market.

Most Negroes have automatically been excluded by this fact alone.[18] Estimation of the proportion of Negro families able to pay private-market prices for new housing is a complicated matter, varying with both income levels and building costs in different localities. Nonetheless, a rough indication of the proportion of Negro families who might be considered candidates for new privately-financed housing is provided by a recent federal report which shows that only twenty-eight per cent of nonwhite families in the United States had incomes of $7000 or more in 1966. During the height of the post-World War II building boom, in the early 1950s, the proportion was much lower—ranging from five to nine per cent adjusted for subsequent price changes.[19]

This fact would be of less moment had supplementary federal aids been made available on a scale sufficient to meet the housing needs of minority families who

---

[17] U.S. BUREAU OF THE BUDGET, EXECUTIVE OFFICE OF THE PRESIDENT, THE BUDGET IN BRIEF, FISCAL YEAR 1967, at 42 (1966).

[18] While FHA and VA mortgage guarantees enable lower downpayments than are generally available under conventional financing, these are of no help to families whose incomes are too low to meet monthly costs. Interest rates provided through federally-aided mortgages are generally somewhat lower, but not enough to bring costs down to the level affordable by most nonwhites. Limited exceptions will be found in the special subsidy programs to be discussed later in this article as well as the § 221(h) program, 12 U.S.C. § 1715l(h) (Supp. II, 1965-66), which provides low downpayments, and extended (forty year) terms to aid relocated families in purchasing homes.

[19] U.S. BUREAU OF LABOR STATISTICS, DEP'T OF LABOR & U.S. BUREAU OF THE CENSUS, DEP'T OF COMMERCE, SOCIAL AND ECONOMIC CONDITION OF NEGROES IN THE UNITED STATES (BLS Rep. No. 332, Oct. 1967).

could not participate in the private market. But such aids have been decidedly limited. Throughout most of the postwar housing boom—during which an average of more than one million new private dwellings were constructed annually—the sole federal resource available to aid in improving the housing of low-income families was the subsidized low-rent public housing program. This program, established under the Housing Act of 1937,[20] employs direct federal subsidies to local housing authorities to achieve rents keyed to capacity to pay.

Three decades after its establishment, at the end of September 1967, federally-subsidized public housing had some 660,000 units under management.[21] This is only one per cent of the total housing stock, and about half of a single year's new private construction at current rates. Throughout its lifespan, the public housing program has added an average of only 20,000 units annually—far less than the annual increase in the number of low-income minority households. By no means all public housing units, moreover, have been available to nonwhites. Furthermore, even the minor contribution of public housing to the improved housing of racial minorities has been made chiefly within the boundaries of the central cities and rarely in the suburbs—further enhancing the development of the ghettos.

In the past several years, increased public concern for the housing of low- and moderate-income families has added some weapons to the federal armament—for the first time providing a modicum of encouragement to private effort to enter this previously unrewarding field. But the first of these new measures was not enacted until the early 1960s. In the interim the postwar housing boom, spurred by federal incentives to private enterprise, had produced many millions of new private dwellings in suburban areas—on terms which restricted them almost solely to whites. During this period, the housing needs of expanding Negro and other minority population were met chiefly by succession to the older, often decaying dwellings left behind in the central cities by whites moving to the new homes being built in the suburbs.

The Housing Act of 1961 initiated a new form of federal encouragement to private construction of housing for families unable to pay normal private-market rates. This is the FHA 221(d)(3) "below-market-interest-rate" program.[22] It lowers housing costs through direct purchase of mortgages by the Federal National Mortgage Association at interest rates considerably below those demanded by private lenders. Currently, the maximum rate is three per cent. This interest-rate subsidy allows prices low enough to aid families above public-housing income maxima but under private housing levels. Many minority families are in this previously-unaided category.

The program has been slow to get underway, however. Six years after its estab-

---

[20] 42 U.S.C. §§ 1401-30 (1964, Supp. II, 1965-66).

[21] This figure was supplied by the U.S. Housing Assistance Administration, Dep't of Housing and Urban Development.

[22] 12 U.S.C. § 1715l(d)(3) (Supp. II, 1965-66).

lishment, at the end of September 1967, only 67,100 units had been insured. The present level of appropriation permits adding only about 40,000 units annually.[23]

The Housing Act of 1965 authorized still another form of assistance—direct rent supplements to owners of private housing to enable them to accommodate low-income families.[24] This program for the first time permits low-income families to be integrated with those of somewhat higher incomes within the same housing development. The program was hotly contested in Congress, however; and despite its enactment no appropriations were forthcoming to implement it until fiscal year 1967—when the amount allocated was only $32 million.[25] Only $10 million has been appropriated for the current fiscal year.

In fiscal year 1967, and in a number of prior years, federal programs to aid private housing in combination generated more receipts than expenditures—placing them among very few federal programs which show a "profit." (Premiums charged for insurance and sales of acquired properties and mortgages account for most of this.) Few better commentaries could be made on the degree to which these programs have helped meet the housing needs of those citizens unable to bear the full market price.[26] The excess of receipts over expenditures in these federal aids to private housing was so great ($137 million) as to erase more than half of the $200 million spent by the federal government on subsidies for public housing in the same year.

It has already been suggested that there was a geographic concomitant to the racial and economic selectivity of federal housing programs. To state this geographic factor more fully and explicitly, the new private housing stimulated by federal policies was built chiefly on the open land available on the suburban fringes of the expanding metropolitan areas. The fact that this housing was not available to the great majority of Negroes meant, perforce, that the suburbs became almost exclusively white.

Simultaneously, the expanding housing needs of the Negro populations within the central cities were met (however inadequately) within the central cities, in dwellings left behind by departing whites. Private speculators and "blockbusting" real estate brokers aided the process of racial conversion to their personal profit. The public housing program, limited as it was in magnitude, further enhanced the trend of segregation by the fact that, where it made dwellings available to Negroes, these were generally located in central areas already heavily nonwhite in composition.

The federally-supported urban renewal program, initiated under the Housing Act of 1949,[27] was a foresighted effort to retain and restore the economic viability of central urban areas by encouraging more affluent segments of the population to

---

[23] This figure was supplied by the U.S. Federal Housing Administration, Dep't of Housing and Urban Development.

[24] 12 U.S.C. § 1701s (Supp. II, 1965-66).

[25] This figure was supplied by the U.S. Dep't of Housing and Urban Development.

[26] See U.S. BUREAU OF THE BUDGET, supra note 17.

[27] Ch. 338, 63 Stat. 413 (codified in scattered sections of 12, 42 U.S.C.).

return. It did this by providing federal subsidies for the acquisition, clearance, and resale to private developers of blighted urban areas. From its inception, the urban renewal program was administered with more sensitivity to the problem of racial discrimination than most other federal housing activities. As a consequence, a number of urban renewal projects provided the first racially-unsegregated private housing in their localities.

Nonetheless, the relatively high price levels of most urban renewal dwellings effectively excluded all but a tiny majority of nonwhites from residence. And since they were often located in areas formerly occupied by nonwhite slums, many such projects merely resulted in opening a small white (or nearly white) hole in the central Negro ghetto, while simultaneously causing the external boundaries of that ghetto to expand still further outward.[28]

To sum up, federal housing policy encouraged the growth of the ghettos in two main ways. First, during the major part of the postwar housing boom, federal benefits were largely restricted to whites for both economic and racial reasons; as we have indicated, the economic selectivity was by far the more important. Second, the geographic location of new federally-stimulated construction was such as to enhance segregation by drawing whites out of the central cities toward the suburbs, and permitting the areas they left behind to be occupied by Negroes. Only in the early 1960s, after a decade and a half during which the all-white suburbs and their counterpart central-city Negro ghettos had grown to a point where they presented the nation with a domestic problem of frightening scope and complexity, were federal policies modified. These modifications were in two directions: first of all, to restrict racial discrimination in application of the federal benefits; and second, to assist private developers to serve a wider socioeconomic range. Even then, the measures were so limited in scope that they could not conceivably halt, let alone reverse, the now well-established tide of ghettoization.

Is it too late to undo what has been done? To believe that the point of no return has been passed is to accept the alternatives which have been outlined on preceding pages. It may also be to accept the loss of many of America's most highly cherished democratic protections. Already efforts to repress ghetto violence are producing legislation and police procedures which, carried to their logical extreme, could transform a free nation into a police state. Ultimately, the majority may suffer as much as the minority from the end effects of continued ghettoization and racial conflict.

Would the dissolution of ghetto patterns require forced redistribution of population? In answer, it is only necessary to point out that about half of all American households changed their place of residence during the latter half of the 1950s

---

[28] This problem is discussed in E. Grier and G. Grier, Federal Powers in Housing Affecting Race Relations, Sept. 1962 (an unpublished paper prepared for the Potomac Institute and the Washington Center for Metropolitan Studies).

alone. Residential mobility is so much a part of the "American way of life" that a virtually complete redistribution of the population can easily be achieved within the span of a single generation, and without forcing anyone to move.

Such a massive redistribution has, in fact, largely been accomplished during the two decades since the conclusion of World War II. It has resulted in the present ghettoized pattern. The ultimate form of any future redistribution will depend largely upon the federal incentives which are applied to shape it. Continuation of present incentive patterns can only lead to the further growth of segregation.

What alterations in the pattern of federal benefits would accomplish the elimination of segregated residential patterns most effectively and economically? This question requires further study, and determination of the best means should be an objective of highest federal priority. But it is probable that measures recently placed on the books point the way. More flexible federal benefits; incentive programs which encourage private enterprise to produce housing for lower-income groups; measures which encourage racial and socioeconomic diversity both within particular housing developments and throughout entire metropolitan areas; measures which free housing subsidies from restriction to dwellings in control of public housing authorities or (as in the section 221(d)(3) program) of non-profit sponsors; strengthened prohibitions against discrimination—these appear to constitute the most promising routes for federal intervention. Above all, it will be necessary for far greater funds to be allocated to assist families presently unable to compete in the private market.

These measures in the housing field must, of course, be accompanied by programs to improve the economic capability of minority groups and to overcome the manifold social deficits resulting from generations of selective disadvantage. The end goal of all such programs must, however, be to enable Negroes to take their place in the mainstream of American life—not to solidify the structure of the ghettos. The cost of adequate efforts will be high, but must be measured against the alternatives. There is little question that they are affordable, especially in light of the tremendous expenditures which accompanied the redistribution just accomplished.

Finally, and certainly not least, it will be necessary for the more fortunate white majority to learn to accept racial integration as desirable and, indeed, essential in every area of life. This will require fundamental reorientation of the values and biases which contributed to the direction of present federal policies. Can a democratic nation achieve such a redirection? This is the final unanswered question. Upon the nation's ability to face it and to answer it may rest its own survival.